TO THE DESERT

VAHRAM DADRIAN

TO THE DESERT
PAGES FROM MY DIARY

translated from the Armenian by
Agop J. Hacikyan

Gomidas Institute
London

This book was originally published in Armenian under the title, *Tebi Anabad (Prtsvadz echer orakres)*, by Gochnag Press in New York, 1945. The Armenian original has been translated here in its entirety and appears with the addition of maps, photographs, and family trees related to the author.

The first edition of this book was published in 2003 under the imprint of Gomidas Institute. The second print appeared under the imprint of Taderon Press. This is the third printing by Gomidas Institute.

Edited by Ara Sarafian.

ISBN 978-1-909382-52-7

[Original dedication]
I dedicate this book to the memory of my father,
ARMENAG DADRIAN,
and to the two million of my compatriots
who fell on the road to Golgotha.

[New dedication]
The publication of this book by the author's
nephews is not undertaken with the intention
of condemning the Turkish and Kurdish peoples.
Rather, it is given as a testament to the human
spirit to overcome adversity and as a tribute to genocide
victims past, present, and, regrettably, future.

Table of Contents

Illustrations

Introduction

Narratives of the Armenian Genocide fall into several major categories. Although there is a master narrative encompassing the physical destruction of Armenians in 1915—the murder of young men conscripted in the Ottoman army, the liquidation of community leaders, mass killings associated with deportations, and the destruction of deportees "settled" in Deir Zor[1]—there are also lesser-known narratives. Many Armenians were not deported at all (for example, in Constantinople); thousands of women and children were abducted into Muslim households (that is, they were not killed); many others were deported to places other than Deir Zor, such as the Dadrian family from Chorum.

Individual narratives from this period also differ according to specific circumstances and chance factors. Sometimes Muslims protected Armenians for altruistic reasons or for material gain; many Armenians resisted the genocidal process by offering bribes, converting to Islam, resorting to prostitution, or utilizing escape networks from death camps.[2] Indeed, survivor narratives are almost by definition

1. For typical master narratives, see Vahakn Dadrian, *The History of the Armenian Genocide: Ethnic Conflict from the Balkans to Anatolia to the Caucasus* (Providence: Berghahn Books, 1995); Raymond Kévorkian, "L'extermination des déportés arméniens ottomans dans les camps de concentration de Syrie-Mésopotamie (1915–1916): le deuxième phase du génocide," *Revue d'histoire arménienne contemporaine* 2 (special issue) (Bibliotheque Nubar de l'UGAB: Paris, 1998).
2. For additional models narrating the Armenian Genocide, see Ara Sarafian, "The Conversion and Absorption of Women and Children as a Component of the Armenian Genocide," in *In God's Name: Genocide and Religion in the Twentieth Century,* ed. Phylis Mack and Omer Bartov (Providence: Berghahn Books, 2001); Hilmar Kaiser, *At the Crossroads of Der Zor: Death, Survival, and Humanitarian Resistance in Aleppo, 1915–1917* (Princeton and London: Gomidas Institute, 2001).

deviations from the norm—which was death for Armenians living in Ottoman Turkey between 1915 and 1918.

In Vahram Dadrian's case, his diaries encompass not only much of the genocidal context of the period, but also the specific circumstances that allowed him and some members of his family to survive.

The Diary

Vahram Dadrian started his diary on 24 May 1915, at age fifteen, sensing that something calamitous lay ahead for Armenians in Ottoman Turkey. In the following years he recorded what he saw, felt, and heard about developments around him during the genocide of Armenians. His observations shed light on one of the lesser-known episodes of the Armenian Genocide—the fate of over one hundred thousand Armenians who were sent towards Damascus rather than the wastelands of Deir Zor in 1915.[3] Vahram's diaries also include other people's survival accounts from such theatres of the Genocide as Moush, Harpoot (Kharpert), and Deir Zor.[4]

Vahram knew the significance of keeping good diary-records. He expressed his concern for not being able to write his entries on a regular basis.[5] By June 1919 he had six booklets already written, and he intended to publish them.[6] Since the original diary was written as concise notes, it was expanded by the author between 1919 and 1922 into its present form.[7] It was not edited or elaborated for content.[8] The original diary notes have not been located to date. According to the Dadrian family, Vahram's private papers were sent to Soviet Armenia in the 1950s.

---

3. Vahram Dadrian's diary should be read alongside another diary that parallels his account, the diaries of Father Nerses Tavoukdjian, *Darabanki Orakir* (Diary of Suffering), ed. Toros Toranian (Beirut, 1991). Father Nerses was exiled to the region of Hama from Aintab.
4. His informants include Gadariné (Yozgad), Heghiné (Harpoot), Takoohi (Harpoot), Khacher Aghpar (Moush), Karekin (Trebizond), Sarkis (Moush), Torkom (Rodosto), Stepan (Adabazar), and Pakrad (Diyarbekir).
5. See the entry for 9 Sept. 1918.
6. See the entry for 17 June 1919. The final publication was composed of 377 individual entries.
7. See p. 3.
8. See pp. 3-4.

The Armenian Genocide: South and East of Aleppo

Over two million Armenians lived in Ottoman Turkey at the beginning of 1915. Most of them were killed in the following two years. Their deaths were part of a genocidal campaign to rid Anatolia and Armenia of its native Armenian population and to pave the way for a supposedly homogenous Turkish state.

The destruction of Armenians was cloaked as a "deportation program," ostensibly intended to resettle a troublesome people in the lower Euphrates. By July 1915 this program led to the destruction of practically every Armenian community in the Ottoman Empire.

Many deportation convoys, composed of women, children, and elderly men (the younger men were mostly conscripted and liquidated in the Ottoman army) were destroyed at specific locations along deportation routes. Others were wasted away, with young women and children often taken away to be absorbed into Muslim families. The United States consul to Mamouret-ul-Aziz (central Turkey), Leslie Davis, personally reported on the passage of thousands of emaciated Armenians from further north; he saw young women and children taken away by Muslims; and he observed the corpses of thousands of Armenian deportees around Lake Goljuk, where they were murdered *en masse*.[9] The United States consul at Aleppo, Jesse B. Jackson, who was posted at

---

9. Davis describes one convoy of deportees as follows "I have visited their encampment a number of times and talked with some of the people. A more pitiable sight cannot be imagined. They were almost without exception ragged, filthy, hungry and sick. That is not surprising in view of the fact that they have been on the road for nearly two months with no change of clothing, no chance to wash, no shelter and little to eat. The Government has been giving them some scanty rations here. I watched them one time when their food was brought. Wild animals could not be worse. They rushed upon the guards who carried the food and the guards beat them back with clubs hitting hard enough to kill them sometimes. To watch them one could hardly believe that these people were human beings. As one walks through the camp mothers offer their children and beg one to take them. In fact, the Turks have been taking their choice of these children and girls for slaves, or worse. In fact, they have even had their doctors there to examine the more likely girls and thus secure the best ones." Leslie Davis (Mamouret-ul-Aziz) to Henry Morgenthau (Constantinople), 11 July 1915. National Archives, Record Group 59, decimal file 867.4016/127. For Davis' report on the wholesale massacre of Armenians see decimal file 867.4016/392.

a critical junction along the deportation routes, estimated the size of deportation convoys arriving from Armenia proper at 15 percent of their original number, with better survival rates for convoys from western regions and areas immediately to the north of Aleppo.[10] By 16 July 1915 the United States ambassador to Ottoman Turkey could already conclude that "a campaign of race extermination" was in progress.[11] In February 1916 Consul Jackson approximated the number of Armenian survivors arriving in Syria at over 486,000 people. Most of them were pushed east of Aleppo towards Deir Zor, where they were eventually destroyed.[12] However, around 130,000 were sent south of Aleppo, and over one hundred thousand of them reached Damascus, as far as Ma'an—including the town of Jeresh. The Dadrians were among the luckier ones who were sent south.[13]

Dadrian Family, Chorum

The Dadrians came from Chorum, in what is now western Turkey. They were relatively well-to-do merchants. They, like other Armenians in Ottoman Turkey, were deported from their homes in the summer of 1915. While they were subject to robbery, assault, and murder on their way, they were relatively lucky. Their deportation caravan reached Aleppo with some deaths but mostly intact; and they were sent southwards thereafter.

The family's survival was helped by its wealth, connections, and some foresight of what lay ahead. They used their resources to bribe their tormentors at critical junctures. The family obtained special

10. Jesse Jackson (Aleppo) to Henry Morgenthau, 29 September 1915. National Archives, Record Group 59, decimal file 867.4016/219.
11. Henry Morgenthau (Constantinople) to Secretary of State, 16 July 1915. National Archives, Record Group 59, decimal file 867.4016/76.
12. Hoffman Philip (the U.S. chargé d'affaires in Constantinople) reported the destruction of the remaining Armenians in Deir Zor by September 1916. Philip Hoffman to Secretary of State, 1 September 1916. National Archives, Record Group 59, Decimal File 867.48/296. Two weeks later he related further information from Consul Jackson, that the final massacres at Deir Zor were "arranged and carried out" by the highest authorities. Philip Hoffman to Secretary of State, 15 September 1916. National Archives, Record Group 59, Decimal File 867.48/301.
13. Jesse B. Jackson (Aleppo) to Henry Morgenthau, 9 Feb. 1916, in Hoffman Philip to Secretary of State, 29 Feb. 1916. National Archives, Record Group 59, Decimal File 867.48/271.

consideration from the governor of Chorum as far as possible. And they tapped other resources, such as Ardashes Giulbenkian in Constantinople, who sent them money when family members reached a final place of exile in Jeresh.

Vahram's diary reflects on the fate of his own family members, as they lived and died during the deportation process. His first encounter with mass-scale maltreatment of Armenians took place at Katma, where he saw thousands of Armenian deportees in appalling conditions. He witnessed the dead and the dying buried in mass graves. On one occasion he watched the arrival of three hundred naked Armenians whose convoy had been subject to beating, robbery, and murder only three days earlier. They were left to beg "for a piece of bread to fill their stomachs or an arm's length of cloth to cover their nakedness."[14]

The Dadrian family escaped to Aleppo by bribing camp officials at Katma. They were apprehended, however, and sent south. While in Aleppo, Vahram saw more appalling scenes, as cartloads of Armenians were taken away to mass graves every day. In one scene he describes a little dead girl, who appeared to be sleeping in the street, "her head resting on her emaciated arms."[15]

The Dadrians were eventually settled in Jeresh, where they tried to survive as best as they could. Up to twenty thousand Armenians reached that location, where famine, disease, and epidemics cut their number down. Vahram noted that the Armenian cemetery was soon larger than the cemetery of the more numerous Circassian community.[16] He estimated that the Armenian population of Jeresh was reduced to around one thousand by the end of 1917.[17]

Armenians were constantly kept under the observation of Ottoman officials. They remained subject to abuse from all quarters. At one point they were registered as Muslims, subjected to military conscription, as well as the different whims of officials. Conscripts were put in labor battalions and maltreated and even killed. There were inevitable tensions with the local Arab, Circassian, and Bedouin populations, despite the fact that Armenians actually enriched the local economy. Many of the tensions were due to economic pressures brought about by the world war, such as a lack of foodstuffs or the devaluation of the paper currency.

14. See the entry for 10 September 1915.
15. See the entry for 14 October 1915.
16. See the entry for 14 May 1917.
17. See the entry for 19 November 1917.

While some exploited Armenians as an underclass, others befriended them. Yusuf, the Bedouin chieftain, was one such character.

The Dadrian family helped others where it could, and Vahram continued to contrast himself to others less fortunate than himself. On one occasion he describes the condition of an old Armenian beggar in a "tattered jacket and a pair of torn pants, leaving most of his body exposed."[18] On another occasion he portrays two Armenian orphans grooming each other by catching the insects that infested their bodies.[19] Most of these Armenians probably died in the months ahead.

The Dadrian family's fate during this period represents a survival story of one family. They suffered much hardship and lost twenty-three members of an extended family of forty-two.[20]

ARA SARAFIAN
Gomidas Institute (UK)

---

18. See the entry for 5 Feb 1917.
19. See the entry for 21 May 1917.
20. See the entry for 23 March 1919.

Editorial Notes

This book is a complete English translation of Vahram Dadrian's *To the Desert: Pages from My Diary,* originally written and published in Armenian.[21] The translation has been lightly edited for style and should be read with the following points in mind:

- Vahram uses the Julian calendar at the beginning of his diary but changes to the Gregorian calendar with his entry of 3 March 1918. The Gregorian calendar, which is commonly used today, is thirteen days ahead of the Julian calendar. In a few cases, he notes dates according to both calendars. For example, he gives his birthday as 17/30 April 1900. We have not standardized these dates and they remain as in the original diary.

- Foreign terms used in the text are explained when they first appear in the diary, and are included in a glossary at the end of the book. Additional annotations appear in square brackets.

- When compiling personal names for the index, we attempted to identify people by their family and first names. Where only one of these names was available, we included additional information, such as the gender, profession, and place of origin of individuals. We hope this course proves useful for readers.

- We have appended the following materials to the original translation: New front matter and introduction, maps, genealogical trees, a glossary, and a selective index of proper nouns.

---

21. Vahram Dadrian, *Tebi Anabad (Prtsvadz echer orakres)* (New York: Gotchnag Press, 1945).

Map showing the deportation route of the Dadrian family from Chorum to Jeresh (1915) dur

To the Desert: Insert 1

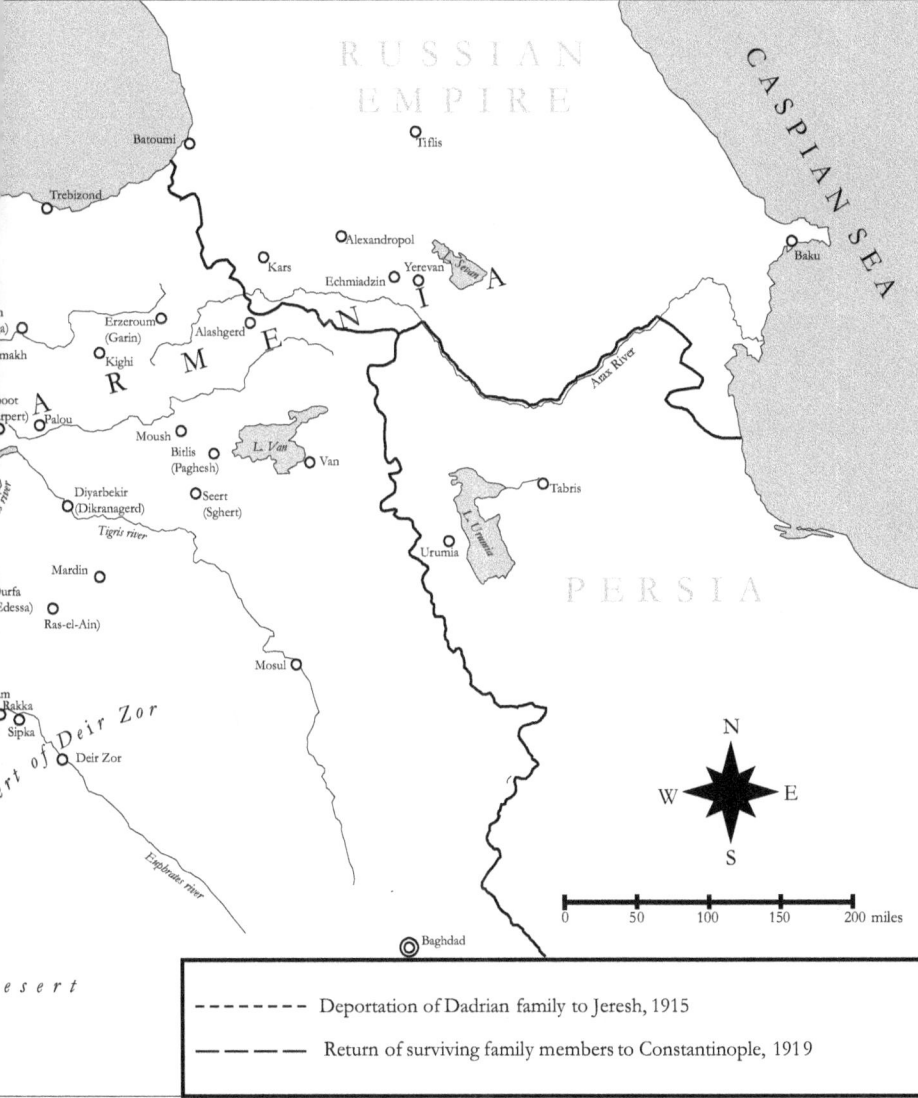

Armenian Genocide, and the return of surviving family members to Constantinople (1919)

- - - - - - - Deportation of Dadrian family to Jeresh, 1915

— — — — Return of surviving family members to Constantinople, 1919

TO THE DESERT

In Lieu of an Introduction

Do you know how deer are hunted? Hundreds of them are penned up inside the woods of a palace. Hunters surround the forest and wait in ambush at all escape routes. When everything is ready, the hunting dogs run the deer out of their pens and chase them through the forest. The animals, unaware of the hidden hunters or the traps set for them, flee with all the strength of their legs.

Suddenly a shotgun resounds through the bushes. Four, five of them fall, and the rest, terrified, turn around and run off in different directions. Again the hunters open fire on them. Those that have been mortally wounded fall; those that are still alive proceed with their alarming escape.

Now they find themselves in front of a precipice. Some fall in; the others continue their escape. More shots, more traps, more massacres and carnage. . . . And that is how it is . . . in the evening the ground is strewn with corpses and with struggling wounded animals that bellow in their agony. If a few have escaped, they are already lost in the thick of the woods; they mourn the memory of an atrocious day, the death of their loved ones.

To get an idea of the *Medz Yeghern* (Armenian Genocide), one need only expand this image. Imagine all of Turkey as a forest, and the three million Armenians as the deer in that forest. All the bloody murderers, thieves, vagabonds, and brigands of Turkey (Turkish, Kurdish, Laz, Chechen, Circassian, etc.) have surrounded this forest, waiting in ambush at each crossroad, along the shores of the rivers, deep in the valleys, and at the approaches to all passages.

Just like greyhounds, the police rout the Armenians from their homes and chase them into reach of the blood-thirsty assassins. And so begins the carnage, without mercy, horrifying.

The terrified people run, trying to escape, to flee, trying to save their lives, running, running. But where are they running to? Snares open up under their feet to swallow them up—and fire descends upon their heads.

By the time the Great War had finished, two million people had been sacrificed: they were laid out on the ground. If there are survivors, they are like the wounded deer, scattered, lost, to the four corners of the world. And the horrific nightmare of the days they have lived dwells at the very core of their souls.

* * *

The martyrology of the Armenians comprises hundreds of events.

Our Armenian brothers were slaughtered—savagely, monstrously—in the cities, the villages, the valleys, and on the roads. The chasms resound with their horrid history.

Our unprotected, defenseless children, drowned in rivers and wells, ripped in two by the legs, have a hideous story to tell.

Our lion-hearted sisters, who fought to defend their honor, who threw themselves from the rocks and precipices, have a revolting story to tell.

Our mothers and orphans, suffering under the scorching sun, hungry, crawling in the cruel footsteps of sickness and disease, have a heart-rending story to tell.

Our intellectuals and writers, in dark, dank dungeons tortured with unimaginable torments and martyred, have a horrendous story to tell.

Our incomparable heroes, who fought against the enemy to defend lives and protect their honor, have an admirable story to tell.

* * *

We, the survivors, what have we been able to contribute to that blood-tainted story? The slaughter of our brothers who were victims of the Genocide, in all its hellish details; the epic tragedy of thousands of our compatriots, in all its heart-rending episodes; the struggle of our heroes as they drew their last breaths, in all its horror; none of these . . . have ever been presented to us in their strict entirety.

A few articles in the press, memoirs, impressions . . . a few books and booklets, and that is it! Everything has been forgotten.

Our million dead could never have imagined, even for a fraction of a moment, that they would have been forgotten so soon.

Tomorrow, when the newspapers have worn out and the books have faded, they will be thrown away like junk. Yes, tomorrow, when the witnesses have shuffled off their earthly existence, the next generation will not be told how this unlucky people were martyred and sacrificed in the year 1915 and the hellish years that followed.

Tomorrow's generation: what am I talking about? What does the present generation—which had the good fortune of growing up behind that fire wall—what do they know about the horrors of the Genocide beyond a confused, faded, general outline?

* * *

In publishing this diary, I have no illusion that I have produced a general history of the bloody carnage that was inflicted on the Armenian people throughout the period of the Great War. That is the task of future historians, who, bit by bit, with the help of the survivors, will expose the Crime in all its chilling convolutions.

Considering, however, that my diary contains not only what I witnessed and experienced, but also what I heard about, I presume that reading it will provide a small idea of the silent tragedy undergone by Armenians who lived within the borders of Turkey, throughout the black days of affliction.

V. D.

P.S.: I would like to take this opportunity to provide a little clarification concerning the composition and contents of my diary.

First, let me say that it was written by a fifteen-year-old boy, and for that very reason it is different from all other published books dealing with the Armenian Genocide, which, without exception, have been written by adults.

Second, all entries were written on the precise day in question, under the immediate impression of the events that took place on that day, and not as they were remembered years later.

Third, the diary encompasses the entire duration of the Great War and the period following it, whereas similar works concentrate mainly on the events of 1915 and make only brief references to the events of the first half of 1916 and those of 1917, 1918, and 1919, which were not much less turbulent for the Armenian nation.

Originally, I wrote a concise diary, because of the scarcity of paper. Then, from 1919 to 1922, I expanded my notes in Constantinople, with a view to publishing them, which, of course, was not possible because of the changing political situation.

During those years in Constantinople, I also wrote the ten stories mentioned in my diary—by assembling hundreds of tiny events which I heard about during the deportations and interweaving them with an entirely new story centered on a hero.[*] Perhaps I was wrong, but at that time my adolescent mind was more interested in what the Turks did to the Armenians than in the Armenians as such or where they came from.

From that time until 1936, when I left Constantinople, I had no opportunity to go over my diary. Later, when it was to be published as a serial in *Baykar*, I went through it and corrected certain grammatical mistakes, without adding anything to its content.

---

[*]. *Kerezmannerou Mechen: Prtsvadz Echer Orakres* [*From the Graves: Pages From My Diaries*], (New York: Gotchnag Press), 1945. This title has recently been translated into English and appears under a new title, *Forsaken Love*. See Vahram Dadrian (Ara Melkonian and Ara Sarafian transl. and ed.), *Forsaken Love*, (London and Reading: Taderon Press, 2006).

Part One

TO THE DESERT

Hayastan, Armenia, your tribulations are few! Few are your afflictions! Your cities are still standing; your churches are still standing; you are still surrounded by the rejoicing of brides and bridegrooms; children still cry in their cradles; fire still crackles in the stove; smoke still rises from the chimney; your elders still walk proudly erect; iron still shines in their hands; the helmets on their heads still shine; your daughters are still adorned in purple and rainbow-hued dyes; they still wear golden necklaces about their necks and bracelets on their arms. But now all this is ended. Your cities shall henceforth be deserted, your buildings unfinished, your churches half-demolished; your houses shall be bereft of all signs of life . . . the glad sounds of weddings and merrymaking will give way to the grieving voices of mourning and the clatter of guns and the rattle of chains; the tinkling of your bangles and bracelets will be drowned out by the cracking whips of slavery. Yes, your brave ones will become slaves in their own country and slaves on foreign shores. And your daughters will become maid-servants in their homeland and in bitter exile. When you turn your face eastward, you will see the enemy; when you turn it westward, you will see the enemy; you will ask for help, and you will receive hatred and contempt. You will turn your eyes to Heaven, and thunder and hail will pour down upon you; and your children will continually pierce their mothers' hearts by killing each other.

—Tzerents, *Yergunk* (ninth century).

11 May, 1915

This seems like a good time to begin keeping a diary, something I have been meaning to do for some time now. Our national existence has never been in so much danger as during these disastrous days. The present is dark and the future undecided. The days are filled with catastrophic events.

I don't think it's out of place to talk about a few past events first— to give a little background.

* * *

I was born on 17/30 April 1900 in Chorum.

Chorum is a commercial center with a population of 30,000 and is in the Province of Angora (Ankara).

There has been an Armenian community in the city for around 60 or 70 years. Most of the Armenians emigrated from the regions of Cilicia and Yozgad, and others came from Marsovan and Amasia. There are now about 150 Armenian families there; they have a church and two schools: one for girls and one for boys.

My parents are from Germir. It is a small town near Talas, an hour's distance from Caesarea. My father is well known: he has been a member of the Board of Managers for a long-time.[*] He is a respected and distinguished man. He is in the wholesale corn, wool, and opium business, in partnership with a Turk.

As I write these lines I have just turned fifteen. I finished the local elementary school last year, but this year I am still going to the same school, as they have added another grade to it. It is strange what fortune has in store for us. Last year, when my father got back from his trip to Europe, he told us that he was planning to sell his business in Turkey and move to France with the family. He wanted me to go to a good French school and specialize in electricity. In fact, on the recommendation of a friend in Marseilles he had already registered me in a school. A month after he got back, however, the Great War was declared, and this shattered all our plans. Now, instead of going to school in France, I go to our Armenian national school.

The Great War . . .

For not quite a year, the events and developments leading up to the war had been piling up. The first time I heard about the war, I felt as if I had known about it for ages. I remember well how my father told us the news on the day that general conscription was announced. We had gone to our vineyard for the vacation following the end of the school year. It was about half an hour from the city. In other years we went much further for our vacation, at least a day or two from the city, where there were forests, lakes and springs, and fresh air. Last year was an exception: we went to the vineyard to take advantage of our newly

---

[*]. After the 1908 Constitution he was unanimously elected member of the provincial assembly by the townspeople; he resigned, however, for personal reasons.

built country house. At the same time, it was easier for my father to go in to the city to look after his business.

We hadn't even been there for two weeks. One evening, my two sisters (ten and four) and my brother (one) were standing with me on a nearby hill to watch for our father's return, as usual. My father was always right on time, and usually he came into sight on the road at that particular time, riding his chestnut horse. He'd wave at us and come galloping up to us. Then he'd get off his horse and kiss us one after the other, giving each of us a little present. Then, hand in hand, we'd all walk back to the vineyard, where my mother and grandmother would be waiting for us.

On that particular night, however, as the minutes passed and the daylight hours began to run out, nobody appeared on that deserted road. We were all worried. Waiting. Then suddenly we spotted our father, riding a different horse. He didn't wave to us or gallop up to meet us. Something must have happened. As we waited for him, our hearts beat faster and faster. Then at last he was there. He got off the horse. His face was solemn; deep within his eyes there was an unaccustomed grief. It was the first time I had ever seen my father so distressed. And his upset state seemed to fill our young souls with the dread of an approaching danger.

In answer to our questions, he told us that general conscription had been declared and that our horse had been confiscated by the government on the same day.

"What's conscription, father?" we asked anxiously.

"It means preparing for war," he replied.

Later, in the vineyard, he explained things to us, ending with these words: "We can't stay here any longer this year. We have to cut our vacation short. We wouldn't get any peace at all from the draft dodgers or from those who pass by or from all the vacationers. We have to go back to the city."

First thing the next morning we collected together our belongings and, leaving all the pleasures of country behind, we returned to the city in gloom.

Something unusual was going on in the city. The streets were filled with the deafening beats of drums and the town criers were shouting in their sharp, loud voices that all men between the ages of 21 and 45 had to join the army.

There was no immediate danger for our family because I was 14 and my father was 47. Of course, we were not happy. It was as though a mighty earthquake were shaking the foundations of our happiness.

* * *

That was the day we lost our peace of mind.

Event followed event—each more disturbing than the other. Every day the deteriorating situation reminded us that things would only get worse. Nothing could happen today that we had not already guessed the moment Turkey entered the war last year.

On the day when the soldiers were being sent to the front, the entire population of the city gathered at the garrison, to wish well to those who were leaving. We were also there, as we had many compatriots among those who were departing.

After the prayers and good wishes, the leader of the Union and Progress Party made a speech. He was a young officer. His words chilled the hearts of the Christians who were there: "We are going off to fight and, God willing, we will smash the heads of all the *giaours,* infidels, who are the enemies of our faith and our homeland."

After the ceremony my father, who was sitting next to the governor because he had taken on the job of supplying food to the army ever since conscription, brought to the governor's attention that he shouldn't have permitted a speech like that. The governor said he was sorry for the tactless incident and assured him that saying things like that would not be allowed in future.

The same things were repeated, however, on the day that the *jihad* was declared, and this time in stronger terms. There was a meeting at Ulu Jami, to which the city's Greek and Armenian dignitaries were also invited. Those who spoke there insisted that there was no difference among Christians, regardless of their nationalities: they were all malicious enemies of the Muslim Turks.

A fanatic Turk who was there asked the speaker this question: "So what are we waiting for? Let's begin cleaning up the *giaours* inside the country first, and then turn our attention to those outside . . ."

* * *

And now we see that they have already set their plan in motion— they are already in business.

They claim that the Armenians of Zeitoun have rebelled, and the result has been huge massacres there. They say the same thing about the Armenians of Van. We don't know how true these reports are, but we can see that the Turks are very worked up.

One thing is clear: that special assassinations and acts of barbarism are taking place every day in the far reaches of the provinces.

Reports have already reached us that the government has rounded up all of the Armenian intellectuals in Constantinople and exiled them.

Today, we heard that war tribunals have been formed in all of the big cities, and soon the foremost Armenian leaders and dignitaries will be tried and condemned to death, as well as everyone who has had dealings with Armenian political parties, whether close or distant.

The storm is on!

Fear of death has gripped our hearts.

We all feel that a horrible tragedy threatens our very existence. What can we do, though? We are like sheep penned up in a slaughterhouse. We are helpless and cannot escape our destiny.

* * *

Today is Sunday. There is no school. I went to the vineyard with my cousin Aram. When I got back I heard that my father and one of the city officials, Parsegh Tabibian, had been arrested, and that they would be sent to the war tribunal in Caesarea. The news terrified me. It was no surprise, though, considering that the persecution of Armenians was getting worse with every passing day.

I rushed to the prison. My father had retained his cool, but it was obvious that he was worried. He said that they would be sent to Caesarea early tomorrow morning.

In the evening, my father obtained permission from the governor to spend the night at home. The news that my father and Tabibian had been arrested spread all over the city with the speed of lightning. It caused a great deal of sadness among the Christians and some of the Turks. In the evening our house was filled with relatives and friends.

Why had my father been arrested? No one could suggest a definite reason. Many said it was because of his trip to Europe last year. Others, because he had founded a new chapter of the Armenian General Benevolent Union in Chorum and, since that association was under the control of Boghos Nubar Pasha at the time, the government might have considered it a seditious organization. There were, of course, other theories. My father used to help the Russian prisoners of war and the Russian-Armenian exiles who were in the city at that time. They were kept under strict supervision. The Russian consul in Samsoun had stayed with us after diplomatic relations between Turkey and Russia were severed and he was on his way home. In addition, my father had given both moral and financial help to the Jesuits who were expelled from Marsovan (Marzvan) when they passed through Chorum. Was that why he had been arrested?

Is it possible to interpret a noble, humanitarian gesture as political wrong-doing? Especially in the case of someone like my father, who always contributed to every worthy cause and helped everybody, regardless of religion or nationality. All of the charities—the Red Crescent, the Navy Campaign for the Needs of the Military, etc.—had my father's name at the top of the list of contributors, despite the fact that many of Chorum's Turks were much wealthier.

It's a good thing that there are no Armenian political parties in the city and that my father doesn't belong to any of them. But of course deep down he has always supported everyone who works for the good of the Armenian nation, and has helped them in any way he could.

25 May, 1915

It was raining cats and dogs this morning when, escorted by two mounted policemen, a closed carriage pulled up at our door. After saying good-bye, my father and his friend got into the carriage and left.

The road went past our school. I followed them as far as the school. There we had a second for a last good-bye! The carriage continued on its way between the two policemen who accompanied it. I watched it disappear from sight. Then, controlling my sobs, I went to my classroom.

2 June, 1915

There was a bandit in the mountains of Chorum who went by the name of Yusuf and who had been robbing people for years. The government spent a lot of time trying to capture him, but they never succeeded. Because they couldn't bring him in themselves, they offered a reward of 100 pounds to whoever brought in Yusuf's head. Now, a new law has been passed which allows Yusuf and all bandits like him to be pardoned and set free, provided they join the *chetés* (irregular troops). One of our Turkish neighbors took Yusuf the news and a few days later he came down to the city and was received by the governor with great honor. A few days after that, everyone condemned to life imprisonment was also liberated. Under Yusuf's command, all these murderers formed an army of assassins.

These killers all behaved like spoiled children after they were pardoned. They roamed unhampered all over the city, insulting and beating up Christians with no fear of punishment, and at times threatening them by saying that they had been set free to wipe out the Armenians. Recently they started fooling around our school and beating up the boys. Because of this, at 2 o'clock this afternoon the principal called the students and staff together, spent five minutes explaining the dangerous situation, announced that the school was shutting down, and told us to leave for home that very minute. In the meantime, he advised us not to remain in the streets too long.

We all felt sad as we stood up, cast a last glance at our desks and blackboards, and left, tightly clasping our scribblers and books under our arms.

17 June, 1915

It's impossible to describe the fear and emotion we have felt during the three weeks after my father's arrest. Every day we heard of prisoners who had been led to the gallows, and scanned the list of their names in fear, thinking that perhaps my father's might be among them.

We have received only one letter from my father. It was only a couple of lines, letting us know that he and his friend Parsegh were in prison in Caesarea. He did not write much; he was probably worried about censorship. He wrote enough, however, to let us know that he hoped soon to establish his innocence and be released.

Last night, when the same closed carriage stopped in front of our house, it was again pouring, just as it had been on the day he was arrested. His friend was not with him. He had to remain in jail in Caesarea.

My father was arrested because the police had entered the house of a person accused of being a *komitaji* (*i.e.* a member of a secret revolutionary organization), and among his papers they had found a certain list, which contained the following item: "Chorum. Paid by Armenag Dadrian. 25 pounds." Another reason was his trip to Europe, for which the government suspected there were political purposes—as though my father had gone there to have a meeting with Boghos Nubar Pasha, etc.

My father explained that the guy who had been accused of being a *komitaji* was a simple businessman, that the payment was for a small purchase he had made, and that his trip to Europe was purely for business—to buy new machines for his new flour mill—and he succeeded in freeing himself. On the other hand, his close friendship with one of the members of the war tribunal and the number of gold pieces that changed hands also contributed substantially to the final decision to set my father free.

There was great joy and exhilaration in the city when it was learned that my father had been released and was back home. This, of course, contradicted and reversed what the Turks had been saying against the Armenians: that if someone like my father, who was considered a good and exemplary person, could become a traitor, who knows what an ordinary person might do?

All night long, my father endlessly described the types of torture and brutality he had seen in the jail in Caesarea. Hundreds of prisoners had been crammed into one room, which was scarcely big enough for more than a few people. The floor was wet, the walls damp, the ceiling covered with cobwebs and thick dust.

Next to them was the torture room. From morning till night they heard the heart-rending cries and sobs of their friends as they were tortured. They counted between two and three hundred consecutive lashes to the feet of each man. Beneath the horrendous shrieks and screams they also heard the sounds made by their unfortunate friends as they collapsed to the floor. Their tormenters stuck red-hot irons to their bodies and used nails and needles on the most sensitive parts of their anatomies. They also applied boiled eggs to their wounded armpits. Meanwhile the rest of the prisoners sat in the other room, listening to all the screams, wails, and shrieks, as they waited their turns.

The door would open. In were thrown those who had just been tortured, half-alive, unrecognizable. And fresh victims were taken out to be tortured and crippled.

It was a horrible sight: all around were people with injured heads, swollen faces, eyes falling out, nails pulled out of both hands and feet, bodies covered with burns. They sobbed noiselessly and at last many of them died quietly in a corner.

During the night the prison door would open suddenly and a policeman would enter, holding a large piece of paper. Slowly and laboriously he would read the list and order those whose names he had read out to leave the cell. Many of these would be asleep and unaware of the black destiny that awaited them. The others would wake them up. Others were wounded so badly that they couldn't even move, but the jailers dragged them out. Those who were left behind had no idea why their friends had been taken away. Were they going to be tortured? Or led to the gallows? Or perhaps set free? They all listened, breathless. There was absolutely no noise from next door, the torture room. They lay awake all night, turning over various conjectures. And then they peeped out of their tiny windows, and there they were! The gallows had been set up in the prison courtyard and from them dangled the friends who had been taken out the previous night.

A few days later the prison door would open again. The same officer would come in and read a list of names. A shiver would go up the spine of each prisoner, thinking that his name could be among the ones the guard was reading out. After reading all the names on his list, the man would once more, in the same sepulchral tone, tell those whose names he had read out to leave the cell.

This time nobody would move.

"Get a move on! Now!" the beast would roar, thrashing his whip threateningly in the air. "I could kill all of you on the spot. Those whose names I've read out must leave immediately."

These prisoners, now condemned to death, would stand up one by one, bid good-bye to their friends, and leave on tottering legs.

The next morning their bodies also swayed dangling in the middle of tripods.

29 June, 1915

Today the police searched the houses of a few Armenians under suspicion. They were looking for weapons and revolutionary publications. My father sent one of his employees to our home to get rid of books like that.

We got rid of about 30 books from my bookcase: *Out of One Jail into Another, Sparks, The Fool, Armenia's Wound* and also pictures of Armenian *fedayin* (freedom fighters) that I kept so carefully in my bottom drawer. I found it impossible to burn them, so I put them in a tin box and buried it in a corner of the garden.

When my father got home this evening, he asked me if I had carried out his orders. I confessed that I had buried a few books and the pictures in the garden. My father got angry and told me to destroy them all at once.

After it got dark, I went to the garden with a spade and a hoe, dug up the tin box, and burned its contents in the fireplace.

5 July, 1915

Although members of Armenian political parties, intellectuals, and dignitaries have been arrested and murdered everywhere, the only mass murders or massacres we had heard of so far were in Van and Zeitoun.

We told ourselves that the Armenians of those two cities had been massacred because they had rebelled, and so we comforted ourselves by supposing that people who didn't raise a fuss were in no danger. Today, however, it became evident that the government was pursuing a policy of exterminating the Armenians and had already massacred the entire Armenian population of the six eastern provinces, with no consideration of either gender or age.

Here is what happened in the province of Sivas, and especially in the city of Sivas. A woman from Marsovan, one of our accountants, told us about it today. We got goose pimples from hearing about the extermination of our unfortunate brothers.

First they arrested all the well-known Armenians of the city and put them in jail. Then they deported all the women, old people, and children who were left. While they were on the road, Turkish peasants seized all the beautiful women and put the rest to the sword. They did not spare either the elderly or the children from the carnage. The killers acted with such incredible barbarism that some of them grabbed infants by their legs and split them in two before the eyes of their crazed mothers.

Then they let out all those who were in prison and told them to march in groups to a camp near Malatia. Some Circassian marauding bands and *chetejis* who had been placed all along the road attacked these prisoners, killed around 5,000 of them, and threw them into the valleys and ravines.

6 July, 1915

We live in constant fear and terror. The situation is more serious than anyone might think.

Today the foremost Armenians in Chorum had a secret meeting with my father at our house. My father has sympathetic contacts in government circles and meets with Governor Galib Bey every day.

In reply to my father's question whether the Armenians of Chorum were in any danger, Galib Bey had answered as follows: "No, we can be absolutely certain of that. There were deportation orders only for the six eastern provinces, and they have already been carried out. If they were going to be extended to the entire Armenian population of Turkey, they would have been executed at the same time everywhere in the country."

Then my father had asked the governor what his position and attitude to the Armenians would be if a second order arrived for the Armenians of our city.

"The Armenians of Chorum have always been very loyal to the government and have never been involved in political parties," answered the governor.

"But if the order arrives?"

"Naturally at that time I'll do whatever I can, and with little loss of time, to keep you out of danger."

On the other hand, a great many reports arrived from the six eastern provinces, confirming what we had already heard. We have learned that within the regions of Malatia, Harpoot (Kharpert), Diyarbekir, Erzinjan, and Erzeroom there are no Armenians left.

8 July, 1915

The news from Marsovan is awful.

The four wagon drivers who deliver flour from our mill to Samsoun returned from Marsovan yesterday. It takes one day to get to Chorum from Marsovan by wagon.

They say that a week ago the government rounded up all the men from their homes and shops and imprisoned them in the military barracks. Then a town crier went through the streets and announced that all the men between 15 and 17 years old had to report to the garrison, and that those who refused to do so would be sentenced to death and their houses burned down.

They all reported. After collecting the entire male population of the city, they took them in groups of about 200 a couple of hours outside the city, and on the road to Zilé, they slaughtered all of them —after taking all their money and valuables from them first, of course.

Then they put the women, the old people, and the children on the road and sent them off to Mosul. Before they reached Vezir Kopru the mob attacked their convoy and, after choosing all the beautiful young women and setting them aside, they put the rest to the sword.

The wagon drivers say that the same thing also happened around Zilé, Amasia, and Ourfa (Edessa), under almost identical conditions. Every Turkish peasant has filled his house with looted goods. And there isn't a city dweller who hasn't taken his share either of the massacre or of plunder—a beautiful woman, a little boy, or a girl.

12 July, 1915

The Armenians of the Black Sea region have also been deported under extremely cruel conditions. They were all forbidden to take any money or provisions for their immediate needs.

We have many relatives and friends in Samsoun. As soon as my father heard they had been deported with no money and no clothing, he sent one of his employees to them with money, food, and clothing.

Fear and terror began to reign again in Chorum. So much for the governor's conviction that the deportation orders were only for the six eastern provinces, as Samsoun was not in these provinces.

19 July, 1915

Our employee came back from Samsoun today. He brought back everything my father had sent for the Armenian deportees; they have slaughtered all the Armenian men and the women are being sent to Malatia, where it was impossible to trace them.

Today we are mourning the deaths of our loved ones, who left us and never returned, victims of Turkish hatred and savage vengeance.

We now feel that there is no escape; the same tragic fate awaits all of us.

25 July, 1915

The waves of death have quickly widened and have now reached the gates of Chorum. It is now certain that we will not be spared the tragic fate planned for all the Armenians in Turkey.

I went to my father's business this morning. A bit later I saw a policeman and a couple of gendarmes standing in front of our door. The policeman came in and asked me where my father was. When I told him he was working in his office, he went in to see him. He saluted my father and told him that the governor would like to see him.

"Very well then." My father was busy writing a letter. "Do you mind if I finish this first?"

"Go ahead, please," replied the policeman politely.

My father finished the letter, left a few instructions with his secretary, and headed for the door. Seeing the armed gendarmes there, he smiled sadly and remarked: "You didn't need these people. I would have gone without these gendarmes."

The policeman did not answer. Without further ado, my father stationed himself between the two armed soldiers and walked off, leaving us in a state of great anxiety and sadness.

"No doubt it's about Caesarea again. He won't get off so easily this time!" said one of the employees.

A bit later the arrest of two other Armenians gave a different turn to the employee's theory. Had the deportation order arrived, perhaps? Was the Armenian population of Chorum also going to be ordered to leave? If that were the case, why didn't the police capture or arrest every Armenian they encountered?

The mystery didn't last long. They first collected the foremost citizens of the city, then they came back again to our business premises to take us all out, lock our shop and offices, and lead all of the Armenian employees off to jail. As I was only fifteen years old, they left me behind.

I was extremely affected by what had happened and rushed home to tell my mother about the tragedy. When I got home, I realized that my family had already heard, not only that but also that children younger than I was had also been arrested. It seems that it was a miracle that I had been left behind.

I scarcely had time to rejoice, for the police arrived to search the houses in our neighborhood. They arrested three neighbors and took them to prison too. We were again lucky that they didn't visit our house; otherwise they would have taken me as well.

So here we are; we spend our days in terror. Every time someone knocks at the door we think that the police have come to fetch me.

26 July, 1915

When I woke up this morning, my mouth was dry and my tongue all white. I had hardly slept all night; evil thoughts kept turning over in my mind. I kept asking myself why they were arresting and detaining the men. Did they intend to massacre or deport them? If we remembered what had happened in Marsovan, Amasia, Samsoun, and Sivas, there was nothing we could do but wait for our death knell to sound. Fortunately, we still had some hope: a hope inspired by Governor Galib Bey, that in the event of a deportation order for the Armenians of Chorum he would try to save them at all costs.

Galib Bey repeated this promise yesterday, when my father and other prominent citizens were taken to see him. He showed them a telegram he had received from Angora and told them that he had no choice but to arrest the men; he would, however, do his best to ensure that not a single Armenian would suffer, within the limits of his power, of course.

By evening we had sold our furniture for the measly sum of 10 liras. Every time the door bell rang I ran up to the attic, terrified, and hid in a recess. The police came looking for me twice today, and returned empty-handed each time.

The beds have been sold, so tonight, for the first time, I slept on the floor.

28 July, 1915

The police came to search our house again today, but they didn't think of checking the little corner where I was hiding in the attic. After the police left, my mother went to the jail for news of my father.

She returned in an hour, happy and sad at the same time. She was happy because it was obvious that the men would be deported with their families. Where and how were not important: it would be all right as long as they weren't taken away to be exterminated. She was also sad, because we had to leave today, and my father's Turkish friends, who had promised to help us financially, had gone back on their promises.

"Sell all the furniture," my father had told us, "because we're leaving today and we absolutely must have money to travel."

Fortunately, the government allowed us to sell our furniture in the afternoon, and the streets were full of buyers. So we opened our door and invited them in. There were about 600 people in our courtyard and garden and on the first and upper floors. We took in 20 liras for 9 rooms full of furniture. When my father returned home everything had been snapped up and it was all over.

Fortunately, my father borrowed 100 pounds from one of his Turkish friends, so we don't leave completely threadbare. A little later my father's Turkish employees arrived with three closed carriages and parked them in front of the house. They are rented carriages, because our personal vehicles are in Samsoun at the moment.

We collected the bare necessities together and climbed into the carriages. My grandmother, her sister—another octogenarian like her—and father's nephew Arshag got into the first carriage, in which we also had our provisions. A sackful of *baksimad*s, which we had prepared for our relatives deported from Samsoun. In the second carriage were my paternal aunt and her three children, Haig, Aram, and Haygouhi. And, in the third carriage, my father, my mother, my sisters Manoushag and Arpiné, my brother Souren, and me.

I wanted to have a last look around the house before we left. My room—how sad—I had spent the most beautiful nights of my life there, sleeping, dreaming. The living room was also quiet and deserted. My study room, with its desk and books. The dining room, where we had thrown so many parties and had so many celebrations.

I opened the doors of all the rooms one after the other and, after a quick glance, shut them again. All of the rooms were sad—each sadder than the others. I went out on the balcony and gazed at the garden, which lay spread beneath my feet. The fountain that my father had brought from somewhere three hours away and paid for in person. It sputtered away continuously, but the flowers were faded; they had been neglected for the last three days. There wasn't even a bird in the trees, as though they had guessed the tragedy that was striking down the family in this house and had all run away.

Destitution, loneliness, and sadness everywhere.

My emotions would not allow me to continue my visit. I went out and entered the carriage, which left immediately. It had a hard time making its way through the crowd and the disorder in the streets.

The Turks cast hateful looks at us. Not yet satisfied, they picked up some of the furniture that had been loaded onto the carriages as if they wanted to buy it, but their intention was to grab them and keep them for free.

A light rain was falling. We went slowly through the streets. I looked at our house, then briefly at my school and the church as we passed in front of them. In half an hour we arrived at the garrison road, where hundreds of carriages were already parked. They were waiting for others to arrive from the city.

In half an hour everything was ready. The carriages started to move, surrounded by policemen. The mob was still following us, hoping that once we were outside the city limits there would be looting and slaughter. As time passed some got discouraged and went back, and finally we were alone with our escort of guards on that deserted road.

Our convoy advances noisily . . .

The city gradually falls away behind us and finally disappears in the misty rain.

I stuck my head out of the window and watched the scenery go by. My heart grieved for the happier times I had spent in these places, before I tasted the bitterness of life. We passed the three-story building of our electric mill, which is beside a river, under the shade of poplar trees, off to itself; it watched us, as though saying good-bye to us. It was to buy equipment for this mill that my father had gone to Europe. Hardly half of the machines had arrived when the War was declared and the roads were closed, and the factory remained half-finished. Seeing it all abandoned, I asked myself if I were not at that moment exactly like the mill—born in abundance, nourished with hope, and then left unfinished.

I couldn't bear to look outside anymore. I pulled my head in and noticed for the first time that my mother was crying. My father was trying to console her, but I saw that he was also terribly moved, and the words stuck in his throat.

At that moment I realized the horrible reality that had been like a dream for the last three days. We have been exiled . . . Our wealth is gone; gone is our dignity, esteem, and honor; we are no longer masters of our destiny, but are now the prisoners of these policemen, who are taking us who knows where? And who knows why? In the evening we arrived at the Tutunji Oghlu *khan*. Twenty families from among us settled down in the few rooms of the rickety building. The rest spent the night outdoors, and so ended the first day of our deportation.

29 July, 1915

When I opened my eyes this morning, it seemed at first that I was still at home and that nothing had happened. Like waking up from a nightmare. It lasted only a minute. The sight of the ceiling, all smudged with smoke and dust, brought me back to reality.

The sun was only a few minutes over the horizon when everybody was up. We all rushed out to get a breath of fresh air. I also got dressed as fast as I could and went out holding my side, which was very sore. I had been sleeping on something hard. But what really caused me pain was the fact that there was no water. We all got into our carriages without washing and continued our journey.

By noon we were all dying of thirst. We kept asking our driver if we would come across water soon.

"Yes, within half an hour," the man would reply. He was not much bothered, though, as he was fasting for Ramadan.

The half hour went by, then another hour, and then another . . . there was no sign of water on the horizon. The sun poured down its burning heat, getting hotter and hotter with every passing minute. As we approached a hill the driver turned to me and said: "Just over the top of the hill, at the edge of the woods on your right, there's a spring. Run there quickly, so you can fill your container before everybody else rushes there."

I jumped down from the carriage at once and ran toward the spring. The other side of the hill was deserted, and the spring was not that close, but I could see where it was by the green grass and bushes in the distance. As I drew closer to the water, I saw three Turks dressed like peasants, sitting under a tree and chatting. My sudden appearance took them by surprise for a few seconds. They stopped talking and watched me for a few moments, as if astonished. Then they got to their feet, looked around, and began walking in my direction.

Why were they coming up to me and what did they want? I suddenly noticed the evil glint in their eyes. I was sorry I hadn't been more careful. I didn't know what to do, but just then the carriages came over the crest the hill. People from the convoy started rushing in our direction with buckets and other containers. When the peasants saw this, they made a hundred-and-eighty-degree turn, ran into the forest, and disappeared.

This is the second day we've been on the road. I've escaped a big danger. Who knows what the future has in store for us? If we survive, that is.

This evening we reached Aladja. Again we spent the night in a khan. My father has done many favors for the chief of this town over the years. When he heard that we were passing through, he came to meet us and arranged for us to be made comfortable.

Today many carriages turned over on the road, and many people were injured.

30 July, 1915

This morning we left Aladja. While we were going along one street, my father showed us a house that belonged to us, pointing from the window of the carriage. He told us that we also owned another house, right behind it. We could scarcely see the front of the house and the garden beside it. The carriage moved on past it and turned at the corner. "What's the use!" we exclaimed. In Chorum we also owned two houses besides the one we lived in, as well as a bakery and a vineyard, but now we were going away and leaving everything behind. Our only concern at the moment was saving our lives.

I wanted to get used to walking, so once more, as I have done for the past two days, I got out of the carriage and walked for an hour. I looked down a length of straight road and was filled with emotion as I saw how large our convoy had grown. We have been joined by 25 to 30 families from Aladja. Hundreds of carriages, filing along one after the other like the cars of a train . . . all pressing forward. People were walking on both sides of the road, all of them tired and sweating, all of them supporting the carriages on that rough terrain so that they wouldn't turn over and topple into the ditch. In front of the caravan, behind it, and on both sides of it rode about 30 policemen, all using their whips on the poor souls who were incapable of walking fast and couldn't even keep up with the horse-drawn carriages. I couldn't watch as those men and women were beaten over and over again. I knew a lot of them. I climbed back onto our carriage and submerged myself for hours in painful, agonizing thoughts.

This evening we heard a loud, heart-rending cry from the end of the caravan. All at once the carriages halted and people started running where the voice had come from. Our school principal's carriage had fallen into the ditch and was completely destroyed. They pulled his old father, who had fainted, from under a heavy pile of goods. After stopping for half an hour we again got on the road, and we stopped for the evening at Arap Seyfi. From here on, we stopped for the night wherever we happened to be when it got dark.

31 July, 1915

Still no water, either to wash in or to drink. Today the road was filled with difficulties. Some carriages passed by, creating a huge cloud of dust behind them which thickly covered the faces and clothes of those walking on both sides of the road. The horses are foaming at the mouth with exhaustion and have a hard time pulling their loads.

Today another sad thing happened. The eight-year-old child of our teacher, Nishan Khoranian, disappeared. The parents searched in vain. They couldn't remain behind the rest of the convoy in order to search further. The police whipped all those who fell behind. So the parents trudged forward, sobbing, their eyes constantly looking to the rear. They probably would have been less distressed if their child had been killed.

In the evening we arrived in Yozgad. When the Turks heard that we had arrived, they came and stood on both sides of the road to watch us pass by. They were surprised that such a huge crowd could stay together and travel like this without being slaughtered. The Armenians of Yozgad had all been massacred outside the city. The Turks give us the "news" that we will enjoy the same fate in the morning, shortly after we leave town.

Bombarded by threats, insults, and extraordinary confusion and uproar, we came to a large inn and went inside. The doors were shut immediately behind us, cutting us off from contact with the outside world.

Late in the evening, a policeman came to see us. This policeman owed my father a favor. He informed us that we would be searched tomorrow, and anything above five pounds in money or jewelry would be confiscated. The news created a great deal of anxiety among the people. The deportees started to hide their money and jewelry in secret places as well as they could. We put some of our money into an earthen jug, some into loaves of bread, and some between the linings and the soles of our shoes. Because of all this activity, we didn't get to sleep until morning.

1 August, 1915

My cousin Parsegh has been doing his military service in Yozgad. Today he came to visit us. The doors of the khan were shut, so we were able to exchange only a few words with him from the window. Because of the strict police surveillance, he couldn't even say good-bye to his mother, sister, and three brothers, and left with tears in his eyes.

Usually we leave early every morning, so we were very worried this morning when our departure was delayed. A little later we heard from our friendly policeman that the governor of Yozgad had telegraphed his counterpart in Chorum, expressing his surprise that we were still alive and traveling in good health and asking what he should do.

His instructions arrived this afternoon. The governor of Chorum said that we should be allowed to travel on, without the slightest violence. The executioner of Yozgad was not satisfied, however. He had evil in mind. Consequently, a while later the doors of the inn opened and in he came, accompanied by a couple of high-ranking officers and a *hodja*.

They stood in the middle of the courtyard holding pencils and notebooks, and one of the officers announced loudly: "Males over thirteen years old, stand on one side; the rest of you, stand on the other side."

We did what we were told, which took about five minutes. We waited for the next order, our hearts in our mouths.

"Women," the governor said, tuning to the women's side, "if you agree to convert to Islam, we'll let you go home. The Sultan offers you this favor to spare you the difficulties and hunger that your men will suffer. Do you accept?"

"If we had wanted to stay at home we would have accepted this offer already, there, on the spot, and we wouldn't be in this situation now," answered some of the women's voices. "We don't want to be separated from our husbands and children. We will follow them with all our hearts, wherever they go."

"It is, in fact, a great sin to do favors to infidels like you," the *hodja* barked, most put out. "You can go to *djehennem*, (Gehenna, Hell) all of you. Go wherever you want. May God's curse be upon you."

Half an hour later the doors of the inn opened and the caravan was on its way, this time under the surveillance of new policemen. The police who had accompanied us from Chorum to Yozgad had already gone back home.

With great fear and anguish, we followed the same road that the Armenian population of Yozgad, about 10,000 strong, had traveled a week earlier. On the road we met a group of hideous *chetejis* (irregular troops), eight of them. As they went by, they leered at us enigmatically.

Despite the fact that we never stopped for the evening until dusk, today the police accompanying us ordered us to stop around two in the afternoon, in the middle of some fields belonging to a village called Topchu. The fields were a bit outside the village. We were all terribly scared, but we did what we were told and got out of the carriages.

The chief of police summoned a few prominent men from our city—my father, Hagop Dadrian, Krikor Toramanian, Sarkis Tintonian, Mgrdich Aslanian, Harutiun Gulbenkian, and Hagop Shirinian—and warned them that he would exterminate all of us if 500 pieces of gold were not put into his hands at once.

My father and his friends explained our situation to the chief, telling him that we had been put on the road in a rush and had no opportunity to take any money with us. If we had had a few pieces of gold, we would have spent them on the road for bare necessities.

The chief of police couldn't care less. He was adamant about his demand and insisted that he would order the massacre to begin if he didn't receive the sum of money he had asked for. After a great deal of difficulty the chief was persuaded to accept 200 pieces of gold instead of 500.

They started to collect the money right away. Nobody could produce more than 50 pounds. The rest my father and his friends took from their own pockets and gave the money to the chief.

We spent a terribly emotional night, as if the black ghost of death were hovering over us.

2 August, 1915

Our school principal's father, who was crushed under an overturned carriage two days ago, died, and so his suffering came to an end. A strange coincidence: a baby was born in our caravan today.

The police bother us constantly. Whenever we go through valleys and dangerous regions, they order us to stop the carriages and threaten us with slaughter if we do not make up the 500 pieces of gold that they initially demanded. Today we paid another 150, and that shut their mouths.

We stopped at the village of Seyyah this evening. We had a hard time finding bread in this place. Wherever we went, they slammed the doors in our faces: "Be damned, infidels!" they shouted. A few who did manage to find bread paid four times its worth for it.

From the savage hatred and fanaticism of the local people, we conclude that day by day we are driving farther into those areas where people are more incensed against Armenians than in the Chorum region.

3 August, 1915

Our insecurity increases more and more every day. As we crossed a bridge we saw corpses: naked and swollen, some of them washed up on the sand by the current.

The Turkish police and drivers pointed them out to us, laughing loudly and telling us that those corpses were the inhabitants of nearby regions and that we would have soon been like them if we had not paid them the ransom they had demanded.

Three hours later, all along the road, we saw male corpses and breathed their foul stench, which completely polluted the atmosphere.

This evening we stopped for the night in a place called Serchali Tekke. Here we were joined by the second convoy from Chorum, approximately 20 families. They had also saved their lives by paying the same ransom to the police.

During the night about 50 cavalry *chetejis* surrounded our caravan. They got off their horses and walked through the crowd of people, examining all the women and the furniture and insulting us, saying that we were quite chunky morsels but it wouldn't take them long to swallow all of us. Proudly showing us their gold watches, rings, and other valuables, they said that their horses' saddlebags were full of such objects. In a way they were revealing the enormous crime that they were returning from.

The minutes were agonizing. My father and his friends at once went to the officer in charge of the police and begged him to get rid of the *chetejis*.

The commanding officer talked with the head *cheteji* for about a quarter of an hour, then sent them away, delivering us from a horrible nightmare. Nevertheless, we couldn't sleep all night, afraid that the thugs would come back and kill us all.

4 August, 1915

We left before sunrise, quickly putting as much distance as possible between us and that hellish region, where we had suffered the unassuageable sweat of death for more than ten hours. Once again we came across corpses on the road. The chief of police pointed them out to us and again asked for money, and this time he was within his rights—after all, he managed to save us from the bandits yesterday.

We went through Boghazlian this afternoon. Fifteen minutes outside the city we saw a gendarme who had just killed a man and was still standing near him. The dead man was lying on his face and was dressed in dark city clothes. The gendarme was resting the butt of his gun on the dead man's back and calmly watching our caravan go by, while the shoulders of his victim still twitched with the spasms of death.

Then we passed through Boghazlian. The Armenian population of this place and the surrounding villages had all been slaughtered. The Turks of the town watched us in amazement and muttered: "Look how lucky these people are. They can travel, alive and healthy, with their women and children . . . Who is letting them get away with this?"

We too were amazed at our luck as we passed through the deserted and spoiled Armenian villages, filled with corpses. Death has extended its arms over everything. In spite of the fact that Turkish peasants and *chetejis* constantly surrounded us, looking for an opportunity to butcher and loot, it seemed that a supernatural force was protecting us, and we continued our way without obstacle through these blood-soaked regions that only a short while before had been the burial ground of hundreds and thousands of our kinsmen. What could be the explanation of this supernatural force? Is it perhaps the result of the order given by the governor of Chorum, or the influence of the gold pieces pressed into the palms of the police every day? We don't know, but we are still breathing and that's all we care about.

Boghazlian was scarcely half an hour behind us when there was a sudden commotion. A policeman galloped up to us from the city and wanted to see my father. He pulled up quickly beside our carriage, verified my father's identity, and said that the deputy governor wanted to see him.

"Me? Why? What's wrong?" my father asked in surprise.

"I don't know. Please follow me," answered the policeman.

Everybody stood in the middle of the road and watched as my father got out of the carriage and left with the man. He had no idea what this unusual circumstance could mean. Hours passed, but still my father did not return. The later it got the more anxious we became, especially whenever our thoughts returned to the corpse we had seen just before Boghazlian . . . Before long we were filled with great happiness, when the carriages behind us passed forward the good news that my father was returning. The others were even happier than we were because Armenag *Effendi* was the only person in the caravan who could lead them and obtain favors from the police.

This is what happened: the deputy-governor of Boghazlian—and fortunately the monsterous Armenian-devouring governor who had given the order that all the Armenians of the region should be annihilated was away that day—had seen our convoy passing through town and wondered who we were, where we came from, and how we had managed to survive without being massacred as we crossed the death-belt. So he had sent a mounted policeman to fetch one of the prominent members of the caravan so he could find out. When the policeman arrived, he apparently asked who the leader was. Everybody told him that it was Dadrian Armenag.

And so the policeman had come to bring my father to the deputy-governor in Boghazlian. There, after the deputy had obtained the necessary information from my father, he sent a rush telegram to the governor of Chorum, saying that he suspected we had been sentenced to death but that we had succeeded in surviving by bribing the police who accompanied us.

The governor, Galib Bey, remained faithful to his promise and told the deputy to allow us to continue our journey in safety. After that telegram arrived my father was set free and returned to us.

The caravan began to move again. We spent the night in a field, in which there was a huge well completely filled with corpses. The police told us to cover the corpses with earth so that we wouldn't have to look at them. I did, however, notice the tip of a man's foot and the thin arm of an adolescent sticking out, despite the earth thrown on them.

5 August, 1915

On the road there were two more corpses. They were stark naked and lying next to each other. There were blood stains on one's knee and similar stains on the other's back .

Armed peasants carrying sacks follow us on donkeys. They hope to slaughter and rob us. The police—who have now become our friends—chase them away with the butts of their guns. These rude yokels think the police are joking, and they continue to follow us like ravenous dogs, forming a second convoy behind ours.

Today, however, the police tricked us. One of them, who had fallen behind, suddenly began whipping his horse and rode up to us, all the time shouting, "Good news! Good news!"

We were stunned. We wondered what had happened. The policeman, all covered with sweat, drew up to us and said that orders had been received that the Armenians from Chorum were to be settled in Caesarea and the surrounding area.

There were no bounds to our happiness. In no time at all the people collected a handkerchief-full of money—mostly loose change—and gave it to the policeman. A little later, though, we were told that what he had done was just a joke.

We don't mind this kind of joke. Let them take whatever we have, provided they protect us from the thieves who are following in our footsteps, hoping for their share of the pie.

We spent the night in a large stone building on the banks of Kizil Irmak. The banks of the river are covered with hundreds of corpses, both men's and women's. It is impossible to drink from the river or breathe the air.

Here again the inhabitants of the neighboring Turkish villages came out, armed with hatchets, axes, and huge knives, and surrounded us. It seems they make a habit of massacring the caravans that camp on the banks of the river.

The police fired into the air a few times to frighten them off. The murderers left but took up positions on the other side of the river, where they waited all night long, hoping that the police would eventually change their attitude.

We couldn't sleep all night. But in spite of that, there were many incidents of robbery. A policeman pulled one of our woolen blankets off my grandmother and disappeared. We saw the theft, but not wanting to create a scene, we didn't say anything.

6 August, 1915

Early this morning we got up and continued on our way. The thieves who had spent the night on the opposite bank of the river closed in on us again and took advantage of the police's inattentiveness to begin grabbing everything they could lay their hands on—carpets, hats, shoes, clothes, etc.—threatening to kill anyone who resisted. At last, though, the police came and forced the thieves to run away for good. One person had disappeared from the caravan during the night, a blacksmith. They think he went to get a drink from the river and was killed by the thieves.

At noon the police stopped us and ordered the men and women to separate. We separated from each other in a large field, the men on one side and the women on the other. The police carefully counted all the men, one by one, then they did the same for the women, and then they began talking among themselves, which lasted for quite some time. In the meantime, we waited in total anxiety, knocking our brains out with worry. Finally the police chief called my father and two other prominent men and asked them how we would pay him back for protecting us from undeniable dangers and saving our lives so many times since Yozgad.

My father and his friends thanked him for his timely kindnesses and promised that they would again raise money this evening to reward him as he deserves.

After that the order was given for the men and women to rejoin each other. We got back on our carriages and carried on.

In the evening we arrived at a deserted place called Dibsiz. It is two hours from Caesarea, a marshy steppe. They collected money from the wealthy tonight, and the proceeds were delivered to the police. They took the money and left, transferring their duties to a fresh battalion of policemen who had just arrived from Caesarea.

7 August, 1915

We had only been on the road for a few hours today when the police ordered us to camp again in a huge open space on the edge of a forest.

"Form a circle! Quickly!" roared the police chief, bringing his whip down cruelly on Father Anania, because the priest had driven his carriage the wrong way. "Make a perfect circle . . . Haven't any of you served in the army?"

Not a single soul escaped a beating, and eventually a perfect circle was formed. Then the chief of police summoned the leading men from the caravan, led them into the depths of the forest, and apparently said: "I see that you are traveling as though you were going to a wedding, with all of your family and furniture, and in great comfort. You are God's chosen people. The Armenians here were also Armenians like you, but they were massacred. Now it's your turn. They didn't transfer any specific number of you to me . . . If I wanted to, I could have you all wiped out this very minute. Go get me 300 pieces of gold; if you don't, I know how to squeeze money from you."

"But chief," my father and his friends replied, "just take a look at our carriages! Do you think they are carrying anything of value? All that's in them is beds, blankets, clothing and underwear, provisions, and so forth. We left our homes in such a great hurry that we didn't even have time to take the money in our shops with us. Spare us. We don't have that much money to give you. As a matter of fact, the policemen who accompanied us before you robbed us of everything we had."

"Don't talk nonsense!" the policeman apparently told them. "I know how much you paid them before we took over . . . I am asking for less than they took from you. Take your pick. Either pay 300 gold pieces or you'll all be killed. And if that happens, you can be sure that I'll be able to get 3,000 gold pieces out of you, not just 300!"

"Of course we'd rather pay 300 pounds than lose all of our lives," my father and his friends replied. "But we are not able to pay you. You know that. Do what you want. We leave it up to your conscience."

"Then go get 200 pounds. I feel sorry for you. Just be thankful I'm in a good mood today," the detestable police chief repeated.

It was very hard to get together this last sum of 200 pounds. The people knew that it was the price for their blood, but they no longer had anything to give. As for the rich people, they had given so much already that their wallets were also empty. In the end, however, the use of scare tactics and threats made it possible to get the money together, and it was wrapped in a handkerchief and delivered to the chief of police.

My father said that when he passed the money over to the policeman, the latter counted it quickly, and seeing that it was a pound short—probably he had miscounted in his haste—he threw the handkerchief in my father's face, complaining that people were cheating to get away with paying a pound less. My father knew that nothing was missing, but he apologized, took a pound from his own pocket, and gave it to him.

It rained hard all night. We stayed in our carriages, and were soaked to the bones. Everybody who slept under the carriages was covered in mud.

We all looked dirty and miserable.

8 August, 1915

Today, many of the Turkish carriage drivers did not want to go any farther, despite the fact that they were paid in advance to take us from Chorum to the border of the province of Angora. They had agreed to these conditions at the start of the trip but they had probably been hoping that after Chorum they would be able to slaughter us and go back with their carriages loaded down with furniture and maidens.

Once they realized that the situation did not exactly measure up to their calculations and that their expectations would not be realized, they wanted to unload the carriages today and go back. They would have carried out their plans if the police hadn't objected.

Because of this situation, we were prevented from leaving until around noon today. Two hours later we met the Armenians of Talas, riding on donkeys and in one-horse carriages. They were traveling just like us, but we didn't know where. Two hours after that we also met 2,000 young men traveling in rows of four in the opposite direction. In answer to our questions, they told us that they were Armenians from the provinces and had been deported from Constantinople. When we asked them where they were going, they simply replied:

"To be killed."

In the afternoon we met some people from Boursa. Their convoy was advancing on foot—they were tired human skeletons, with no strength left for walking.

This evening we arrived in Indje Sou. On the road the Turkish drivers killed an Armenian, but we didn't dare to tell anyone about the killing. The life of an Armenian is not even worth as much as the life of a chicken.

9 August, 1915

We left Indje Sou this morning. Half an hour out of the city the road began to climb steeply. To make things a bit easier on the horses, I got out of the carriage and was walking ahead a little, when I suddenly heard a sharp scream from behind me. I turned and saw that six Turkish peasants armed with cudgels and one with the thick axle of a cart were trying to snatch the coat my mother used to cover herself at night. When I heard my mother's call for help, I ran to our carriage as fast as I could, started tugging on one end of the coat, and shouted at the thieves: "Let go! You have no right to take it!"

One of the peasants sized me up with a terrifying look and spat through his teeth: "Get lost! Scram! . . . I could tear your mouth open like a piece of canvas."

I ignored this threat—inexperience, I guess—and kept tugging on the coat, when I suddenly noticed that one of the monsters was getting ready to attack me with his cudgel. There was no way I could avoid the blow. The cudgel landed on my head, a second blow fell on my shoulder, and a third on my back.

I don't know what happened after that. Half an hour later I found myself in our jostling carriage. My father, unconscious, his face covered with a bloody cloth, was lying next to me, and next to him sat my mother. She was constantly changing the cloth that covered my father's face. My sisters and my brother were frightened and squatted in a corner of the carriage, watching my father and at times watching me solemnly.

My entire body ached, as though my bones had been crushed. I didn't cry, though. The bloody appearance of my father had paralyzed me. I no longer had the strength to cry out.

A bit later I heard from my mother that when the thieves threw me to the ground and continued to beat me, my father sprang from the carriage at once and covered me with his body to protect me. Then the blows poured down on him, and one of the enraged peasants hit him in the face with the axle he was holding so violently that my father fell down unconscious. We would both have been dead if the police had not heard the shouts of the onlookers and come to save us. When the thieves saw the police coming they ran away, naturally remembering to take the coat with them. Our blood-soaked bodies were carried to the carriage, and soon the caravan began to move again.

This evening we arrived at a vast inn. I got down from the carriage, limping, and we carried our father to a room in the basement. He is still unconscious and has a deep cut on his nose that won't stop bleeding. We have no way to treat him.

10 August, 1915

We spent a tormented night, but we were still alive when we got on the road again this morning. After several long fits, my father finally regained consciousness. The wound on his face looks horrible and is still bleeding now and then. He still travels lying down in the carriage with his head wrapped in a bandage. We sit quietly next to him, afraid to talk or move, trying not to disturb him.

This evening we arrived in Karahissar, where we spent the night at another inn. We carried my father to a room and put him to bed so he could rest. I was getting ready to go to town to buy a few necessities from a pharmacy. Unfortunately, at that moment, the police ordered us to get ready to get on the road again at once. We moved my father back to the carriage, but within five minutes there was another order to stay. This time we moved back to the khan, but there was no further opportunity to go into town because the police were spreading rumors that we would soon be leaving again—but they were joking as usual.

11 August, 1915

The first thing I did this morning was to go to the market to buy drugs, a hat, and a pair of shoes, as the thieves in Indje Sou stole my hat and shoes when they attacked us.

My father is a bit better today. We washed his wound with antiseptic, covered it with cotton, and wrapped it in a bandage before we left.

As we travel deeper into Anatolia, the anger and violence against Armenians increase. The Turkish peasants refuse to sell us bread and barley for our horses. This evening they even set a trap to rob and kill some Armenians in the caravan, but they did not succeed.

There is a Turkish village about 15 minutes from the khan where we were staying. Some peasants on their way there told us that we could get bread and barley in the village and offered to take anyone who wanted to go there with them. A group of Armenians, not suspecting a trap, went with the peasants. Half way to the village, though, the Turks suddenly attacked them with their sickles and would have killed them if the Armenians had not been alert and able to escape.

Many caravans have stopped at the same caravansary. There are names written in pencil on a wall in one of the rooms, and also the following ill-boding sentence: "There are 502 (or 562, it isn't very legible) of us, and they'll slaughter us all right here."

12 August, 1915

After quite a tiring journey we stopped in a field near Nigde. As if the inhabitants of the city had been waiting for us, they came in groups and spread through the crowd. They showed no hesitation about picking up anything they liked and offering to buy it for next to nothing. If the owner of the object refused, they taunted him, saying: "What good is it to you? You'll be killed soon anyway."

The situation was critical. As more and more armed people arrived and the crowd gradually grew larger, we asked the police to put us on the road again. Otherwise everything, including our lives, honor, and belongings would have been in danger during the night. (Needless to say, these were not the same policemen who accompanied us from Caesarea. They were replaced at Indje Sou, and the ones from Indje Sou were replaced in Karahissar. They change from city to city. Whenever they hand over the convoy to the next group of guards, they always tell them how much head tax they have collected from us. In other words, they make sure they know enough to do the same. Anyway, the new guards had just received their money from us, so they couldn't refuse our request and let us get on the road again. It is night . . .

Everywhere is silent, except for the clatter of our carriages, which shatters the silence all along the stony road.

In the carriage just ahead of ours the wife of one of the eminent men of the city, Mgrdich Aslanian, was in labor. She was having a baby. Every time the carriage went over a bump, she let out a heart-rending scream. Listening to her filled us with sadness and concern. But we couldn't afford to stop, not even for a second. The crowd from Nigde was following us. At last, not long afterwards, we heard that the woman had a baby girl and is now comfortable.

We kept on going. Suddenly we heard an uproar coming from the carriages behind us. A group of thieves hiding under a bridge attacked the unprotected men and women. By the time the police arrived from the head of the convoy, there were two dead and seven injured lying on the ground.

The carriages continue their cacophonous run. Everywhere it is dark. There are thousands of us—trying to escape . . . From out of the darkness bullets are fired over and at the sides of the carriages. Sometimes a sharp scream . . . sometimes a painful cry . . . pierces the night. No one looks back, no one looks forward, but everyone runs . . . We run . . . for hours and hours . . . until we put the danger of death behind us.

The exhausted travelers throw themselves down in a field. We are not far from Bor. There is no water, no bread—but who cares about such details now?

13 August, 1915

We got ready as early as possible and hit the road before dawn. We passed through Kiz Hissar and arrived in a place called Kolsuz this evening. On the road we met the Armenian peasants from Injirli. They were traveling in miserable conditions, some on foot and others in small carts. Among them a very beautiful young girl with blonde hair caught my attention. She was sick and lying in a cart, and her old grandmother was walking next to the cart, constantly goading the oxen.

Today, on the road, we also saw locusts, which covered everything with their green bodies and thousands of them were crushed under our feet and wheels.

The sight of them made me think: weren't we a lot like those creatures, scattered everywhere, abandoned on every road, while bloody heels crush us without mercy and kill us?

14 August, 1915

The drivers who have driven us this far from Chorum did not want to continue any farther. They sold their carriages and went back. We could buy only two carriages instead of three, but managed with some difficulty to put everything into the two of them and continued our trip. We are happy to be outside the boundaries of Angora at last. We think we have escaped the danger of mass murder, although naturally not the danger of individual killings, as we were again attacked by the Turks today.

We brought the convoy to a halt in fields near Ulu Kishla this evening. The Armenians from Konia and its environs also spent the night there with us. The police threatened us. They wanted to take us to the deportation station in Ulu Kishla and send us by train to Aleppo. But we had heard that this was a trap for confiscating all our goods at the first station and then leaving us with nothing for the rest of our journey, so we bribed the police to allow us to travel by our own means.

We have no more money. We began selling my mother's decorative gold pieces to pay our expenses as we travel on.

15 August, 1915

Now we have to drive our own carriages. We take turns with Arshag driving our carriage. The road is in such a bad condition that we progress with great difficulty. All of the other drivers are as unskilled as we are. The number of accidents has increased in the last two days. And today we broke the record for overturned carriages. If the road ahead of us is as mountainous and as difficult, no doubt we'll all end up with broken carriages and won't be able to reach our destination.

At noon we went through a deserted Armenian village. Its bell tower could be seen through the trees. The fruit on the trees had ripened and fallen to the ground. A little farther down in the village we stopped to bury a cobbler's daughter. The little girl had fallen sick and died during the journey. Her corpse had slipped off the carriage, and if the people in the carriage behind them hadn't noticed, her parents would have kept going, unaware.

The number of people who have died since we left Chorum is now over 30.

Again this evening we stopped in a field and spent the night repairing our carriages and binding our wounds.

16 August, 1915

Since this morning we have been traveling on mountainous roads. They wind endlessly and are in terrible condition. On our left rise towering majestic rocks, and on our right are deep ravines. The slightest wrong move could send you down in no time.

Around noon we were all out of our carriages holding the reins of the horses and were advancing carefully when we suddenly noticed a man coming around a bend in the road, brandishing a huge sword in his hand. A minute later hundreds of other men also came round the same bend, all brandishing swords, while thousands of invisible throats poured forth a deafening roar that exploded in the mountains and valleys.

"*Le illahi illallah . . .*"

Our anxiety and fear were indescribable. We didn't know who they were and why they were coming. In a moment a huge crowd had came round the corner and was rapidly approaching us. They were all dressed in rags. They had bare chests and legs, and wore no hats.

We were petrified and couldn't move—we didn't know if they were coming for us or if they were also travelers.

This bizarre crowd of people gradually got nearer. There were ten or twelve people at the head of the crowd, brandishing swords in the air and shouting: "Allah, Allah!" The rest of the crowed followed them, in the meantime repeating in muffled voices, "*Le illahi illallah . . .*"

Fortunately they were not armed, except for the ones at the front of the crowd, who were carrying swords. Singing and hopping up and down to the rhythm of their songs, these people soon reached us. As we were among the first carriages at the front of the convoy, they glared at us savagely and showered us with incomprehensible insults as if they were speaking Arabic. One of them came close to our carriage and was getting ready to grab a bag. Just at that moment, a cavalry officer who was accompanying them happened to pass, and he drew his revolver and ordered the man to drop the bag. The order was obeyed instantaneously. It was a miracle. . . . the first time we had met somebody along the way who protected us!

The crowd passed us and disappeared. We learned from the police that they were Arab soldiers—even though they didn't look like soldiers—who were on their way to the Dardanelles to fight the British.

This evening we met some Arab refugees. They were in miserable condition and were being led to the interior of Turkey. At first we thought that they had been robbed on the road, but later we heard that these poor blessed people always went around naked and barefoot, even in their own country.

To think that we are going to the land of these barefoot people, and we expect to find kindness there!

This evening we passed through Bozanti, about half an hour outside the city, and camped on the edge of a cedar forest. There we met Armenian refugees from Konia and Akshehir.

Until today we had at least a vague idea of where we were going. Whenever we asked the police where we were going, they replied, "Aleppo." We all wondered how they would ever manage to settle such a huge crowd of refugees in that city.

Today the mystery was clarified when by chance we met an Armenian soldier on his way from Aleppo. We asked him what the Armenians were doing in Aleppo. The soldier told us that the Armenians were being sent from there to the desert . "What can all those people do in the sand?" we asked, thinking that by desert he meant an endless expanse of land covered with sand.

The Armenian laughed at our naïveté and explained that we shouldn't think only of vast expanses covered with sand. A desert can also be land covered with stones, bushes, and thistles.

"You can travel through those deserted expanses for days and weeks on end without ever seeing a single living soul," said the soldier. "Sometimes there are serpents crawling underfoot, sometimes you hear the sound of a hungry beast in the distance, and sometimes you see an eagle in the sky, gliding on spread wings. These are the inhabitants of the desert. After traveling across these deserts for weeks on end, you may come to the real desert, covered with sand, or to places that have water and are inhabited. There the Bedouins, Chechens, and many other races plunder and kill without fear of being pursued by the government. As you get farther away from the desert, you come to the Fellah villages, where the people are less savage. They also are thieves, however lazy and fanatical. Then you come to big cities, where the people are more or less civilized."

"And when you get away from the big cities, you come to Fellah villages again, then the Bedouins, and after that barren wildernesses and deserts covered with sand?"

"Yes."

"What will the Armenians do in the desert? Will they find means to make a living?"

"I don't think so. The Arabs live in such appalling conditions that they dig up corpses from the graves so they can use their shrouds as clothing. If such people don't rob you of everything you have, consider yourselves lucky. To top it all off, the climate of the region is unbearable and there is disease and illness everywhere."

This Armenian soldier's information about the Arabian desert grieved our souls. We were happy that we had escaped mass murders, but now we think that we are all being driven out into the desert to be buried under the sand!

17 August, 1915

Today, for the first time since we left Chorum, we did not travel. We rested. From morning to night there was continuous activity in the convoy. Some repaired their carriages; some sewed up their torn shoes; some washed their soiled clothes and underwear; others washed themselves in the river; some rested, shaved, and cooked a hot meal for the first time in ages.

After repairing the broken wheel of our carriage, we took the horses to the river and washed them, and then rested in the shade of the thistles. At night we built a bonfire and sat around it discussing tomorrow's uncertainties.

18 August, 1915

Our trip today would have been very difficult if we had not let the horses rest all day yesterday. We were continually climbing the sides of steep mountains. We were worried because at any minute we might have been crushed under heavy stones falling from the top. The Turkish soldiers who are building roads up there deliberately send huge rocks crashing down the side. They consider it an act of bravado and laugh out loud. These rocks, as huge as meteorites, roll down so very fast that they uproot all the vegetation on the slope of the mountain. If any of them were to collide with a carriage, it could send the vehicle and all the people in it rolling into a precipice. Fortunately, the total damage caused by this mad cruelty was only one broken arm.

The road was better this afternoon. We passed through steep rocky passages with Greek writing on the sides. It said that in the old days half of Alexander the Great's victorious army passed this way.

What a contrast between those armies and our convoys!

Some camels were approaching from the opposite direction. Our horses shied, Arshag made a wrong move, and our carriage turned over. I happened to be sitting in the front part of the carriage at the time, so I could see the danger and had time to throw myself out. The other members of our family, however, tumbled with the carriage and had injuries to their arms and legs. My father, who had hardly recovered from the wound on his face, was injured again. Fortunately this injury was less serious than the other. And we were most fortunate that nothing really serious happened to the carriage.

Tonight we arrived in Mezar Oluk.

19 August, 1915

Here we met many arrested Armenians my father got to know when he was put in jail in Caesarea. They were shackled together and were being taken to Diyarbekir to be tried at the war tribunal. They told us that Parsegh Tabibian, who was arrested with my father in Chorum, had been taken from Caesarea and killed on the road to Diyarbekir. They were not very sure whether they would arrive there alive either.

One of the prisoners explained that he had been caned 450 times on his feet. He took his shoes off and showed us his feet. Although more or less healed they looked more like chunks of flesh than feet. First they had pulled out the poor man's nails and then cut off his fingers And his legs were covered with scars.

Another one showed his chest and forearm, which had been burnt by red-hot iron rods. Although without exception they had all had been tortured in prison, they still counted their blessings that they were alive . . . that they had not been sent to the gallows. A half hour from Mezar Oluk, lying in a field by the edge of the road we saw the corpse of a young man. There was a bullet hole in his skull. His blood-soaked hair added an awful aspect to his lead-colored face. The killer had left him in only his socks and drawers.

This evening we camped in a field near Tarsus.

20 August, 1915

We slept the night . . .

This has turned into a common expression, used all the time even if we don't close our eyes all night. We didn't sleep last night either, but this time it wasn't out of fear that the *chetejis* might massacre us. It was impossible to close our eyes because of the lice.

This field was occupied by Turkish soldiers before us. The ground was swarming with the little beasts they left behind. They were so many that in a tiny square we could easily count twenty or more. The police have brought us here deliberately, so we can catch Typhus and die.

What fiendish imaginations! What else will they think of to wipe out this unfortunate people?

On top of all these evils, our executioners have declared that we are not going to leave today.

21 August, 1915

Today again we did not leave. We, who needed so much rest, begged the police to take us away from this place. We scratch all day, until we bleed.

The police do not allow us to go to town to buy a few things that we need. We all try to stay out of the field and we spend most of our time bathing in the river. In the evening we return to the same damned field, our heads bent in sadness.

We had tasted all kinds of hardship and torture, but we had never thought of this one!

22 August, 1915

Some good news came today. Our torture in that flea-pit had come to an end and we would get on the road immediately.

We yoked the horses as quickly as we could and used our whips as we raced our carriages out of that accursed field, as if the ground burned our feet. But what's the use? We are carrying our unwelcome guests with us. They have now penetrated our clothes, bags . . . every fold. They give us no rest with their sharp bites.

When we got to Yenidje we bribed the police to let us stay there the whole day, so we could get washed. Today, I'm not feeling well. I think lack of sleep for the past two days has affected my health. There are many others like me in the convoy. They are not feeling well at all. The weather is extremely hot in this region. As we advance we feel that we are going deeper into Hell.

"If we get sick because of the weather here, what will become of us when we get to the desert?" we ask each other.

The worries of our day-to-day existence are so many that we don't even think about tomorrow.

23 August, 1915

Our convoy got on the road again today, but about ten families among us who had sick people obtained permission from the police to stay here for another day.

Today, I feel a bit better. I had an accident around noon. It could have been quite serious. While wandering around the confines of the station with my cousin Vahram Toramanian, I felt an animal creeping up my trouser leg. I caught it before it reached my knee, and it began to struggle in my hands violently. The station employees heard our screams and came to remove it from my trouser leg. It was a green, monstrous-looking, fearsome lizard. The local people said that it was the poisonous kind. I was lucky the animal didn't get a chance to bite me!

24 August, 1915

At the precise moment when the sun began to rise at the end of our road, we left. We traveled into the sun. It sat at the end of the road and watched us.

At noon we went through Adana. On the other side of the stone bridge we stopped in a field. We rested for about half an hour and had our lunch with yogurt and bread.

The Armenians of Adana are also being deported, so we have seen several carriages as well as people traveling on foot. In spite of rushing, we were unable to catch up with the caravan of people from Chorum. At night we slept at the gate of a khan called Mufti Effendi, under the feet of camels.

25 August, 1915

At noon we passed through Misis. We stopped at a cafe and had some hot tea and then continued on our way again. After a couple of hours we caught up with the caravan we had separated from the previous day, on the bank of a river.

From this spot one can see the ramparts of a place called Yilan Kalesi. It was apparently built centuries ago by the Armenian kings of Cilicia. If only those kings could come back today and see the pitiful condition of the people they abandoned such a long time ago!

After bathing and washing in the river and resting for a short while, we continued on our way. The heat was unbearable. The horses were panting and gasping so hard they could hardly pull the carriages.

In the carriage in front of us one of our friends, Nishanian, was dying. We could see him. He was lying on his back, snoring. His young wife was so frightened that she got off the carriage and walked behind it, checking now and then to see if her husband were still alive. After a painful two hours, his snoring stopped. This evening we buried our poor friend Nishanian in a field near Hamidiye.

26 August, 1915

After four or five hours of traveling we camped in a field. Our trip today was short, but it was one of the most painful stretches so far, because of the extreme heat. This evening we buried another woman in the shade of a tree surrounded by greenery in the middle of nowhere.

27 August, 1915

One of the worst things that can happen, because it causes so many problems, is for a carriage to break down. Every day we keep an eye out for carriage accidents. While our second carriage was crossing a deep ditch, one of its wheels broke. We would have been stuck there if we hadn't had another carriage at our disposal. We moved my grandmother and her sister and part of our furniture to our carriage. My paternal aunt and her children and the rest of the furniture went to friends' carriages. Our vehicle is so crowded that we are almost sitting on top of each other. To prevent tiring the horses I walked for the whole trip today. In the evening we arrived in Osmaniye.

Here vast areas are filled with deportees and their tents. Deportees from all corners of Turkey—people from every village and every city. Some have arrived in carts and others on animals or on foot. They all lie here, exhausted, under roofs made of rags. They have been waiting for days and even months for their turn to leave for Aleppo on the train.

Many families from our convoy—those who couldn't walk—wanted to stay here, but the policeman responsible for keeping an eye on them wouldn't let anybody cross to the other side of the barbed wires. The government has given strict orders: the refugee station at Osmaniye must not become congested with new deportees.

28 August, 1915

This morning before getting underway again, we went into the city to have our wheel repaired. When we returned, we saw that the police had already used their whips to put our caravan on the road, except for nine families whose carriages were also broken. A policeman kept an eye on the families who were left behind. We immediately put the wheel on the carriage. When the owners of the other carriages had also returned from the city, we all left in great haste, and caught up with our group within an hour.

Our trip today was extremely tiring. We climbed the Taurus Mountains all day. Because the trip was so long, the horses were exhausted and could no longer pull the carriages. We stopped every fifteen minutes to give the animals a chance to rest. To prevent the carriages from sliding backwards, we put stones behind the wheels.

Everyone, young and old, walked in the sun, dusty and sweaty. Only the old and the feeble rode in the carriages. The others walked all day, forever scaling the steep rocky peaks—anyone watching from a distance might have compared it to an agonizing walk up Golgotha.

We didn't reach the crest of the mountains until just before evening. Then, however, as soon as we began to go downhill, there was another unforeseen difficulty. Going down was more dangerous than going up. Now the horses and carriages crowded and pushed each other. They might have caused many dangerous accidents if we hadn't placed pieces of stone in front of the wheels to prevent the carriages from barreling downhill.

Anyway, before too long there was such an accident. The horses belonging to one of our friends, Garabed Turkujian, shied, and with dizzying speed began galloping down, dragging the carriage with them. Besides Garabed, this carriage contained his mother and sister. Although Garabed pulled back on the reins with all his might, the animals couldn't stop, as the carriage itself constantly pushed them forward.

It's impossible to describe everyone's fright and alarm. On one side of the road there opened a bottomless abyss. Everything, the horses and all the people in the carriage, would disappear into the precipice unless there was a miracle. And there was a miracle. The strap hitching the horses to the carriage broke. The animals felt themselves suddenly free and ran as far as a precipice the right side of the road, their front legs hanging in the emptiness . . . And the carriage slid down, crashed into a rock on the left side of the road, and came to a halt.

At once everyone rushed, some in the direction of the carriage and others toward the horses, which were still hanging over the abyss by the side of the road. They were trembling with fear. Fortunately, the passengers, though injured, were still alive. And the carriage was still in usable condition. After taking care of immediate repairs and arrangements, we resumed our journey.

To get out of the way of the stampeding horses, hundreds of people had thrown themselves against both sides of the road, resulting in deep scratches and injuries. I am among the injured. When I saw the horses and the carriage coming toward me at such breakneck speed, I threw myself into the bushes along the side of the road. I cut my forehead on a sharp branch. Although my nose and my head were bleeding, I was pleased to have escaped with such minor injuries.

Very late at night, shattered and damaged, we all arrived at the foot of the mountain chain and, exhausted, we lay down on the shore of a river.

29 August, 1915

During the night three of our sick people died. Two men and a woman. After we buried them, we got on the road again. While we were crossing Kanli Gechid, another sick person died. We also buried him, and continued the journey.

We had a fairly difficult journey today, because of the roughness of the mountain roads. This evening we arrived in Hasan Beyli, where, just like us, some Armenians from Adana were camping

Here we experienced another mishap. At night our bag was stolen from under my mother's head. She was using it as a pillow. We had our food and some silverware in it. Naturally, when she felt someone pulling on the bag, my mother woke up, grabbed the bag, and shouted for help. But the thief snatched the bag away from my mother and disappeared into the darkness. When we reported the theft to the chief of police, instead of looking for the thief he reproached us for being asleep!

Two people from the convoy who saw the thief run away told us that the man was wearing a policeman's uniform. . . . This was probably the man who had come up and asked us for some *pagharch* during the day. When we gave him some he saw what was in the bag— the silver spoons and forks. It seems that he didn't consider us respectable enough to be using silver cutlery.

30 August, 1915

They have also exiled the local Armenians here. Their houses have been destroyed and the lumber is now for sale. No doubt they have done the same thing to our houses, to make sure that we can't ever go back there, even if we survive.

Today we didn't travel. We took advantage of that circumstance by buying flour and preparing some provisions for the rest of the journey.

31 August, 1915

We are crossing regions where there are thousands of soldiers, highwaymen, and fugitives. They suddenly block the road, attack the carriages, steal everything they can lay their hands on, and run away. Those who resist or dare to run after them are threatened with daggers.

The police are incapable of protecting us. Besides, which of us should they protect? There are only twenty of them and more than a thousand of us.

I walked for more than three hours. This evening we arrived in Islahiye, all of us dead tired. After watering the horses and eating a piece of bread and some grapes, we slept.

1 September, 1915

Since we are now getting close to Aleppo, the police aren't rushing us so much. So we didn't travel today either.

We went into the city this morning to buy a few things. When we got back we heard that our friends Mrs. Terzian and Miss Kesikbashian had passed away. The latter was a beautiful, educated girl. She had become ill while crossing Boghazlian, out of fear that the *chetés* would kill us and rape the women.

We buried them in the middle of a field. Every day we leave one or two unfortunates behind us. The number of dead is now over seventy.

But we no longer really mourn for them, since we don't know what may happen to us tomorrow. Every passing day our money gets less, our clothes get more and more worn out, and our provisions get scarcer. The number of sick people increases, the pain and worries multiply. We are headed for the desert. We don't know what kind of tragedy or destiny is waiting for us. We envy everyone who dies and is freed or liberated. We don't consider ourselves lucky to live a few more days or weeks. On the contrary, we are the unfortunate ones—by postponing our deaths we only suffer more in the meantime.

2 September, 1915

We yoked the horses and got on the road around noon. We were hardly fifteen minutes outside the city limits when we heard a familiar tune. A company of soldiers marching not far from us were playing "*Lousin Chgar*" (There was no moon) on their flutes. . . . How ironic! After stealing everything else from us, were they now stealing our melodies too?

We immediately found ourselves on another road full of steep rises and descents. An endless road. We were going through Kurdish regions, where the people were no less barbaric than the savage Turks.

As we had been in Bozanti, we were also stoned here. We were showered with huge pieces of rock. Fortunately we didn't suffer any serious damage.

Today I was a bit careless again, and it might have cost me my life. This was the second time I've escaped death since we left Chorum.

At noon, we stopped for a rest in a field not far from a Kurdish village. There the police told us that tonight we would be stopping in a deserted place and that if we didn't want to go hungry we should provide ourselves with food in the village. (The police don't want us to go hungry because for the most part they eat our food.)

Following this announcement by the police, I and a friend of mine set off for the village, accompanied by a Kurd. We wanted to buy some barley for our horses. The Kurd led us to his home, which we entered without any suspicion. But as soon as the door closed we realized our mistake. There was no barley or anything else for sale. The Kurd showed us a little door at one end of the room and told us to go through it to get the barley. We didn't know what to do. We couldn't decide whether to go in or not. It might well be a trap, or perhaps the Kurd was honest. At any rate, the Kurd's strange movements and gestures and the way he talked to his wife in Kurdish aroused our suspicion. So we asked him to get the barley and bring it to us where we were.

Both husband and wife protested and got angry at us for worrying unnecessarily. They wanted to take us into the room with the little door by force and show us the barley. We protested and were still arguing with them when suddenly we heard knocking at the door— loud and strong fists banging insistently on the door.

After a moment's hesitation, the man and his wife decided to open the door. All at once several people from our convoy burst into the room. They had apparently had seen us leave with the Kurd from afar, and had run after us to take advantage of the opportunity we had discovered. . . . But now the Kurds refused to sell anyone barley, insisting that our doubts and mistrust had hurt their pride . . . .

We breathed long and deep on leaving the Kurd's home, but we went back to the camp with empty bags. A little later we started moving and came to another place, and even before I got to know its name, there was another accident. This time one of our horses lost a shoe. A farrier was trying to put it on. And I was helping him, holding the horse's leg and watching what he was doing, when the hammer struck my left eyebrow. The cut must have been quite deep, because I started to bleed profusely. My father washed the cut with *oghi* (ouzo), bandaged my wound, and made me lie down in the carriage. After I had rested for an hour, he took me to the station-restaurant and, to reward me for my ordeal, he treated me to a serving of meat and potatoes.

3 September, 1915

The road was extremely dangerous today. We expected to be attacked by Kurdish bands at any minute. The carriages proceeded one right after the other, without the usual two carriage-lengths between them. This is also dangerous, and could have cost us quite dearly.

If the carriages are following each other too closely, one right behind the other, and the carriage in front of you decides to stop, you aren't always able to stop your own carriage right away, and the front of your carriage crashes into the back of the one in front of you . . . And in no time at all there is a pile-up of 10 or 15 carriages.

I knew how dangerous it is to sit in the back of a carriage. Not a day went by that such an accident didn't occur. Today, though, I was terribly tired, and I was sitting in the back of our carriage. Suddenly the carriage in front of us stopped and something heavy hit my back with great force. Fortunately, I quickly threw myself forward, and that reduced the impact; otherwise my spine would have been crushed.

This afternoon we had another problem. One of our horses got sick and couldn't walk. This slowed us down,and we fell quite a bit behind the rest of the convoy. We were in an area full of Kurdish bands. The policemen were with the main body of the caravan, and we were left unprotected on the road. Fortunately, fifteen or twenty other families were also lagging behind. Some had problems with their carriages, others with their horses. We hobbled along the road with them and arrived in Rajo this evening without encountering any evil—that's where the rest of our caravan had camped.

After dark a Circassian chieftain and a soldier arrived, used their whips on anyone near them, and ordered us to pack up and leave at once. Since it would have been awfully dangerous to travel at night along roads infested with Kurdish hordes, we gave the two men a bribe of fifty pounds and this enabled us to postpone our departure. There was plenty of water not very far from the station. We couldn't even get a drop of it, because Turkish soldiers blocked access to the spring and abused anyone who tried to fill a bottle.

Tonight we went into the village, bought a horse, and gave our sick horse to the first person we met.

4 September, 1915

We are still crossing Kurdish territory. In a few days we'll cross the Arabian border. While we were still in Turkish jurisdiction we were afraid of being slaughtered. Now we are afraid of being robbed. What will we be afraid of as we go through Arab territory? Of starving to death or catching some terrible disease?

This evening we were in Tahta Keopru. We spent the night in a field next to the bridge. On the opposite shore we saw several Armenian families making a fire, probably to cook their dinner.

We did not go over to ask where they were from. Along the road we meet thousands of deportees. They all share the same story and have the same tragic destiny. They are leaving just like us, kicked out of their homes. They travel one after the other, in carriages, in carts, on donkeys, or on foot. They all journey in the same direction, to the same destiny. Those who fall on the road from exhaustion, and those who have no strength left, nevertheless keep pressing forward, carrying their crosses—where and for how long we don't know.

5 September, 1915

For me it was a gift of providence that we didn't resume our journey again today. I have a terrible headache and am suffering from yellow fever. From morning till night I lay in the shade of the carriage and watched the river that rushes a little further down, without a drop of water to cool my burning heart. I didn't blame the river or these mountains that they can't bring my fever down, even a little bit, with their cold water and cool air.

By a process of association of ideas, my mind shifted from inanimate to animate objects. I started thinking about the Christian nations. I asked myself if Austria and Germany were unable, like this river, to alleviate our suffering. Have all feelings of pity and compassion dried up in their stony hearts?

As I lay on the ground beside the river in the shade of my carriage, I couldn't stop thinking about this and I prayed from the bottom of my heart that if their hearts have indeed turned to stone, even worse things might happen to them.

6 September, 1915

After traveling for five hours we arrived at last in Katma. We have heard about this place for some time now. This is the gate to Aleppo, and all the caravans from all corners of Turkey have been sent here. The government has created a refugee station here to prevent overcrowding Aleppo and causing a famine there with the great masses of refugees who arrive every day. This is where they organize the movement of the deportees from Aleppo to the desert.

Every day, for every ten who leave a thousand arrive. As a result, the refugee station at Katma has gradually filled up and spread beyond the horizon, covering the entire region with a multi-colored blanket of tents.

An immense crowd of carriages, horses, donkeys, mules, and people stretches in all directions. A deafening roar of brawling, cursing, sighs, cries, and laments fills the air. On both sides of the road skeletal arms are held out, begging for a piece of bread. As we moved forward we felt that we were sinking in an inextricable ocean of blood and tears, pain and suffering.

An awful stench filled our noses. Stinking, unburied human and animal corpses are everywhere. In addition, the excrement of thousands of people in an open field has polluted the atmosphere so much that it's impossible to breathe. We moved forward, holding our noses and shutting our eyes, through the excrement and the field of human corpses. Before long we stopped at a place at the edge of the tent city that had been reserved for us.

The police told us that our journey had come to an end and that we could stay here as long as we wanted to. We had previously begged the police to let us rest for a day or two. Now, on the other hand, we begged them not to make us stay here. But all in vain! They had accomplished their mission. They delivered us over to our luck and left, in order to lead new convoys to the same Hell.

We had no choice but to get out of the carriage. Since we will have to stay here for a few days, we put up our tents. Now we can't smell anymore. Fortunately, our noses have become desensitized. The flies, however, are unbearable. They are as numerous as the parasites of Tarsus. They descend on us like black clouds. The exposed parts of our bodies are covered with so many stinging bites that it's more than anyone can endure. We wave our hands around continuously to shoo them away, but there are just too many of them. Thousands of them cover our clothes and food; and they are so stubborn and shameless that once they have found a place to land they will never abandon it.

This evening we started to breathe a little more easily when we put a light on in the tent. All the flies swarmed over the lamp, as if covering it with a black veil. After we had got rid of the flies and rested a bit, we went to the nearby stream, washed, and cleaned ourselves. We brought back containers of water, and for the first time in ages we made a fire and cooked a hot meal.

The night, however, was horrible. We walked quite far from the tents to relieve ourselves. Everywhere we went, though, it was almost impossible to find a spot to step. As we walked through the field, we suddenly sensed that there was an open pit before us. Even though it was dark, we could see a corpse at the bottom of the pit. We let out an awful cry and backed quickly away. There, right in front of us, was another pit, another corpse. There were corpses everywhere: holes with the unburied corpses of men, women, old people, children . . . all of them naked and not even covered with shrouds . . . some lying face-down on the ground, others on their sides.

We ran, terrified, to the tents, remembering what the Armenian soldier in Bozanti had said: "The Arabs live in such appalling conditions that they dig up corpses from the graves so they can use their shrouds as clothing."

And to think that we are still only in Katma: in other words, only on the threshold of Arabia!

7 September, 1915

I opened my eyes to the sweet sound of a religious melody. I imagined myself in church for a moment, but I immediately came to my senses when I felt a battalion of flies biting my eyelids, as if trying to dig my eyes out.

I dressed at once and ran out of the tent. I saw an outdoor church in the neighboring field, where hundreds of people were all singing *Der Voghormia* (Lord have mercy).

May the Lord have mercy on us, but what lord? If we had a lord or protector we wouldn't be in this situation.

At noon we went to the market set up on one edge of the station by some clever and enterprising refugees. These people made an agreement with the police that allowed them to go all the way to Kilis and bring back goods to sell—things like bread, cheese, eggs, salt, sugar, fruit, vegetables, cereal, etc.

Then we walked around the tent city, which has no beginning or end. My pen is unable to describe the poverty that reigns over the place. Armenians from every city and village, those who have managed to survive, have came here and fallen, hungry and completely exhausted. Deadly diseases have followed hunger and nakedness. There isn't a single tent that doesn't have one or two seriously ill people. In one place, three young boys are lying on a piece of rag. In another, a mother has stripped the cover off a comforter to use as a canopy and has put her ailing son in its shade. Now he is delirious, suffering from a high fever. The flies, like huge crows, swarm over the youngster's face. The mother sits by the boy's pillow and tries to shoo away the flies with a piece of cloth.

Over there a child holds a piece of bone in his hand, hoping to find a bit of meat and gristle on it. From one corner we hear the stifled sounds of crying and moaning. We ask what is the matter and discover that a mother has died.

We walked around for more than three hours. We saw death in seven different places. We also met a young man carrying the white-haired corpse of a woman away from the camp. He was probably going to bury her in the field. Nobody was following them—no mourners! In another place we saw another dead person; two people were burying him, singing the liturgy. This one had five mourners, as well as a poor priest. He murmured prayers under his breath as he walked, and had the hem of his worn-out, discolored coat tucked into his belt.

There were countless sick people, people asking for help, and beggars. One would have to have unlimited wealth to be able to make even a ripple in this ocean of misery.

We returned to our tents, saddened and filled with anxiety, because the same destiny awaits us. We didn't feel like eating, even a bite, all day.

8 September, 1915

Today was the fourth time I escaped death. This morning, we took the horses to the stream to water them. The horse I was riding waded into the water to cool off. After we had gone a few meters, I realized that the horses' legs were getting stuck in the slippery muck on the bottom.

I whipped the horse, to urge him out of that dangerous place. But instead of turning around, the animal rushed forward and sank into the mire. Only the horse's neck and the upper part of my body were sticking out of the water. As though that wasn't enough, the more I tried to save myself, the deeper we sank into the swamp.

We were getting caught in quicksand, like a scene from *Les Misérables*. No one could help us. And, as hundreds of people looked on, we would have sunk to the bottom if the horse hadn't sensed the danger and made a supernatural effort to leap back.

That fatal leap saved our lives. The animal extracted itself from the mire and with a second leap threw itself breathless out of the water.

I got undressed and spread my clothes on the stones to dry. An hour later, clutching my wet diary, I returned to the station.

9 September, 1915

Every day and every hour new deportees arrive. Our tents, which were originally on the edge of the refugee station, were now in the center.

Countless people have got lost trying to find their tents or their way through this labyrinth. No one knows his neighbor. Many of those searching laboriously for their tents pass them several times without recognizing them. These large pieces of cloth (so-called tents) look so much alike that they are hard to tell apart.

As more refugees arrive, a pitiful picture is gradually revealed. After being on the road for months, walking and, like us, escaping massacres, all of them have at last ended up here. But it does them no good—all of them are emaciated, wasted, and ruined. What the Turks and the Kurds left unfinished will be accomplished by illness here in Katma.

Today the Catholicos of Cilicia honored us with a visit to our camp. My father knew him, because a few years back he made a sizable donation to Father Khat, the delegate, for the renovation of the Palace of the Catholicos in Chorum. Our city was under the jurisdiction of the Cilician Diocese.

Two high-ranking priests accompanied Catholicos Sahak, as well as six prominent men from Sis and Adana. His Holiness informed us that they had appealed to the mayor of Aleppo to find a solution to the tragic condition of the Armenians in Katma. Unfortunately their pleas were ignored.

Those who were present asked: "What will happen to this people? Where will we go? Where will we end up? If the government doesn't help, doesn't give us food or work . . . what do we have to look forward to?" The number of people present kept increasing as more and more refugees heard that the Catholicos had come to visit the camp. But what did Catholicos Sahak know, and what could he say or answer? He held up Christ as an example, and in his sad, trembling voice advised us to bear our cross with the utmost patience, even to Golgotha.

This evening, they bribed the Katma police and my father took the train to Aleppo with them. They said they would try to find a way to save us from this horrible situation.

10 September, 1915

To escape being attacked by flies, we took our bread and headed for the stream. There we learned quite a bit from the Arabs who sat by the water, with the help of five refugees who had been in Katma for some time and had improved their knowledge of Arabic to some extent.

I noticed that the majority of Armenians had learned the following three words: *dakhilek* (please), *khubes* (bread), and *jivan* (hungry), and had no intention of learning more than that. Those who are reasonably wealthy learn *vahid, tneyn, tlati* (one, two, three) first, and keep going until they can count to a hundred. Then they learn the names of the most needed items, which they want to buy, as well as the words for "yes" and "no" and "good" and "bad," from which they are able to construct hundreds of phrases and sentences. The ordinary Armenian refugee has no trouble mastering the expressions *yella ruh* (get lost) and *inael abuk* (a curse on your father), because he or she hears them from the police a thousand times a day!

Close to evening about 300 almost naked Armenian refugees approached—all in a state of extreme hunger, fatigue, and exhaustion. Without exception they all had wounds: some on their heads, others on their arms, the rest on shoulders. We had never seen such a tragic collection of badly suffering people.

We found out that they were attacked by Kurdish bands three days ago. The latter killed 67 Armenians, then tortured and robbed the rest, taking even their underwear.

These poor people now arrived in Katma, after walking, hungry and thirsty in the scorching sun and the dust and leaving behind people who died along the way. They now begged for a piece of bread to fill their stomachs or an arm's length of cloth to cover their nakedness.

We helped them as much as we could. And they—married women, maidens, old people, youngsters, infants, adolescents—all of them emaciated and destroyed, like ghosts escaped from the grave, resumed their walk as we looked on.

I realized how tragic the destiny of the Armenians was. Of course, these too were people like us, with feelings and intelligence; like us they also had ideals and ambitions. How do they feel now, knowing that a horrifying end awaits them?

11 September, 1915

I was repairing my shoes in front of the tent when I suddenly heard a pitiful cry:

"Fire! Help! Help! Fire!"

Fire in the tent city . . . Unheard of! I immediately got up and ran in the direction of the cries.

I hadn't taken more than ten or fifteen steps when I saw the fire. The tents were burning so fast that it took no more than a minute for one of them to catch fire and disappear completely. One moment a sudden flame flared up somewhere; the next moment a black column would appear in its place, which was now completely deserted, as if denying that only a few minutes earlier there had been a tent there, under which an unfortunate family had taken refuge.

The wind was blowing away from our tents. Blazing, fiery pieces of cloth, sheets, bed covers, and shirts were flying through the air. As they fell on other tents they enkindled them also into sudden flames. It was most discouraging and hopeless to see the situation these people were in—their helplessness in face of this unprecedented tragedy. There was no way of stopping this evil. In fact no one had time to think of a solution, as the calamity continued to hammer away at them, without giving them a chance.

Fortunately, in half an hour the fire reached an open space left by the departure of some more fortunate families, and died out by itself.

No lives were lost, but the caprice of nature destroyed more than 70 tents.

12 September, 1915

We received a letter from Aleppo, from my father. He informs us that with great difficulty he has been able to obtain permission for ten people to leave Katma. He enclosed the written permission with the letter and told us to leave immediately. Since we do not have permission to settle in Aleppo, my father advises us that when we arrive at the city limits of Aleppo we should send our carriages to a nearby khan, get a horse and buggy, and meet him at the Frat Hotel in the vicinity of Bab-iul-Faraj. He has rented a few rooms for all of us there.

As soon as we received my father's letter we began at once to get ready, and this evening we got on our way with ten other families. The commandant at the edge of the tent city checked our papers, found everything in order, and let us pass.

In spite of our joy at leaving Katma behind, our journey today was rather emotional: first because of the precarious roads and second because we don't know what lies ahead of us.

This was the first time since we left Chorum that we traveled without a police escort—and we were traveling through areas where there are frequent robberies and rapes and killings.

Some time after midnight something unfortunate happened— something we have always dreaded most. The front wheel of our carriage broke. Not wanting to endanger their own lives, our traveling companions didn't stop to help us repair it. They continued their journey, leaving us and our broken carriage alone in the night.

Fortunately, after a couple of hours another carriage came along. The driver was a kind Armenian from Adana. He gave us nails, an axe, and the other tools we needed. Then he left in a hurry, telling us that if we eventually caught up with him we could return the tools then. We quickly repaired the wheel and left as fast as we could. Within three hours we had caught up with our friends and the kind driver, who were out of the danger zone and were awaiting our arrival.

Just before dawn we entered Aleppo and, following my father's instructions, we went to the Frat Hotel.

13 September, 1915

We were terribly cold last night. My father treated us to hot tea and biscuits in the ground-floor cafe of the hotel. Then we went upstairs to sleep a little. But it was impossible to shut our eyes. There were more than thirty people in one room. People were constantly coming in and going out, stepping on our arms or legs in the process. Finally, fatigued and weary, we sank into deep sleep. Barely two hours later we awoke because of an unusual commotion. A policeman, learning that we were Armenians, arrived to take us to Sebil.

Sebil was a train station in Aleppo, and from there refugees were sent to Deir Zor, the all-consuming desert. Going to Sebil meant walking to inescapable death. Every Armenian who arrived in Aleppo was obsessed with evading that awful destiny and, if it was not possible to stay in Aleppo, with going anywhere at all but to that notorious place.

So you can imagine our turmoil when the policeman showed up, whip in hand, at the door of our room. He kept threatening to take us to Sebil, and to make matters worse he refused to take a bribe. After my father had tried every trick in the book, he finally succeeded, with the help of the innkeeper, in getting rid of him by paying him a considerable amount of money.

After he left we breathed easy, but we couldn't get back to sleep after that—we were not sleepy any more.

All day we heard again the endless clamor of swearing and pleading, intermixed with the sound of whipping, from the street. When we ran to the windows and watched secretly from behind the curtains, we saw a group of Armenians being rounded up by the police and dragged off to Sebil.

14 September, 1915

Just like the Archangel Gabriel, a policeman appeared early this morning.

"Let's go, *yallah*. You're going to Sebil."

We had just got rid of him when another policeman showed up, threatening us in the same words. We crossed his palm with three pieces of gold and sent him also to Hell.

The gendarmes along the way passed on to one another the news that they had discovered a gold mine, and the police here were doing exactly the same thing. They came one after the other to rob us. If we stay in this hotel a few more days, no doubt the entire Aleppo police force will parade in front of us!

Fortunately, at last, close to evening we managed to find a five-room house in a quiet part of the city. And tonight, without accident or mishap, we moved here.

It is a one-story stone house. The rooms are dark and damp, and they open onto an asphalt courtyard. Two families have to live in each of the tiny rooms, but we are pleased that, since the owner of the house is an Arabic speaking Armenian woman, at least there should be no danger of being betrayed.

15 September, 1915

Having heard that the police aren't harassing Armenians anymore, we went out today. We wanted to see the city and buy some immediate necessities.

During our wanderings, we came across the Armenian church. The picture it presented made our blood run cold. It is impossible to imagine such extreme poverty and misery.

Beginning on the neighboring streets, right up to the churchyard, inside the church, and even on the altar lie thousands of sick people, all of them fading away, dying, drawing their last breaths. One sobs and asks for water, another breathes in a tragic wheeze, the body of another twitches and writhes. And another . . . his teeth are chattering. And sitting near all of them are a mother who has lost her mind . . . a father . . . a confused orphan . . . a young woman suffering from deep depression and disappointment—they don't know what to do to ease the pain and suffering of their loved ones. Many of the suffering have no one to care for them . . . and some of them are dead, their eyes still open, their pupils shining like pale glass, producing terrifying emotions in those around them.

The municipal rubbish carts are deafening as they creak their way up to this human wreckage. Two employees walk among the sick and go up to all whose faces wear the shadow of death. They grab the body by the shoulders and feet and carry it to the carts.

The cart leaves, loaded with corpses thrown at random one on top of the other. A second one follows it . . . Then a third, fourth, fifth . . . and so these municipal carts carry more corpses—Christian corpses— than garbage to the dump sites of Aleppo.

We could stay in the churchyard no longer. Fighting back tears, we returned home, and did not go out for the rest of the day.

16 September, 1915

We made it from Chorum all the way here thanks to our money and my mother's jewelry. Now we have spent all the money; from now on we have to use the jewelry. We began to sell it, but no one pays its true value. Fortunately, in answer to our request, my father's Armenian and Greek friends in Samsoun and Constantinople cabled us 100 Turkish pounds. So far we haven't heard anything from my father's Turkish friends in Chorum.

The day we left a crooked Turk refused to pay us the 100 pounds he owed us, callously declaring that we would be slaughtered on the road anyway, so we wouldn't be needing money.

But he told us that if we were lucky enough to survive, we should let him know where we were and he would send us "more than he owed."

Relying on this promise, when my father arrived in Aleppo he cabled our address to him, expecting that the man would keep his word. Instead of money, the Turk sent the following telegram: "As all your property and effects have been seized by the government, there is no money to send you."

My father sent the following cable in reply: "I am not asking for any share of what belongs to me. For the sake of our twenty-two years of friendship, please send money out of your own pocket."

It has been three days since my father's telegram to the Turk, but there is still no news from Chorum. The worthless villain still refuses to keep his promise. Does he really care? When will he ever see us again, to be ashamed of his shoddy behavior?

17 September, 1915

Despite our precaution, the police followed the carriage while we were moving the furniture from the khan to our house, and found out where we are. Two of them visited our house today. Cracking their twisted ox-leather whips over our heads, they barked: "*Yallah ruh* . . ."

Yallah ruh is every Armenian's nightmare. We have scarcely settled into a place for a few days when a whip cracks in the air and the uncouth voice of a policeman shouts: "*Yallah ruh* . . ."

We have become like the wandering Jew: walking, walking, without end!

18 September, 1915

As usual, friends of the police came to visit us this afternoon to get their share of the plunder. After they left, my father had a meeting with the *moukhtar* (the neighborhood elder), gave him a considerable amount of money, and managed to postpone our deportation for about a week.

Today we wandered around the city a bit more. Municipal garbage carts file continuously through the streets, exposing their tragic loads to the passers by. In the space of an hour we saw four of them go by, one after the other, raising a totally uncivilized din. From one of the carts dangled the arm of a corpse, constantly bumping and scraping against the iron rim of the revolving wheel.

19 September, 1915

We have heard some good news. Disabled women, as well as military families and children under fifteen years of age will be able to remain in Aleppo. If this news is true, thousands of unsupported women and orphans will be spared the dangers of being deported to the Arabian desert.

The elderly and the children were the ones who suffered most from the deportation. Unable to endure the fatigue and deprivation of the road, they swallowed the bitter goblet and fell, covered in blood, under the jack-boots of the gendarmes and the hooves of the horses.

We don't have to think hard or look far to imagine the tortures the Armenian grandmothers suffer. Every day our eyes are filled with the sight of my grandmother and her sister. Despite the fact that they traveled in a carriage, they no longer have the strength to speak or move. They are ill, always lying down and begging for death to deliver them from their unbearable existence. What a total mockery of destiny! They who wanted so much to live longer so that they might enjoy watching our happiness are now praying for death.

20 September, 1915

Our wandering steps again led us in the direction of the Armenian church. We go there as though drawn by the tragic state of our unfortunate compatriots, hoping to see an improvement in their lamentable condition.

Sick people . . . dying people . . . dead people . . . and next to them the living dead, whom starvation has turned to skin and bones.

With a terrifying clatter the municipal carts arrive empty and depart completely filled.

"Driver!" shouted a kid of barely ten years beside us, "there's another dead man here. You forgot him."

The driver muttered a few words in Arabic.

From the way he spoke we thought he was trying to say that his cart was full; that they would have to wait for the next one.

"We're not even worth anything as garbage," a woman remarked when she saw the driver refuse.

"We're worse than garbage," responded her neighbor: "Can't you see? Even the garbage man doesn't like us!"

21 September, 1915

The way of handling money here is rather peculiar. We didn't know about it and we still wouldn't if we had not made a bet with a young man from Diyarbekir.

Our ignorance has apparently cost us quite a bit. But how were we to know? The local people profited from our ignorance, so they didn't set us straight.

Until today, whenever we bought something and the shop-keeper asked for ten, we gave him ten. But we should have paid only eight instead, because what the shop-keeper asks for is the price if you buy on credit: for cash purchases you are entitled to a twenty-percent discount.

The young man from Diyarbekir, who just happened to be there while we were doing our shopping, explained things to us, at the same time mentioning that all the Armenians from our region made the same mistake.

We thanked our compatriot for explaining this custom to us, then, on learning that he was from Diyarbekir, we asked how he had managed to stay alive. We had heard that the Armenian population of the six eastern provinces had been completely wiped out.

His name was Pakrad. He told us that it wasn't true that they had all been annihilated.

"About ten percent were miraculously saved, including myself," he explained.

"But how? Please, tell us!" we urged with interest.

Pakrad did not deny our request. And for the first time we heard the following story about the slaughter of more than 150,000 Armenians from that prosperous province.

* * *

When you consider the anti-Armenian policies of the government, it was only natural that the Armenian population of a thriving province like Diyarbekir would be no exception. As early as the day after war was declared, the local Turks and Kurds began to show their hostility, openly declaring that the time had come to settle old accounts.

The young Armenian men of the province had already been conscripted and sent to the front. The first thing the government officials and the military did was to have their evil way with the defenseless wives, sisters, and fiancees of the conscripts.

Some Armenian soldiers heard what was going on, deserted their barracks, and returned to the city to fight these enemies from within and protect the honor of their families.

As a consequence, the government began searching houses to find these fugitives and look for dangerous weapons and books. As they didn't find either, they arrested all the prominent Armenians of the city: doctors, members of political parties, government employees, clergymen, etc.—around a thousand people. They put them in jail and began to torture them to make them confess non-existent offenses.

To give you an idea of the savage way in which these people were arrested, it is worth mentioning the arrest of Pakrad's father, Apraham Agha. A corporal and two policemen entered Pakrad's house, grabbed the old man, and asked:

"Where's your son?"

"I don't know. He was drafted six months ago," replied Apraham Agha.

"We've heard that your son belongs to a dangerous organization and keeps weapons at home," said the corporal. "We'll search the house. But we advise you to save us unnecessary effort and show us at once where he keeps his weapons."

"What are you talking about? God help me! My son has never belonged to any such organization," my father shouted in shock. "And my house . . ."

The whip suddenly came down on the old man.

"Shut up, you impudent old fool! You ought to be ashamed, with your white hair. Ashamed of lying, at your age!"

"But I swear . . . in the name of God that . . ."

"I get it!" roared the executioner, turning to the policemen, "we have to kill these pig-headed people if we want the truth! Tie his hands!"

The policemen pounced on the old man like a pair of wild beasts, slapped him around a bit, then tied him up.

Pakrad's mother and his twenty-year-old sister threw themselves at the corporal's feet, begging them not to torture the husband and father.

The corporal kicked them out of the way and left the room with one of the policemen to turn the house inside out.

Fifteen minutes later they returned, with four or five "dangerous" books in their hands. The corporal ordered Apraham Agha to follow them. The poor man was so shocked and injured by their cruel blows, however, that he collapsed to the floor unconscious. The police poured water in his face to revive him, took him by both arms, and dragged him from the room.

"But where are you taking him?" cried the mother and daughter, again begging. "Why are you taking him away? What has he done wrong?"

The police pushed the mother and daughter aside, ignoring their pleas, and took their prisoner out into the street. A large crowd had already gathered to see a *komitadji* being arrested.

As soon as the policemen and their victim were out in the street, the poor Armenian was showered with curses and swear words:

"Ho! Ho! Kill him, execute the dog!"

"No, no, we want to know what he has done wrong, first."

"What? Done wrong . . . wrong . . . wrong?"

"Clobber him! Kill him! Destroy the traitor!"

The crowd swelled in huge waves and roared like an enraged beast:

"His crime? His crime? His offense? His crime?"

The corporal gestured to the crowd to shut up. "Listen! Look here. Look what we found in his home," he yelled, lifting a geography book into the air. "You don't know how to read, so you don't know how dangerous this book is. But I won't have to say much before you can draw your own conclusions. In the hands of our enemies this book is a more terrifying weapon than all the guns and cannons of the army.

This book gives the locations of all the cities, villages, rivers, and roads in Turkey. All of them meticulously portrayed. Anybody who goes through this book can find not only the plan of every city, but also the location of every house and whether it belongs to a Christian or a Muslim. They have marked each one with a cross or a crescent, so that one day when they rebel it will be easy for them to tell a Muslim household from the others."

Grumbling from the mob—arms into the air in defiance!

"Oh, oh, oh . . . clobber him, kill him, let him rot, the traitor."

"Please calm down. Not so fast," the corporal ordered with authority, "I haven't finished yet. Look. Here's another book." He held up another book—a physics text. "It tells you all you need to know about how to make gun-powder, bullets, and dynamite. These conspirators' homes are filled with books like this. Both the young and the old read these books and learn what to do to destroy our country. But thank God and the Sultan that we have been vigilant and were able to uncover their plot at the last minute. Now it's *we* who will destroy *their* homes and put *their* children to the sword."

The policemen had a hard time clearing a way through the violent crowd. They finally succeeded and, pulling and pushing their victim, they took him off to jail. In the meantime blasphemies, threats, and insults rang out in the streets.

As for the tortures used in the prison . . . even their description is horrifying and shocking. Various unheard-of methods of brutality were used. Red-hot irons were thrust into victims' hearts. Others had their skulls crushed in presses or their nails pulled out with pliers or their noses, tongues, and ears cut off.

If they were still alive after being tortured for days, they were ordered to take to the road. There Kurdish and Turkish brigands surrounded their caravan and axed them to death.

Then the government started making mass arrests, sending women, children, and the elderly over the same road that the men had been sent over. In the meantime the looting began—they plundered houses, shops, and churches.

Street scoundrels, vagabonds, porters, and peasants, led by a fanatic sheikh or a dervish, entered the cathedral. Some put chasubles, copes, and other vestments on their backs, others put diadems and crowns on their heads. Some wore servers' gowns, others lit the chandeliers and candlesticks . . . Some poured out of the church clutching thuribles, chalices, and other sacred vessels. They roamed the streets sounding the cymbals and fly-flaps and treading on pages torn from the Bible and on holy pictures.

They grabbed the primate and dragged him through the streets until midnight, shouting insults all the while. Then they stripped him, made him lie prostrate in front of a mosque, and broke his teeth, pulled out his eyes, burned his face, pulled out his hair and beard, and cut certain parts of his body off. Finally they poured kerosene over him and burned him alive, until there was nothing left but ashes. While all this was going on, soldiers beat their drums continuously, to muffle the heart-rending cries and screams of the victim.

Those who left in the caravans were massacred, some an hour outside the city limits and others after a torturous few days' journey. Good-looking women and maidens were taken captive by the executioners. Children under three were thrown into the Tigris river. Hundreds of innocent infants were snatched from their mothers' arms, beheaded, and thrown to the dogs.

When Pakrad heard about his compatriots' tragic fate, he dropped his rifle and ran back to Diyarbekir. But it was too late! His father had already died in jail, and his mother and sister had been sent off to the desert.

Disguised as a hunch-backed old man, he joined a caravan of 800 people and traveled with his compatriots, hoping that sooner or later he'd find his mother and sister. After unheard of torments, no more than 100 people arrived in Ras-el-Ain. There Pakrad heard from a compatriot that the Circassians had already disposed of all of the caravans from Diyarbekir. His sister had been raped by one of the executioners and then abducted by an Arab gendarme.

On learning that this gendarme was from Aleppo, the young Armenian escaped from Ras-el-Ain and arrived in Aleppo with a refugee woman to look for his sister. Unfortunately, his search has been in vain, as he knows neither the name nor the address of the gendarme.

* * *

Pakrad's story devastated us. We thought we had suffered, but we couldn't compare our experiences to what the population of these six provinces had gone through.

Pakrad guessed what was going through our minds. "But all the same, I have suffered nothing at all," he said. "Since you want to record this in your diary, let me introduce you to Mrs. Takouhi, and listen to her too.

"Who's Mrs. Takouhi?" we asked with interest.

"A woman from Harpoot (Kharpert); we escaped from the Ras-el-Ain Refugee Station together."

"Yes, we'd like that," we said, "but first, come to our house."

Pakrad came back with us. When we got here we gave him an old coat and a little parcel. And my father pressed a gold piece into his palm.

22 September, 1915

Pakrad kept his promise and came to see us today. He took me and my cousin to one of the remote quarters of the city. He lived in a basement room there with his "adopted" mother, Mrs. Takouhi.

Mrs. Takouhi is barely 50 years old, but suffering and affliction have aged her before her time and have turned her into a skeleton. She has been suffering from malaria for a week. One day she has a high fever and the next day she feels perfectly fine. Today she was feeling reasonably well and so agreed when we asked her to tell us about her epic experiences.

* * *

Needless to say, the police in Harpoot began to search houses and arrest prominent citizens as they had in other provinces. The prisons were filled with intellectuals, teachers, party members, doctors, and businessmen.

The Harpoot police chief was a bloodthirsty monster, who never missed an occasion for torture. Under the pretense of making them confess and finding out where they had hidden their weapons, the prisoners were beaten constantly. They poured boiling water on some people. They also put nails in people's stomachs or nailed their hands together. They used red-hot irons to flog prisoners. Or poured salt into their wounds.

Many prisoners could not endure such pain and suffering, and died in prison. The rest were chained together to be deported and martyred.

After they got rid of the foremost citizens in this way, they began the mass arrest of men. They put a caravan of 3,000 men on the road;

among them Mrs. Takouhi's husband and her older son. Father and son, arms tied together, left and never returned.

Thinking that the police would come and take away her second son, Vartan, who was 17, Mrs. Takouhi sent him and her daughter Vartouhi, 15, to the house of her sister, Mrs. Heghiné, which was only a few streets away. Ever since the deportation of her own husband, Mrs. Heghiné had lived alone in the house, and so, for the time being, was exempt from being searched by the police.

Also staying in the house were Mrs. Takouhi's young daughter-in-law, Aroussiag, and her two children, Meliné and Krisdiné. They lived in uncertainty, wondering how the storm that was sweeping the nation would end.

One day there was a knock at the door. Thinking a policeman had come to arrest Vartan, the daughter-in-law and mother-in-law went to the window. They were filled with fear when, from behind the curtain, they saw a man in a turban, armed from head to toe, and with half of his face covered. The daughter-in-law and especially her two daughters had a foreboding of a great tragedy, and began to tremble.

Mrs. Takouhi advised them to remain cool, and at the same time encouraged them to hope that the unknown man would soon go away, since no one was answering the door. But their presumption was in vain. The turbaned man kept knocking at the door, over and over again, calling Mrs. Takouhi by name.

Unable to stand it any longer, she went down, stood near the closed door, and asked:

"Who is it? What do you want?"

"Takouk Hanim, open the door! It's Rushdi Bey," replied a familiar voice from the street.

"Rushdi Bey? But why are you dressed like that?"

"I'll tell you later. Open the door!"

Mrs. Takouhi opened the door, because the visitor had been a close friend of her martyred son.

"Ah, we were so frightened! We didn't recognize you," the woman said with emotion.

"Don't be afraid. I've come to protect you," said the Turk. He climbed the steps without even being invited in.

The little girls were amazed at the man's unusual weapons and clothing, and hid behind their mother.

"Don't be afraid, my dears," said Mrs. Takouhi to reassure them. "Rushdi Bey was your father's friend. He has come to help us."

"Yes, yes," affirmed the Turk, leaning his long stick against the wall. "Come, children, I came because of you." Seeing that the children still hesitated, he added, "Have you forgotten your father's hunting buddy. You used to put your arms around my legs and say 'Rushdi Bey, bring us back a live bird!' Come, it's me—the same Rushdi Bey. Things are a bit complicated, so I look a bit different. Sniper shots come from all directions, and if I don't wear a turban somebody might think I'm an Armenian and kill me by mistake, turning me into an idiot-martyr." Then he turned to their mother and said: "What can we do, madam, we're living in difficult times? It shouldn't have been like this but we can't do a thing. May God punish those who made these things happen."

"There's no need to remain standing, Rushdi Bey. Please sit down," said Mrs. Takouhi, concluding that the Turk had come to see them as a friend. "We don't exactly know what's happening out there. Are they still arresting people?"

"No, that's over now. There are no men left to be arrested," the Turk replied.

"What has happened to the deportees?"

"They were all sent to Ourfa (Edessa). . . . God willing, you may soon receive good news from them."

"What will happen to the women and children who are still in the city? Do you know anything about that?"

"The government plans to send the rest of the people to the same place as the men."

As he spoke Rushdi Bey kept looking at his friend's wife, who was not taking part in the conversation.

"But why isn't the lady saying anything? Is she sick?"

"Yes," replied Mrs. Takouhi. "Her husband's deportation was a great shock to her. She cries day and night, and that's why she's a bit sick."

"Come here, children," said the Turk, pretending to be deeply moved.

"Come here, don't be afraid of me. A curse on everyone responsible for this situation!"

Meliné had been watching the visitor's friendly conversation with her grandmother and was reassured. Blushing, she approached the visitor and kissed his hand.

"Long may you live, my daughter!" exclaimed the Turk, caressing her golden hair. "I like polite little girls like you. Call your sister. Tell her to come here too."

"She's afraid of you," stuttered Meliné in embarrassment, her eyes focused on the floor.

"But why? Don't you know I'm your friend?"

"Yes, but you look different. Why aren't you dressed like my father?"

"Well, my girl. One day, when everything has settled down, I'll dress like the Rushdi Bey you used to know. Go on now, call your sister. Tell her not to be afraid of me."

Encouraged by Rushdi Bey's warm words, Krisdiné also went and kissed her father's friend.

"Bravo! Now that you're a good girl, I'll love you too," retorted Rushdi Bey. And sitting her on his knee, he kissed her.

Krisdiné was repelled by the smell of *oghi* on the Turk's breath, and turned her head away in disgust. Rushdi Bey pretended he had not noticed and kept on talking in a shaky voice.

"A pair of angels . . . you can't help feeling sorry when you think that tomorrow on the deportation road, hungry, exhausted, and weakened, they'll fall into the dust and be crushed under the hooves of the horses . . . what a terrible destiny!

"Madam . . . Madam . . . what's your name?"

"Aroussiag."

"Mrs. Aroussiag, I have shared bread and water with your husband, Vahan, for many years. I can never forget his kindness, especially around two years ago, when he saved me from total ruin. I'd be betraying our friendship if I left his wife, his children, and his mother to their fates, without help during these dark times. And so I've come to take you back home with me and keep you there, under my protection, until the storm is over. When your husband sends you news from Ourfa, I'll send you to him in safety, or perhaps I may even succeed in bringing him back here. At any rate, at the moment the most important thing is your safety. I have come to take care of it."

"We don't want to go to your house," the two children cried, interrupting the Turk.

"We appreciate your thoughtfulness," said both of the women at the same time, clearly alarmed at their friend's veiled proposition. "We are eternally grateful that you haven't forgotten us in such difficult times and have offered us your kindness. But Rushdi Bey, we'd prefer to remain here in our own house."

"Oh, I get it . . . you're worried about your furniture. There's nothing to worry about. Now I can station a couple of policemen in front of your door. No one will dare touch anything that belongs to you."

"If you're concerned for our safety," said Mrs. Takouhi, forcing a smile onto her pale face, "please tell the policemen to stay in front of our door and protect us from anyone who tries to bother us."

"Oh, what you're saying is impossible, Takouk Hanim. After all, the government has certain laws, and we're obliged to obey them. All Armenians will be deported. That is an unavoidable reality. If you remain in your house, the police will come with their whips to kick you out and they'll drive you like sheep all the way to the hellish Arabian desert. We can't prevent that. But if you are with me in my home, I can assure you that even if the army comes, let alone the police, they will never be able to take you away from me."

As he spoke, the Turk unconsciously caressed the dagger that hung from his waist.

"Let's go to my house," he said, showing signs of impatience. "We have no time to think, to linger, to hesitate . . . any minute the police may come and I could not interfere."

"Rushdi Bey, we accept our destiny. Whatever happened to the other Armenians, may the same thing happen to us. We cannot leave our own house," answered Mrs. Takouhi.

Suddenly the Turk became enraged. He realized that all his efforts to persuade these Armenian women were in vain.

"You infidels don't deserve kindness!" he said brutishly, pulling Mrs. Aroussiag by the arm. "But I feel sorry for you. Come, cover your head and follow me." Then, turning to the lady of the house: "Takouk Hanim, if you wish, stay here and keep an eye on your furniture. But I'm taking your daughter-in-law and her children home with me."

"No, we're not going anywhere!" screamed the girls, running away from the Turk and hiding behind their mother's skirt.

"Rushdi Bey, please stop joking," said Aroussiag, shaking to free herself from the grip of her husband's friend. "Don't you see that you're frightening the children?"

"They're frightened because you're resisting," replied the Turk calmly.

"Once you start moving they'll follow you peacefully."

"Will you take us with you by force?" asked Aroussiag, her face now ashen.

"Yes!" answered Rushdi Bey with demonic determination. "Yes, if I have to, by force!"

An evil smile gleamed in the miserable man's eyes. He had now exposed his true colors. He was enraged, his legs and hands were trembling, and his teeth gnashed with unprecedented savagery.

"I'm not taking a single step, force or no force!" the Armenian woman said proudly, scorning her adversary's threats and violence.

"You will!" in a low voice.

"But Rushdi Bey," interrupted Mrs. Takouhi, "why should you want to force us? Since we don't want to go, please leave us alone."

"I know that you're all going to meet violent ends, Takouk Hanim. If you want me to tell you the truth, I will . . . Vahan, your husband, and all their friends have already been massacred by the *cheté*s (irregular bands). I learned this from a band member who came back to the city after personally taking part in the massacre. And don't forget: the same fate is in store for you. The government doesn't distinguish between male and female. The order is for everybody. Anyone who calls himself an Armenian will be slaughtered, regardless of age or gender. I want to save you from that tragedy by taking your daughter-in-law as my second wife. If she accepts my humanitarian proposal, the lives of not only her but of her two daughters and yourself will be saved."

When Aroussiag and Mrs. Takouhi heard the sad news that their husbands were dead, they were horrified, and the children let out heart-rending shrieks and burst out crying.

The Turk watched them for a while, then shrugged his shoulders and said: "Your screaming and crying won't change anything. No matter what you do, you can never escape the fate in store for you. Come with me, or you'll die."

"Then we'll die," answered the women, with admirable determination.

"I won't let you die," answered the Turk with a touch of sadness in his eyes.

"In spite of your obstinacy, I will save you."

Having said this, he leapt at the young Armenian woman with savage, animal-like passion, trying to take her in his arms.

By moving quickly, Aroussiag managed to escape the attack, but could not shake him off completely. With another giant leap, the monster got behind her and pinned her arm.

"Rushdi Bey, even if it means my death, I'll never go with you."

"You will! You will! Do you hear? You *will* come with me." With a barbaric yank the hyena twisted the woman's arm and, ignoring her screams, sank his sharp teeth into the soft flesh of her shoulder.

Without warning, she slapped him with all her might.

Aroussiag freed herself with a supernatural effort and ran from the room. The Turk ran after her with uncontrolled fury. There was a short skirmish. Suddenly the dagger flashed. All this took place in such a sort time, Mrs. Takouhi had no time to intervene. She heard a terrifying scream, then the thud of a human body falling to the floor.

"Die, you stinking whore!" roared the monster, putting his dagger back into its sheath. "I knew that ungrateful dogs like you did not deserve kindness; but I thought I'd at least try."

After delivering this eulogy on the woman he had killed, the murderer came back into the room, took the two girls by their hands, and dragged them out. Mrs. Takouhi, out of her mind and speechless with terror, dropped to the floor.

* * *

A quarter of an hour later the neighbors arrived. They had seen Rushdi Bey leave with the two crying girls and immediately concluded that something was wrong. They saw Aroussiag lying lifeless at the top of the stairs and Mrs. Takouhi unconscious on the floor of the room. They brought her around and she was so feeble that they took her to her sister's house.

Mrs. Heghiné was a strong and courageous Armenian. When she heard about the awful crime and rape, she immediately went to see one of the influential aghas of the city and asked him to rescue the two kidnapped orphans.

Sabri Bey had an old score to settle with the murderer, so this presented a perfect opportunity for him to get one up on him.

Accompanied by two policemen, he went to his opponent's house and, without bloodshed—since Rushdi Bey was not home—he seized the orphans and delivered them to their rightful guardians.

In tears Meliné and Krisdiné ran into their grandmother's arms and told how Rushdi Bey had tortured them to stop them from weeping over their mother. The more they cried, the more the hard-hearted Turk had pinched them and struck them on their tiny hands with a stick. Realizing that the more they cried the more they would be tortured, the children tried to close their mouths and stop crying, and sat, motionless and quiet, in a corner.

The Turk had reached into his pocket and produced the jewels he had taken off Aroussiag after he had killed her. He gave them to his wife, daughter, and son, saying, "One for you and one for you and . . ." All the while the criminal's wife and daughter squealed with admiration at their share of the jewelry. His ten-year-old son, Ali, pushed away the pieces of gold he was given, saying he wanted a riding horse, not stupid toys like this.

"Don't be angry, son. If you want a horse, I'll get you one tomorrow," said Rushdi Bey.

"But Father," said the spoiled little brat, "make sure it's a white one, with a nice saddle . . . and a whip with a silver handle."

"All right, dear boy," said the father. "From now on all the possessions of the damned Armenians belong to us. We can do whatever we want to them. The government and our religion both assure us that we won't be punished, either in this world or the next."

"Hurrah!" exclaimed the little urchin, clapping his hands happily.

At this gleeful demonstration, the father exclaimed: "Good for you, son! May I always see you like that. Let's hear you swear at those faithless people . . . Let's hear you swear."

And the scoundrel insulted the parents of the two orphans in unspeakably vulgar terms. Rushdi Bey's wife and daughter were thoroughly amused, pointing out to each other the two orphans, who were trembling with fear.

Fortunately, the next morning Sabri Bey rescued them from their imprisonment. Otherwise, they could easily have suffocated in that polluted atmosphere.

But their joy did not last long.

That evening, when he returned from his plunders, the criminal Turk heard that Sabri Bey had taken the orphans away. He guessed what was behind Sabri Bey's act. The evil-doer had never considered that an Armenian slave would have the guts to protest and would be able to make a complaint and get back what he had stolen and considered his property. On the one hand, the wrath triggered by the rebellious spirit of the Armenian and on the other, his humiliation before his wife and children made him thoroughly enraged and out for revenge.

That same night, after putting his shoulder against Mrs. Heghiné's door and forcing it open, he found himself face to face with the woman of the house in the inner courtyard. He asked:

"Where's your sister?"

"She's not here. What do you want? What gives you the right to force my door like this?"

"You took the girls away from me, and now, to top it all off, you're lying. Bring them here, or I'll kill you."

"Rushdi Bey," said Mrs. Heghiné in a flattering tone, "please calm down. Why are you treating us so hard-heartedly? You, who are such a good friend of the family. You've killed the girls' mother. .What else do you want from us? We've suffered enough pain, anguish, and worry already. Rushdi Bey, please leave us alone to mourn our dead."

"I haven't come here to listen to nonsense. I'm here for the girls," the Turk barked violently.

"They're not here."

"I'll go upstairs and look in every single room for them." And the criminal pushed Mrs. Heghiné out of his way and rushed upstairs, causing a racket with his heavy boots on the steps.

When they heard their kidnapper's voice, Meliné and Krisdiné were terrified, and they ran and hid in different corners of the house. The monstrous Turk entered the room where Mrs. Takouhi had been put.

"Are you here, you witch?" he roared, bringing his whip down on her. "I'll teach you what it means to take children away from me!" Then, seeing that Vartouhi was in the room and was running to her mother to protect her: "Oh here's a fine piece . . . I hadn't noticed. Tell me, what's your name, girl?"

"Why are you hitting my mother? She's sick," Vartouhi protested with justifiable fury. "Spare us, at least for the love of my father and brother, Rushdi Bey."

"Don't remind me of your father and brother, infidel," reprimanded the Turk impudently. We now know what kind of people you are. You and your entire nation are the enemies of our country and race. It was a mistake to consider you friends and treat you as such. Don't talk to me about friendship anymore."

"Does that mean you want to treat us as enemies?" asked the young girl with emotion.

"Yes. You declared war on us, you fought, and you were defeated. You are now our slaves. You no longer have the right to ask us for mercy."

"What are you talking about, Rushdi Bey? When did we ever declare war? Who did we fight?"

"Enough! Show me where the girls are. I'll take you prisoner . . . I'm telling you."

"We have no girls to give you," said Mrs. Heghiné, running up to him and placing herself between him and the girl. "Please go away and get lost."

"*Hanim*, I advise you to get out of my way immediately, or you'll regret your insolence," warned the savage, giving her a violent blow on the chest. Then, clumsily pushing Vartouhi out of the room: "Now let's see you walk, wretched girl."

"Please, Rushdi Bey, I beg you."

"Don't beg, walk."

"Are you going to take me by force? I won't go."

"You will."

The monstrous Turk pulled out his dagger and brandished it threateningly before the girl's eyes, hissing through his teeth, "Walk, or I'll stretch you out on the floor too, just like the newly-wed."

Just then a young boy came out of the adjacent room.

It was Vartan. He could no longer put up with the atrocities being inflicted on his family. In an instant he had grabbed a chair from the middle of the room and smashed it over the criminal's head.

The monster, stunned by the violent blow, swayed a bit, lost his balance, then rolled all the way down the stairs.

As he tumbled down, the dagger he was holding in his hand was thrust into his chest. The detestable Turk let out a painful roar and was spread out at full length at the foot of the stairs.

The people of the house jumped over the corpse and took refuge with distant relatives. They were still recovering from these troubles and outrages when they were forced to leave for the desert.

* * *

The caravan moved forward.

They went through villages, cities, mountains, and valleys, constantly exposed to attacks by armed peasants all along the road. In the region of Severeg they met other deportees, and they joining together to form a caravan with no beginning and no end.

A few days later, this innumerable mass of refugees was surrounded in an extremely dangerous place by peasants and guerrillas armed with daggers and hatchets, who began to rape and slaughter them without mercy.

The alarm and confusion was horrible.

Everyone was confused, not knowing what to do or where to escape.

The frightened screams of girls throwing themselves into their fathers' arms, the pitiful shrieks of children clinging fast to their parents' legs, the discouraging cries of elderly fathers trying to reach out to their precious children and loved ones, the heart-rending laments and moans of mothers forced to witness the rape and slaughter of their children, and the blasphemies and sighs that formed on the lips of thousands and thousands of unfortunate victims as they rolled in pools of blood that slowly flowed through rocks and stones.

The executioners—unfeeling and ruthless in the face of their victims' suffering, vast as the ocean—slew mercilessly, stopping only when exhaustion made them incapable of lifting their arms any more.

The villagers left with their booty, taking with them the women they had kidnapped. The *cheté*s separated the men who were still alive out from those who had been massacred, took them behind a nearby hill, and shot them all.

Their mothers heard their children being killed and started running frantically in that direction. The executioners turned the muzzles of their rifles on them, and many mothers fell bleeding, shot in their foreheads and chests, on the corpses of their beloved children.

Then, using their whips as a threat, the police collected all the women who had hidden in the fields, beat them severely, and put them back on the road, heading for the desert. Mrs. Takouhi and her daughter were among those who survived. On the day they left the city, her daughter, Vartouhi, had disguised herself as an old woman, cut her hair, and painted several wounds on her face, and that's how she escaped the whipping of those criminal Kurds, who were weeding out the good-looking women. Mrs. Takouhi's sister, her son, and her two grandchildren were slaughtered before her eyes.

Approximately 500 people were left, supervised by 20 policemen. They were naked, barefoot, wounded, injured, and dirty; for days they traveled in the sizzling sun without bread or water, bearing in their hearts their anguish over the deaths of their loved ones.

The police deliberately made them travel through deserted areas so that they would be unable to find bread and water by the road. Occasionally they passed near a cool stream or spring. No sooner did they try to quench their thirst and wet their parched lips than the whips started cracking in the air.

"Move on. We don't have time to wait for you."

Those whose thirst was too strong tried to get a drink of water anyway, and the butts of the policemen's guns were suddenly brought down on their backs. They dropped to the ground, half dead.

As if not satisfied to plunder, the police gradually began to act savagely. They searched women's bodies, their secret parts, in the hope of finding hidden diamonds, gold, and money. Hearing that some women had swallowed gold, they slit open the stomachs of those they suspected. More than 50 women were slain by the beastly actions of these monsters. They found gold in the insides of only three of them.

And the caravan kept moving, through corpses and graves, subjected to constant plunder and murder. When the deportees tried to pick grass or roots to fill their sour stomachs, which had been empty for weeks, the whips cracked, followed by a torrent of threats.

"Walk, or we'll butcher you all."

* * *

After days of traveling like this, the caravan arrived at the shore of a river. The road continued on the other side of the river. But how would they get across? There were no boats and no bridge. In fact the police had brought them there on purpose, so they would all be drowned trying to cross the river.

They came to a halt at the river and dared not move another step. The river was deep and seemed to have a swift, violent current.

The police began beating them with the butts of their guns, breaking noses, jaws, and heads. The blows were sometimes so strong that under their impact a few fell lifeless to the ground. Heart-rending screams, weeping, and pleading were all in vain. The rifles kept pounding down on the deportees.

Death ahead of them—death behind them! To no avail they threw themselves into the river, hoping that a miracle would get them across to the opposite bank.

Like a foaming monster the river devoured them all.

Only a few got across, either by swimming or floating through the mass of swollen corpses that had filled the river. Among the fortunate ones was Mrs. Takouhi. And Vartouhi? She could see her nowhere. The foaming waves had snatched her away from Mrs. Takouhi.

The poor mother dropped to her knees and beat her chest. She was on the verge of losing her mind. She kept pulling out her hair. After losing her husband, son, daughter-in-law, sister, and grandchildren, she had now lost her only daughter as well. Life meant nothing to her anymore. What did she have to live for after that? Wasn't it better to die and be freed at last from this miserable existence? Mrs. Takouhi was in just this mood when she heard a frantic voice:

"Mother!"

It was a familiar voice. The mother, terrified, turned to the voice and spotted several corpses, like pieces of straw floating on the current of the river, at times sinking and at other times borne along on the waves. And her daughter was among them, firmly clutching the leg of a corpse, like a shipwrecked person hanging on to a broken mast.

When Mrs. Takouhi saw her daughter's disastrous situation, it was as if she acquired supernatural strength. In a fraction of a second she had thrown herself into the water, and she reached her daughter at that very instant when the latter fainted and was loosening her grip on the leg. Mrs. Takouhi grabbed her daughter by the hair, pulled her through the water, and brought her to shore, where she herself fainted in the bushes, next to her daughter.

* * *

After herding the people into the water, the police rode off on their horses and crossed the river by using a bridge just half an hour away. Scarcely forty women were lying on the sand, exhausted, hungry, and absolutely terrified.

Rifles and whips were used to get these miserable skeletons to their feet, then they chased them with their horses to make them run.

Mrs. Takouhi and Vartouhi were forgotten where they lay behind the bushes. A little later, when they regained consciousness, they saw their friends running like wild animals before the mounted policemen, trying to avoid their savage blows. After running for some time, they fell down breathless and, regardless of how many blows they received, they couldn't move a moment longer.

Mrs. Takouhi and her daughter experienced a short but mistaken burst of euphoria when they saw the police riding away from them, leaving their victims where they were. But this elation did not last long. A bit later they saw the executioners returning. . . . and this time they had bundles of dry grass in their arms.

What was the purpose of these bundles? It wasn't hard to guess. The police spread them on the corpses that covered the ground, set fire to them, and watched them burn for a brief moment, then got on their horses and disappeared. In the meantime, thick smoke filled the air, as if the black curse of the Armenians were being written in the bright blue sky.

Mrs. Takouhi and her daughter watched in horror as this scene unfolded. They were so crushed and weakened it was as if they had no more ability either to think or to feel. They were like zombies. Mother and daughter stayed there all night, in nightmarish torpor. The next day, a little recovered from their fatigue, they got up and leaned against each other as they walked through the deserted fields, without knowing where they were going or why.

Within a couple of hours, Vartouhi stopped, almost at her last breath, and whispered:

"Mother, I can't walk any more. My eyes have gone dim, I feel dizzy, my heart is beating faster and faster . . ."

"Don't be afraid, daughter," the mother consoled her. "There's nothing wrong with you. Yesterday you were a little scared . . . that must be the reason."

"No, Mother. My condition is serious."

Vartouhi was physically broken down and psychologically destitute. She took refuge in her mother's arms like an injured bird.

The mother sat in the shade of a tree with her daughter's head on her lap, not knowing what to do. Hoping to find a village not too far away where she might be able to get help, she put her daughter on her back and began walking along the road. After walking for scarcely five minutes, she stopped, breathless.

"Oh, I'm dying, I'm dying," Vartouhi sobbed.

The mother bathed her daughter's burning forehead in tears and remained encouraging:

"Dont be afraid, Vartouhi; don't be afraid, your fever will soon come down and then you'll feel fine."

But Vartouhi heard no more. Her pale cheeks burned with fever. She babbled constantly. She was delirious. In her sick imagination she saw the jaundiced faces of the police and the irregular soldiers. They had come to slaughter her, to choke her, to burn her alive. She kept shouting, sobbing, screaming, and that night, at last, in horrible affliction, she drew her last, innocent breath.

Stung deeply in her motherly heart, Mrs. Takouhi wept for a long long time over her daughter's corpse. Then, realizing that it did no good to cry, she dug up the earth with her fingers and nails, buried her daughter's body, then ran away like a madwoman, stretching out her arms before her and with disheveled hair flying in the wind.

* * *

When I got back home I thought about Mrs. Takouhi's story for a long time. It seems that every Armenian has had horrifying experiences like this.

I tried to visualize the churchyard and the thousand miserable people sleeping there; the hundreds of thousands of sobbing unfortunate people under the tents of Katma; the teeming crowds along the roads, some already massacred, others dragging themselves along; and I thought: who knows what stories they could tell if we could only make them speak?

"No, no, they mustn't speak. Isn't what we have gone through enough to discourage us also from wanting to listen to them?"

"But why shut our ears?" I asked myself a little later. Regardless of how wretched their stories were, wasn't it our duty to listen to them and put their stories down on paper?

Yes, I have decided that no matter how difficult that task might be, I must listen to the stories of my unfortunate relatives and record them. This unspeakable suffering and frightening tragedy of the Armenian people must echo forever. Future generations must read these lines and think of ways to prevent the horrifying stories of their people from ever happening again.

23 September, 1915

Today we heard bad news. Because of his tolerant attitude to Armenians, the mayor of Aleppo has lost his post. It seems that the government is going to increase its policy of persecuting Armenians. We saw evidence of this today in the posters glued to the walls, announcing that all Armenians must register at their local police stations within a week. Those who disobey the orders will be heavily fined and thrown into prison.

We don't know what to do. If we register, there is no doubt they will deport us from here as soon as they can. And if we don't, we'll face heavy penalties.

24 September, 1915

While we were wandering around the market place, we saw some policemen arresting Armenians. Those who are arrested have no chance of ever seeing their parents, wives, and children again. They are immediately taken to Sebil, and from there they are sent to Deir Zor. That's why there are so many fathers, mothers, wives, husbands, sisters, and brothers who have been separated from each other: they have been deported separately, to different destinations.

Since we were afraid of being arrested, we left everything unfinished and returned home panting.

25 September, 1915

The *moukhtar* (elder) of our neighborhood came and ordered us to get ready to leave. Our permission to stay for a week expired today.

Since the orders were extremely precise, we paid double to obtain the necessary permission to delay our departure another week.

At the moment we're all imprisoned in the house. We can't even go out to make alternative arrangements.

30 September, 1915

After a long illness, the wife of my paternal uncle, Hagop Dadrian, passed away. Although Hagop Dadrian was really my father's cousin, we used to call him uncle and respected him as a father. The death of his wife, Mrs. Hayganoush, caused us great pain. Porters came and took her away to be buried. Nobody could go to the funeral because the police were arresting Armenians in the streets.

This evening we went to the local police station to register.

2 October, 1915

Today was a very emotional day for us. The *moukhtar* of our district and two policemen came early this morning and wanted to take us to Sebil. No matter how much money we offered, they refused us permission to extend our to stay. We had no intention of leaving Aleppo and wanted to gain time by postponing our departure date.

We showed the police those among us who were sick and told them that under the circumstances we were not able to travel. Regardless of how hard we tried, it was impossible to soften their hearts of stone.

At the last minute, a certain Hovhannes Giuleserian, a local Armenian and a friend of Mrs. Zarifi, our landlady, came to our help. Apparently he knew a lot of people in government circles. Speaking in Arabic, Giuleserian finally won over the people who had been hassling us. He also promised to do his best—naturally by bribing high-ranking officials—to get us exempted from police surveillance.

5 October, 1915

Orders have arrived from Constantinople that Armenian Protestants are not to be deported beyond Aleppo. Giuleserian delivered this news and suggested that we register as Protestants to make it easier to arrange our stay in Aleppo. He is looking after it.

Since my father didn't think there was anything wrong in being registered as Protestants, he went to governor's office with Giuleserian and got Protestant certificates for ten families.

Therefore, as of today, by the strength of the Holy Spirit, 64 Armenian Apostolics have become Protestants . . . only on paper, of course!

12 October, 1915

The persecution of Armenians has eased a little. After eighteen days of voluntary imprisonment in the house, we got my father's permission to go out.

The first thing we did was visit Pakrad and Mrs. Takouhi. Ever since the day we heard their stories they had become a subject of daily conversation. We wanted to know what they had been up to since our last visit.

I got a silver coin from my father, and a friend and I headed for the house where they were living. We went through a deserted courtyard and stopped in front of the basement room.

We were suddenly worried when we saw that there was nobody in the room. We looked around, disturbed. An Arab—later we learned that he was the landlord—rushed over to us and asked who we were looking for.

"The madam and the mister," we said in broken Arabic.

"They've gone," the man said with an expansive movement of his hand.

"Where?"

"The police . . . Sebil . . ."

"When?"

"A week ago."

We stood there heart-broken for a minute, as if we had just learned of the death of two friends, and then, without wandering around the city, we went back home, still in deep thought.

13 October, 1915

The military authorities confiscated our carriages and sent them to Rakka to transport wheat. Two trustworthy men from Chorum went with the carriages. They planned to steal the vehicles at the first chance they got and bring them back. Today they came back with the carriages, at the same time bringing us heart-breaking news from the Arabic regions.

They have taken more than 100,000 people there and distributed them in groups of 50 or 100 families in the villages. The local people are extremely savage and are thieves, and from the day they arrived they began to plunder several deportees, who had already been plundered and robbed of almost everything. According to these men, there is neither food nor drinking water in these villages, no employment, and no houses to live in. The desert climate is unbearable. Misery and illness are everywhere. Every day Armenians drop like flies from cholera and dysentery. Everyone is deeply discouraged and nobody knows how to find a way out of this tragedy.

14 October, 1915

Corpses are common sights in the side streets of Aleppo, especially early in the morning, before the garbage collector has passed.

Today we took part in a heart-rending episode, which caused us a great deal of pain. A girl of hardly ten years—her marble-white body could be seen through her tattered rags—was sitting on the steps of a stone house, sleeping calmly, with her head resting on her emaciated arms.

Her unusually jaundiced appearance and her immobility attracted our attention. We went up to her and took her hand, when suddenly . . . we were holding a stone statue. We were terrified. She was frozen. The poor orphan was not sleeping. She was dead.

15 October, 1915

The news that Armenian Protestants wouldn't have to leave Aleppo is not true. The police arrest Armenians and take them to Sebil without ever asking whether they are Protestant or Apostolic or Catholic.

It's enough to be white and unable to speak Arabic. For the police, such a person is condemned, and must go to Deir Zor.

Today my cousin Haig and I were almost caught and sent to Sebil. We had sold our two carriages and had been paid. We were on or way home when we noticed the police approaching us with a group of arrested Armenians. When we saw the danger Haig and I turned around and began running in the direction we had come from.

A policeman, sword in hand, shouted, "Catch them! Catch them!" and started chasing us. Fortunately, there was no one in the deserted street to catch us. We escaped by running around one or two corners.

We took refuge in a *khan* (inn), hid under some carriages, and got home two hours later, having taken a good deal of care to get there.

16 October, 1915

Despite all his efforts, Giuleserian has not yet obtained a permit for us to stay in Aleppo.

"There are possibilities for military families, but for people like you the law is extremely precise," he said to us today, in explanation of his failure. All the same, he assured us that he would use supernatural means to succeed, and that if staying here should eventually prove to be truly impossible he would try to send us to Damascus—although that region is also full up and now shut. It's not a bad idea, going to Damascus. The other day, one of our friends, Kevranbashian, who has a good position in one of the stations in Damascus, came here to get his relatives and take them back with him. From what he said, we know that the climate is mild and it's possible to find a job. Kevranbashian, who visited us again today, said that my father's close friend, judge Ali Riza Bey, is the president of the genocidal tribunal (*yeghernatad adyan*) in Damascus. In Damascus a government official of Ali Riza Bey's caliber can be very effective. Therefore, if we cannot manage to stay in Aleppo, going to Damascus is the lesser of two evils for us.

17 October, 1915

A great deal of tragic news has arrived from Deir Zor. Some of the Armenians who were taken there escaped and returned to Aleppo. Here they were arrested and sent back to Deir Zor. They escaped again and were deported again, and so some families have been to Deir Zor and returned to Aleppo at least three or four times.

According to what they say, death is inevitable for Armenians in Deir Zor unless they can find ways to get away from there.

18 October, 1915

Tonight my grandmother was in agony. Her sobbing and moaning kept us awake all night.

My paternal aunt and her little girl, Haygouhi, are also lying in a corner of the room. They are both sick.

You'd think our room had been turned into a hospital. Today I also have a headache.

19 October, 1915

Toward evening Giuleserian came and told us that there was no longer any possibility that we would be allowed to remain in Aleppo. Despite the fact that through Giuleserian the police have received quite a bit of money, they still threaten to deport us to Deir Zor if we do not leave the city within 24 hours. Giuleserian has managed to get written permission from the police for us to go to Damascus.

The only sad part is that we won't all be able to travel together, because transporting sick people to Damascus is strictly forbidden. My grandmother, my aunt, and Haygouhi are still sick and don't even have the energy to move.

Fortunately, Giuleserian has succeed in obtaining a second permit from the chief of police, which allows my grandmother, her sister, my paternal aunt, and her two youngest children to remain in Aleppo, as they are considered members of a military family. (Haig and Arshag, who are over fifteen, can't be included in this permission, and will come with us).

Given the circumstances, we have absolutely no choice but to accept our destiny. We think that if we settle in Damascus we will perhaps be able to send for them to come and live with us. We spent the entire night in preparations. The other nine families from Chorum will go with us.

20 October, 1915

We left my grandmother and aunt everything they might need and enough money for three months. After heart-wrenching goodbyes, we left.

When we arrived at the station we found about 800 people who, like us, had bribed officials to obtain permits to go to Damascus. They were all waiting for the train to arrive. After a little while a train consisting of twenty cars came. We were permitted to get on and make ourselves comfortable. With an unusual amount of commotion and pushing and shoving we rushed for the cars. In that huge crowd countless people ran into each other, pushed each other, or were crushed under heavy bales and shoes.

We also made our way forward through this confused mayhem: pushing and stepping on others, falling and letting ourselves be carried along by the current of the crowd, being shoved right and left, sometimes forward, often backward . . . at last we also succeeded in getting aboard a second-class coach.

We had hardly settled on the benches when a municipal doctor and about ten policemen also entered the car to look for sick travelers.

The policemen took all the patients pointed out by the doctor off the train, while telling the families of these sick people that if they didn't want to be separated from them they could get off too . . . Eventually they reached our compartment. My uncle's little son, Piuzant, has been a little under the weather since yesterday. Afraid that the policemen might see him, we immediately hid the boy behind the curtain. But the policemen saw him and took him off the train.

My uncle could not abandon his five-year-old child, so he got off the train as well, leaving us to our care for his old mother and his other two little children, who lost their mother only three weeks ago. Realizing that they were now going to be separated from their father and brother as well, they started crying out in terror, "Father! Father!"

The police paid no attention to the complaints of the families who had sick people, but took 22 people off the train. In the meantime we thought that we had already suffered our share of savagery and would soon be leaving, but unfortunately the merciless employees of the railway now came and told us that it is forbidden for Armenians to travel in cars intended for people; so we had to take our things to the freight cars.

"But our tickets are for third class," we objected.

"It doesn't. You aren't allowed to travel in first, second, and third class cars," they replied, with no trace of concern.

"If that's the case, why did you sell us these tickets . . . and then why didn't you tell us in advance, so we could have gone directly to the freight cars?"

But who listened to us, to our objections? With the help of the police they took us off the cars where we had already settled down and led us to the livestock cars. There were about 140 people in each car, which was designed for only forty. We were on top of each other and thoroughly squashed. We could only take a few covers and some food with us. The rest of our belongings were moved to other cars, and as soon as everything was ready the doors were shut with a giant slam and we were on our way.

It was like being imprisoned in a huge closed trunk. There was a little opening in the door of the car, through which a bit of air and light entered. At one point, with a great deal of difficulty, I managed to make my way to that opening to breathe some fresh air. What I saw outside cut my breathing off like the edge of a knife.

We were traveling through a huge field full of dome-shaped huts, like the ones you see in pictures of how the cannibals of Oceania live. They were all over the field. Black people, almost naked, were crawling in and out of the mud and straw huts like serpents. They let go blood-curdling cries as they pointed us out to each other . . .

"Strange," I thought, "that only a few hours from a civilized city like Aleppo, in an area through which a train even passes, there are people living in such primitive conditions. If it's like this here, what must it be like in the depths of the desert?" I couldn't bear to watch or think about them anymore. Others were shouting at me: "Hey, young man, get your head out of the window, or we'll all be suffocated to death."

I apologized and went back to where I had been sitting. In my sadness and terror, I had forgotten that the air, which I had monopolized for a brief moment, had to be shared with 140 people.

Tonight it was impossible to sleep because of lack of space, the polluted air caused by the cramped conditions, and the constant shaking of the cars. At one point, as if all this were not enough, a sudden noise was added—thunder and lightning—and heavy rain beat down on the roof of our car with a deafening clamor.

Sometimes the train stopped at a station. The moment the doors were opened, thousands of refugees who had been waiting there at the same station for months in the sun and rain rushed onto the cars— some hoping to find a place, others hoping to find a member or two of their families who had been separated. They called out the names of their lost relatives. People who were already in the car also shouted out names, thinking that perhaps they might find a relative or a compatriot among the crowd waiting there. At the station in Hama we also looked for my cousin Eugene. We had heard that he had escaped the Samsoun massacre and had taken refuge there.

"Eugene, Eugene . . . Eugene Soghomonian from Samsoun," we shouted with all our might.

But alas, what hope was there really of finding a lost relative in such a situation? Before long the doors were shut and the train plunged into darkness.

* * *

Around noon we arrived in Rayak. Since the gauge of the rails got narrower there, we changed to another train. On this train they used wood instead of coal, and as a result it is very difficulty to pull the cars at the end of the train. Every time the train has to climb a slope the locomotive stops, the train is divided into two or three sections, each section is pulled to the top of the slope separately, and then the sections are put back together to resume the journey. This entire operation reminds us of a mother cat transporting her kittens.

We heard that the cars carrying the rest of our belongings were held up at a station along the way. Apparently they will be sent on eventually.

All our beds, underwear, and clothing are in those cars. We were discouraged at the thought that this was one more way of robbing us, who have been robbed ever since Ulu Kishla.

It was hard to control our emotions as we passed through station after station where refugee families invariably rushed to our cars, hoping to get a place to travel for themselves. They told us that while they were on their way to Damascus at their own expense, the government had commandeered their trains to transport troops. Despite a promise that they would be able to continue their journey on the next train, these people had been waiting for months . . .

While passing Baalbek I put my head out the window for a second in order to catch sight of the famous ruins, when suddenly I pulled it back in again, letting out a painful cry. A live coal from the chimney of the train had fallen on my neck. Immediately before that other burning coals had apparently fallen on my hat and shoulders. I hadn't felt them, as they had not yet burned through to my flesh. Like a crippled tortoise, we were advancing slowly and with a great deal of difficulty. In the meantime other sparkling pieces of coal were flying through the air. The train went on, and at last tonight it stopped at a station lit by electricity. "Damascus."

We thought we had come to the end of our journey, to our destination. We were impatiently waiting for the employees to come to open the doors of our prison when the train blew its whistle and its wheels started turning again.

But where were we going? We looked at each other amazed and couldn't answer our own question.

The train went on for about half an hour and then came to a halt in a shady area. We heard that we had arrived at Kadem station, the name of which is synonymous with Sebil in Aleppo, the only difference being that from this station Armenians were sent to the desert in Hauran . . .

What did we have to do with Hauran? We explained to the station employees that we had taken the train from Aleppo to go to Damascus, and that the permit we had obtained proved our intended destination.

The chief of police of the station smiled at our naiveté, tore our permit to pieces, and threw it away.

"The municipality of Aleppo has no jurisdiction to meddle in the business of the municipality of Damascus."

"If they had no authority to issue it, why did they do so?"

"How do I know? Go ask them."

The policeman's reaction amazed all 800 of us, and voices were raised everywhere.

"Oh Giuleserian . . . Giuleserian, why has he betrayed us? Why didn't he tell us that the permits he got from the Aleppo police station didn't really mean a thing?"

Or had he, perhaps, also been deceived? Or was he collaborating secretly with the police in order to rob Armenian refugees? We had no time to think. At the moment the central question concerned the conditions that threatened our health: the police wanted us to get out of the cars, where we would freeze, as it was like winter outside and we had nothing to cover ourselves with.

Before long another bribe solved the problem. The chief of police permitted us to spend the night in the cars. That we did until dawn. We waited sadly, thinking about our hopeless vagrant situation.

22 October, 1915

At dawn we all got out of the wagons and stood in the sun to warm our bones.

A little later the police led us to a place, not far from the station, where thousands of refugees had pitched their tents or settled under the protection of olive trees, willingly awaiting their turn to be taken to the desert. Armed policemen surveyed these refugees quite attentively so that no one would escape their outdoor prison.

We spread the cover that we had brought with us in an open area and sat on it. The sun, which we had looked forward to so eagerly this morning, began to scorch us like fire scarcely an hour later. The refugees who knew the place told us that this is the law of the desert— at night extremely cold, in the afternoon extremely hot.

My father wrote a letter to his friend Ali Riza Bey today, asking him to think of a way to save us from this hopeless situation.

We spent the night in the tent of a kind refugee.

23 October, 1915

Other contingents, cheated like us, gradually arrive from Aleppo and are taken off at the Kadem station camp. We wonder what will happen to my grandmother, her sister, my paternal aunt, and her two children if the permit they were given is as worthless as ours.

Today the police savagely beat a young refugee as he had tried to escape to Damascus. The poor guy has broken bones and lies in a pool of blood on the ground, crying continually. His heart-rending cries and sobs break our hearts.

One of the women objected to the police, saying that no one should beat a human being so savagely. The police answered:

"What are you saying, woman? We have orders to kill all Armenians who try to escape from the refugee station. Just thank God that we felt sorry for the guy and decided to beat him up instead of killing him. We really can't treat you any more humanely than that!"

24 October, 1915

Here there is neither food nor drinking water. A dirty Arab has opened a shop where he sells rotten provisions for twice and sometimes three times the usual price. Besides, he has so little stock that there's hardly enough for a third of the people. We get water to drink from a strange well, which is actually a hole that opens into an underground stream.

Gradually new convoys of hungry and sick people arrive. They won't allow us to go to the city to buy bread or medicines.

Today my father's Turkish friend came from Damascus and visited us. According to him, the city is so crowded that the mayor has declared that any official who in any way helps Armenian refugees get into the city will be punished severely. On the other hand, he said that he could save our family alone, but my father wouldn't agree to this, insisting that there must be an arrangement for at least ten families. After this Ali Riza Bey left, saying that he was not terribly hopeful, but would do his best.

This evening my paternal uncle arrived by train with his young son, who was feeling better. This seemed a miracle to us, because we already thought we had lost them forever. Their sudden return to us cheered us up considerably, but the news he gave us equally saddened and changed our mood. Giuleserian had played the role of a body-snatcher, and on the day following our departure the police had come for my sick grandmother, her sister, her daughter, and the two grandchildren, Aram and Haygouhi, and taken them to Sebil. When my uncle had heard this evil news, he had searched for them, but unfortunately had found no trace of them . . .

25 October, 1915

Today we received a letter from Ali Riza Bey, the president of the genocidal tribunal. He regrets that all his efforts to obtain permission to take us to Damascus have failed.

At noon some policemen came and told us to get ready to leave this evening by train to Deir Zor.

"We have nothing to get ready but a cover," we told them. "Isn't it possible for us to wait a few days, until our belongings arrive from Rakka?"

"No, it's not possible. You leave this evening. If your belongings arrive we'll send them after you," said the policeman.

None of our pleas and begging helped in the least. They allowed only three families from Chorum to remain at the station, as they had seriously ill people.

We eight families (Artin, the carriage driver from Chorum, succeeded in getting on the train in Aleppo with his wife, and they were now traveling with us) and numerous other families from Caesarea, Marash, Aintab, Sis, and Adana—a total of 300 people—bought tickets this evening and got on the train. Being deprived of our belongings, with a single cover to go into the desert with, had deeply depressed us. We sat on the hard benches of the cars and brooded. Suddenly, one of our compatriots who had stayed behind in the station came running to us to tell us that our belongings had already arrived and were in the station warehouse.

We still had fifteen minutes before the train left. At this news we all jumped out of the cars and, disregarding the police and the shouts of the station employees, who were all thieves, we headed to the warehouse, picked up a few bundles, and returned to the train. The rushing and pushing and shoving that comprised our warehouse experience can only be understood by those who have tried to save belongings from a fire.

We had hardly climbed back into the cars when the train blew its whistle and left. We wiped the sweat and dust from our foreheads and were happy for a while, congratulating each other on finding our lost belongings.

Happy . . . but is it possible to be happy, when with each passing minute we felt that we were leaving civilization behind and heading into the scorching desert? Reality, however, soon woke us up and delivered us over to sad thoughts again.

Tonight we passed several stations where always, as in all of the other places, there were thousands of refugees who were temporarily being detained there. These poor people were so cold that some were warming their hands against the hot sides of the locomotive.

We wondered about the condition of these people, about what might happen to them . . . people who don't even have a coat to protect themselves against the biting cold of the night and the stinging heat of the day.

"Why did the executioners of the Armenian nation have to create groups of bandits to wipe us out?" we asked ourselves: "Weren't the desert heat, the cold, famine, illness, and misery enough to accomplish that goal?"

26 October, 1915

This morning the train stopped at Dera station, which is an important stop on the Hijaz railroad. That's where the desert of Hauran begins, and we'll be settling in some of the villages there. We picked up our luggage and went to the refugee station. Several families had set up their tents there and were waiting to be chosen by the council of the village they would be going to so that their expenses would be taken care of by the officials. We also set up our tents and waited our turns. This evening something strange happened. Some policemen came and ordered us to form a circle in a nearby field. With no idea of what was going to happen, 2,000 people—grownups, children, women, and adolescents—stood next to each other in the field and formed the circle, as ordered.

After we had been standing there for about half an hour, we spotted a government employee approaching us in the company of a policeman. The policeman was groaning under the weight of a bag. The employee entered the circle, opened the bag, took out a handful of coins, and stopped in front of each of us, placing forty *para* in the palms of the grownups and twenty in the palms of the children.

We didn't understand the purpose of what they were doing. Was this some kind of joke? Were they mocking our misery? But then they revealed the height of their impudence by forcing us to shout three times, "Long live my *Padishah*."

The Armenians offered three-fold praise to the sultan who had destroyed them, wishing him a long life; then, holding back their tears, they went back to their tents.

27 October, 1915

This afternoon we went into town, to get an impression of the inner provinces of Arabia. Despite the fact that Dera is an important station, there was no life in the market place. A few shopkeepers squatted in front of their businesses and drank coffee or *narghile* or yawned lazily. There was nobody in the streets but us; the town was *dead* in the real sense of the word.

This afternoon the order came, and twenty families left on camels for the places they had been assigned to. As traveling by camel was a novelty for Armenians, many of them fell off and there were a few minor mishaps. This evening the police came again and ordered us to form another circle so we could receive our daily ration. Those who were in need of forty *para* went to get it. We didn't leave our tent.

28 October, 1915

There is a shortage of water and bread here also. There is a bakery shop at the station, where you can buy bread early in the morning. Anyone who gets there a little late comes back with no bread. The local inhabitants don't sell bread because they don't have enough even for themselves.

As for the water, it is not drinkable. It comes from a dirty well. It is murky and looks like mud. There are red worms in it. We sift it through a piece of white cloth three times before drinking it, and then only a little at a time, because it is extremely bitter.

Today we couldn't find any bread, even at the bakery shop, because the troops leaving for Palestine have confiscated all the bread. Suffering from hunger, we went to the governor's house to demand that he either provides us with bread or sends us where we were supposed to go, without undue delay.

It was our bad luck that Governor Abdul Kadir Bey was apparently sleeping. He got angry at us for disturbing him and kicked us out, saying that we had no right to meddle in the business of the government.

This evening, as punishment for our protest, we were deprived of one *para* of our daily allowance.

29 October, 1915

This morning it was decided where we would be going. We'll be settled in a Circassian village four days away from here.

In this region there are ten or twelve Circassian villages, about five or six hours away from each other. The inhabitants emigrated from the Caucasus about half a century ago and settled in the region of Dera with the consent of the government. The fact that these people usually choose areas with lots of water and large, open fields made us feel better, especially when we considered that the Circassians were much more civilized than the Fellahs of the desert.

An hour later our conjectures proved true, especially when the police introduced us to seven carriage drivers from Jeresh who had come to Dera today and were getting ready to go back. One of these carriage drivers, who could speak a little Turkish, told us that not only was their village an oasis in the middle of the desert, but that it was also the only place in all of Hauran that deserved to be called a paradise.

In order to get to this magical country, we immediately hired the carriages of these Circassians, supplementing them with four donkeys and twelve camels bought from the local Arabs. Just past noon our eight families from Chorum got on the road, under the surveillance of two policemen.

We remembered how the Armenian soldier in Bozanti had described the desert. We especially remembered when, after travelling quite a way from Dera, we found ourselves on a endless barren plain. There was neither elevation nor the green of vegetation in sight, but a never-ending, monotonous flat expanse. A rocky and thorny path had been created by the constant coming and going of animals and human beings since time immemorial. This path extended, like a straight line drawn down the middle of the steppe, all the way to the horizon. Despite our progress across this plain, there was no evidence either that the road would ever end or that the scenery would ever change. We felt as if we were always in the same place, trapped on this forbidding steppe.

The sizzling rays of the sun burned our heads and shoulders and blinded our eyes. A suffocating wind seared the skin of our hands and faces. As if ahead of us the doors of a furnace had been left open and its fiery blast were blowing in our faces.

"What kind of wind is this?" we asked our carriage drivers.

"This is the excessive heat of the simoon," they answered. It is the bane of the desert inhabitants, its vegetation, and its beasts.

Fortunately, it was soon evening.

Before nightfall we arrived in Rimta, an Arab village. The peasants refused to sell us bread and water, insisting that they didn't have any extra. Since we needed water more than bread, we roamed the streets looking for a well. Whenever we did find a well, it was either furnished with a locked iron cover or, if it were open, was completely dry. We spent the night in an abandoned police building at one end of the village. Although we were squeezed together, 39 of us, we shivered with the extreme cold until morning. The excessive, hellish heat of daytime became a terrifying ice-cold wind, which blew through the cracks around the windows and the door and numbed our senses. Often we were so confused that we struck matches, thinking that we could warm ourselves with their momentary flames.

30 October, 1915

We woke up frozen this morning, and basked in the sun like sluggish flies, just to warm up. After collecting a bit of strength and reviving ourselves, we loaded the camels and took to the road.

We had a relatively peaceful journey until noon. The torture began once again this afternoon: first because of the heat, and second because of the path, which became harder and harder. The camels could not walk, and kept falling with their loads. Forgotten were the heat and the parching wind: we spent a lot of time getting the camels back on their feet, looking after injured passengers, and tying bales together.

My cousin Haig, who has been sick for the last three days, was completely exhausted today and couldn't stay on the camel. We made him lie down in our carriage and my mother, sisters, and brother got out of the carriage and were distributed among the animals. I was sitting on a camel and I took my little sister and my brother, put them into saddle-bags, and that way we managed to suspend them on both sides of the camel. My father, who was sitting on our third camel, took my other sister. We put our mother on a donkey, but as she was not used to riding, Arshag walked beside her until he got tired. Then he would come and sit on one of our camels and I or my father would take turns performing the same task.

Our traveling companions were in exactly the same situation: some of them traveled on camels, donkeys, and in carriages, and others on foot, with their furniture and belongings loaded onto pack horses.

All day long we continued our journey: falling, getting up, helping to get fallen camels back on their feet, staying close to those who needed help, always swaying with the creaking of the carts and burned by the scorching rays of the sun.

This evening we arrived in Irbit, a little province in the jurisdiction of the government of Dera. Jeresh, our eventual destination, is in the same jurisdiction.

We spent the night more or less peacefully, because Irbit lies in a valley and is not much affected by the cold wind. However, we had another adventure tonight. Thieves would have taken our camels, carts, and their loads if the Circassians hadn't foreseen the danger. Since we thought that the attempted robbery had been organized with the collaboration of our camel drivers, we kept our eyes open all night long.

31 October, 1915

We went to the government building this morning and officially registered as "honorable" citizens of Jeresh.

A young man known as Minas from Sis had come from Jeresh some time ago looking for employment, and he told us quite a bit about our future homeland. According to him, Jeresh was founded on the ruins of an ancient city—it is a town of 150 houses, and the only place in the desert with a water spring. The climate is hot and not terribly wholesome. The population consists mainly of Circassian farmers and a few Arabs from Damascus, who are mostly merchants.

Because of its market, Jeresh occupies an exceptional place in the desert and has become a sort of capital. Fellahs and Bedouins, who live mostly in tents, come to Jeresh from the surrounding villages to buy and to sell.

The village is governed by a leader who has an assistant, a barbaric Kurdish sergeant major with 10 hungry gendarmes.

According to Minas, within the region of Hauran there are 20,000 Armenians, of whom around 600 families—mostly from Marash, Aintab, Kilis, Zeitoun, Caesarea, Sis, Adana, Deort Yol, Hadjin, and Yazdi—live in Jeresh, half of them in houses and the rest in the surrounding caves.

Among the refugees, only those from Sis and Caesarea have modest means. Of the others, those who have skills find jobs in the local market and those who have no professions and are in good health become laborers and grow vegetables, while those who are frail go about in the streets completely discouraged and holding out their hands to their luckier compatriots, because the Circassians are stingy and uncompassionate, and the Damascus Arabs are fanatics and uncharitable: they wouldn't give beggars the crumbs from their tables.

Minas' information gave us a very bad impression, as the descriptions of the Circassian carriage drivers had given us a completely different picture of Jeresh and its delightful inhabitants.

In deep thought we loaded our belongings and took to the road.

Our journey today was more difficult. As we get closer to the depths of the desert we feel that we are approaching the borders of Hell. The dry searing wind burns our faces and the sun scorches our woolen clothes, like rays emanating from an evil spirit and focused on us by a magnifying glass.

The hot wind has made the camels nervous. They turn their long necks to right and left, roaring loudly. And sometimes they just lie on the ground, emitting foamy liquids from their breathing or breathless mouths, or trying to bite anyone who dares to approach them.

The sick are in pitiful condition—especially Haig, who constantly asks for water, but where can we get water? All the wells on the road have dried up and our reserve was used up long ago. We give him oranges to quench his thirst, but he refuses and asks for water.

After a crushing journey, we arrived this evening in a village called Husun. As we made our way through the streets, we were greatly surprised to see a church in the village square. There was a cross on top of it. The villagers told us that it belonged to Orthodox Arabs, and that there are apparently a few other villages like that in Hauran.

Before the war, French missionaries opened a school and built a church here, with a view to converting the Orthodox Arabs to Catholicism. Nowadays there isn't a trace of these missionaries, and the school has been partly destroyed. However the few rooms that are still standing served to shelter the exhausted bones of several Armenian refugees that night.

We spent the night lying on the hard benches and desks. In the middle of the Hauran desert a church, a cross, a school, and desks! What will we come across next?

1 November, 1915

As a matter of interest, we went to church this morning. The service was in Arabic. The intermittent repetition of the word *Allah* by the priest gave us the fleeting impression that we had entered a mosque by mistake. The simultaneous sight, however, of icons, crosses, and lamps assured us that we were indeed in the temple of a people who worshipped at the foot of the cross.

After leaving the church we reloaded our carts and camels, took our stock of bread, oranges, and water, and set off on the road. As on most days, our journey was comfortable until noon. But after that we were faced with difficulties, especially in the rocky valleys on the other side of the flat steppe.

The camels, which were used to walking on sandy terrain, proceeded with a great deal of difficulty on these stony roads, and often they slid and fell the moment their feet struck a tiny obstacle. During these frequent falls the leg of one of the camels was dislocated. This became a good reason for the camel-drivers to take the loads from the backs of the camels and declare that they would go no farther with these accursed Armenians.

After paying for the injured camel we were able to talk the Arabs around. This process, however, took hours and hours. At last they started moving again, but on condition that no traveler over the age of five would ride a camel.

We had resolved our feud with the Arabs, but we still had to contend with the constant moaning of the sick people. Every time the carriages hit large pieces of stone there were heart-rending cries, as they shouted that their ribs were being crushed.

As if we didn't have enough to worry about, we soon began to run out of water; our stock of oranges was depleted and the people began to be grilled by the sizzling rays of the sun.

The earth burned our feet. The rocks were scorching. An amazing, peculiar vapor rose from the ground and dried our throats. The scorching wind blew incessantly and its lethal breath baked our bodies. "Water, water!" people cried from everywhere, especially the sick and the little ones, including my sister, Arpiné, in a pleading voice that grieved our hearts.

"Patience . . . there's a well beneath that rock over there," the police inevitably replied to our endless questions.

We would quicken our steps to get there as fast as possible, but when we arrived we would find to our horror that the well was dry.

"There's another one an hour away," the camel-drivers would say.

"Is there any water in it?"

"*Inshallah.*"

When the Arab says *Inshallah* it means there's no hope. And accordingly, when we arrive there an hour later, we are not surprised to find that there isn't a drop of water in the well.

"Don't give up. In two more hours we'll come to another large well," the carriage drivers say this time: "Walk! Let's hope there's water there."

Walk . . . but how? The sick are suffering from thirst and would prefer to be left to die on the side of the road instead of being shaken about endlessly on this rough road.

We stopped for a while to give them a rest. Then, wanting to get to the water as soon as possible, we started moving again. During our race the camels kept falling, tumbling donkeys refused to obey, the oxen revolted, shaking off their yoke, and the Arabs and Circassians swore continuously. Soaked in blood and sweat, hungry and parched, covered with dust, constantly pushing the carts, picking up the loads of the camels, pulling the donkeys by their reins, helping the sick, encouraging the children, arguing with the carriage and camel-drivers, burned by the sun, scorched by the hot wind, and exhausted, we kept walking, we fell down, we stood up, we fell again, we walked again, and at last, demolished and destroyed, we arrived at the big well.

There was no water there either, but fortunately there was a tree. A tree in the desert is as rare as ice in Hell. Almost numb, we spread ourselves under its shade and remained motionless for a long long time, until we heard our hearts beat regularly once again.

Suddenly an Arab came out of a crevice in a rock (Arabs always show up suddenly from the most unexpected places). From his appearance it was plain that he was a herdsman, although no cattle or pasture could be seen anywhere nearby.

"*Khayo, moy, mafish?* (Countryman, is there any water?)," we asked him. "Bring us some water and we'll reward you generously."

The herdsman nodded positively. Then he took a tin container and part of the reward from us and left, telling us to wait about an hour for him.

The hour passed and then another, but no one was yet in sight. Had our tin container and money disappeared? Was he perhaps a thief and had gone to call his friends? Evil thoughts kept tormenting us as we suffered more and more from the heat and thirst, when suddenly a joyful cry was heard.

"Good news! The Arab is coming back!"

Even the coming of the Messiah wouldn't have caused us such happiness as the arrival of this barefoot Fellah. Especially since he was carrying the container on his head rather than letting it hang from his arm. This was a sign that the container wasn't empty, because Arabs carry heavy items on their heads.

As soon as the good herdsman arrived, we discovered that what he had brought was more like mud than water. As usual, this mud was also full of red worms, but no one paid any attention. We all drank until there was none left. The water affected the parched heart of each of us the same way as a drop of water would affect a red-hot iron. The sick people and children stopped crying, and after a long rest we were able to get to our feet and continue our journey.

As the day was wearing on, we ceased to suffer from the heat, but as darkness descended new difficulties popped up. We could no longer see where we were walking and we were worried more for the camels, which kept falling, than for ourselves, as the road rose steadily toward rocky peaks. Over and over we had to make the camels stop while we ran to help the donkeys lying in sweat on the dusty road. We lightened their roads—by carrying them ourselves—and then had to chase up the oxen, which would stop, exhausted, and refuse to draw the carts.

When we got out of the rocks we breathed a sigh of relief.

Far in the distance, down in the valley, we could see light. The carriage drivers pointed it out to us, saying that it was the village we going to, the village of Jeresh.

Oh! At last we were here! We sped in the direction of the light. From a distance we began to hear the barking of dogs. For a while we thought we were getting closer to the village, but the more we walked the more we descended and the more we clambered around rocks and bushes, as if we were getting no closer to our goal, not even a step.

A little later we even heard the welcome bubbling of a stream. Water! The flowing water was also at the bottom of the dark valley.

We quickened our steps. No matter how tired our legs were, we lengthened our steps with supernatural efforts. We ran breathlessly, and at last, dazzled, we stopped before an indescribable scene.

There it was, the water, in front of us, bubbling up from the bottom of a pool, pouring out so abundantly and so pure. With the donkeys, camels, and carts, we entered the spring all the way up to our knees and, burying our sunburned faces in the water, we drank greedily, we washed, and we drank again, without even giving a brief thought to the fact that the water had lost its clearness because of the dust on our animals' feet.

And when at last we had extinguished the fire in our hearts, we came out of the pool, walked to the edge of the village, and dropped in an open space, completely shattered, hungry and exhausted.

Part Two

IN THE DESERT

2 November, 1915

When we opened our eyes this morning, we saw lots of Armenian refugees. They had surrounded us and were pointing at us, saying, "People in pants have arrived."

It was their remarks about our clothing that first drew our attention to the unusual way our compatriots were dressed. Their clothes were different from ours. All of them, young and old, wore linen gowns and plum-colored hats, had woolen belts around their waists and shoes that resembled slippers. Some of them were also barefoot. Some of the older ones wore jackets over their gowns, and these were the only pieces of modern clothing they had.

These were refugees from Marash, Zeitoun, and Aintab. Then we learned that when they called us people in pants they meant rich people. In their villages, European clothing was worn only by the wealthy.

After the Armenian refugees, the Circassians came to have a look at us. They wore *kalpak*s of black leather and on their feet thin, light jack-boots. Their waists were generally confined by belts adorned with silver ornaments, from which dangled their ever-present daggers. Then came the Damascus Arabs: the shop keepers, fat and fleshy examples of townspeople, not wearing any shoes or socks. And finally came the Fellahs and Bedouins: with bony, sinewy faces and black beards, savage people with neither shirts nor shorts.

After getting to know the inhabitants of Jeresh superficially in this way, we looked around and discovered why we had become such a center of attention. We had arrived at night, in the dark, and without knowing we had camped near the village square.

The sun had already risen when we got up and headed for the village to rent rooms to live in. Two hours later we finished that chore. Everyone in our group had found something according to their means.

The house we rented has two rooms and one kitchen. Eight people will live in one room and in the other will be my uncle's family, six people.

The rooms are empty and have no furniture. At noon we moved our belongings in. On one side of the room we put our bedding, in another corner our bundles of underwear, and in another the food baskets. Haig made his bed in the only corner that was left, and in the middle of the floor we spread a little carpet, just to sit on.

It sounds unbelievable, but this little Circassian hut seemed like a palace to us.

We think that our roaming like gypsies, in the sun and the thick dust along the road, has come to an end. Jaundiced-looking policemen will no longer threaten our lives, no longer rob us, no longer shower us with blows from their whips, yelling "*Yalla ruh*." No more will the terror of massacre hang over our heads like the sword of Damocles; no more will they separate men from women before chopping off their heads; no more will the nightmare of being raped haunt the depths of our souls. No more will we have to fear spending the night unprotected and unsheltered on mountains, in valleys, or in fields; and no more will we suffer anxiety over not finding a piece of bread or a drop of water.

We have been saved from all the suffering and exhaustion of the road, which constantly taxed and wore our moral and physical strength. How many of us will have the good fortune to greet the real dawn of freedom? We don't even think about that anymore. Because even if we die, it will now be with our eyes closed and our legs stretched out.

3 November, 1915

A policeman came this morning and summoned us to the government building to register as citizens of Jeresh for the second time.

We all went, except those who were ill. An employee asked for our papers. Those who owned such things handed them over to him and those who didn't declared their names, ages, and places of birth, and the secretary recorded everything carefully in a copy-book.

While he was taking down the information we gave him, two things caught our attention. First of all, he wrote down that we had all been born in Jeresh . . . Then, a special effort was made to change every man's age: if he was young he was registered as older and if he was older, he lowered his age. Thus my age was recorded not as fifteen but as eighteen, and my father was registered as forty-four instead of forty-eight. When we objected to the sergeant-major, he said: "We can't change what has been written . . . both of you are the right age for compulsory military service."

Military service? . . . We didn't really understand what he was getting at.

4 November, 1915

Haig's condition gets worse and worse. At last his illness has been diagnosed: he has typhoid fever. The plague of the Armenians of this region! Every day three or four people die of this illness. Once a person is infected with it, it's hard for him to get on his feet again. In addition to being dangerous, it's also contagious. Once it gets into a home, the entire household becomes bedridden. Not only does the village lack drugs to treat the disease, but there isn't even enough nourishment to sustain the patients.

Poor Haig lies in one corner of the room. He asks repeatedly for yogurt. He thinks that if he swallows a spoonful of yogurt he will be cured and will get to his feet.

The majority of the Circassians keep goats and sheep in their houses, but they don't sell the milk, even if you pay the equivalent of its weight in gold. We ask the Arabs who come to the market to bring us milk from their villages. They agree and ask for payment in advance, and once they have the money in their pockets they are never seen again.

In the meantime, the patient suffers from extreme fever and waits in vain for the yogurt.

5 November, 1915

Today we explored the village quite a bit.

The many different costumes of the crowd at the market seemed rather strange to us, as did the rifles. Everybody wears a cartridge-belt across his chest and carries a German or English rifle on his back. And the variety of swords, daggers, and diamond-hilted daggers is infinite.

People's distrust of each other is so obvious. The Arabs who come here to do their shopping are all armed because of the insecurity of the roads. The Circassians and the Damascus Arabs are also armed against possible attacks by these thief-like people. They want to be ready, just in case.

At the slightest misunderstanding or discussion between two people, the rifles come off the shoulders, the daggers out of the sheaths.

In this armed crowd we Armenians are like mice that have been put into an iron cage with wild beasts.

* * *

In order to get a clear understanding of the situation of the Armenians in the desert in Hauran, one needs to know a few concise facts about the different peoples of the region. We usually call them all Arabs, but they are quite different from one an other from the points of view of traditions, characters, customs, and perceptions. These differences are as noticeable as the differences between a Chinese and an American.

The Arabs of Hauran can be classified into three major categories, according to the extremity of their politics: the Bedouins, the Fellahs, and the people from Damascus. Or tent-dwellers, villagers, and city people, respectively.

The Bedouins can be divided into two categories: the black ones and the dark ones; or the savages and the semi-savages respectively.

These two classes are quite prevalent and live in extremely primitive conditions. They travel constantly, moving from one place to another, with their goat-hair tents loaded on their camels and driving their sheep in front of them. Their wanderings take them in a huge circle from Hauran to Mecca. In winter they go far away, in the direction of Hejaz; at the end of spring they return to Hauran, where they have planted crops. After harvesting their crops they reseed them and leave again on their usual route.

Because of this constant movement, they have nothing but the shirts on their backs. With their families loaded on camels and donkeys, they roam from one desert to another and camp wherever they are when night falls. They feed themselves on lamb, camel meat, and butter. They dry the camel's dung and use it as fuel, its urine as water, and its hair and beard for clothing.

They don't have the slightest notion of cleanliness. They don't know how to do the laundry. Their tents stink and their clothes, which they put on the day they bought them, they take off only when they are completely worn out and turned to rags.

Some of them, especially the black ones, are so retarded that they can count only up to twenty. Their vocabulary consists of 150 to 200 words. Their ignorance knows no limits. Some of them have never seen a piece of paper and think that paper is a kind of cloth. They neither fear God nor respect the prophet. They don't suffer guilt and aren't ruled by any law or government.

They obey only their chieftain, who is the ruler, the judge, and the policeman of this community. What the head of the tribe wills is everything. He can punish a person with death if that person has committed a crime against the good of the community. If he has committed a crime against a member of another community, instead of being punished, he is rewarded. The only thing these savage people take pleasure in and spend time on, besides their daily occupations, is waiting at street corners with their rifles on their knees, to rob unarmed travelers or threaten them with death to get what they want. From their point of view there is no difference between an Armenian and a Fellah, so long as they possess something that can be stolen.

They are usually dressed in a shirt resembling a night gown—the men in white and the women in dark blue. Some wear a woolen overcoat over their shirts, which is called an *aba*, and when it's thin it's called a *meshlah*. The men cover their heads with a white cloth held in place with an *agil*, like a black serpent coiled twice around. If a woman is married she wraps the upper part of her forehead in a blue cloth and if she is a widow she goes bare-headed.

Husband and wife walk around barefoot, just like their camels. The wealthy ones, though, have rawhide sandals or yellow jack-boots with wide cuffs, but they usually carry them around their necks (the shoes tied to each other, hanging from their shoulders, so they don't wear out) instead of on their feet. Neither men nor women have pockets on their shirts. Therefore they tie all of their little items—such as coins, comb, tobacco, flint, etc.—in a corner of their head covers. The largest denominations of money they carry are usually *medjidiye*s (silver coins). They don't like gold coins because they are afraid of getting false ones. They carry these silver coins in a leather belt worn under the shirt. They wear a second belt over the shirt, from which hangs the inescapable crescent-shaped dagger. In addition, the head of the community also carries a sword, which is a symbol of princeliness among the Arabs.

* * *

The Fellahs are quite dark-skinned and live in villages near their fields. Compared to the Bedouins, they are more civilized. They are also ruled by their own chiefs, the only difference being that through them they pay taxes and give soldiers to the government, although at a nominal rate.

In the Fellah villages it is sometimes possible to find a mosque or a school, although the people don't know much about education and religion. Their entire knowledge consists of the precepts that Mohammed is the prophet and they are Mohammedans.

The clothing of the Fellahs is not much different from that of the Bedouins. They wear the same shirts, the same woolen overcoats, the same yellow jack-boots, the same head covers, and, of course, the same daggers and rifles that have become part of the dress code of the inhabitants of the desert.

All Fellah and Bedouin women tattoo their hands and faces with ugly pictures. The Christian Fellahs have crosses tattooed on their foreheads or chins, to distinguish themselves from their Mohammedan relatives. All of the women wear bracelets on their arms and legs and sometimes rings in their ears and noses. The latter custom is more popular among the Bedouins, whose earrings are sometimes so big that the "beauties" are obliged to hold them up with their hands while they eat.

The Fellah woman takes care of all the daily chores. She tills the earth, seeds, reaps the wheat, and transports it all the way from field to home, from home to mill, and from mill to home again. In order to do the shopping for the home, the woman puts a bag of wheat on her head and takes it to many far-off places, first to sell the wheat and then to buy things and carry them home the same way: by placing them on her head. While the woman works like a virtuoso, her husband for his part is plotting and scheming how to steal another community's horse or donkey. As stealing is considered a heroic act, a young Fellah or Bedouin has a difficult time finding a young girl to marry if he does not demonstrate the results of his heroism at least occasionally.

The Fellahs also have no notion of cleanliness, and they wallow in dirt. It is amazing, though, that despite their extreme filthiness they are never sick and enjoy much better health than the clean city people.

If these people, the Fellahs and Bedouins, marry, their pride resides in their women. The honor of a woman, even an enemy woman, is inviolable for these people. A woman of their people or nation can travel alone for days without being attacked and raped. The Fellahs and the Bedouins rob women, but they never rape them.

* * *

The Arabs who lived in the city, whom the Circassians consider the lowest class of all the inhabitants of Damascus, suffered from hunger and so came to Hauran, where they could cheat naive people. They are white and to some extent civilized. But they are from the East and have all the bad qualities of the Easterner, such as cheating, jealousy, evil-mindedness, fraud, immorality, etc.

Like the Circassians, they are fanatical Muslims, but not so irritable as the Circassians. Feuds among themselves are common. The wives of the Damascus Arabs go around with their faces veiled and try to avoid men they don't know. They don't have their bodies tattooed like Fellah or Bedouin women. They prefer to adorn themselves with jewels and gold ornaments. The men wear striped silk belts and silk head covers, and on their feet wooden clogs decorated with mother-of-pearl.

The difference between a Damascus Arab and a Bedouin or Fellah is that the latter two are enemies of the Armenians and ready to steal whatever they can from them. The Damascus Arabs, however, are enemies because the Armenians are Christians and competitors in business. They continually plot against the Armenians and incite the ignorant Circassians, Fellahs, and the Turkomans who live in a village three hours away from Jeresh, and their hatred of the Armenians is no less than that shown by the blood-thirsty Turks of Anatolia. After all, our situation here in the desert of Hauran duplicates the situation of the Turks and the Kurds. Who knows what else we, who have been obliged to live side by side with these variegated elements, shall yet see and endure, before we emerge from this Hell on earth!

6 November, 1915

At the market we are gradually getting to know the Armenian community of Jeresh. There are quite a few wealthy families. Among the Caesareans are the Chamchian and Kehyayan families. My father knew Chamchian's brother in the jail in Caesarea, where he was led to the gallows. Among the people from Sis there are Kegham, Minas, and the famous Garabed Geovderelian, about whom we had read in a book about the massacres of Cilicia, by Arshagouhi Teotig. The local people call Geovderelian *Sheykh Ermen* because of his tall physique and beard. Among those from Zeitoun is the teacher, Hovhannes Aharonian. And those from Marash include Sarko and Setrag, brothers and dedicated patriots. From Aintab there is the gun-smith Kapriel, a brave and dedicated young man. And those from Kilis include the famous miller, Khurshid.

Those from Yozgad—from the nearby regions of Caesarea—are mostly women whose husbands went to the United States before the war. These poor people make a living by carrying wood from the mountains or water from Circassian homes. The people from Kilis are millers; those from Marash, Zeitoun, and Hadjin are farmers. Those from Aintab and Adana are skilled workers; as for those from Caesarea, Sis, Chorum, they are well-off at the moment and don't do anything.

Three months ago, in other words, before the first arrival of Armenian refugees, Jeresh was a small village with humble, dilapidated houses, no trees and no vegetation. Despite the fact that water runs abundantly through the village, the local people had never come up with the idea of making a garden or a water mill, which is so indispensable for farmers. They traveled for days to have their wheat ground, and they had to wait there for weeks before it was their turn.

Immediately after their arrival, the Armenians built eight mills along the river. Then they created and planted around fifty vegetable gardens, where they grow all sorts of vegetables, according to the season.

The skilled workers have opened about forty shops, where they make their livings as cobblers, gun smiths, comb-makers, felt-makers, farriers, iron-mongers, butchers, etc.

Because of the shops, water mills, and vegetable gardens, the little village of Jeresh has become a profitable business town. Every day hundreds of Fellahs and Bedouins come from afar to have their wheat ground or their broken rifles repaired, their pots mended or their horses shod.

As the neighboring population flocked to Jeresh, the town became an important market in the middle of Hauran desert. People also come here to sell or barter their crops, olive oil, fat, and sheep. By emphasizing commerce on the one hand and by building bright and modest buildings from which to earn their daily bread on the other, the Armenians have expanded Jeresh and brought life to it. They have beautified it and truly made it the capital of Hauran. Instead of appreciating the contribution made by the Armenians, however, the local people hate them, thinking that the Armenians have come and reduced the supply of everything in their town.

"Ever since the infidels came, the blessed abundance of the country has been reduced," they say, and think that the Armenians are responsible for the rising prices of sugar and kerosene.

These people are so uneducated they can't even figure out that the high cost of living has been caused by the war, not by Armenian immigration. But because the high cost of living coincided with the arrival of the Armenians and their settling in their country, all of them, especially those from Damascus, think and repeat the same song, planting that cockeyed idea deep in the minds of the natives.

In total there are about fifteen to twenty families from Damascus, and that is more than enough to poison the entire Hauran and turn the people against the Armenians. If others look favorably on Armenians and do business with them, this can stand in the way of the dishonest dealings of the merchants from Damascus. They are used to buying the produce of the local people very cheaply and in return selling them what they need at ten times the price. But now the Armenians buy the crops of the Circassians and Fellahs by paying an honest price for them, and by repairing broken items they create a situation where these poor people don't have to buy new ones from the shops of the Damascus Arabs. The hatred and the anger that these shopkeepers, who are so accustomed to usury and oppression, feel for the Armenians is understandable. But how can one explain the animosity of the Circassians, Fellahs, and Bedouins, when they are totally satisfied with us and have no reason to complain?

Melun Ermen, this is what we are called: really a cursed nation, not liked even by those who are grateful to us.

7 November, 1915

Today I do not feel very well, but all the same we went to visit the hill on the other side of the valley, the ancient ruins of Jeresh. For the first time, my attention was caught by the size of the Armenian cemetery. It has been only three months since the Armenians settled here, but our cemetery is much bigger than that of the Circassians, who have lived here for half a century. Making our way through several piles of earth, we entered the area of the real ruins.

Columns, standing or fallen to the ground, half-ruined palaces, large amphitheaters, ornate doorways, triumphal arches, half-demolished domes, halls lined with columns, vaulted cellars, cobbled avenues, remnants of bridges sitting in the valley, half-demolished ramparts, and everywhere heaps of stones rising high into the sky—it seems that Jeresh was a huge city in the old days. Then, over the years, it was destroyed by successive battles and earthquakes.

First we visited the race track. Then the two amphitheaters. In the large one we counted enough gradually increasing steps to easily accommodate 20,000 people. This large amphitheater remains almost intact. One can still see the place reserved for the king and the cages for beasts and people sentenced to death, which opened onto the arena. Who knows how many people were torn to pieces by savage beasts or how many fought and received the laurel there? The spectators seated on these stone benches applauded hysterically, creating a thundering and tumultuous atmosphere with their cries and shouts.

Ancient glories . . . There is absolutely nothing left today, except a few heaps of stones on which serpents and lizards crawl.

Then we visited the temples adorned with columned courts, palaces decorated with mosaics, and the huge triumphal arch. Everywhere there are sculpted capitals, large stones with Greek inscriptions, granite columns and pedestals. On both sides of the large avenue one can count more than 100 standing columns, each so large that at least three people would be needed to encircle it. For hours we visited the pools, the tunnels, and the caverns, in some of which there were graves made of single slabs of stone that had remained intact or had half-collapsed covers.

Then we went up on the fortifications and from one side we looked at the ruins of the old city for a long time and from the other the newly-spreading, living homes of the new city, where the people looked smaller than ants.

Confronted with this picture of the vanity of life and the world, we wondered how so much poison, passion, and hatred could boil in the hearts of these people who seemed smaller than atoms.

8 November, 1915

Haig's condition is getting worse and worse every day.

Lost in unconsciousness, he raves deliriously. Perhaps a small amount of medicines could save his life. There is nothing we can do but wait with our arms folded.

9 November, 1915

After days of torment, Haig drew his last breath. His final defeat at last occurred in the room where we had watched him battle death.

The poor boy, scarcely twenty years old, got on the train in Aleppo only three weeks ago—he never thought that he was going to a place where he would fade and disappear so quickly and at such a young age. He had such a desire to study, to get on in life. With his innate alertness and modest disposition, he had a bright future. But now all his hopes and aspirations have vanished into thin air and he lies in a corner of the room, eyes half-closed, staring out at the world—as though he could see the members of his family about whom he dreamed so much.

Tirelessly we watched over his death bed, as if it were a magic mirror that reflected an image of his uncertain destiny. For all we know, one day we also might get sick, and close our own eyes after such a hopeless struggle, while those around us are upset and stunned as they silently watch us struggle, incapable of doing anything.

Death has no mercy. It spares no one. Its hundreds of thousands of microbes fly like invisible arrows. How can we be sure us that one day we won't be pierced by its lethal bullets?

I was thinking about these things at Haig's bedside when they came to take away his body. Two men laid him down on a stretcher, grabbed hold of both ends, and took him away . . . It was raining a bit outside and, heavy as a tombstone, darkness descended on our hearts.

10 November, 1915

We have cases of stealing and robbery every day. The Arabs rob even the rags off the poor refugees.

Today we heard that they had robbed Setrag of Marash, who had gone to Dera to buy some things for his grocery store. The thieves not only stole Setrag's money and clothes, but they even tried to kill him as well, stabbing him twice: once in his shoulder and a second time in his thigh. Fortunately, Setrag was able to escape and return home.

The Armenians want to live by sweat and labor. The others, however, don't think we deserve even that.

11 November, 1915

We visited the gardens near the village and admired the miracle that the creative hands of Armenians have produced in these rough, godforsaken regions. They have grown all kinds of vegetables. The local population, who had never had the opportunity to eat anything but peas and broad beans, now devour with great relish squashes and egg plants, tomatoes and cucumbers, turnips and carrots, without appreciating the Armenians who produce them.

We talked with gardener Khacher Aghpar for more than two hours. Despite his quite advanced age, he looked strong, energetic, and healthy. This old mountain lion from Zeitoun works day and night with his daughter-in-law and two grandchildren, and makes hardly enough to put food on their own table. The Circassian landowner takes almost all the results of Khacher Aghpar's toil instead of rent. Despite this, he has the pride of his people. He doesn't want to complain about his difficulties to anybody.

We asked Khacher Aghpar to tell us his memories of Zeitoun. He shook his head in refusal and began to curse the Catholicos of Cilicia, who, because he listened to bad advice, had brought about the surrender of Zeitoun. He didn't say much and we didn't insist, leaving it to a more opportune moment, when he was in a better mood.

Khacher Aghpar is a perfect example of a mountaineer. With his aquiline nose, thick eyebrows, and kind eyes, he resembles our patriarch Haig. In his ruined state I can see my nation's history, with its magnificent past, its gloomy present, and its uncertain future.

12 November, 1915

Today, they found the body of a murdered Armenian about an hour's distance from the village. The killer left him stark naked at the side of the road.

The women from Yazdi who go to the mountains to collect wood saw the corpse and came back to tell everybody. Two young Armenians went at once and brought back the body, which was laid out on the market square in an effort to discover who the dead man was.

A bullet had entered his forehead and come out the back of his skull. Everybody who had men working away from the village came to check, and left in terror. No one claimed the body. This afternoon the same young men took the corpse away and buried it among the ruins.

13 November, 1915

It feels as if winter were here. It rains continuously. The local people say that once the rain starts, it lasts for at least forty days.

Fortunately, we were able to find ourselves shelter before the rainy season started. But what about the deportees at the Dera Refugee Station, where so many families are still waiting outdoors or under the shelter of tents? According to what Setrag from Marash says, the governor has still not been able to satisfy his desire for revenge on the Armenians, and they have even stopped distributing their daily allowance of 40 *para*.

14 November 1915

The ceiling of our room drips continuously.

Despite the fact that we have placed more than twenty containers at various strategic points in the room, there are still puddles in one or two places.

We are kept awake all night by the drops falling on our faces. Today we called the landlord to ask him to find a way to improve the situation.

"It's impossible to repair the roof before the rain stops," he said.

Does that mean we'll have to put up with this wetness for forty days?

15 November, 1915

My mother got sick yesterday and today my father is also feeling unwell. I don't feel terribly well either. Is it possible that we are coming down with what Haig had?

16 November, 1915

To be safe, I didn't go out today. I'm running a fever and have a headache.

My mother's sickness seems serious. It is quite clear that she has typhoid fever.

17 November, 1915

This morning I couldn't get out of bed.

Three of us are sick in bed in the same room: me, beside me my mother, and beside her my father.

The roof continues to leak. The sound of water dripping into containers gets on my nerves. My sisters and brother are kept busy emptying the containers as they fill up.

The wife of one of our compatriots, the carriage driver Garabed Artin, sits with us as a nurse. Her name is Mariam. She covers our burning foreheads with towels soaked in cold water. My fever is so high that the water gets warm on my forehead and evaporates right away. My mother's and father's temperatures have also gone up. There is no doubt; the three of us have typhoid fever.

18 November, 1915

My sister Manoushag is also ill.

Our situation is gradually becoming critical. The water from the roof is pouring in like water-falls in three different places. The drops fall on our covers, pillows, and faces. There are two plates on each side of my pillow and four on my cover. The same on my mother's, sister's, and father's covers. If we make a careless move the plates spill and we get soaked.

What I hate most is when it drips into the plate and then the drops splash out again into my face. This is too much to endure, but we have no choice—we have to put up with it.

19 November, 1915

When I woke up, I noticed the diary under my pillow was wet because of the continuous downpour of never-ending rain. I am writing these lines on a dry piece of paper and will eventually recopy it.

Today my little sister, Arpiné, also got sick.

20 November, 1915

My mother is hovering between life and death. Her heart is fluttering to the point of stopping. She can't breathe. Just as Haig constantly craved yogurt, she keeps asking for cognac. She believes that a bit of cognac would cure her. But where can we get hold of cognac?

My father is delirious.

My sister and I still have fevers. Mariam changes the towels on our foreheads without stop.

21 November, 1915

We have heard that a certain Arab physician has arrived in Salt. It is a little town to the south and it takes about a day to get there on horseback. We sent a Circassian to bring him to our village.

We are all at the brink of death.

22 November, 1915

My condition is getting worse and worse. At times I feel drowsy and I sleep. I talk in my sleep. When I wake up I ask our nurse if I've said anything during my sleep. She tries to reassure me that I haven't. She probably wants to make me believe that my illness isn't too serious.

23 November, 1915

It has not rained since yesterday. Today, at last, we had a clear, sunny day.

They took all our wet pillows and covers out and spread them in the sun; but we stayed in bed, wrapped up in dry clothes, until the bedding dried.

Arshag and Artin Aghpar were pulling a stone roller over the roof to pack down the wet earth. It felt as if they were pounding on our heads with a piece of wood. The noise was so nerve-wracking! It's better, though, to put up with this noise for a while than to get soaked and be tormented by the dripping rain.

24 November, 1915

The Arab physician from Salt arrived today and examined us. He recommended that we sweat. They put bottles filled with hot water in our beds at once, but this didn't really help, as the room was too cold.

All the poor man has brought with him is a bit of quinine and some tincture of iodine. He has no other medicine.

25 November, 1915

I won't be able to go on with my diary. My hand is no longer strong enough to hold a pencil. I feel as if I were hypnotized. I'm so drowsy that I forget everything around me.

Before I lose my clearness of mind completely, I want to describe these final hours. Who knows? Perhaps I might fall asleep and never wake up again.

It's dark outside. It has started to rain again. The raindrops beat forlornly on the windowpanes. The ceiling has started to leak once more, in exactly the same spots. Five of us lie next to each other. Only Arshag and my brother Souren are still on their feet.

Souren is playing in a corner with his mosaic stones. He is unaware of what is going on around him.

Arshag is busy emptying the water containers. He also complains that he does not feel well and is weak.

My mother sighs over and over again with grief and is so bothered by the heat that she keeps trying to throw off her cover. Mariam, who is sitting between my mother and me, alternately covers my mother up and changes the wet towel on my forehead.

My father has lost consciousness and sleeps deeply. On the other side of my father, my two sisters are burning with fever.

The picture is heart-rending. I could not look at them any longer. I pulled my wet cover over my head and began to weep silently.

"Vahram!"

It was my father's voice. I stuck my head out from under the cover and looked at him.

"Are you calling me, father?"

He didn't reply. Was he sleeping, perhaps? No. His eyes were closed. He was whispering something. I listened:

"Send money," he was muttering, "or we will all starve to death in this desert . . . If they have confiscated my wealth, send it by yourself, from your own pocket . . ."

Although asleep, my father was repeating the contents of the telegram he had sent from Aleppo to his heartless friend. Then he moved his hand as though he were writing, and some time later he whispered almost inaudibly, and then fell silent.

And now he is in a deep coma.

I pulled the cover back over my head and shut my eyes.

3 December, 1915

I opened my eyes like a person regaining consciousness.

Mariam was sitting next to me, putting balls of flour into my mouth. I looked around me, all confused. I was in the room where my uncle's family lived. Besides me, my sisters and my brother—the latter also sick—were in the same room, lying in separate beds.

"Where are my father and mother?" I asked the nurse in a subdued voice.

"Your mother's in the other room," replied Mariam. "Your father . . . went to Damascus."

"Why?"

"They can't cure him here. We sent him to the hospital there."

"How is my mother?"

"She's comfortable. Like you, she's getting better."

"My sisters? My brother?"

"They're also comfortable. They're sleeping."

"Arshag?"

"He went to the market to get some oranges."

"What are we doing in this room? Where's my uncle's family?"

"They rented another house a week ago and moved there."

"A week ago? What's the date today?"

"December the third."

"What? Have I been asleep all that time?"

"Yes, you were always either half-asleep or asleep."

"I want to go and see my mother."

"No, don't move. If you get out of bed, you'll get sick again."

"Then tell my mother to come here."

"She can't. She has to stay in bed too, just like you."

I tried to sit up in bed a little . . . It was as if my limbs had been shattered. They no longer belonged to me. I lay on my back without moving. A little later I lost consciousness again.

5 December, 1915

As a result of my continual pestering, Mariam and her husband moved me back to our room.

My mother was lying in bed, emaciated and worn out. When she saw me she began to sob.

"Why are you crying, Mother?"

"I was worried about your health," she replied sadly.

"Don't be afraid. Look: I'm better now."

" . . . "

"Is there any news from my father?"

"Not yet."

"How did they take him to Damascus?"

"In a carriage."

"Hasn't the driver come back yet?"

"Oh, Vahram, why do you always ask so many questions?" She turned her face away from me. "Why do you go on and on?"

"I'm sorry for tiring you out, Mother."

All day long I gazed at the ceiling in silence, without moving. Fortunately, the dripping has stopped, but the repulsive stains are enough to make my flesh crawl.

7 December, 1915

I got up today and walked around the room, holding onto the wall like a child. First I visited the other room. Although my sisters are no longer in danger of dying, my brother Souren's condition is still serious.

In addition to being concerned about my brother, my uncertainty about what is going on with my father worries me constantly.

9 December, 1915

One of our relatives, Hovagim Berberian, died this morning. He also had typhoid fever. His untimely death made us very sad.

There is still no news from my father.

11 December, 1915

My sisters are now much better and have been moved back into our room. My brother is still in danger. My mother and I are not in bed anymore. We are able to get up and sit in the room.

At noon I had the barber come and cut my hair. When I saw my face in the mirror—the sunken eyes, the protruding cheekbones, the waxen color—I was frightened.

We need a lot of nourishment to regain our strength, but the market doesn't even have the usual milk, butter, and eggs.

18 December, 1915

The week of convalescence went by slowly and monotonously. My brother is better, but there is still no news from my father. I'm very worried.

It was a beautiful day today. For the first time, I went to the market, but I got tired in no time at all, and came back home.

25 December, 1915

I went to the market and sat with Khoren from Aintab, who is a cobbler. A Bedouin came to have his shoes mended. My friend (here all refugees are friends) examined the shoes and told him that for five coins he could resole them. The customer agreed and left, but he asked Khoren to have them ready in an hour. And he came back in an hour. The shoes were ready. He put them on, and as he was getting ready to leave, Khoren reminded him that he had not paid yet.

"What do you mean?" yelled the Bedouin in a threatening tone, "how many times do I have to pay you?"

"When did you pay me?" my friend demanded.

"*Ineal abuk, akurut* (a curse on your father that ever I came here). Are you out to rob us? Just a little while ago, when I brought you the shoes, I paid in advance."

"No, my friend," objected Khoren. "This young man here was sitting beside me. He can confirm that you didn't pay."

"That's right," I said, "you didn't pay."

"*Ya khreb beytek, melun ermen* (may your house be destroyed, you damned Armenian)," exclaimed the savage and then, turning to me, he threatened, "And yours, too, sitting here with your countryman and swearing to his lies!"

"I'm not lying."

The Bedouin grew even more agitated at my reply and tried to hit me with a stick. Just then Misag the farrier ran across the street, grabbed the man's arm, and roared:

"Don't! The boy is just getting over an illness."

"*Setdiyn sene* (literally sixty years: a common expression meaning even if that were true for the next sixty years, I still wouldn't give a damn)!" yelled the Bedouin in a hateful voice. "I'll smash the skull of anyone who lies to me!"

"Excuse them. There must be a mistake." Misag took the man's arm and led him out to the street.

A little later, after Misag had seen the Arab off, he came back over to see me.

"I met your father once. What a nice man he was . . . ." Then, suddenly changing his expression, "Have you heard from Damascus? How is he?"

"No," I replied, terrified. "But why did you suddenly stop while you were talking about my father?"

"No, I didn't stop. I was just thinking about that nasty man, who was ready to use his stick on you."

Misag's explanation didn't quite satisfy me. I went right home. I looked into my mother's, sisters's, and brother's faces, hoping to discern an evil secret in their eyes. But I detected nothing suspicious.

"Mother," I asked after a moment: "Hasn't the driver who went to Damascus come back yet? Why doesn't my father write to us?"

"Don't start again," my mother interrupted reproachfully: "We'll probably hear from him any day now."

"Mother, you're not lying to me, are you? I think you're hiding some bad news from me."

"Vahram, you're talking like a child."

Perhaps I was talking like a child, but my mind couldn't rest. I kept thinking about my father, day and night.

31 December, 1915

Today, at last, I heard the bad news they have kept from me for about a month. My father had died and they had deceived me by telling me that he had gone to Damascus. I had suspected it from their voices and movements and whispered conversations. But naively, deep down I wanted to believe that my father was being treated in Damascus instead of reconciling myself with the idea of his death. This evening a careless word escaped for Manoushag's mouth and I learned the bitter truth.

My father died on 28 November.

"I was at his bedside," said Artin Aghpar. "The departed one loved his family so much that he couldn't stop talking about you, even in his sleep. With his last breath, but in full possession of his faculties, he asked how you all were. Not long after that he died. The next morning we took him to the ruins and buried him there. All members of your family were sick in bed, and no one knew. Since then I go to check his grave every day, just to make sure the thieves don't steal his gold teeth.[*] So far they haven't touched him, and I hope they'll also leave him alone in the future."

---

[*]. My father's sixteen gold teeth had aroused a great deal of interest among the local people. For them this was a novelty.

With infinite pain I listened to the details of my father's death and fell into deep distress and wept. My mother, sisters, and brother joined me in tears. They had already cried in secret from me so many times.

1 January, 1916

The light advanced slowly into our dark room, giving birth to the year and making us mournful—as if we felt its labor pains deep within our hearts.

We thought about how we felt and what has become of us and what will happen next. Last New Year's, when my grandmother blessed our table and wished us a happy and prosperous year we never thought we'd be spending such a tragic New Year only twelve months later. We had more than 25 guests at our table. My father had followed his usual practice and invited some of his employees and a few of our teachers and their families so they wouldn't have to stay at home all by themselves. We were all happy; we sang; we clinked our glasses, joyfully celebrating the new year.

Today we tried to call up their faces one by one, and with great anguish we realized that many of them have departed from this transient world and will never return.

What terrible things have happened during the course of this past year! And to think that they are only just beginning! Who knows how many of us will have the good fortune to see the next New Year? A terrifying, enigmatic mystery!

6 January, 1916

When we bought our famous bedspread we never thought that one day it would play an important role in public life. This morning Sarko, who is originally from Marash, came and asked to borrow the spread for a couple of hours.

"What for?" we asked.

"Everybody saw it the day you arrived in Jeresh," explained Sarko. "Apparently it shows the Virgin Mary holding the Infant . . . We're having a church service in the courtyard of a ruined house and we want to hang it on the wall instead of a curtain."

"Yes, that's right. Today is Armenian Christmas," we replied: "But how can you celebrate Mass without a priest?"

"Apparently there's one in Mejdel (an Arab village a few hours away) and we're bringing him here and he's going to live in Jeresh from now on."

We gave Sarko the spread and he put it under his arm and left, quite pleased. Later, when he returned the spread, he told us that hundreds of Armenians had stood in an abandoned courtyard, bowed their heads before our spread, and prayed, wept, and found solace, just like the early Christians in Rome who prayed and celebrated in underground chapels.

10 January, 1916

To break the monotonous rhythm of the day and to provide ourselves with a modest means of making a living, we set up a table on the market place and began selling oranges. We sold quite a few all day long, but there was next to no profit.

We wrote a letter to my father's colleague Ardashes Giulbenkian, in Constantinople, and asked him to help us financially.

17 January, 1916

Something happened today that reminded us of the era of Abdul-Hamid. A Circassian working in the fields lost his food basket, which he had placed under a tree. By chance, he found a label with the name Hovhannes on it, and he immediately concluded that the thief was an Armenian named Hovhannes. Then he started catching all the Hovhanneses in the village and beating them up one by one to make them confess their supposed crime. Among his victims was the teacher Hovhannes Aharonian from Zeitoun, who is a very honest and respected Armenian.

The local people have the notion that the government has sent us here to be their slaves. Because of this they treat us like servants, often tormenting without reason the poor refugees who have lost their families, the orphans, and the widows.

As though they have done something courageous, they then return to the market and strut around proudly. If any of us dares to find fault with their heartless behavior, they get quite aggressive and threaten to give their critic a good beating.

24 January, 1916

The weather is almost spring-like. This afternoon I put half a bag of wheat on my back and took it to the mill. The miller, Hovsep, like the other millers, is from Kilis. He is a sensitive, educated young man.

When I heard that he had served as an officer of the Ottoman Army on the Caucasian front, I asked him how in the world had he ended up in the Hauran desert, so far from the Caucasus.

When Hovsep had poured the wheat into the hopper, adjusted the millstone, and satisfied himself that the wheat was being ground properly, he came and sat beside me and told how it happened that the one-time officer had now become a miller.

* * *

The Armenians of Kilis suffered less during the deportations than their countrymen in other provinces. Since their town is only a day's journey from Aleppo, they got there without much roaming around, and from there they were sent on to Deir Zor and the vicinity of Damascus. Apparently in the beginning there were no obstacles on the road to Damascus.

However, our friend was involved in several stormy situations. He joined the army on the day war was declared, and was sent to the Caucasian front to exercise his duties as a citizen. Because of his bravery and selflessness, he quickly rose to the rank of first corporal, then sergeant. Perhaps he could have risen higher if the government hadn't applied its anti-Armenian policy. As a result of certain changes on the battle front, he was called back one day and sent to a military camp near Ourfa to train new conscripts.

Hovsep performed his duties with utmost devotion. One unfortunate day, a major came from Ourfa to inspect all aspects of the forces stationed there. His interest was aroused when he noticed Hovsep on the training grounds, teaching his conscripts with extraordinary enthusiasm how to attack the puppet-like soldiers of the enemy.

"Bravo, bravo!" the major shouted, approaching him. "If you keep up with such vigor, the army will have no shortage of qualified soldiers!"

"We're trying, sir," answered Hovsep, standing at attention.

"Your efforts deserve recognition," added the inspector with a pleasant smile, "What's your name?"

"Hovsep."

The major's face darkened.

"What kind of name is that? Are you a Kurd?"

"No, sir. I'm Armenian."

"Hmm . . ." And he added, as though talking to himself: "Who would have thought that the world still contains Armenians?"

Then he suddenly turned his back and walked away, muttering under his breath: "*Siupan Allah*! We keep killing and butchering them, and they still become officers and order us around!"

That night as Hovsep lay in bed trying to visualize his old mother, young wife, and two sons, he remembered the Turkish officer's behavior and words.

He had received no news from his family for a long time. He grew quite agitated.

Suddenly the door of his tent opened and in walked a corporal and two soldiers, without asking or receiving permission.

"We have our orders for your arrest," said the corporal, walking to the tent pole, where Hovsep's rifle and sword were hanging .

At once Hovsep jumped out of bed, stood before the corporal, and said: "You have no right to confiscate the sword of a superior officer. Please get out of my tent. If there are orders to arrest me, they must be carried out by the military police."

"We don't need them to arrest a dirty Armenian," answered the corporal, signalling the two soldiers with his head: "We are more than capable of carrying out that order by ourselves."

Before the corporal finished speaking, the two soldiers attacked their prey. Suddenly the flickering light of the lamp in the tent went out. In the dark four people fell to the floor, one on top of the other.

Hovsep was quickly overcome. A savage hand grabbed his neck, thrusting bloody nails into his flesh. A piece of dirty rag was stuffed into his mouth. He was kicked and hit with canes. Painful blows rained down on his head and stomach.

"This is how we punish the treacherous Armenians," bellowed the corporal, slapping the prisoner across the face. Then they pulled him to his feet, tied his arms, and pushed him out of the tent.

"Get a move on!"

"Leave me alone," said Hovsep, making himself understood with great difficulty because of the rag stuffed in his mouth: "Let me go. I demand to see the commandant."

"We are the commandant. Walk!" the soldiers answered forcefully.

They passed the guards without difficulty and went out the gate, leaving the camp behind and heading in the direction of the valley, about fifteen minutes away.

In a deserted place they laid Hovsep on the ground. One of the soldiers sat on his legs and the other immobilized his arms. The corporal pressed his knee into the Armenian's abdomen and pulled out his dagger.

"How do you feel now? I think we'll skin you alive."

Hovsep let out dreadful groans and squirmed under the corporal's knee.

"*Bism illah*," yelled the corporal, slowly gliding the sharp edge of the knife over the victim's throat. "How does that feel? Good?"

Hovsep writhed in terror, letting out muffled cries.

"No!" said the corporal with a monstrous smile, "if I skin you now it'll all be over quickly; I want to torture you slowly. Get up!"

The soldiers pulled the half-dead Hovsep to his feet and dragged him away. Two hours later, in another deserted place, they laid him down again and started performing the same ceremony, threatening to skin him. And an hour later they did it again!

Every time they repeated their farce—if it can be called a farce—Hovsep, who was petrified with terror, had no way of knowing whether that time would be the last. Or perhaps the soldiers had orders not to kill and were simply amusing themselves. At any rate, they played their roles so realistically that Hovsep's heart could have stopped at any moment, whenever he felt the sharp knife touch his throat.

Subjecting Hovsep to such merciless treatment, the soldiers took him, eventually, to Aleppo, and there they threw him into a military prison.

The jail was a humid cellar and was full of Kurdish and Arab deserters. For a moment Hovsep felt relieved to be out of the hands of his torturers. Before long, however, he realized his precarious situation and began to reflect on the wrongs these people had done him.

The fact that the soldiers had arrested him without a written order and brought him to prison made him suspect that this was all a hellish scenario arranged by the inspecting major. But what was the purpose of the scenario? Hovsep couldn't come up with an answer.

"This is how we punish treacherous Armenians," the corporal had said. But he had never engaged in treachery. Sunk in anguish, he collapsed in a corner of the prison. A bit later a jail-keeper with a harsh face came and put iron chains on his legs and arms. Hovsep did not resist. On the contrary, he closed his eyes and buried himself in deep lethargy.

Four days went by and nothing changed. During all that time Hovsep didn't eat, drink, or speak. His cell mates wanted to console him and distract him by talking about various things. But Hovsep continued to brood and didn't even hear the questions they asked him. At the end of the fourth day, in the evening, this harmless, tranquil young man suddenly snapped. He got up, went to the door, and started to bang and shout at the same time: "Open up! Let me out of here . . . Take off my chains! I haven't done anything wrong."

His face taut with hatred, his lips foaming, his eyes flaming with anger, he screamed: "Open up! I want out of here . . . I have a mother, wife, and children waiting for me out there!"

The other prisoners were horrified. They were afraid to go near him. Hovsep banged the door with his chain until the military guards came and took him to another cell.

What happened after that? Hovsep doesn't remember very well. Some time later, when he regained consciousness, he found himself in a hospital bed. He was astounded and tried to get up, but discovered that they had put him in a straitjacket.

"Who brought me here and why have you tied me down?" he asked a military nurse who was not far from his bed.

"Have you forgotten everything you did? Don't you remember that you started to throw everything you could lay your hands on?" replied the soldier reproachfully.

"Me?"

"Yes, you. Look where you bit my finger two days ago."

"But how come? Didn't I just get here today?"

"Today? Aren't you the one who lost his mind in prison?"

In prison . . . Oh, yes. Hovsep remembered what had happened, and broke out in a cold sweat.

Two soldiers came that same evening, dressed him, chained his hands, put him into a carriage, and took him back to the jail he had left a week earlier.

* * *

During this time the murderous major did not remain idle. After having his victim thrown into jail again in Aleppo, he sent a cable to the commandant of the Caucasian forces, informing him that Sgt. Hovsep, who had been sent to Ourfa, had lately been involved in suspicious dealings with a number of undesirable people, that he had learned that his disloyal acts had been discovered, and had disappeared from camp one night.

After receiving a reply telegram from the commandant of the Fourth Army ordering him to capture the guilty soldier and punish him accordingly, the major sent another cable, this time to the military authorities in Aleppo, asking if there were anyone of Hovsep's name among the imprisoned deserters. If there were, he asked them to send him immediately to the war tribunal.

Hovsep was unaware of all these machinations to ruin his life, and went through physical and psychological crises in jail. One night he was startled awake by a series of kicks in his ribs.

"Get up, animal! Are you deaf? I've been calling your name for two hours." Hovsep got to his feet, rubbing his eyes.

"Put your shoes on and come with me,"shouted the chief jailer bitterly.

"Where are we going?"

"Silence! Make it quick."

Hovsep quietly followed him. In the courtyard he saw Arab and Christian prisoners, about twenty of them. They were tied together with a long chain. A policeman came and chained Hovsep to the last soldier, at the end of the line. A corporal read out the prisoners' names. They counted and counted again, *tamam . . . tamam* (that's right), and got on the road, under the surveillance of three policemen on horses.

They traveled over rough, winding roads. The prisoners were alarmed for a moment when they got to the edge of the city and saw the citadel where deserters were usually shot. Fortunately, though, they don't stop there. They passed the fortresses and continued north. Within half an hour the city had disappeared behind them.

They walked for three days without eating or resting, trying to keep up with the horses. On the third day, Hovsep could walk no farther. The bottoms of his feet were bruised and his legs were swollen. On top of this, the heavy rain made their shoes and clothes much heavier.

Unable to walk, he nevertheless tried to remain on his feet. He staggered for a moment, swayed, and collapsed on the road.

"Get up!" ordered the chief policeman, edging his horse near him, "Now! Get up!"

"I can't," pleaded Hopvsep in a weak voice.

"You're lying. Liar! You've got to get up," roared the policeman threateningly, raising his whip in the air.

"Even if you kill me here and now, I cannot stand or take another step," Hovsep answered, with the indifference of a dying man.

On their leader's orders, two policemen got off their horses, grabbed Hovsep by the arms, and made him stand up. But the next second, when they let go of him, they watched him crumple like a rag.

"Drag this son of a bitch until he croaks!" yelled the executioner, directing his words to the prisoners.

They set off on the road again, pulling Hopvsep through the mud and stones behind them.

They couldn't make much progress that way, however. After a short while they all stopped, exhausted, and said that they didn't have enough strength to drag their half-dead friend any farther.

"He's done for anyway," they told the chief. "Leave him here to die by himself."

"But I'm responsible for delivering him to the war tribunal," the merciless creature answered. "I have to take him."

"In that case, put him on your horse and take him that way," suggested the prisoners, with justifiable alarm.

"Yes indeed, that would be very nice," exclaimed the chief mockingly. "While the government official walks, the condemned deserter rides on horseback!"

"If you don't want to walk, you have no choice but to leave him on the road. We can confirm your story, saying that he was dead. What else can we do? He is not a cow that we might skin and take the hide to the judge."

Confronted with this complex situation, the policemen consulted each other for a long time. Then they examined Hovsep and came to the conclusion that he was already on the brink of death. They brought their whips down on him once more and left him behind.

Hovsep stayed there, unconscious, for a long time. Before evening a group of Kurdish mule-drivers noticed him and came closer to see what he was doing on the ground. Hovsep told them in Kurdish that he had been attacked by highwaymen. Then he begged them not to leave him there without help or food. Hopvsep spoke such fluent Kurdish that they couldn't identify his real nationality, so they put him on one of the mules and took him to their village, about two hours away.

An old mule-driver took him home, removed his muddy clothes, and put him in a comfortable bed, while his old wife prepared some medicine and her daughter-in-law laid a fire to warm up some soup.

As soon as Hovsep ate the soup, he felt a merciful warmth envelop his body. His eyelids grew heavy with sleep. He soon fell into a deep slumber and was transported to the land of dreams.

It was almost noon the following day when Hopvsep woke up, full of joy. The pain of his wounds had almost disappeared and his fatigue was gone.

In another part of the room milk was boiling over the flickering fire, exuding its sweet scent in the air. A tray of flat bread, fresh cheese, and eggs was waiting for him. His clothes had been washed and dried and put next to his bed.

He couldn't believe how astonishingly happy he was. He immediately got out of bed and got dressed. Just then someone knocked loudly on the street door. Fearing bad news, Hovsep cocked his ear to the door and soon heard the coarse voice of a policeman addressing the old woman who opened the door: "Apparently there's a deserter here."

"There must be some mistake," the old woman protested. "There's no deserter in my house."

"Since when have you started protecting Armenians?" asked the policeman, in an admonishing manner.

"Who's an Armenian?" asked the daughter-in-law, who by then had joined her mother-in-law.

"Your guest."

"But he's a Kurd!"

"That's a lie. He has lied to you."

The policeman pushed past the amazed daughter-in-law and old woman and ran into the room, where he saw Hovsep.

"Come with me, you scoundrel!" he bellowed. "You lied to these simple people when you told them you're a Kurd. I'll teach you what it means to malinger and pretend to be sick on the road . . . Didn't you think we'd come back this morning and would search the village when we didn't find your corpse? On the double! Let's see you walk—or I'll kill you."

When he finished speaking, the policeman came closer and brought down his whip on Hopvsep's head. The Armenian sergeant cried out in anguish. Just then he spotted a dagger hanging on the wall. He soon had it in his hand, and in less than a moment he thrust it into his opponent's chest. The monster let out a savage roar and fell, while the Kurdish women stood in the courtyard, petrified. Hovsep ran out of the room and fled the house.

He roamed about in the mountains for a while. Because he was familiar with the roads of the region, he arrived safely in Aleppo. He managed to find one of his compatriots and learned that his family had been deported in the direction of Damascus. He then continued his search in Damascus, where he discovered that his people had been sent to the Hauran desert. Finally he came here and found them, but his happiness did not last long. Within two months his mother and his little son died of a cruel illness.

Three months ago, with the help of one of his relatives, Hovsep opened his mill. Now in its solitude and monotony, Hovsep hopes to rediscover peace in his troubled body and soul.

31 January, 1916

We have no money left. There is no more gold or jewelry to sell. We are selling our extra clothes and shoes to buy wheat.

We moved from our house to a much cheaper rented place today to save money. The place we rented is an unconnected room adjoining the sheep fold of Husein Bey, one of the leading men of the village. Although we have no kitchen facilities, we don't really mind, thinking that the way things are going we might not find food tomorrow, and thus there won't be anything to cook anyway.

This evening we heard some sad news. One of the wealthy people from Sis, Kegham, has also died. He was a young patriot and had a noble heart. He was engaged in his own country and a week after their engagement he and his fiancée were deported here.

The grim reaper relentlessly mows down this suffering, afflicted people. Over the last three months, more than 500 people have died of typhoid fever.

7 February, 1916

Today we took advantage of the good weather and went to see the ruins again—to visit the graves and copy the inscriptions on the stones. On our way back we saw the caves and the hundreds of families who live there in absolute misery. We were appalled. Most of them are hungry, ill, and half-naked—some of them sitting or lying down on mattresses, some thinking and others sobbing.

As a matter of interest we entered one of the caves. An old man was sleeping in a one-piece stone grave . . . next to him an old woman was cleaning grass roots . . . in a corner a child covered in tatters was chewing on some orange peels . . . while at the opening of the cave a young woman was roasting pig-chestnuts over the fire.

The air was so full of smoke that we could hardly make our way out again without being asphyxiated. We walked quickly past the rest of the caves—almost everywhere the same sad, heart-rending picture.

The amazing thing is that we also saw families of Fellahs in these caves, living under almost similar conditions. If the owners of this country suffer the same misery, what can the poor Armenians do? They are not familiar with the place, not used to the climate, not trusted by the inhabitants, and do not know the language spoken by everyone around them.

14 February, 1916

Mr. Giulbenkian sent us 30 pounds from Constantinople. We were elated to see that we still have one kind friend who cares for us in these difficult days. The cheque is drawn on the agricultural bank of Irbit. Tomorrow my uncle will go to Irbit to cash it.

21 February, 1916

Most Circassians are filled with hatred for Armenians, but there is an exception: Shevket Bey, a close relative of our landlord—and the head of their family—is trying to do his best to improve the harsh conditions that the Armenian refugees live in.

Shevket Bey's brother Reshid was educated in Damascus. He is an enlightened young man and our only friend among the entire population of Hauran.

Reshid Bey is our age (there are six of us: my cousins Levon and Vahram Toramanian, Apraham Geyigian, Arshag Kaishian, my friend Vahé Vartanian, and me). He enjoys our friendship enormously. Every time he goes to our landlord's house for a festive occasion, he has us invited too, so that we can listen to and watch their singing and dancing, which is very lively, all the more so because of Fatma, the landlord's daughter, who accompanies on her accordion.

Reshid Bey came to visit us today and proposed to take us somewhere interesting. We had heard about the place, but only in stories and tales. The six of us followed our Circassian friend for over an hour and finally stopped before a huge rock, on the summit of which, at a first glance, we noticed nothing unusual.

Reshid Bey drew our attention to little dug-out holes, which were about two feet apart and ascended like stairs all the way to the summit. By placing his feet carefully in these holes, he climbed to the top and told us to do the same. Following his example, we climbed about twenty meters and found ourselves facing a thick bush growing from a large crevice in the rock.

Behind the bush was a square hole. We bent down and went in, finding ourselves in an enormous empty room. As though this weren't enough, on the other side of the room we also noticed a passage, which extended horizontally into the heart of the mountain. In an attempt to discover where it led, we crawled along it for quite some distance. As the lack of air bothered us, however, we turned around and came back. Reshid Bey didn't know when or why or by whom that room had been dug out of the rock. We thought it had been excavated centuries ago by the former inhabitants of Jeresh for military reasons, to be used as a hiding place. At any rate, it's the result of long and difficult labor, with a mysterious passage leading we don't know where or for what purpose.

28 February, 1916

The Kurdish corporal was certainly aware of what was coming next when he deliberately changed our ages when we were registered in the village records. Today we learned the purpose of that forgery: the Armenians are going to be drafted.

As though illness and misery were not enough, we now have to worry about military service! It's very strange, though. What does the government expect from such a small number who have been bled dry, while they leave millions of strong, healthy young Arab men[*] comfortable and undisturbed?

If the purpose is to strengthen the army, which is falling apart, the deported Armenians represent neither strength nor superiority in numbers. It is evident that the government wants to deliver the last blow to the Armenians, who are living out their last days in the desert after being afflicted by massacres, disease, and hunger.

When a working man who provides for his family is drafted, there can be only one result: his entire family is condemned to death. And we are quite aware of the fate of the Armenian soldier. First he is disarmed, then he is given a hoe and a spade and sent to build roads. In the end, when he isn't needed anymore, he is disarmed once again and killed beside the road or bridge he has built.

It is because there is a shortage of labor battalions that Armenians are again being drafted. There's no doubt that once these newly conscripted soldiers fulfill their duties they'll meet with the same fate, the same tragic end that has been the lot of their unfortunate brothers.

We brooded all day long. The Turks' Allah seems starved and looking for new victims.

6 March, 1916

As evening was falling we witnessed a tragi-comedy that revealed how the local population use the name of Armenians for their personal profit.

There has been a food shortage in this region for the last two months.

Despite the law passed by the government that ten kilograms of wheat should never sell for more than 10 coins on the market, it is impossible to find wheat at even double that price.

In these circumstances the Damascus Arabs convinced one or two Circassians to complain to the authorities that a certain Fellah had been selling wheat to the poor refugees at double the price. To refugees who are selling the shirts off their backs in order to be able to eat a piece of bread.

---

*.   The Circassians, who are known for their Turkophile attitude, have not supplied even one soldier to serve in the armed forces. The Fellahs not only don't supply soldiers, but don't even pay taxes. The Bedouins are not even registered. As for the Damascus Arabs, they have bribed the police and do nothing but business.

It seems that they also made a few good promises to the person in charge, because a couple of policemen immediately opened the Arab's store-house and began to sell wheat at double the price. The unfortunate thing in all this is that once inside the shop, which was opened for the poor Armenian refugees, Armenians can't get even a grain of wheat. The police find a reason to refuse every Armenian who shows up to buy:

"You are rich. We opened this place for the poor."

If the person asking for wheat is a poor man in tatters, they say, "You'd better wait a little, until it's your turn." And if he has been waiting for a long time they say, "You have a lot of provisions at home. You're trying to buy more so you can sell it again and make a profit. Get back, or I'll beat you." And since nobody can step back because of the huge crowd, the whips lash out in all directions.

A certain brave young man from Zeitoun by the name of Kevo grew incensed at the policemen's monstrous treatment, pushed himself forward, grabbed the whips from the officers' hands, and shouted: "Don't beat us! We're already dead . . . all we ask is wheat in exchange for our money."

"Wheat is wasted on you. You damned animals. Go and eat grass!" roared the policeman's friend, and he brought down his whip on the young man's head.

The store-house was sold out in no time flat. They sold more than 5,000 kilos of wheat. Almost all of it was bought by the Damascus Arabs. Now they invite us into their stores, advertising wheat for 35 coins. When we brought it to the attention of one of the store-keepers that it was cruel to sell it for that price when he had pretended to be an Armenian and bought it for 20 coins, he was furious.

"Ungrateful dogs!" he jested. "What more do you want? If we hadn't had the store-house opened, you wouldn't be able to buy wheat even for 45 coins!"

13 March, 1916

Approximately seventy Armenian soldiers who went to Irbit five days ago for their medical examinations came back today, on condition that they should be ready to leave when called. Our three relatives, Arshag, Levon, and Apraham, who are among the soldiers who returned, said that there had been a mistake: only men over twenty had been called for a medical, whereas men who are twenty are also subject to military service.

And they saw my name on the lists posted on the government building. I'm listed as 20 years old and my grandfather, Nishan Dadrian (who is actually my grandfather's brother, but we call him grandfather) is listed as 54 years old. I'm really 16 and my grandfather is 69.

We had heard of a father and son serving together in the same army, but for a grandson and his grandfather to be called up at the same time can only happen in Arabia!

20 March, 1916

For the past few days inspectors have been registering the name and birth date of every Armenian refugee. Since the deportation they have registered us at least twenty times. We don't exactly know what devilish intentions the government has in mind when it counts us over and over again.

According to the optimists, the government has benevolent intentions: the Sultan will declare an amnesty, and every Armenian will go back to his or her birthplace. But according to the pessimists, the government is trying to establish the exact number of remaining Armenians in order to improve their extermination methods.

In any case, it's obvious that there is something afoot concerning our fate.

27 March, 1916

Today they discovered two rooms buried under our courtyard. An Armenian worker was digging in preparation for building something, when suddenly the ground caved in and the poor man rolled into the void that opened at his feet. When we heard his shouts for help, we got a ladder, climbed down, and found ourselves in a room with plastered walls. Fortunately, the Armenian worker was not injured, although he was terribly frightened. We lifted him out and entered the second room to see what it was like. There was nothing there, except an earthen water jug and a dove-shaped lamp. This section of ancient Jeresh was inhabited by common people; houses in excellent condition are often discovered beneath the earth. Often they find money and valuable furniture in these houses. Hoping to find that sort of thing, our landlord shook the water jug, but in vain; instead of a fortune, earth poured out into his palm. But he had no reason to complain about his luck. He was having rooms built to rent to Armenians, and what should miraculously open up under his feet but a couple of rooms!

Only the Armenian complained of what had happened. Apart from the fear and pain this surprise cave-in caused him, it also cost him his job—for the simple reason that the landlord no longer needed him to build new rooms!

3 April, 1916

What we have been dreading has finally happened. Today they called all the Armenian soldiers and sent them on foot and in the rain in the direction of Irbit.

We (in other words, my three cousins and I) got permission from the corporal to leave on horseback tomorrow and join our friends in Irbit. As for my grandfather, he was exempted: when the corporal saw how old he was, he was convinced that his name had been included on the list by mistake.

The condition of the soldiers who left was tragic. Almost all of them were dressed in tatters. Most of them not only lacked shoes, but didn't even have a little bag of food under their arms.

Around 300 women and children were gathered at the far end of the village, on the road to Irbit. Old fathers and mothers embraced their departing children; young sisters and brides pressed their brothers and husbands to their breasts; little boys and girls held firmly on to their fathers' legs, all of them emitting heart-rending cries that could easily have drawn tears even from stones.

"Where are you going, brother? Who's going to look after me?" a little girl sobbed.

"Who will bring us bread when we're hungry, father?" cried a dehydrated child.

"Everybody at home is sick. Who's going to look after us?" wept a tormented old woman.

The scene was heart-breaking, the separation difficult. Those who were leaving knew that they'd never return, and those who were staying felt that a horrid fate awaited them. But nothing could be done to change things. They had to be separated, especially when the mounted policemen began showing signs of impatience.

So there was one last embrace, one last hug, warm kisses and goodbyes, and that was it. The procession started on its way.

The dense crowd that had come to see them off followed their loved ones with tears in their eyes until they disappeared around a bend in the road. Then they scattered in all directions because of the rain, which had become much heavier and was soaking everybody.

Just then the sky darkened and took on a foreboding appearance. Rolling clouds, one after the other, thunder and some other, unexplained noise, shook our very existence.

4 April, 1916

The four of us future soldiers left around noon for Irbit. My uncle and an armed Circassian accompanied us. My uncle is coming to see if he can postpone our military service. If he can't save all of us he will try to save at least me. The Circassian will show us the way and at the same time protect us from the attacks of highwaymen.

The moment of leave-taking was terribly emotional. All our relatives and acquaintances were gathered at our home, which lay on our way. We were all deeply depressed as we hugged each other and then left. As we rounded the hill, I looked back for a moment and saw my mournful mother, my sisters, and my brother once more. They were surrounded by friends and watching us in sadness. I couldn't hold back my tears if I looked at them much longer. I turned my head and continued along the road.

The six of us rode for a long time, each lost in personal worries and thoughts. When we arrived at Nayimé, an Arab village, our mood changed a little. A joyous wedding was in progress.

The Fellahs were gathered in the village square, dancing to the harsh rhythm of a drum and making strange noises, like roosters (the well-known *halali,* which was sung on festive occasions). A little farther along, the crowd had gathered around a large bowl and were eating cracked wheat and boiled meat with their hands. They were wiping their greasy fingers and hands on their beards and the exposed parts of their bodies. In yet another spot, the people were passing a container of *tan* (liquid yogurt) from hand to hand, everyone drinking from it most avidly until they quenched their thirst.

The Arabs gave us some water in honor of the bride and groom. We also passed the jug from hand to hand, drank a bit, thanked them, and left.

Late this evening we arrived in Irbit. Instead of presenting ourselves to the military authorities, we stayed at Haygazun Bzdigian's home. My uncle had got to know him when he came to Irbit about a month and a half ago. He is one of the leading men from Adana. He is quite well respected here within regional government circles.

Mr. Bzdigian shares a room with three bachelor friends. They very kindly provided us with a bed and a blanket. Five of us spent the night lying next to each other across the width of the bed, and had strange dreams.

5 April, 1916

We followed Bzdigian's advice and didn't go out today. This morning he and my uncle went to see a few officials at the government building.

We waited for them to return until evening, imagining all kinds of things in the meantime. They returned after dark and reported that their contacts had not yet produced any definite result.

6 April, 1916

Today we were once more imprisoned in the room. It rained very heavily all day. There are posters stuck to walls in the streets that announce once more that all Armenians between the ages of 20 and 50 must register with the military authorities My uncle and Mr. Bzdigian went once more to the government building and returned this evening. They were disappointed and sad. Not only had they not been able to settle our situation, but they had also found it impossible to correct my age in the records.

7 April, 1916

The Armenian soldiers who left Jeresh on foot arrived here in pitiful condition last night, and this morning they were sent to Dera; from there they will be moved to Tfliye.

The south of Hauran is an unhealthy region, inhabited by the Bedouins of Beni Sakhar. These savages continually set fire to or raid the Fellah villages, with a view to plundering their belongings. What will become of Armenians among such people needs no explanation.

We still haven't presented ourselves to the military authorities. My uncle and Mr. Bzdigian are making supernatural efforts to save us at all costs. In order not to impose upon Mr. Bzdigian too much, we rented a room today and moved into it tonight under cover of darkness.

8 April, 1916

My uncle came back at noon and announced philosophically that since all his efforts had proved fruitless, he had no choice but to hand us over to the military authorities.

There was no way out of it. We would also be sent to do military service in the Tfliye desert. We shouldered our bags and followed him meekly, without uttering a word. We had climbed more than halfway up the hill leading to the government building when my uncle stopped suddenly, turned to us, and said: "Boys, let's go back."

Thinking he was joking, we stared at him in amazement.

"I'm not a superstitious man," he continued, "but everything I have ever done on a Friday, my whole life long, has failed. Today's Friday, and it's an unlucky day. Let's go back home. I'll hand you over to them tomorrow."

"We're not in the mood for such beliefs," we replied, smiling at his superstition. "We've already climbed almost three-quarters of the way up the hill. Who wants to do the same thing all over again tomorrow, climbing this steep road? We're almost there, so let's go and do it now."

"No," insisted my uncle. "Let's go. Don't be lazy. Tomorrow you can climb again. No, not today."

We stopped objecting. We slowly walked down the hill, again in absolute silence, and returned to our room.

9 April, 1916

This morning, to our great surprise, a Circassian we know knocked at the door and walked in.

"Come, bring the old man in," he said in a weary voice, and sat in the entrance to the room.

"What old man?"

Filled with curiosity, we went out into the street and were all surprised to see my grandfather in a pitiful state, sitting—or to be more precise, half-lying. He was so exhausted he couldn't hold himself straight—on a donkey.

We carried him into the room at once and made him lie down on his back on the floor.

Speaking in fragments, my grandfather explained that the Kurdish corporal had broken his promise and sent him here so the local commandant could see with his own eyes that a mistake had been made. My grandfather had left accompanied by the Circassian and, after traveling all night, had arrived here.

Seeing his sleepless state and extreme exhaustion, we postponed our visit to the government building. We wanted him to get a few hours of rest and then we would all leave together. He awoke almost six hours later. We got him dressed and were ready to leave when there was another knock on the door. This time it was Mr. Bzdigian, beaming with joy. He rushed into the room.

"Cheer up, children! I've got good news for you. Jemal Pasha has postponed the conscription of Armenians by six months. I saw the telegram. It was with the governor of the province. The moment I saw it I ran here to tell you the good news."

Not even a criminal on his way to the gallows would have been so happy on receiving a pardon. We were absolutely thrilled. We immediately stowed our military kits in a corner of the room and went out, to walk around freely and breathe the freer air. At the market we met other Armenian deserters. They had also heard the news and come out of their hiding places. They couldn't stop congratulating each other.

A little later, however, something happened to change our mood. In a vacant lot we saw a very young and pretty Armenian girl. She was sitting there alone on a long piece of grindstone. Three young Arabs surrounded her, making lewd jokes. The girl was shouting angrily and seemed to be threatening them. Then, noticing a slice of bread held out to her by one of the youths, she suddenly burst into loud laughter. She immediately got to her feet and walked with her seducer, leaning on his arm, into a deserted street.

"She's deranged by illness," said Mr. Bzdigian, realizing our distress. "She's an Armenian refugee from Aintab and has no one to look after her. Her name is Victoria. This happens every day. Pitiless shop-keepers, employees, and gendarmes all take advantage of this poor girl's hunger and mental state."

10 April, 1916

In spite of his extreme fatigue, my grandfather looked rejuvenated. He wanted to return to Jeresh even before we were ready, to give everybody the news of the postponement. So we got ready this morning and decided to leave with the Circassian on horseback, all seven of us.

As we passed through Husun on our way, we met some Christian Arabs who had some Easter eggs dyed red. They were hitting their eggs against each other to see which would break first. That made us realize that today was apparently Easter. So we bought bread and eggs and rested for about an hour, then got back on the road. This evening we arrived at the notorious well where we had to lie in the shade of the only tree and wait for the Arab herdsman to bring us the murky water. This was during our first trip to Jeresh. We were thirsty this time too, but we didn't suffer. Whenever we got thirsty we got off our horses, lay on the ground, and drank the rain water that accumulated in the holes made by the hooves of the camels.

This evening, after dark, we arrived at Jeresh, but by an altogether different road, which was much shorter than the one the policemen deliberately made us travel on, and much more comfortable.

The moment the news of our arrival spread through the village, all of the Armenians left their houses and caves, assembled in the little square across from our house, and praised the name of Jemal Pasha with bravos and wishes that he might live a long life.

After a week of soul-destroying events and experiences, we spent a worriless night, stretched out in our soft beds beside our loved ones.

17 April, 1916

The Armenians who were drafted returned from Dera yesterday. There were a mere 22 Armenian soldiers of the 500 who went from here and nearby villages with the first expedition to Tfliye.

The families of those who returned are beside themselves with joy— if it is possible for an Armenian refugee to feel such an emotion as joy. The families of the others are in deep mourning and curse their luck. There is, however, a great deal of hope that the rest will also return.

24 April, 1916

The starving Armenians were happy today. They saw their first crop of barley. The price of wheat, which had skyrocketed up to 75 coins for 10 kilos, suddenly dropped to 40. They think that within a few weeks it will come down to its original price (20 coins). But even then, there are a great many people who find it impossible to scrape together even 20 coins.

Those families that were once considered well-to-do are now in great difficulty. At the market we meet venerable fathers, heads of families, whose foreheads are creased with deep furrows. They have come to sell their underwear, clothing, shoes, copper plates, and many other items so they can buy a handful of wheat. What will they do then? What more can they sell? It is frightening.

If there is any consolation at all in this misery, it is that the local people buy whatever the Armenians sell—so what if they pay less than what it's worth? Another good thing is that they know nothing about fashion or fine clothes—they buy anything that is offered for sale. It's quite frequent to meet a Fellah in the streets who is wearing an Armenian woman's wedding gown, or, for that matter, a Bedouin walking around in a fur coat, as though on the way to a fancy-dress party.

1 May, 1916

Circassians don't like the sight of Armenian refugees sleeping in the streets. They complain that from morning to night these Armenians panhandle in front of their doors, disturbing their comfort and peace with their endless pleas and demands. They are right, to some extent. But what choice do these unfortunate deportees have? A person who is drowning will grasp on to a serpent! They know that they will receive more beatings and animosity than bread. But, having no other choice, they have to take the risk.

In the end the Circassians complained to the Kurdish corporal and asked that all Armenians in dire circumstances should be deported from the village.

The police rounded up 120 people today. Under the blows of their whips, they sent them all on their way, intending to send them to an area of the desert so forsaken that they won't have anyone to disturb.

4 May, 1916

We have received more money (20 pounds) from Constantinople.

The last time we were able to have it cashed at the bank by a proxy. This time I have to go myself. I'll probably go to Irbit with my uncle and the Circassian guide this afternoon.

Although we set out yesterday evening in order to avoid being bothered by the weather, it was an extremely hot night. To quench our thirst we were obliged to eat the eight cucumbers we were taking as a present to Haygazun Bzdigian since they are considered real rarities in Irbit.

The entire area between Jeresh and Irbit is covered with Bedouin tents, and stealing is commonplace. With that in mind, we proceeded with caution, sometimes taking a detour to avoid the robbers' tents and pastures. Fortunately, we had no incidents and this morning, at dawn, we arrived in Irbit.

5 May, 1916

When we woke up it was almost noon. Our attention was drawn by an unusual tumult and alarm in the narrow street where our hotel was located. We ran to the window and saw hundreds of naked and barefoot refugees. Despite their hear-rending cries, the police were pushing and thrashing them to make them enter a vacant stable across the street.

A while later we were informed that, like the unfortunate ones of Jeresh, these were also victims of evil and misery, and on the governor's orders they also were being exiled to a forsaken corner of the desert, about two days away.

Before long they were all crammed into the stable. The police locked the door and left.

My uncle and I were curious to see what would happen next, and remained standing near the window. Next we saw a young deportee push his head through a hole and gaze at the roof, as if planning a way to escape. He soon changed his mind, though, when he noticed the thick vegetation near him. It was as if he had discovered a huge treasure chest. The young man withdrew his head from the hole, came out onto the roof through it, and began to pick the grass hurriedly, eating it voraciously and stuffing his pockets at the same time.

A little later a second person came out through the hole, then a third, a fourth, a fifth . . . more than 10 people altogether, who devoured the grass greedily, taking care that the people below them wouldn't learn of their discovery. However, new faces—all of them emaciated and skeletal—gradually kept peeking out, witnessing their friends' lavish banquet, and trying to take advantage of it, causing a fight, alarm, and plunder.

For a moment we were afraid that the roof would cave in under the weight of these hundreds of people. Fortunately though, the pillage was soon over and they all went back inside the building, except for one or two people who hung down from the edge of the roof like goats, trying to pick the grass growing in the crevices of the wall.

We looked at the roof, which had now turned into a piece of wasteland. It had been covered with thick untouched grass only fifteen minutes ago. We were appalled and asked ourselves if they were rational people like us or dumb animals who scratched each other's face for a sprout of green. In Jeresh there were also people wading in misery, but we had never seen or heard of such a thing happening there.

We had not yet recovered from our horror when the police came riding back on their horses. They opened the stable door and took the people out.

Now there were no protests. They all went quietly and complacently, picking up from the ground orange peels, onion skins, and all sorts of other things that man could chew and the human stomach could digest.

6 May, 1916

We went and cashed the 20 pounds at the Agricultural Bank, but instead of gold pieces we got paper money, which is worth 30% less. After converting these bills into pieces of gold and silver, we set out for Jeresh in the evening. The sky was overcast. We traveled all night long in thick darkness. We were afraid that at any moment a thief might attack us from behind a bush or a rock and grab our money and clothing and the horses for which we were responsible. Fortunately, our return also ended safely, and this morning we arrived home, alive and well.

8 May, 1916

The new tenant in our courtyard is a widow from Adana who has two grown-up daughters. They were rather well off when they arrived here. They were able to live a modest life on what they had, hoping that before their means of livelihood were exhausted peace would return and they would be able to go back home. What they had hoped for did not come to pass. They spent all their money and began to sell what they had brought with them as necessities. Then they ran out of those too. Now the three of them work in harsh conditions to provide themselves with daily bread.

Both daughters are well educated. They speak French and English, play the piano, and are skilled in embroidery. In this desert, however, who cares about their fine education? Like the women from Yaghde, they also go to the mountains to collect wood and haul it back to the village to sell.

Tonight, however, they both returned empty-handed. While they were cutting wood a Bedouin stole their rope, hatchet, and the shirts off their backs. The older one has become sick as a result of her fright, and has taken to her bed. The poor girl obviously didn't know about how virtuous the Arabs are, otherwise when the Arab removed her underwear she wouldn't have been so frightened, to the point of getting sick!

15 May, 1916

Hunger and misery on one hand and the animosity of the locals on the other are forcing the Armenians to abandon the villages where they have settled and leave for Damascus to seek their fortunes. They put their rags on their backs and go, hoping to get into Damascus, where the men can practice their occupations, the women can work in factories, and the little ones can be put in orphanages. The emigration is mostly from the neighboring Arab villages. Jeresh maintains its large Armenian population because refugees from far-off villages come and settle here in secret. They have heard that there is a real need for skilled workers here.

22 May, 1916

The weather here is so unhealthy that typhoid fever devastates the region in winter and malaria in summer. I've also been suffering from malaria for the past four days, and I'm already weak. The only remedy for this illness is quinine, but unfortunately it is not something that is available to every Armenian, considering that it costs 45 coins a gram.

Fathers who work to give their children their daily bread are in a difficult situation if they ever have to stay in bed for a week or so. First, their family members have nothing to eat. Then, as they cannot afford to buy drugs and nourishment, they can never be cured. And the longer it takes them to get better and go back to work, the worse their situation gets.

Khoren the cobbler has also become a victim of this well known vicious circle of cause and effect. This means one thing: another family has dropped into obscurity.

29 May, 1916

Because of the scorching summer heat, all of the snakes, scorpions, and poisonous insects of Arabia have become active. Only two days ago a gardener from Marash was found dead in his hut. He had been bitten by a poisonous snake and died instantly.

At night we sleep in fear and we open our eyes in terror at every little noise we hear in the room.

Last night we killed a huge snake in our courtyard, and last week a strange animal, as big as a kitten, that looked like a chameleon.

Lizards crawl up and down the walls of our room and insects buzz all night in the rafters.

5 June, 1916

Disasters follow one after the other. We hear that in Dera they have begun to convert Armenians to Islam. Already close to 1,000 people have accepted the "True Faith" under threat. There is no limit to the delight of the Damascus Arabs and the Circassians, who are busy preparing lists of women they would like to marry the moment they convert to Islam!

Worry, fright, and alarm are rampant, especially among women and maidens who have no one to protect them. They are barely over the fear of being raped while traveling, and now they risk being imprisoned in Muslim harems.

This painful news forces us to conclude that the government is determined to exterminate the Armenian nation completely, and that no obstacle or difficulty will ever stop them from realizing this hideous intention.

12 June, 1916

When I went to the market, I heard that six of the Armenian soldiers who were sent to Tfliye had returned, looking miserable. A little later I met Moushegh from Sis. He was one of the six who came back. He was telling a group of people about the horrible conditions they had endured there.

These soldiers were stationed in a barren field farther down the coast of the Dead Sea, almost in the middle of the Amman and Ma'an Railroad. There 800 of them joined another 300 who had arrived earlier.

They had to carry water from a well three hours away. It was filthy by the time it reached the tents in the unbearable heat, and was fit for nothing but bathing. Bread came from a place two days away and there wasn't much of it. There was so little that they could eat it only once a day.

It was the task of these Armenian soldiers to get heavy hammers early in the morning, walk quite a distance, sit in the scorching rays of the sun by the edge of a road, like galley-slaves, and labor continuously, breaking stones. There were huge piles of stones in front of each soldier; farther along Turkish soldiers sat in the shade of a tent and watched the labor detachment carefully. Anybody who stopped for a short break would immediately feel the whip, and those who attempted to escape were shot on the spot.

In the evening when it got dark, these poor souls returned to camp, where they could eat a piece of bread as hard as stone and drink some murky water. After devouring what was available, they would drop, already half-unconscious, to the ground, there to remain until they got up the following morning and began the same torturous routine all over again.

In two months more than 150 of them died of hunger and sunstroke. There is no doubt that hunger would have killed them all if they hadn't thought of a way to escape.

The plan was devised by a young man from Hadjin named Soghomon. It was an excellent plan but they had to wait for the right moment to put it into operation.

When that moment arrived they were ready. One night it was their turn to go and fetch water. Under the surveillance of two soldiers, ten of them grabbed goat-skin bottles and headed for the well. In order not to arouse the guards' suspicions, the soldiers walked all the way to the well in silence, saying absolutely nothing to each other. Once at the well, they began to fill the bottles with great self-control. The guards sat a bit back from the well and dropped their rifles to the ground to roll their cigarettes.

"Friends!" Soghomon called suddenly. He thought the time had come for action. "Four or five of us will die, but the rest will survive. Now! Let's attack the guards and take their weapons!"

The young man from Hadjin had hardly finished speaking when they all left their bottles and rushed the guards. The guards were taken by surprise by this sudden attack but they soon reached for their rifles and began shooting at the insubordinate crew. The two or three who were nearest fell, covered in blood—among them their leader, Soghomon—but those who were behind them pounced on the enemy, and a severe fight took place. In the course of a fairly lengthy struggle several more shots were heard and two more of the rebels were killed. In the end, however, the Armenians were able to consign the Turkish guards to perpetual silence.

"Then, with no time to lose, we fled north," explained Moushegh. "Two days later we arrived at the tents of the Bedouins of Beni Sakhar. We bartered the rifles we had seized for bread. We bandaged our wounds and took to the road again, and here we are."

"But what about those who are still in the camp?" asked Ruhji Bedros from the crowd: "Don't you think that the Turks will take revenge on them?"

"Let them do what we did," said Moushegh with a shrug. "Our people got themselves into this mess by always thinking of 'those who remain behind.' Just ten policemen led hundreds of thousands of young men to the valleys and slaughtered them like sheep. They could easily have killed their executioners, but they didn't, thinking that the Turks would take revenge on the unprotected people left behind in the villages and towns. And what happened in the end? They all died: women and children as well. Wouldn't it have been better if they'd died like heroes, even if the others died with them?"

Nobody spoke a word. It seemed there was some truth in what this boorish Armenian was saying. Perhaps we wouldn't be in this brutal situation now if our entire nation had thought like this country fellow and his friends.

19 June, 1916

Bedouin shepherds grazing their flocks from one place to another have made it all the way down here and are camping only half an hour from the village. I heard that several Armenians had bought milk from them at an exceptionally low price. I took a container and went to the shepherds as well.

Even as I drew near their pasture I realized that I'd made a mistake. First of all, no Armenian ever went there alone. Second, they always dressed very poorly, in worn-out clothes, when they went. Not only was I alone, but I was also wearing European clothes, and I had a gold ring with a precious stone on my finger. It was given to me by my mother when I finished school. It was too late to turn back, however. They had already spotted me. So I collected my courage and approached them with their usual greeting: "Peace on you, countrymen. I've come to buy milk."

"*Ehlen* and *sehlen* (welcome)," the Bedouins replied hospitably.

There were four of them. One of them took my container and went over to the sheep and the others remained with me, looking with interest at my unusual clothes. Before long, one of them found the courage to speak,[*] and he pointed at my costume and said: "Aren't you uncomfortable in those clothes?"

"No," I replied, "I'm used to them."

"Where is your village?"

"Over there, very, very far."

"Why did you come to our land?"

I couldn't tell the Bedouin the truth. He must not know that the Turkish government had brought us here to exterminate us.

"Because," I murmured, "an enemy invaded our country."

"Then why didn't you kill the enemy?"

"We couldn't. There were too many of them."

"Does that mean that when the enemy is numerous you run away?"

This cheeky shepherd's question was so equivocal that I hesitated briefly before answering. If I said "No," what was I doing in the Hauran desert? If I said "Yes," wouldn't I betray the weakest component of our national character?

"Enough of this," I said, changing the subject. "Just take a look at what your friend is doing. He's milking the sheep, but he's also pouring water from the leather bottle hidden under his arm into my container!"

---

[*].   These savages are extremely shy for the first few minutes whenever they
       meet a stranger. Later, though, they gradually gain courage and become
       so shameless that they can even kill the person.

The Bedouin realized that I had seen him cheating and no longer tried to keep it secret. He gave a terrifying shout and started counter-attacking me: "Do you expect us to fill your container with pure milk for the price you're paying?"

"You don't have to fill my container. Just fill it with the amount I've paid for," I replied calmly.

"No, give me more money. Then I'll fill your container."

"I don't have any more money."

"What's this?"

Suddenly the savage grabbed my right wrist so firmly that it felt clamped in a vise.

"It's a ring," I said, trying to free my hand.

"A ring!" exclaimed the shepherd, with ill-boding pleasure, his eyes glittering. "Take it off. Let's see how beautiful it is."

"It doesn't come off," I said, keeping calm. "They put it on my finger when I was a little boy and since then my finger has grown a lot thicker."

"You're lying. You don't want to take it off because you're afraid we'll steal it."

"Why should I be afraid? You're not thieves, are you?"

Now the other two shepherds, who had been quiet until then, joined the conversation: "If it doesn't come off your finger, how did you get it on . . . Just watch! We'll get it off!" Having said this, they jumped on me, pushed me to the ground, and began pulling on the ring with great force. The pain was unbearable.

"Leave me alone! Let me go!" I cried, writhing under the weight of the four powerful men—because now they had been joined by the swindler, the one who had been milking the sheep.

"Cut his finger off and that'll be the end of it," ordered the first shepherd with dreadful determination.

I noticed the dagger that had come out of its sheath, and at the same time I heard a sharp voice, which petrified the evil-doers.

"*Hola*! What are you doing to the boy?"

The thieves stopped, stupefied at the sight of the gigantic man (Khurshid the miller), who had a big pail in his hand and was running up to them threateningly. They pretended it was all a big joke and laughed: "Your countryman is such a sissy . . . we just wanted to see his ring . . . The uproar he made could be heard for miles!"

Khurshid shut them up with an admonishing look, took my milk container from them, and signalled that I should leave.

"Lucky for you I passed this way as I was repairing the sluice-way," my liberator from Kilis said when he left me at the end of the village. "My boy, what you did was very thoughtless!" Don't you know that the Arabs are capable of killing, even for something worthless?"

I was so shaken with fright and emotion that I couldn't open my mouth to thank him. I left him without uttering a word, and headed directly to Misag the farrier's, put my hand on the anvil, and said: "Please take this ring off my finger."

P.S. I am writing these few lines at night by the light of a lamp. My mind burns like a red-hot piece of iron, not so much because of that savage Bedouin's criminal actions as because of his just observation. What *are* we doing in this inhospitable country? No matter how strong our enemy, wasn't it essential for us to remain in our homeland?

26 June, 1916

Our business on the market was interrupted by conscription. Today we made a renewed effort, and opened a fruit and vegetable store with Levon and Vahram.

Mr Giulbenkian has sent us another 35 pounds from Constantinople The paper bills are now worth only 60% in coins, so we'll get only 20 pounds. We are, however, most grateful to him.

3 July, 1916

The heat gradually builds to an extreme. It's impossible to go out around noon. The earth burns your feet like the floor of a furnace, even if you step on it with your shoes on. An egg becomes hard-boiled if you leave it in the sun for two or three minutes.

Now there is a cholera epidemic. It makes us long for our typhoid fever or malaria. At least some were cured from those illnesses, but no one ever survives cholera. Once it attacks one member of a family, there is no hope for the rest. Only in Jeresh, twenty people die every day.

Everyone in our family is suffering from marsh fever. Sometimes I, sometimes my mother or my sisters or my brother, sometimes all of us together develop a very high fever and have to stay in bed. We spend all the money we have on quinine, but we still can't keep our eyes open.

Today I and Manoushag are sick in bed. We are running a very high fever. Our mental anguish increased when we heard a woman moaning and sobbing bitterly and mournfully on the lower floor.

The girl from Adana who became ill about two months ago after being attacked in the mountains by thieves has apparently died. We wonder why people cry for the dead. Isn't that what will happen to all of us one day soon?

10 July, 1916

The Muslim problem is getting more serious. They have arrested the Armenian priests living in the Hauran and taken them to Dera. Today they also arrested the only priest in our village.

The poor man, who is quite old, has been sick and hasn't left his hut for a week. This morning a policeman went to his hut and ordered him to get ready to leave immediately.

Terrified, the priest's wife and daughter pleaded: "But sir, don't you see that he's sick in bed. How can he travel in the condition he's in?"

"I don't care whether he's sick or not. I have orders and I have to take him away," replied the gendarme.

"But please! Look at him!"

"Don't talk so much or I'll take you away too!"

The old priest realized that pleas or requests would make no difference. He got to his feet, put on his clothes, and with faltering steps followed the pitiless officer.

We assume that the government is rounding up the priests in order to facilitate the conversion of Armenians to Islam.

17 July, 1916

I've been determined for a long time to hear the story of Khacher Aghpar from Moush. Today was a good day for it. He came to our store, sold the produce from his vegetable garden, and was sitting there for a rest.

This time he couldn't put me off with his usual objection that he couldn't spare the time because he had to get back to his garden. It was burning hot outside and he had no choice but to wait until the heat decreased. He therefore agreed to our request, took a deep breath, and told us his story.

* * *

The Turkish government did not forget its long history of defeat by the people of Zeitoun. It was always looking for occasions to overthrow this coveted, freedom-loving people. The Great War offered them the occasion they had been seeking.

Before the oppression of Armenians in the provinces began, individual assassinations and violence started to occur in Zeitoun. First they wrongfully arrested and beat to death an Armenian named Nazaret Chavush, considered by the people of Zeitoun to be their prince. Then they also trapped three or four of the other princes and killed them too, after submitting them to lengthy torture. At the same time, soldiers tortured and raped their wives and daughters.

This was more than enough evil for the people of Zeitoun, and they hoisted the flag of rebellion. Upon the advice of the Catholicos of Cilicia, however, who warned them that an uprising might endanger the safety of Armenians in the provinces, they kept quiet, accepting all the hatred and evil.

But the government was not satisfied with what they had done so far. On the pretext of seizing weapons, soldiers forcefully entered Armenian homes, tortured the men, dishonored the women, and frightened the children.

The population of Zeitoun ran out of patience. A group of brave young men—including Khacher Aghpar's only son, Avedis—grabbed their guns and killed everyone who had raped Armenian women. They then went up into the mountains and took refuge in an ancient Armenian monastery.

This was exactly what the government had hoped for: to incite the people to rebellion and then use their revolt as an excuse to exterminate them all. At once an army, 10,000 strong, arrived from Marash, surrounded the town, and demanded that the rebels surrender.

A delegation of Armenians from Zeitoun raised a white flag and went to see the commandant, to explain that they did not agree with what these fifty hot-headed youths had done but were unable to capture and deliver them to the government. The soldiers then surrounded the monastery where the stalwarts were staying and, after a long gunfight, succeeded in setting fire to it.

The brave Armenians ran out through the flames and attacked the enemy.

They sacrificed ten men—among whom was Avedis—but they killed at least ten times that number. They cut through the enemy lines and disappeared into the night, taking with them the heads of their slain friends so the enemy would not be able to identify them and take revenge on their families.

These poor people forgot that the Turks are not endowed with the virtue of differentiating the guilty from the innocent. In addition they are perfectly capable of slaughtering peaceful people and their delegates under the "protection" of a white flag.

The Turkish commandant first took revenge for his defeat on the Armenian delegation. He had them arrested before the military action began. Later he secretly killed them all, ordered the arrest of all the prominent men of the city, and at first chance put 300 of them in chains and exiled them to an unknown destination.

A few days later, the police who took away these worthies returned, swimming in wealth: gold watches, rings, tobacco boxes. They took charge of a second caravan and left again.

After cleaning up the leading citizens of the city, they divided the rest of the 20,000 people into groups of 2,000 and put them on the road, sending some to Konia and Sultanie and others to Aleppo and Rakka. By the end of April not one stone was left standing on top of another.

Khacher Aghpar, the pain of his martyrized son still in his heart, joined the convoy for Aleppo with his wife, daughter-in-law, and three little grandchildren. They took with them only what they could carry on their backs. The police forced them to walk quickly. They almost had to run. Children, the sick, and even mothers in the pains of labor were whipped and fell powerless under the steps of the police, and were often trodden upon even by their own loved ones as they tried to escape the police bayonets.

* * *

For days they traveled in the same conditions. Khacher Aghpar, leaning on a stick, walked with the crowd, sometimes carrying his tired grandchildren on his back and often tasting his share of beating and whipping.

One day as they were passing near a forest, they met a German officer and his wife and young daughter. The three of them had rifles and were dressed for hunting, and they had a greyhound with them.

When the people saw the black cross decorating the officer's chest, they ran up to him excitedly, fell at his feet, and started pleading: "In the name of Christ, tell these policemen not to torment us. We are hungry and tired. We beg of you, please find a way to help us."

Although the officer's wife and daughter understood nothing, they were extremely moved by the pitiful condition of the crowd. The German officer, however, grasped the situation. He took a notebook out of his pocket and hurriedly wrote a few lines, tore the page off, gave it to Khacher Aghpar, and told him to deliver it to the quartermaster of the military storehouse that was two hours away. Then in broken Turkish he urged the police to be more merciful to the poor deportees and, his conscience satisfied, he continued on his way with his wife, daughter, and the dog.

It was almost sundown when the caravan slowed down and with shaky steps arrived at the military storehouse. About ten carriages loaded with trunks, bags, and barrels were continuously coming and going. Soldiers were moving heavy loads from the carriages to the storehouse and from the storehouse to the carriages. A young officer standing amidst the bustle was giving orders left, right, and center.

Thinking he was the quartermaster, Khacher Aghpar approached him respectfully and with a deep bow delivered the German's note to him. The Turkish officer, a typical example of a Young Turk, haltingly read a few words, and then impatiently asked the bearer of the letter what it was all about.

A policeman jumped forward and explained the problem under his voice.

"Very good, very good," said the officer, turning to Khacher Aghpar. "Go right across and camp in the field that's surrounded by trees. As soon as I finish my work I'll come and take care of your problem."

The people, blessing this kind-hearted son of the Ottoman army, went to the spot indicated by the officer and fell dead-tired on the ground. An hour later the officer kept his word and approached the caravan with the police chief to see if they had settled down comfortably.

"We have a bit of extra meat we can give you," he said proudly. "Just be a bit patient. The soldiers are preparing it now."

"But sir, even a bit of dry bread would be enough for us," came the touching reply of hundreds of voices in unison.

"Unfortunately, we have no bread, and the meat was about to go bad. You are welcome to it," replied the quartermaster.

"Thank you very much. We are most grateful," murmured the crowd.

And encouraged by the officer's compassionate behavior, they surrounded him, asking many things they wanted to know: "What will happen to us, sir? Where are we going like this, and how long will it take? . . . We have traveled for days, hungry and thirsty, with the aged, the children, and the sick, roaming about in the sun on roads that have no end. We have no strength left to keep on walking . . . Bury us alive and free us from this life . . ."

Everyone was moved and affected and started crying like children.

The Young Turk, truly touched by this unanimous expression of pain, tried to console them: "Don't cry, compatriots; I'm hopeful that the Sultan will pardon all of you. The guilty have already been punished. The innocent will be able to go back to their region."

"May God hear your voice, my child! May God grant you a long life, and your children also," answered the crowd, wiping their tears.

The night was already advanced. Before long they were immeasurably delighted to see flaming wood fires in twenty different spots near the storehouse. Even though the darkness was thick, the flames revealed several soldiers putting kerosene cans filled with water and meat on the fires.

People who had been hungry for days felt their nostrils distend at the aroma of the boiling meat. Dimmed eyes glittered in the presence of cooking food. Pale faces were rejuvenated, intoxicated by the imminent delight.

At last they heard the voices of the soldiers in the deep silence—the bearers of good tidings!

"Armenians, Armenians, hurry up! Come, your food is ready!"

The crowd stood as one person and rushed to the burning wood fires. There were seventy or eighty people around each fire. They couldn't wait for the food to cool down a bit. They didn't even think of taking the boiling kerosene cans off the fire. They pushed each other out of the way, dipped their hands into the boiling water, tore off a piece of meat each, and threw it into their mouths. The policemen and the soldiers watched their distorted faces from a distance and burst into loud laughter.

Within a quarter of an hour there wasn't even a trace of meat left in the cans. The people, blessing the members of the kind-hearted officer's family, started to return slowly to their campground and lay down on the ground to sleep peacefully and get up completely recovered in the morning.

Khacher Aghpar leaned his back against a tree trunk and was getting ready to shut his eyes. He noticed a little boy a short distance away, sitting on the ground and busily chewing on a piece of bone. It aroused the curiosity of the old man, since there was not even a fragment of bone in the food they had just eaten. He approached the child. "What's that? Give it to me," he said, and took the bone away from the child.

He had hardly glanced at the bone in his hand when he froze on the spot he stood on. The bone was nothing less than a man's finger, with the fingernail still on it.

The Turkish officer had fed them human corpses, perhaps the corpses of their compatriots who had been butchered in the region. Without another thought Khacher Aghpar put the human finger in his pocket in horror and disgust and ran from the crowd . . . Meanwhile, the child was in tears, blaming the old man for grabbing his snack away from him.

* * *

After such hideous experiences, Khacher Aghpar's caravan finally arrived in Aleppo. At that time the city was not so crowded and the road to Damascus was still open. Khacher Aghpar's family and fifty other families were sent to the vicinity of Damascus, and the rest to the desert of Deir Zor.

As if they had not suffered enough misfortune already, they had a train accident near Zahle. They were traveling in freight cars with many other refugees when suddenly the silence of the night was broken by a blood-curdling cry: "Help . . . Help . . . Fire . . ."

Bewildered, people rushed to the windows, but they couldn't see a thing. Where was the fire? Was it in the front or the back? It was impossible to tell. Instead of stopping, the train was hurtling forward at breath-taking speed. They were passing through orchards and the engineer was afraid of setting fire to the trees.

A little later, when they were going round a curve in the track, they saw that the two front cars were blazing like brush-wood, ignited by the sparks that poured out of the locomotive.

Because of the galloping speed of the train, the fire quickly spread from one car to another and the travelers were jumping out to save themselves from the flames. Then suddenly, with a deafening clamor, the train rolled off a bridge.

The car in which Khacher Aghpar was traveling and the two cars attached to the locomotive landed on a deep layer of earth and remained there, jack-knifed. They were not injured. Nevertheless, the travelers in these cars received several bruises on different parts of their bodies.

These fortunate ones eventually succeeded in getting out of the cars in which they were imprisoned and rushed to help their unlucky friends, who were burnt and were moaning horribly from under the wrecked and shattered cars.

They worked until dawn to pull burnt bodies with broken legs, crushed skulls, or unrecognizable faces out from under the wreckage. Another blow to the children of the unfortunate and persecuted Armenian nation!

In the morning high-ranking railroad officials arrived at the scene of the tragedy. They made a lengthy examination of all the overturned cars; the locomotive, which could no longer be used; and the ruined bridge. They took notes and measurements, and left, without showing the slightest interest in the sobbing survivors of the accident.

Three hours later more officials arrived, this time from the military. They also examined the cars and the rails, prepared a long report, and left.

"What about the injured?" asked some of the survivors, running after them: "Please think of something to do for us . . . we have no medicine, no bread, no water. Nothing at all."

"That's no concern of ours. You have to apply to the authorities," answered the officer with frozen indifference.

"But where are the authorities? . . . aren't they aware of the accident?"

"I don't know."

They waited in that valley for days. No medicine and no bread arrived. The seriously injured died. Those less injured recovered. After waiting in vain for about a week, those who were still alive got up and dragged themselves, limping, to a nearby village, in the hope of finding some kind of hospitality there. But the peasants were all staunch fanatics, and threw stones at them until they chased them out of the village.

They walked all day and at last they reached a station where many Armenian refugees had pitched their tents. They joined up with them and waited for months until they got their turn to be moved to Dera. And from there they came here. A week later Khacher Aghpar lost his wife, who had fallen sick on the road. And two months later, one of his grandchildren also died.

Khacher Aghpar now works in his vegetable garden with his daughter-in-law and two grandchildren. His only regret is that he didn't hoist the flag of rebellion and die like a hero in the impregnable mountains of his own country, like his son.

25 July, 1916

It has been a year since our souls were plunged into mourning.

The arrests in Chorum began a year ago today. Since then we haven't had a day of relief. We have traveled through mountains and valleys, always in danger of being slaughtered or robbed. We have seen the countless bodies of our assassinated brothers left on the banks of rivers and in fields. We have felt the guerrillas circling around us like bloodthirsty vampires. We have been persecuted by rampaging peasants armed with daggers and hatchets. We have opened our wallets as if opening our veins and have emptied them to place our last silver coins in the palms of the gendarmes. We have witnessed the deadly misery of hundreds of thousands of refugees in Osmaniye and Katma. The tragic condition of the emaciated and exhausted as they lay sick in the streets of Aleppo. Then Damascus, the Hauran desert, sunstroke, frost, winter, rain, sickness, death, famine, and all sorts of tribulation.

It's impossible to calculate the loss that the nation has borne. Only in our region, where there were 20,000 Armenians when we arrived, not even a quarter are left, and they are mostly wasting away, their ability to endure gradually diminishing with every passing day.

The deplorable thing is that we have no hope whatsoever of being freed. The soldiers continue fighting without the slightest sign of fatigue. The government is unstinting in its search for new methods of exterminating the Armenians completely. Nature and disease cause a great deal of damage and guerrillas and Arabs complete what they leave unfinished, in the fanatical belief that whoever harms the Armenians pleases God.

31 July, 1916

The other day the police beat Harutiun the blacksmith with iron and hammers for no good reason. Today, we heard that the poor man, who had been vomiting blood, has died. He has left behind a widow and a sixteen-year-old daughter.

Beating people to death has become the fashion recently. The life of an Armenian is not worth a chicken's.

7 August, 1916

Bedouin nomads have been camping on the road to Jeresh and Dera for a month. They pillage constantly, causing terror among both Christians and Muslims.

Three days ago our Circassian landlord was attacked on his way back from Dera. The thieves ambushed him and killed his horse. Huseyin Bey succeeded in dismounting from his horse, opened fire on the attackers, and escaped safely, finding refuge in a nearby Fellah village.

Today Setrag from Marash ran the gauntlet under similar conditions. He goes to Dera every month to buy everything he needs for his store. Ever since he was robbed, he arms himself when he travels. So when the Bedouins fired on him he shot back, and he saved his life, his horse, and the goods he had bought by fleeing.

If there is any consolation in this, the Arabs are not very good shots, despite the fact that they begin using rifles and guns at an early age. If they were skilled marksmen, you can imagine what our situation would be like.

14 August, 1916

The question of Armenians converting to Islam gains momentum from one day to the next. After the arrest of the village priest, my uncle Hagop Dadrian, Djamdjian and Kehyayan of Caesarea, and Minas and Garabed Geovderelian of Sis were arrested five days ago. In the neighboring villages they have also arrested a few influential people to prevent them from campaigning against conversion.

Today we received a letter from my uncle, who is in Dera. He informs us that they have imprisoned him without any interrogation.

In prison he found Haygazoun Bzdigian and other well known personalities who had been take there from Irbit and other places. They heard that our village priest died on the road, before arriving in Dera.

"Although we have to buy bread to eat from outside sources, we're comfortable in jail. The policemen don't disturb us much," writes my uncle.

The poor Armenian! He was so very afraid of being tortured in prison that when they don't beat him he thinks he's in paradise!

21 August, 1916

The committee in charge of converting Armenians to Islam arrived here yesterday evening. There are five of them: the Mufti of Irbit; an Armenian named Aram, who was formerly the president of the Ipranosian Company in Mersin; two government officials; and a policeman.

They set up shop at the village hall late last night and summoned all the Armenian *moukhtars* (elders) of the village—every Armenian has a representative—and informed them of the government's decision.

The turbaned *hodja* of Irbit apparently made quite a long speech, emphasizing that the government is doing us a great favor by converting us, "because when we are all faithful children of the same religion and country, there will be no reason for hatred and resentment."

"I therefore recommend that you accept the government's proposal," the *hodja* concluded. "If you refuse, you should realize that it will be you who suffer in the end."

After this veiled threat from the Muslim clergyman, the Armenian member of the committee spoke, explaining that they have been visiting all the villages of the Hauran over the past two months, converting all the Armenians to Islam.

"The whole thing is nothing but a mere formality," he said. "Your name is changed only on paper. Just because you have accepted Islam, no one will ever force you to go to a mosque or make your daughters marry Turks."

"If that's the case," replied Sarko the butcher, "then let us give you a list of all the Armenians in the village and you can write in an Islamic name for each of them."

"May you live long! After all, that's what we all wanted," exclaimed the members of the committee.

The *moukhtars* left the village hall to tell the people the news. Today those who know how to write Turkish worked late at the village hall, preparing the list in question. Late at night the members of the committee took the list and left, pleased that they had been able to convert the Armenians of the village.

28 August, 1916

On the evil advice of the Damascus Arabs, the local Circassians presented a petition to the inspector, stating that by accepting Islam superficially the Armenians were helping the government realize its goal to abolish religious diversity in the country. "They should either become real Muslims or get the hell out of our country, where they have brought nothing but disease and a high cost of living," the petition said.

This blessed bunch have forgotten how much Armenians have contributed to civilization and progress in this country. People who a year ago hadn't even heard of socks, handkerchiefs, shoes, shirts, or watches, today wear socks, use watches, and adorn themselves with jewelry, and yet they say Armenians have brought nothing to their country.

How about their chicken coops, sheep folds, uninhabitable rooms, and uncultivated fields, which have now become real sources of revenue by being rented to the refugees as homes, shops, mills, or vegetable gardens. It is even redundant to explain how much these people profit from our presence. But people are stupid; they have become instruments in the hands of the shopkeepers from Damascus, and are cutting off the branch they're sitting on.

4 September, 1916

The prominent citizens of Jeresh who were taken to Dera as hostages came back a couple of days ago.

According to them the conversion of Armenians has been carried out most rigidly in the cities and provinces. In Dera there have been cases of forced marriages, and in Damascus they circumcised the boys from the orphanage and took them to a mosque.

"But this is also a great kindness to the Armenians on the part of Jemal Pasha," they say. "The order from Constantinople was to exterminate all Armenians, with no exceptions. By converting the Armenians of Syria, however, Jemal Pasha has been able to write to Constantinople that there are no Armenians left among the population. On the other side of the desert no one with an Armenian name is left."

The news of the martyrdom of thousands of Armenians in Deir Zor filled our hears with terror. We have hundreds of relatives, friends, and compatriots there. Have they all been killed? Even the thought of it numbs the mind.

11 September, 1916

For the past few days the Bedouins have been getting more violent. They have pitched their tents around Jeresh and are causing a lot of damage to the vegetable gardens of the Armenians during the night.

Early this morning our compatriot Artin Aghpar came to see us, wrapped in rags, and asked for some clothes to cover his wife's nakedness. Last night armed thieves entered their garden and stole not only their bed, clothes, shoes, etc., but they also took their crop, which took the couple months of hard work to grow.

Then the Bedouins entered the next vegetable garden, which belongs to Khacher Aghpar, raped his daughter-in-law, and wounded our old friend in the leg when he tried to offer resistance.

Furthermore, after stealing their belongings also, they went to do the same thing to Samuel from Deort Yol. As the man tried to run away with his wife they wounded him in the head.

In her flight the terrified wife dropped her wrapped-up newborn child without noticing. Much later, after the thieves had left, they went back to the garden and found the poor child asleep under the egg-plants.

18 September, 1916

We constantly expect Bedouin raids. They skinned alive the Fellah sheikh of a nearby village called Sof and drove away the sheep of Chetiné. They are threatening to do the same in Jeresh, with which they have an old feud.

About 150 Circassian youths from distant villages have come to protect their relatives. There is a war-like atmosphere in the streets. They have raised barricades and put guards at every window and door.

The Circassians distributed some of the old rifles to Armenians and told us not to leave our homes.

25 September, 1916

Thinking that the danger was over, we went out today and went to the market to open our shop. But hardly an hour had passed when we heard a gunshot, followed by tumult and confusion. People were running about in alarm. The passersby told us that in the next street a Bedouin had sold a goat to a butcher from Damascus this morning and then had returned to reclaim the goat without returning the money. The butcher, naturally, had refused, and that was why the savage had fired.

When they heard the shooting, hundreds of Bedouins who were in the market-place grabbed their guns and rushed where the fight was. Armed Circassians and policemen did the same. And thus began a commotion in which it was impossible to tell who was being shot at and who was shooting.

Realizing that the situation was serious, we shut the store immediately and ran back home.

There, our landlord and his wife, daughter, and brothers were building a low wall along the street, to prevent intruders from getting in that way if there was a Bedouin attack. We joined them immediately and speeded up the construction by helping them carry stones.

We were still working an hour later, when we heard a salvo of gunfire and the piercing screams of women and children. We wondered for a moment whether the attack had started, but a Circassian soon came running in our direction, shouting that we should not be alarmed: the Bedouins were leaving with two goats instead of one and were firing in the air as a sign of victory.

2 October, 1916

Fearing that they might have left only to prepare for another attack, we did not sleep all night, having hidden our belongings in case of a raid.

The Damascus Arabs and the Circassians patrolled the street until dawn. A few Armenian youths joined them, and all were armed with pistols and clubs.

It is strange to see the alliance of the Circassians and the Damascus Arabs with the Armenians. Only a month ago they were demanding the deportation of the Armenians from the village, whereas now that they find their lives and belongings are in danger, they accept the importance of the Armenians for the protection of the general multi-ethnic community.

Having been spared Bedouin pillage raids, we are now terrified by another, much more horrifying danger. The Kurdish corporal has said that he is thinking of exiling the Armenians to the region around Lebanon, where we would be a homogeneous group.

This is exactly what they did in Deir Zor: "a homogeneous group" . . . all together in one place . . . Are they planning another massacre for the people of the Hauran? Every Armenian is deeply worried.

9 October, 1916

Our room has become a hospital again. I have been in bed for the past six days, suffering from malaria, and so have my sisters and brother. My mother is the only one on her feet. A palm branch in her hand, she sometimes fans me and sometimes her other patients.

Consumed by the burning fires of fever, I think how happy I would be if someone would give me a piece of ice. I held a huge iron key in my hand, trying to absorb its metallic coolness. But my hand soon made the key hot. I put it aside and tried the kitchen tongs, then the pots and pans one after the other, so that they also could lend me some of their coolness.

Sometimes my fever climbs so high that I realize I am uttering nonsense. In my sick imagination I believe that they have taken all my internal organs out and thrown them into a pit. I feel as if I am a bag made of Indian rubber and filled with air. I keep asking my mother why they have taken out my heart, lungs, and stomach. From my bedside my mother assures me that no such thing has happened.

"If I'm talking nonsense, how come I am still conscious?" I ask: "If I can think and I realize that I'm thinking, it means I'm not hallucinating."

Then I fall into a deep state of lethargy and fall asleep. But my sleep is also troubled. I believe I am stretched out at full length on a railroad track and a train runs over me, with all its clamor. The cars keep clattering over me, clattering for hours, endlessly clattering.

* * *

With a startled shake I opened my eyes, as if an incredible miracle had taken place. Suddenly I was transported from under the train into my bed and I saw many people around me. They were watching me eagerly. Among them I recognized Aram the barber, who was smiling at me, holding a strange instrument. I felt that my mind was clear and my temperature normal. My neck was itchy. I tried to reach it with my hand but the barber grabbed me by the hand and said: "Don't touch it. I've drawn some blood."

Before long I was back to normal and wondered if that sick person who only a short while ago had been uttering nonsense with all the conviction of someone who is completely conscious could really have been me.

Aram told me that I had escaped a serious danger caused by some blood complication. In fact, I could have died of a cerebral hemorrhage if they had not helped me in time.

"Maybe I escaped certain death," I said, "but I'm not celebrating."

"Why?" asked the barber in surprise.

"Because," I replied, "I think of every Armenian as a little roulette ball. The Turkish government has dug hundreds of holes in our way. Massacre, deportation, galleys, imprisonment, conscription, forced labor, Islam, exile, misery, hunger, illness, and many other misfortunes—each represents one of these holes. We're like the little balls, skipping over holes by jumping up and down, but we fall into one of them in the end. My ball fell into the hole of illness, and at the last minute, by some miracle, it hopped out again. But what is there to celebrate? Isn't it a fact that it will keep on bouncing foolishly along?

16 October, 1916

We have been forced to close down the store because of police extortion. They collect bills worth 40 coins in the market and then they come to buy something for about 5 coins and ask for change of 95 coins. If we refuse to pay, we are punished for taking the money, and if we pay 100 coins for a bill that is worth 40 we lose the profit on a whole day's work.

Sometimes we find it a lot simpler just to tell the buyer: "We don't want money. Take what you've bought and keep your money." Then they get angry, however, and tell us that they don't need our charity, insisting on getting change.

Anyway, that's the situation. And their purpose is not to purchase anything, but to swindle us.

Because of the devaluation of paper money, you hear people fighting, arguing, and beating each other at the market every day. The local people follow the example of the police when they shop at Armenian stores or deal with Armenian workers. And if an Armenian makes a mistake and pays the rent for his room in the same paper money as his landlord has paid him with, a fight begins—"See how the *giaour* has tried to cheat us . . ."—and they beat him to death.

Obviously it's impossible to do business under such conditions. So we closed our store, thinking it better to eat one slice of bread less than to add another worry to our troubled lives.

23 October, 1916

Some Armenians here belong to a religious sect. They read the good book day and night, trying to predict things from the prophesies of Daniel and the revelations of St. John.

According to these blessed people's interpretations, the year 1335 in the Arabic calendar was going to be a tragic year for the Turks: the Ottoman Empire would collapse and peace would descend on all suffering Armenians.

For the prophet Daniel says that there will be a "thousand three hundred and five and thirty days . . . till the end" [Daniel 12:8-9]. And these 1,335 days are nothing less than the Islamic year 1335.

Many naive people waited for that prophetic year with the greatest impatience. They were firmly convinced that they would all be saved that year. But the year 1335 came and has even been over for a few days, and there is nevertheless still no sign of the collapse of the Empire.

It was tragic to see the disappointment of Ruhji (Spiritual) Bedros and his followers. Now they are looking in the Book of Revelation for other dates on which to base their hope of deliverance.

It is not for nothing that Christ said: "Blessed are the poor in spirit . . ."

30 October, 1916

What we knew about the bloody carnage of Deir Zor had come to us in bits and pieces, but we had no way of knowing how true the reports were. Today we heard the real story from a couple of Armenian deserters who arrived here after an adventurous journey.

One of them, Karekin from Trebizond, is my age, and the other, Sarkis from Moush, is three years older. Both of them, however, have suffered so much that they look the same age.

I got to know them by chance this evening. I saw that they were new in Jeresh and were trying to get information about the village from Panos of Kessab, who lives in a corner of the sheep fold where our house is, with his wife and little boy.

After a modest meal we sat in the courtyard and listened first to Sarkis. The following is his story.

* * *

One day Moush exploded with the bombshell that in Paghesh (Bitlis) 3,000 Armenian soldiers had been disarmed and massacred on the road to Palou.

The news of the massacre filled every Armenian's heart with deep pain and discouragement.

A group of Armenians who had foreseen the carnage, had escaped from the army, and were being looked for by the government took refuge in a monastery. The authorities sent soldiers to capture them. A bloody fight took place and, as at Zeitoun, the Armenians inflicted heavy casualties on the enemy, broke through the besiegers, and escaped to Sasoun.

Angered by their defeat, the Turks brought the corpses of the soldiers who had been killed to Moush and started threatening the Armenians. The governor made a provocative speech when they were buried, publicly promising to cut off the heads of 1,000 Armenians for every hair of every slain soldier.

Terrorism in Moush began then and there.

First they arrested 500 prominent men of the city. After torturing them savagely in jail, they took them to a place about two hours away and burned them alive on specially prepared piles of wood.

Among the unfortunate people who formed this convoy was Sarkis' older brother, Onnig, whose only offenses were his long hair and the fact that he wore glasses. But the blood of so many people did not cool the vengeful governor's heart. He brought a huge army (20,000 strong) from Harpoot (Kharpert) and ordered them to surround the city.

Since the previous week, criminal Kurds and Turks, smelling fabulous opportunities for pillage and massacre, had been coming down from the surrounding mountains and filling the city—all of them waiting for the Friday *namaz* (prayers), which meant so much to them.

At last the day that they were waiting for arrived. Savages who had not prayed even once in their lives went to the mosque that day. The crowd was so big that the mosque was soon full, and as people continued to arrive they gradually spread out to the courtyard and into the nearby streets.

A fanatic *hodja* went to the pulpit and, after referring to a few passages from the Koran, finished his sensational sermon as follows:

"Behold the infidels, who are opposed to our religion and people and country, our accursed enemies! They want to demolish the foundations of our glorious Empire. Thanks be to Allah, however, they have not succeeded in their diabolic schemes. Now it is your turn, brave disciples of Mohammed. Hit them, break them and kill them, uproot them without compassion. Their wealth, lives, honor, and everything else are yours. Go! May Allah give edge to your swords!"

And with horrifying roars the crowd spread out into the Armenian neighborhoods.

Meanwhile, the Armenians, on the other hand, had not been sitting idle. Sensing the danger, they assembled in churches and stone houses, determined to exact as high a price as possible for their lives. With his mother and two sisters (14 and 16 years old), Sarkis took refuge in a house near theirs. It was surrounded by high walls, a courtyard, and was an excellent strategic location.

Besides them, there were another 150 Armenians, who had already moved there before they arrived. The old, the children, and the sick went down into the cellar. The rest—everyone who could hold a rifle—took positions behind the windows and doors.

A little later shooting began in the city. A mob of butchers came and surrounded the house, shouting savage war-cries. During the first few minutes of the fight the windows shattered with a huge crash. Bullets came in and stuck in the walls, breaking all the frames and pictures hanging on the walls into pieces.

The Armenian combatants took up positions behind furniture piled in front of the windows, but did not fire back at the enemy, saving their ammunition. They shot only when the enraged mob tried to climb over the wall to get into the courtyard. Anyone who succeeded in getting up the wall let out a stifled cry and fell head-first either into the courtyard or into the street.

The battle continued all day and all night, at times rather intense and at other times abating, without any result.

The governor, seeing that the mob would not be able to take care of the Armenians, called in the army to take charge of the situation the following day, and the soldiers started to bomb the Armenian neighborhoods. More than four cannons fired shells continuously for four days, not resting until they had destroyed the entire Armenian quarter.

The house where Sarkis had taken refuge was set on fire by the enemy onslaught many times and was ruined completely in the end. The brave Armenians, despite having to fight the enemy, were nevertheless able to put out the fires.

The mob followed the soldiers' example and tried to set fire to the house. They started to throw burning rags at it. Some brave Armenian women got onto the roof, caught the rags, and quickly threw them back at the arsonists. Discouraged by their attempts to start a fire, the mob tried to storm the street door of the house, but whoever tried to cross the threshold was mowed down by the vengeful bullets of the brave Armenians.

This unequal fight between a bunch of stalwarts and twenty times their number of bloodthirsty aggressors lasted four days. During this heroic struggle the Armenians were running low on ammunition, and 32 of the 50 fighters were either wounded or killed—among them Sarkis' older sister—so they couldn't hold out much longer. On their fourth night of defending themselves they ran out of ammunition completely. When their besiegers realized that they were no longer putting up a fight, they stormed into the courtyard, set fire to the building, and retreated to a distance to watch their victims burn.

Suddenly a column of fire rose in the darkness. It momentarily lit up the terrifying faces of these monsters in the dark as, with devilish smiles, their axes raised high in the air, they waited for anyone who might run out through the flames, ready to pounce on them at once.

When they saw these devastating flames, the women, children, and adolescents ran from one room to another, hoping to find a way of saving themselves. Any who, in their panic, found themselves in front of a window fell breathless under the bullets that poured in from outside.

A disheveled young woman grabbed the bars of a window and started shaking them, hoping to tear them down and throw herself out. The mob stopped shooting, in order to savor her desperate cries.

Gradually the flames spread and set fire to the woman's hair. The unfortunate Armenian, now completely beside herself, pushed her legs through the bars one by one and in vain tried to get out. The flames soon surrounded her and a couple of motionless legs hung from the window, dangling in the emptiness.

To save their wives and sisters from painful deaths, the men stabbed them and then committed suicide by thrusting the daggers into their own chests.

Other groups of them drank poison. Women threw themselves into the flames with their infants in their arms. They preferred to die honorably rather than surrender to the vile enemy.

Fortunately, it did not take long for death to release the brave Armenians. A little later the building caved in with an enormous crash, and its burnt ruins at last entombed the sorrowful mourning and weeping of the Armenians.

The mob shouted in victory and rushed forward to hack to death anyone who was still alive.

At that very minute three people suddenly emerged from the smoke, sparks, flames, and dust. Shots were fired at once and hit them from behind. Two of them died, but the third managed to disappear into the night.

That third man was Sarkis.

* * *

Just by chance Sarkis was wedged between two beams but was able to pull himself out of the burning ruins with only minor injuries. Then he ran through the deserted and ruined streets as fast as his legs would carry him.

He came to a neighborhood where the Armenian houses had not yet been destroyed. A motley crowd was busy plundering the houses, as though they were a colony of ants and the houses their nests. Hundreds of grasping thieves entered the houses and came out loaded with chairs, tables, beds, rugs, sewing-machines, pots and pans, furniture, and trunks, in other words anything and everything that the other looters left behind.

In the rush, butter oozed out of churns, syrup leaked out of jars, cracked wheat spilled from torn sacks. Lamps and mirrors broke, and china shattered into pieces.

Sarkis watched all this, stunned. For a moment he considered mixing with these criminal looters in order to cover his tracks. Then, thinking that he might be recognized and torn to pieces, he gave up the idea and turned into another street.

But he had taken scarcely a few steps when a heavy hand descended on his shoulder.

"Wait, where are you going in such a hurry?"

Sarkis tried to free himself from his captor with a sudden shake, but in vain. The soldier—for it was a soldier—put his bayonet against Sarkis' chest and barked menacingly: "Walk!"

Sarkis offered no resistance, but walked quietly with the soldier. And was taken to a jail. On the way he met several other soldiers; all with bayonets fixed to their rifles and searching the ruins for Armenians who might be concealed in hide-outs.

About 400 people were captured that way. Now they are in jail, stuffed on top of each other, and don't know what awaits them next.

A bloodthirsty Turk, who had years of experience in banditry was now the chief of the gendarmes, had the prisoners brought into the courtyard and there he killed them with unprecedented brutality. He gouged the eyes out of one, thrust a red-hot iron into the ears of another, had someone else shod with horse-shoes, and set fire to another's hair and beard.

"Hafiz!" he called out to one of the executioners: "You've studied history. You should know what kind of tortures our ancestors used to kill their slaves. Tell me a method that the Tamerlanes or Attilas might not even have thought of. I want to kill all of these accursed Armenians with unheard-of tortures.

"Don't worry, sir. Leave it to me."

The prisoners who overheard this conversation panicked when they heard the executioner's footsteps approaching them. A moment later the prison door opened. The prisoner behind the door had no room to retreat. The hyena called Hafiz caught the first Armenian by his collar, as if catching a chicken, and led him from the room. The prisoners waited breathlessly inside, bathed in a cold sweat. From the loud exchanges of the policemen they learned that they had undressed their victim, made him lie down on the stairs, and tied him firmly by the arms and legs.

Suddenly a blood-curdling scream pierced the silence, making them all shudder.

"For God's sake, please have mercy on me . . . I'm burning. Please save me . . ."

"What's that you're shouting, *kiafir* (infidel)?" taunted the bandit chief.

"I'm dying, I can't stand it!"

"Does it hurt much?"

"Yes, too much . . . "

"Hey boys," the executioner called his assistants, "do you hear that? it hurts too much . . . . Take the fire off his chest and put it on his navel."

"Oh, God, my bowels . . .," yelled the victim.

"What's that? Does it hurt again?" the wicked rascal asked with cruel sarcasm. "My friend, how delicate you are! I didn't know. Hey boys, turn him over and put the fire on his back."

"Aye . . . aye . . . ooof . . ."

Gradually the voice of the victim died away. The bitter smell of burnt flesh filled the air, reaching the farthest corners of the cell. Then they heard the sound of heavy jack-boots approaching the door.

* * *

By killing fifteen or twenty Armenians every day with unprecedented tortures, there is no doubt that within a few weeks this devil of a monster would not have left a single Armenian alive there, had not a young officer turned up one day to protect them.

The policemen, who had already confiscated the valuables of the Armenians, brought the prisoners to the prison yard, made them strip down to their underwear, and handed them over to the officer.

Under the surveillance of twenty soldiers this white-clad group got on the road, looking like convicts sentenced to death, and after walking for a long time they stopped in a dense forest.

The soldiers undid the hands of a dozen prisoners, gave them spades and shovels, and ordered them to dig a trench between two trees, eight arm-lengths long and one arm-length wide, piling the earth on one side.

"The accursed Moscows (Russians) are coming," they said, and laughed: "Let them come . . . And if they make it this far, they'll suffer the consequences."

When Armenians heard that they were digging the trench in preparation for combat (and not as their own grave), they were happy and worked with enthusiasm, in the meantime praying and wishing from the bottom of their hearts that wherever the Russians were they would come and free them with a surprise attack.

After that trench was dug, the soldiers gave the spades and shovels to the second dozen prisoners and ordered them to dig a second trench two meters away, parallel to the first and again between two trees.

Then a third, a fourth, and thus more than 25 trenches—when the digging was finished, the soldiers tied the prisoners' arms together, twelve people in each group, and then tied these human chains from tree to tree in such a way that they stood immobile on the edges of the trenches they had just finished digging.

The young officer moved forward, put his finger on an Armenian's heart, and said to the soldiers gathered around him: "Aim right here, so they die at once."

A soldier stood at the end of each row of condemned prisoners and passed from one victim to the next, stabbing them with his dagger. The Armenians let out muffled cries and fell into the trench .

"Aim exactly at his heart, just like that, at the heart!" roared the officer, inciting the soldiers. "Take care! Right at the heart."

A dagger also glittered over Sarkis' heart. He cried out pitifully and fell on his back.

* * *

When Sarkis regained consciousness, he realized that his heart was beating like that of a breathless pigeon. He rubbed his eyes and found himself in a terrible situation. A layer of earth and grass covered his body and there were a dozen or so corpses on each side of him, lying helter-skelter—the head of one was resting on Sarkis' stomach, the leg of another was right under his chin.

Just to make sure that he wasn't dead, he tried to move, but did not succeed. First of all, he had lost a great deal of blood, and then his arms were tied to those of the corpses.

How long he had remained in that position he did not know. Considering that the corpses had not yet rotted and that it was daylight, he surmised that it had been either a few hours or a whole night since the horrific crime.

His first thought was to find a way out of that foul-smelling grave. But how could he manage to undo the knots around his arms? Also, he was wearing nothing but a bloodied shirt.

Since the soldiers had tied them above their elbows, he could use his hands freely. He couldn't extend his forearm, however, because of the deadly weight on both sides, which forced him to remain immobile. He had only one weapon: his teeth. His head bent on his shoulder, Sarkis made supernatural efforts to get the knot on his arm into his mouth. And at last he succeeded. He bit on the rope for hours until finally he bit through it. Then he pushed the corpses away with his feeble arms and climbed out of the trench. He had no strength left. He could move no more. And he fainted again and lay there on the ground.

It was already dark when Sarkis regained consciousness. This time he managed to crawl away, and he headed into the depths of the forest, where he knew there was a spring. When he got there, Sarkis plunged his burning forehead into the water and lay for hours next to the spring.

That pure water and the grass were an elixir for this young Armenian. After ten days, like a ghost rising from the dead, he got up and dragged himself along for an hour, until he reached a cave. He spent another week there, until he recovered completely and was able to flee that hellish country, where he had twice escaped certain death.

As he was walking through a wide valley, his attention was drawn to a flock of crows and vultures in the sky. With a wild din they were swooping down and then soaring high up in the sky over almost the same spot. The blowing wind carried a foul stench to his nose. Curious, he walked in that direction and stopped, horrified, before a hideous scene. The bottom of the valley was covered with female corpses, all of them dismembered, one more terrifying than the other.

Ravenous two-legged monsters had visited the site before these ravenous birds . . .

Young adolescent girls with their breasts cut off; young women with their vaginas stuffed with stones and branches; girls scarcely 12 years old lying in pools of blood. Even in their eternal silence they proclaimed the ghastly butchery they had been subjected to.

Here and there women's heads hung from trees by their hair. These women must have offered resistance, leading the assassins to cut off their heads to make examples of them for the rest. In one place lay a pregnant woman whose abdomen had been slit wide open with a dagger. The bloody barbarians had poured the fire of their hatred even on the embryonic creature within her. In yet another place there was a woman who had been disemboweled—but this was the work of jackals, as there were still twelve gold pieces glittering . . .

Sarkis could not bear to look on this horrendous scene of carnage any longer. In all of history, nothing like it had ever been recorded.

For days he walked through deserted, uninhabited fields, gardens, and villages where there was neither noise nor movement. In these once joyful fields of Moush, he heard no roosters crow. Nor did he hear the bleating of lambs, the flutes of shepherds, or the melodious voices of beautiful maidens. All of them were gone, and in their place remained ruined houses, charred beams, corpses, and more corpses.

Along the side of the road he saw hundreds of heads mounted on long poles—like road signs indicating the bloody route which the suffering people of Armenia had trodden.

Terrified, Sarkis took another road, but wherever he went he was confronted with the same horrifying landscape of corpses and ruins.

He tried to avoid any other human being as he traveled. He was sure that whoever he might meet in his loneliness would be no less than the vampire in human guise who had sucked the life-blood from his people.

He fed himself on wild fruit and grass. Sometimes when he passed a field he picked a few ears of wheat and ate them. But they were all empty: harvest time had passed and the grains had fallen to the ground. And the harvesters were harvested before the harvest . . .

Sarkis continued on his way, always heading South, never looking back. One day, while he was crossing a deserted glen, he noticed a group of people on the opposite side of the road. At first he thought they were wandering gypsies, but on closer examination he found that they were women who had escaped the massacres.

These were the first living Armenians he had seen since being buried alive. And so it was with joy that he crossed over to his compatriots and received from them some bread and rags, allowing him to fill his stomach and cover his nakedness.

There he met the only male member of the caravan, his friend Karekin. He was disguised as a woman, and this had saved him from several massacres. He and his countrywomen were heading for the place where all the Armenians went after escaping massacres, carnage, and torture.

Sarkis joined them and, after torturous travels, at last, one day, they reached Rakka before they died.

There he learned about the massacres in the province of Paghesh (Bitlis), which took place under horrible conditions. Not a single person out of a population of 15,000 Armenians was saved. The monks—more than 200 friars and close to 1,000 novices—from the surrounding monasteries were slaughtered during the night. The captured Armenian women—even ten-year-old girls—were subjected to acts of debased passion and then burnt amid the straw. The evil fate of Armenian children . . . all of them drowned in rivers or thrown from precipices. Young brides were raped and their infants torn to pieces before their mothers' eyes.

The Turks likewise exterminated the inhabitants (more than 100,000) of the plain of Moush: the men through massacres, the young women by abduction, and the rest thrown into the river Tigris.

Only a few people were saved in Sasoun. Out of 30,000 Armenians who were surrounded in the city, only 3,000 were able, after a heroic fight, to cut through the enemy lines and take refuge in the mountains. There they defended themselves against thousands of Kurdish marauders and the regular government forces for days. Finally, seeing that they were running out of food and ammunition, they tried to fight their way out *en masse*—even the women and young boys, armed with countless stones and knives. They attacked the enemy, but very few succeeded in breaking through the encircling blockade. As for the rest, after bloody hand-to-hand combat, they fell on the field of honor.

* * *

Sarkis and his friend roamed far and wide in the desert of Deir Zor, searching for jobs. No matter where they applied, though, or what they tried their hands at, they couldn't find regular means of making a living.

They worked as porters in various villages and towns; they worked as unskilled laborers, they even became shepherds, tending the flocks of Bedouins and living in tents.

In the winter they suffered from famine, illness and death, but four times more severe and wide-spread than our experience in Syria.

Despite the fact that the winter ended and spring arrived, the conditions of the Armenian people did not change. Sarkis and his friend saw Armenians everywhere who were selling their children, mothers who fed their loved ones corpses, and abandoned orphans who no longer looked human—they wandered around like pack animals—from Deir Zor, Mosul, Rakka, and Baghdad.

To end the suffering of those on the verge of death once and for all, the government came up with a monstrous idea: how would it be possible to bring together all the Armenians then spread them in the four corners of the desert?

The answer was not long in coming. The government knew full well how the famished people thought. If they heard that they were giving out free bread somewhere, they would rush to the place, even if they were a month away.

In every village and town the town-criers announced that flour and money had arrived from America and was to be distributed among the refugees. Those interested should therefore assemble in Deir Zor, to facilitate distribution.

For people in the grip of famine, this news was more than they had hoped for. And *voilà!*—from every corner of the desert diseased living skeletons, pitiable wrecks, began heading for Deir Zor, one after the other.

Among these naive pilgrims were Sarkis and Karekin; like everyone else, they fell into the trap without a doubt that they were going of their own free will.

They had almost reached their destination when by chance, on the road to Deir Zor, they came across a couple of Chechens whom they recognized from Rakka and Ras-el-Ain as bloodthirsty killers.

The presence of these two Armenian-devouring monsters in a place where they were going to receive favors raised some doubts in the minds of the Armenians. Sarkis and Karekin sensed danger at once, and revealed their fears to their traveling companions. But the latter— close to thirty people—laughed at their needless concern and continued on their way, completely convinced of the sincerity of the government. But the two friends turned around and walked in the opposite direction, having decided to wait for a week and see how things turned out.

But they didn't have to wait even for a day. In the morning of the same day, hundreds of Chechen and Enezé highwaymen rounded up more than 60,000 refugees and drove them under cracking whips, along the bank of a out-of-the-way river toward the interior of the desert.

Only then did the people understand that they were trapped, but it was too late for them to run away.

More than 1,000 brutish louts waded into the crowd and began to hit right, left, and center, crushing skulls and slitting stomachs.

Frightening screams, heart-rending cries, violent laughter, and fierce roars resounded. *Yataghans* flashed in the air, hatchets rose and fell, and the ageless dry sands of the desert soaked up rivers of Armenian blood for the first time.

Only about 100 fortunate ones were saved from this horrific carnage. The others were mercilessly slaughtered and thrown into the waves of the river.

The head-men had previously taken around 7,000 orphans from the caravan. And on the day of *Kurban Bayram* (the Muslim feast of sacrifice) they poured kerosene on their tents and burned them all alive—hoping to be cleansed of their sins by offering this sacrifice to the Prophet.

After hearing and seeing this, Sarkis and Karekin fled those accursed regions and, after several dangerous adventures, arrived in Aleppo.

Then, afraid of being captured some day and sent back to Deir Zor, they fled to Damascus one night by hiding under a train car. But there also they found the doors of the city locked. So they continued their journey and in this way arrived in Jeresh.

* * *

Sarkis' story moved us so much that we had no strength left to listen to Karekin's. It was already late at night. We put off hearing the story until another time, gave our guests a blanket, and told them to go and sleep in the vacant area between the sheep fold and the chicken coop.

They gleefully grabbed the blanket—something they hadn't seen for a year—and went to the spot we had designated. But did they sleep? I don't know. As for me, I couldn't shut my eyes all night.

* * *

6 November, 1916

The following is Karekin's story:

One evil day they arrested all the intellectuals, party members, and prominent citizens of Trebizond. Among those arrested was Karekin's father, who was a businessman and liked by everybody. Under the pretext that they were being sent to Samsoun, they were all put aboard cargo ships and the ships left the harbor. That night they returned— the prisoners had all been drowned.

After the elimination of the city's leading citizens, the government issued an order that the rest of the Armenian population, without exception, should get ready to leave for Mosul in three days.

The Armenians were busy with their preparations when policemen appeared in the streets and proclaimed that Armenians were not allowed to sell furniture and had to leave the city immediately. A moment later they moved from words to actions, removing people from their homes by force, forming several caravans of thousands of people, and driving them out of the city.

None of the naked and barefoot people in any of these caravans would get beyond the bloody region known as Gumishkhané. All of them would be mercilessly slaughtered by Laz and Turkish marauders.

Karekin's caravan, which also contained his mother and sister, traveled for two days without incident. In the evening of the third day, they had just camped in an open field when they had the misfortune of meeting a Turkish cavalry captain who was riding toward them, accompanied by two soldiers. When the captain saw them he turned aside, had a short conversation with the police chief, and then approached the crowd and shouted: "Stand up! Separate the men from the women."

The tired crowd, which had settled down to rest, got to their feet. Some quickly swallowed the food they had in their mouths; others dropped scraps of bread from their hands and obeyed the captain's order instantly.

The Turk examined the men for a moment, then walked over to the women, asked the names of those he fancied, and wrote them in his notebook. Then he ordered the people to rest. He joined the police, who were setting a table, putting meat on skewers and slicing melon and watermelons.

After eating a good meal and draining many glasses of liquor in response to toasts, the captain and the police chief rose from the table and walked over to the caravan, and the captain ordered the women whose names he had written down to come forward.

When nobody moved, he said in a gentle, sweet voice, "There's no need to panic. I have something important to tell you. Believe me, it's to your advantage."

"Say whatever you have to say: we're listening," replied a few brave women. "Why do you want the girls to come forward?"

"I'm not a cannibal. What harm could there be in coming forward?" said the officer in brutal reproach.

"Up on your feet!" the police chief ordered impatiently. "It's no use trying to resist. You'll only force the captain to take a different tone with you."

In order to save their parents from further tortures and beating, the girls—among whom was Karekin's sister, Kohar—stood up, hesitantly went forward, and stood before the officer, who had become livid with rage and crossed his arms on his chest.

"Why didn't you do what I told you?" he asked after a short, dreadful silence.

"Please excuse us, sir, but we were afraid," answered a beautiful young woman on behalf of the entire group.

"But I told you that I was asking for your own good."

"Excuse us, sir. Pardon us," the girls stammered, focusing their eyes shyly on the ground.

"Just to prove that I'm a good man who wishes you well, I forgive you all," the officer replied in a sincere voice.

"Thank you, sir. We're grateful."

"Now listen to my advice," he continued, resuming his habitual calmness. "Of course you must have heard why you are being deported. 'To settle the Armenians in the Arabian desert,' you'll probably say; but that's just a reason to pull the wool over your eyes. The real aim of the government is to annihilate the Armenian people completely, and that goal is not far from being realized. I'm sorry for you because of your beauty and youth. If you agree to convert to Islam and come with me to the city, I promise to save you from the horrible slaughter that inevitably awaits everyone who travels on this road."

"Captain, we all know that we have been sentenced to death, sir," replied the brave Armenian girl. "But what good is it to us if we are saved and our parents and relatives are massacred elsewhere? Isn't it better for us all to die together rather than live and suffer the pain of their bitter fate?"

"Miss, from your manner of talking so freely and calmly I gather that you take my words very lightly and that perhaps you think I was trying to mislead you when I referred to the threat of slaughter that awaits you. Listen well to what I say. I'm on my way back from there . . . I swear on my honor that at the end of this road a terrible fate awaits you."

"We want to be martyred with our parents," the girl answered categorically.

"But you'll regret your decision when you see the irregular troops armed with hatchets at the entrance to the narrow gorge. I'm warning you for the last time: are you going to come with me of your own free will?"

"We won't be separated from our parents."

"I get it . . ."

With a bitter expression the officer turned to his adjutants and ordered them to tie up the rebels.

Then the officer suddenly jumped forward.

After a moment of protest, the air was filled with moans and wailing, cries, yells, and screams, mixed with the cracking of whips, the detonation of rifles, the din of soldiers, and the sound of threats.

Then the commotion of the victims and executioners gradually gave way to sobs and whispers. In an hour everything was wrapped in deadly silence and darkness.

* * *

The caravan got on the move again the next day.

As they crossed a river, they looked down from the bridge and saw many corpses abandoned to the whirling motion of the waves, floating down to the deep waters of the Black Sea like logs.

Every hour and every minute, with every step, they moved forward in fear of encountering the irregulars described by the debauched captain.

They knew that the famous army of marauders was created to exterminate the Armenian people. They knew how these diabolic monsters skinned alive the victims who fell into their hands; they knew how these savages could decapitate a person with a single blow of the hatchet, how they could split a human body in two with their swords, how they dismembered or skinned people alive or tied them to trees and sacrificed them.

There was no sign of these monsters, but the road gradually became more mountainous and the number of corpses floating in the river kept increasing, indicating that they couldn't be far away.

Indeed, it was not long before they saw one of the hideous creatures in the bend of a winding part of the road, which was hemmed in by huge rocks. When he caught sight of the caravan he ran down from an elevation to block the road.

He was wearing a gray uniform and carried a hatchet with a short handle, and there was a gun at his waist. The horrible appearance of this executioner filled each of them with the fear of death. Their faces turned white in a flash and their knees began to tremble.

"Halt!"

The deadly order of the irregular soldier filled the air like the poisonous hiss of a terrifying snake. They all stood frozen in their footsteps.

The jackal approached the police chief and talked to him in a very low voice, occasionally glaring poisonously at the caravan he had just stopped. They whispered together for ten minutes, torturing the people and making their blood run cold.

At last the police chief ordered: "All males over ten years old step away from the women."

The men understood the meaning of the order at once. Nevertheless, under the influence of some strange moral force, they moved aside with no objections. Karekin, who had disguised himself as a woman in the dress and white hair of a dead relative, did not move, however.

The police examined the women carefully to make sure there were no males left among them, and used their whips to force them back on the road, making them leave their husbands, brothers, and young sons—approximately 400 people—behind.

On the opposite side of the gorge, on a plateau divided by a deep abyss, they noticed about ten tents, and a while later they saw their loved ones who had been taken from them not so long ago. They were being herded in the direction of those tents by the pitiless irregulars.

Although there was a wide gap between their road and the plateau, they could clearly see ten or twelve irregulars coming out of the tents.

They gathered around their leader and listened to him while the crowd of prisoners passed slowly in front of them, heading for the edge of the abyss. A little later the irregular soldier at the head of the caravan joined his friends. In the meantime, one could hear a regular sharp noise, no louder than the ticking of a clock, and the black mass that surmounted the edge of the abyss like a living fortress began to collapse.

"Machine guns . . ."

Cries from hundreds of female throats echoed from valley to valley.

The police whipped the women to keep them moving along. But those who managed to avoid the police still saw everything that the irregular fighters did.

Other irregulars came out of the tents and joined the first group. They ran over to the wounded, killed those who were still alive with blows from their hatchets, and pushed them into the river, which was at the bottom of the abyss.

After a while the women, who had watched the slaughter of their loved ones, heard horses galloping up behind them. Frightened, they turned to see what was happening. They saw four guerrillas on horseback race up to the police chief and yell rebukes at him.

"Where are you taking the caravan? . . . we haven't received compensation yet!"

"Compensation?"

"Yes, we were ordered to kill the Armenians with our hatchets and swords . . . but we killed them an easier way. They should have to pay for the bullets we used."

"A curse on all of you . . . you blood-thirsty monsters . . . you killed our husbands and our children . . . and now you come and expect us to give you money?" shouted the women, raising their fists in the air. "May you all burn in hell, you bloody beasts! Go away . . . get lost . . . we have no money to give to dogs like you."

"Then give us your jewelry," the irregular shot back with indifference.

"We have nothing, you insane, wicked, senseless creatures!"

"We know how to get compensation."

The guerrillas dismounted, waded into the crowd and, under the pretext of looking for money and jewelry, undressed thirty or so women; then, after killing two of them, they grabbed the ones they liked, about nine of them, and took them away . . .

Three days later, the crowd of women and unprotected children again arrived at the banks of a river. There Turkish and Kurdish robbers surrounded the caravan, chose the beautiful women, and took them into the mountains. Those who resisted were stabbed to death. Others threw themselves into the river—preferring to drown than to fall into the hands of those savages.

On another day armed peasants surrounded the caravan in an open field and took away all the girls under the age of ten.

A little farther down, they saw a mass of naked male corpses in an untilled field. Their executioners had taken everything but a black tie, which was discarded as a useless object near the foot of a corpse.

The next day they passed through a deserted village, the name of which they could not discover, as there was not even a single living soul there. If a horrible earthquake had leveled the village to the ground, they wouldn't have felt so very despondent as they did now, at the sight of deserted houses with their doors and windows all shut up. As they passed in front of them not even the sound of a whisper was heard. The barren, deserted streets were frightening. Even the dogs had run away.

And so it continued day after day, as they passed through scenes of massacre, theft, and death. They continued on their way, along forsaken rough paths and tracks, through abandoned villages, on dilapidated roads. Those whom fatigue or illness prevented from walking with the caravan were shot by the police like diseased dogs.

Karekin's mother was one of the ones who suffered this tragic fate. Unable to withstand the harsh conditions of their march, she fell on the road one day, ready to draw her last breath. Karekin carried her for quite a while, but when he stopped for a moment to catch his breath a brute of a gendarme rushed up to him on his horse and shot his mother before his eyes. The gendarme didn't want Karekin to use his mother's frailty as an excuse to fall behind and then find a way to escape.

The next day Karekin met Sarkis, and the rest of the story is already known.

13 November, 1916

Government inspectors have already come to register the Armenians. We have been told that the government's intention is to move the Armenians somewhere else. A good number of families from

Dera and Irbit have already been put on the road and sent to the northern parts of the Hauran.

If this relocation comes to pass, the Armenians who are still alive will suffer a deadly blow. Everybody here is more or less settled, and it will be extremely hard to go to unknown regions again and try once more to settle and find work.

In order to have some money in our pocket in case there is a surprise forced deportation, we sold our winter wheat reserve today.

The tradesmen are liquidating their shops. But it's hardest on the gardeners. They find it difficult to leave everything they have grown through months and months of hard work completely abandoned.

After all, wealthy or not, we are all living a life that is nothing but a nightmare.

20 November, 1916

The satrap of our village, the Kurdish corporal, put several unemployed families, close to 100 people, on the road to uninhabited corners of the desert the other day, even before receiving the relocation orders. The condition of these poor people was shocking. Many of them didn't even have a shirt to protect them from the cold.

Sixteen of those who left had already been deported from here before. But at that time—seven months ago—the rest were spared relocation because they had regular jobs. But now illness has put them in an impossible situation. They have been sent away as annoying vagrants.

Who knows whose turn it will be next?

28 November, 1916

It has been a year since we were deprived of my father's gentle voice and smile.

He is no more. And to guide our inexperienced steps in this life-and-death struggle we need his wisdom and intelligent advice now more than ever.

He had a pure heart, a heart of gold, which beat for everybody, without any ethnic or family prejudice. He would put himself in danger anywhere, without hesitation. Like the time on the road to Indje Sou when he saw me being beaten by the highwaymen, flew out of the carriage like a fearless eagle, and took all the blows intended for me.

But is it not tragic that in this chaos that has become our life we have never had the chance to visit his grave? Besides, we don't even know where he's buried. Somewhere in the ruins, but under what stone, under what bush?

Father, forgive us! Even if the plot of land that you still occupy in this world has been lost, you can be sure that your memory will remain undying in our hearts.

May these lines transform our gratitude and love into an eternally green wreath on your unknown burial plot.

4 December, 1916

We received two pieces of good news today. The first was that the mass relocation of the Armenians has been postponed, but the second is even more important: Germany has proposed peace. And so, if the Allies accept Germany's proposal, the war will come to an end, and with it the massacres, famine, disease, and, finally, the deportations.

Everybody is happy, especially the interpreters of the good book, who shout triumphantly at everyone they see: "You see! So you were making fun of us? Perhaps our prediction was a bit delayed, but it was a good one!"

We hope that is the case. But there is a worrisome question: Germany and its allies are proposing peace not because they have been defeated, but because they wish to prevent further bloodshed. So if the Allies refuse the conditions of the peace treaty, Germany is still capable of continuing the war under uncertain conditions.

11 December, 1916

Unpleasant news is being circulated, but the news is always contradicted. After waiting very impatiently for a week, today we learned from the newspaper that people from Damascus receive, that Germany's proposal has been refused.

It would have been absolutely crazy for us to expect goodness in this world. At the moment people are more discouraged and morally shattered.

We tried to buy back the wheat that we sold because we feared relocation, at three times the price.

18 December, 1916

Government officials resumed their harassment tactics.

The man at the top has made it his duty to visit the market and fine the Armenian shopkeepers, and then put the money in his own pocket. The corporal arrests Armenians on the slightest pretext and threatens them with deportation until he receives a bribe. The police continue to misuse the paper money. In the village there is neither law nor court, and naturally no court cases.

Today we were at Sarko the butcher's shop. A policeman came by and bought a couple of oranges from Arshag from Adana, who always sits in front of the butcher shop. After putting the fruit in his pocket, he gave Arshag a banknote and asked for 97 coins in change. Naturally Arshag couldn't give him 97 coins and a couple of oranges to boot for a bill that is worth only 35 coins. So he said that he had no change and the policeman could pay him some other time.

But as soon as he said that the whip descended on his forehead and then he was savagely kicked between the legs, in the testicles. He toppled to the ground as if struck by lightning. Then the policeman stepped over him, grabbed him by the shoulder, pulled him to his feet, put the sack of oranges on his back, and, as if he had captured a criminal, led him to prison, beating him all the way.

Now this poor Armenian's wife and children should be waiting for their father to bring home some bread this evening . . .

25 December, 1916

I see starving children in the streets. They stretch out their hands to every passer-by. I also see embarrassed women, who ask for help with pleading expressions. These scenes cause me a great deal of pain. What can I do for them besides giving them a piece of bread? How can a small crumb be any help in the face of such misery, which has spread like an epidemic?

I looked around. On our streets alone I counted eleven beggars, huddling against the low walls to protect themselves from the bitter wind and ceaselessly asking for help. It makes no difference to them if no one pays any attention to their pleas.

With tears in my eyes I see them every day, and I always find new faces among them. The old faces die, disappear, and new ones replace them. In a few weeks they also will disappear and leave their places to others.

This is a horrible tragedy, which we look upon today as spectators but in which tomorrow, perhaps, we may become the actors.

1 January, 1917

The year 1916 has also gone, taking with it hundreds of thousands of Armenians, all of them consumed by famine and disease. It was no better than the previous year, which went by like this one, also taking with it millions of people, consumed by heat and the sword. Good riddance to years like these!

As I write these lines I wonder what I'll write on the first day of next year, provided I'm still alive: "When 1917 went, it took with it all division among nations"? Or perhaps: "It took with it the worries and pains of the Armenian people"? The former is more likely, as there isn't a single spark of hope that the cup of suffering has yet been filled.

How long? How long will it take for the cup of atonement to fill? Will that day ever arrive, to put an end to our hellish existence?

Oh, freedom! How sweet it sounds on our lips. Through the mists of our imagination, we always see your shining beacon. We march, we march, day and night, to reach you. Every day thousands of us fall exhausted on your thorny road. How many? How many of us will succeed in attaining you? Does it really matter, if we all die of exhaustion on your threshold?

8 January, 1917

No doubt there is a curse on the ancient room in our courtyard. The woman from Adana and her daughter have gone. Now another woman from Marash and her four daughters have rented it. They also worked very hard to make a living, until typhoid fever played havoc with every member of the family.

We were all stunned when we heard a sharp cry of grief from there this morning, and ran to see what was the matter. They were all lying under an old blanket. Three of the daughters had a very high fever and were unconscious, the fourth—the one who had cried out—had fainted with her arms around her mother, whose face had turned a leaden gray, and whose eyes were shut.

In the meantime, other neighbors also arrived and had a hard time removing the arms of the unconscious daughter from her dead mother's neck. They put the mother on a stretcher and took her away.

The poor woman's hair hung down from the stretcher and wafted in the breeze like a black flag.

A countless number of people die of hunger and disease every day. Even the streets are full of half-naked hallucinating Armenian women and brave Armenian youths who have fallen on their faces and are vomiting blood.

It doesn't take a prophet to see that we're all bound to the same wheel of fortune, and that eventually we'll all share the same fate.

15 January, 1917

During the week the police put those who had died and were left lying in the streets into wheelbarrows and took them to the ruins. Eighteen of them had died of cold and hunger. The police sent a few young Armenian men to bury them in a common grave.

Today we moved to another house. Our room is damp, since it's in the basement. It has a much lower ceiling, and is much smaller. We prefer it, however, because it is much cheaper.

The first person to visit us in our new home was a woman from Aintab. She was holding her twelve-year-old daughter by the hand.

"Take my child. She's yours," she said between sobs, "I can't feed her."

We were so astounded we didn't know what to say. If we took the girl now, who would come to *our* assistance tomorrow? And if we refused, we had no doubt that the mother would give her daughter to a Muslim.

As we had no choice, we gave the woman a *medjidiye* and told her to keep the daughter until she spends all the money, and to come back if she still has no work by that time.

This woman was followed by a lot of other beggars, who had quickly learned of our new address. It's the same every day. Hundreds of poor people knock at our door. How can we help all of them? We don't know either.

This winter the misery of the Armenian refugees has reached it peak.

22 January, 1917

The number of homeless people is constantly rising. Today on our way to the market we met our former neighbor, Panos Aghpar, among others. He was thrown out by his landlord and disappeared for a long time.

"Bread," he murmured, focusing his feeble eyes on the passers-by.

No one paid any attention to him. On the contrary, everybody was happy that another of these "unwanted" people was disappearing.

We returned home and got our former neighbor a slice of bread.

Panos Aghpar grabbed the bread from our hands and put it in his mouth. He couldn't eat it, though, because he no longer had the strength to bite, chew, and swallow it. Holding the bread in his hand, he kept repeating: "Give me bread, bread . . ."

We asked him where his wife and child were. He gazed at us in bewilderment, and in a voice from beyond the grave moaned: "Give me bread."

29 January, 1917

Bent under the weight of the wood she had collected, she was coming down the mountain, breathless and sweating. Her tender hands and feet were bleeding because of the thorns and stones. I bought her wood, and we went to our house.

She was barely 18 years old, with blonde hair and blue eyes, and she had a very beautiful face. Her polite manners and intelligent conversation aroused my interest. I asked who she was.

"I'm the daughter of a well-known family from Deort Yol," she said. "My father died on the road during the deportation, and my mother and two brothers died in Mejdel, where we settled.

This Armenian girl told us that she had been left alone and had no other means of survival than carrying wood from the mountain with other women from Yazdi, and earning her living that way.

"I have one worry, though," she said, furrowing her brow. "Now I am healthy and can work, but if I ever get sick . . ."

Ah, illness! The dread of those who are alive and well!

5 February, 1917

Today I worked all day long—my fingers were bleeding—at sewing a pair of shoes for myself.

Here all the Armenians makes their own shoes out of a thick piece of cloth and a few feet of rope, which is first folded and sewn to a piece of cardboard cut in the shape of the sole of a shoe. Then the sole is covered with the cloth, instead of leather, and the result is a splendid pair of sandals, which even Christ would covet if He were still alive!

I put on my shoes and examined myself from head to foot, counting sixteen patches on my pants and more than twenty on my jacket. I regretted that we hadn't yet found an easy method to make clothes from scratch. How I wish I could get rid of these clothes, which are fit only for a scarecrow.

"Please pity the poor . . ."

I suddenly woke up from my thoughts and saw an old man in rags who had stretched out his trembling palm and was asking me for bread.

As if this Armenian refugee had come to teach me a lesson, I examined him carefully and saw he was wearing nothing but a tattered jacket and a pair of torn pants, leaving most of his body exposed. In other words, he had no hat, shirt, socks, or shoes. When I compared my clothes to this man's rags, I considered myself a filthy rich big shot and thought how true it is when they say that nobody would complain if he always looked around at those who are less fortunate.

12 February, 1917

They had dug a hole in the ground and turned it into a forge. The woman fanned the flames with a pair of bellows made from a goatskin bottle and the muzzle of a rifle. Meanwhile, her husband was hammering a red-hot piece of iron on an anvil. With each blow of the hammer the anvil sank into the ground, and five minutes later it was buried in the ground.

In the old days the gypsies roamed from place to place and from village to village with their primitive tools. Since it took them at least a couple of years to go around the entire desert, their return to the same village was always a red-letter day for the peasants. Now no one paid any attention to them, because Armenian tradesmen could take care of their needs on the same day, offering the peasants a higher quality of workmanship, and with great care could quick-silver their rusted pots or forge their broken spikes.

Disappointed, the gypsies got on their donkeys in the evening and left.

The Circassians watched them depart with loud laughter; did they remember the days before the arrival of the Armenians in the Hauran when they desperately waited for the gypsies' arrival?

19 February, 1917

Mumtaz Bey, the inspector of refugees, has come to distribute things to help the poor refugees. For three days, three of my friends and I have been at the municipal building, preparing a list of the Armenians living in Jeresh. According to our list there are now 208 Armenian families in our village: a total of 743 people, of whom 500 are in need of their daily bread.

Late this afternoon Mumtaz Bey distributed 50 banknotes to those in dire need. The paper banknote is worth 30 coins at the moment. But the Damascus Arabs are taking advantage of the situation by buying them from the refugees for 25 coins each.

It was something to see the joy of these Armenians, as they grabbed their money and ran to the bakeries or other stores to shop. Some of them have been feeding themselves on grass for the past two months and haven't tasted any sweets for a year and a half. Most of them bought bread and syrup made of grape juice, and ate with insatiable appetites.

On seeing the enthusiasm of our compatriots we hoped the following: that at least this act of kindness on the part of the government, which is a drop in the bucket compared to the priceless fortune seized from the Armenians, might not turn out to be another meaningless farce, like the one in Dera.

26 February, 1917

The Armenians deported as a result of actions taken by the Circassians and the Damascus Arabs returned to the village yesterday. All of them were like living shells: in pitiful condition. For around three months, they (120 people) had roamed from one village to the next, despite the cold and the rain, trying to find temporary refuge. But wherever they went they were received with hatred and beaten with sticks.

Today the police expelled them again, saying that it was forbidden for new refugees to enter Jeresh.

"But we are registered in this village; other villages turn us away. Where can we go?" asked the poor deportees.

"To hell," replied the police.

The Armenians asked for permission to live in the caves near the ruins.

"But if you ever enter the village to beg, I'll break your legs!" the Kurdish corporal threatened.

They left. In all of Arabia they can't find a piece of stone to lay their heads upon.

5 March, 1917

While we wait for bread, we are feeding others.

The refugee inspector, Mumtaz Bey, has not left since the day he distributed money to the needy. He told us that he was waiting for a fresh shipment. The money he was expecting did not arrive until today. Mumtaz Bey and his horse have been our guests for the last 18 days. He is staying in a room for which we are raising the rent. Every day his table is laden with different dishes. We could feed five orphans on the barley given to his horse alone!

With the conviction that you don't spare a hen when you expect a duck, we make all these sacrifices within our depleted means, but the duck does not arrive and Mumtaz Bey does not move even a tiny bit.

They say there is always some good in every evil. But now it seems that evil is the result of the kindness shown by the government.

12 March, 1917

At last Mumtaz Bey, the refugee inspector, left yesterday. His presence had become an unbearable burden on the well-to-do members of the community. He left after wasting half of the distribution money on himself. The shameless man didn't show the least hesitation in sharing the meager supplies we had laid up for the future. We couldn't tell him to "Get up and leave." He could have become our enemy. And if he received the supplies needed to resume his kindness, he might have refused to do it. On the other hand, we couldn't tell him to stay, because we had no means to sustain and feed him and his permanently hungry horse. All things considered, we were in a difficult situation. Now we are happy, like the man in the proverb who finds the shirt he had lost.

19 March, 1917

The question of working women and young girls is getting more difficult. If they go to the mountains to fetch wood, the thieves rob them; if they stay in the village, they can't work as anything but laborers: i.e., construction work, carrying stones and earth for a couple of coins a day. Not everybody is strong enough for such hard work, which destroys not only these delicate women, but even sturdy men.

Today we learned that our former neighbor, the girl from Adana whose mother died, has now married a Fellah, simply as a means of getting as much bread as she wants to eat. We are afraid that this girl's example may be contagious: that other women destined by unemployment to die of famine may also be infected with it.

26 March, 1917

For the second time I caught an animal climbing up my leg. It was last night. I awoke in a panic, tied a piece of string around it, took off my pants, and banged them on the floor. Then, when I was sure that the animal was dead, I carefully untied the knot and saw that the animal I had caught was a mouse.

Our room is infested with mice. They creep up and down over our faces and pillows, but until now they had never gone so far as crawling under our blankets.

As for scorpions and insects, our room could easily be called a zoo. There's a strange insect that makes such a noise at night that you think someone is fingering worry beads in the dark. Another insect hisses like a goose attacking little children. And the centipedes, millipedes, caterpillars, tumble bugs, and other kinds of creatures are too numerous to count. They crawl all over our bodies all night, often waking us and making us sit bolt upright with their disagreeable feel and their stings.

The hot days are not far away. We'll soon be suffering again.

2 April, 1917

Today is Easter.

We learned this from the police, who seize on such festive occasions to torture people. At this very moment they are going from house to house with clubs in their hands. They are sending back the Armenians from other villages who came to settle here. They have also found a new tactic: they make the Armenian *moukhtars* (elders) go around with them, so that Armenians seem to be punishing Armenians.

The police make the elders point out all the families who don't belong to the community and throw their furniture out into the street. In the meantime, the police beat everyone in the families for having entered the village.

The blood of Armenian mothers and children flows in the street.
Our Easter is red, but not because of red-dyed Easter eggs!

9 April, 1917

My brother Souren, who was suffering from malaria, is much better
now. Now it is my turn again. I have had a high fever for five days. I
feel fine one day and terrible the next. One day I have no fever, and I
scarcely have time to get myself organized when I'm back in bed again
the next day.

I'm dizzy all the time, and my legs tremble. I'm weak all over.

16 April, 1917

I still have a high fever.

After typhoid fever, malaria is the plague of the Armenians in the
desert. It gnaws at the flesh like a worm, until the body dies. Since I
get this disease so often, will I also be one of its victims?

23 April, 1917

It's time for the Bedouins to stir up trouble again: they make the
local people suffer once when they arrive in the Hauran in the spring,
and for a second time as they get ready to leave.

Recently they have become more threatening to the Armenians.
Today Armenian shopkeepers and gardeners complained to the
corporal, saying that the Bedouins buy from them and then torture
them instead of paying.

"If you knew what's good for you, you'd give them what they want
instead of being tortured like that," replied the Kurd. "What do you
want us to do? We can't spoil our harmonious relations with the
Bedouins because of you."

The Armenians also complained to one of the Bedouin chiefs who
happened to be at the market.

"Catch the thief and bring him to me," said the kind old man.

But did he stop to ask himself how an unarmed Armenian could
capture one of those monsters, who are always armed to the teeth?

30 April, 1917

I spend most of my time teaching myself French from a few books
I bought from an Armenian refugee from Adana. But I am still sick
and tired of being unemployed. So today I decided to go back into

business. But I won't open another store. I'll set up a counter in a corner of the market and sell thread, tobacco, pipes, cigarette papers, etc. There are already four Armenians doing the same thing, and they do a good business.

After making this decision, I left the village and cut four pieces of wood to use as legs for the counter. Then I came home and built my table, using a kerosene crate.

So tomorrow I'll start selling. May God protect me from the paper-money problem!

7 May, 1917

On Tuesday night I woke up screaming painfully. I wanted to get up, but I couldn't stand on my feet and fell back onto my bed—it felt as if a long needle had been thrust into my foot. My blood-curdling scream awoke my mother, sisters, brother, and aunt. They were frightened and asked what was the matter.

"I don't know;" I said, "I think I've been stung by a scorpion."

They immediately lit the lamp and searched for the nasty creature, armed with pieces of wood and shoes. In a few minutes they found the scorpion, which was running away, shaking its poisonous tail, across my mother's pillow. They attacked, and squashed it on the spot. Then they put some yogurt on the sting and put out the lamp.

It's five days since that unfortunate accident, but I still can't get to my feet. My leg is all swollen and black.

14 May, 1917

Typhoid fever, famine, and misery continue to claim young lives. Every day five or six people in the village and the caves die. The Armenian cemetery has expanded so much that the Circassians have complained. They say that the cemetery is swallowing up the ruins. So now the dead are buried in "common graves."

Today at the funeral of an acquaintance we saw one of these graves, where three men, two women, and two children were buried one on top of the other, all of them stark naked because their relatives need whatever cloth they have to cover themselves or to sell; others don't want to give the grave robbers a reason to desecrate the graves of their loved ones.

21 May, 1917

At school, when our teacher used to talk about vanished civilizations, we couldn't understand the meaning of the term. How could a civilization vanish? But it's an undeniable fact: the Arabian civilization is excellent proof—there isn't a trace of it in the Hauran today.

How could an advanced people one day revert to a primitive state? Today I was sure I got the answer. At the market I saw a couple of Armenian orphans sitting in the sun not far from my counter. They were grooming each other by catching the insects that infested each other's body in their little fingers.

I wondered what these children and many others like them, who don't know how to read or write or count and, in fact, don't even know their mother tongue, will be able to reflect of Armenian culture and civilization half a century from now, if they are lucky enough to stay alive, and if they go on living like this. And, yes, today I wondered why, when our teacher tried to explain such a simple thing, we couldn't understand it!

28 May, 1917

I hadn't seen Khacher Aghpar from Zeitoun for quite some time. I went to his garden this evening to buy a few things. The old man is still at work with his daughter-in-law and two grandchildren. At night he watches over his vegetables with a rifle in his hand, to prevent them from being stolen by the Bedouins.

In front of Khacher Aghpar's hut we witnessed a sad scene. Two Armenians were carrying a dead man down from the other side of the garden on a stretcher. Suddenly the rope holding the corpse on the stretcher broke and the corpse slid off and fell into the river. The pole bearers stopped for a moment in amazement. Then they took the corpse out of the water, laid it on the ground, and started to repair the stretcher. In five minutes, when everything was fixed, they put the dead man on the stretcher again and continued on their way, leaving a long trail of water dripping behind them.

"The body of the dead Armenian, once anointed with Holy Chrism, is now smeared in muck . . . My God, what next!" muttered Khacher Aghpar, shaking his head.

And it's true that we are living through dark days! There was a time when even dead dogs got better burials.

4 June, 1917

Sitting behind my counter at the market, I repeat over and over the names of the goods I am selling, in order to attract the attention of the passersby: "*Yalla, fetli, abar mshet, defer, ghalyon, diukhan. Yalla, ya khayyo. Fatdal, ya seydi. Shu bitdek, ya yumma. Telahon, ya bint.*" (Here you have thread, needles, combs, cigarette papers, pipes, tobacco. Come, countrymen. Come, gentlemen! What would you like, madam? Come closer, Miss). I repeat these words in all their variations so many times that even at night I say them unconsciously in my sleep.

Despite my efforts, the customers come more often to steal than to buy. They are very stupid, though. They soon give themselves away. Today, however, I had to deal with a very skillful thief. He was a Fellah from Ftdi, a nearby village. I knew his face, as I had often seen him at the market.

He approached my table and examined a clay pipe for a long time. As we couldn't agree on the price, he left. He had scarcely gone when I noticed that a comb was missing from the box. I immediately asked my cousin to keep an eye on the counter, and ran after him.

"Hey there, fellow!" I shouted, getting hold of him in the meantime. "Where do you think you're going, without paying for the comb you took?"

"What comb?" the Arab asked with an astonished look on his face.

"Have you forgotten that you picked up a comb from the table over there just now?"

"You're mistaken, my friend . . . I just looked at a pipe, but I couldn't pay that much and I didn't buy it."

"That's right, but you liked the comb, and you took it."

"In other words, you're accusing me of theft."

"No, of course not. A mature man like you would never steal. I am just reminding you of your forgetfulness."

By that time many curious Arabs had assembled around us to see what would happen. A man who looked like a chieftain, with his eyebrows raised and his hand resting on the hilt of his sword, stepped out of the crowd and said: "*Ya veled* (listen, boy), you are openly accusing this old man, who is my subject, of theft. Do you know how severe the punishment for slander is? I'm going to search him now, and if I don't find the alleged comb, are you prepared to admit to slander and suffer the punishment?"

"Yes," I replied calmly, "but will you let me search him myself?"

"Go ahead, but you see this club? . . . I'll smash your bones with it if you don't find it."

"I'm sure he has the comb," I said, and with that I started to search the upper part of his body. He was wearing a long robe that was tied at the waist with a piece of rope and he couldn't have hidden anything below the waist.

Whatever and wherever I put my hand on, I couldn't feel anything hard like a comb. I even checked his armpits and found nothing.

The accused Fellah was happy to see me fail. The chieftain was showing signs of impatience, and the shopkeepers from Damascus, who love to laugh at other people's misfortunes, started making sarcastic comments, suggesting that I look for the comb between the thief's legs.

"You can't find it, can you?" the chieftain asked, glaring at me sorrowfully.

Imagining the blows which were about to descend on me, I thought of something. Was it possible that this good-for-nothing thief had placed the comb on his shoulder? I checked there immediately. It was there.

"What's this?" I asked, grabbing the stolen comb and holding it before his eyes. "What were you saying just now?"

The shameless thief chuckled in his beard. "I was playing a joke on you," he said. "I was going to surprise you by coming back in three days and paying you."

"Forget your surprise, you miser" I yelled reproachfully. "I'm not in the mood for jokes. Scram."

The Fellah smiled and went away.

The good thing about these people is that they never get angry, no matter how much you insult them. They have no idea of shame and hence no honor. So why would they get angry?

11 June, 1917

There are so many deadly and disabling diseases that no one bothers to talk about the eye ailment that all Armenians suffer from. Because of the desert dust or the glaring rays of the sun, forty per cent of the Circassians have eye problems and three per cent of the Hauran's population are born blind. Naturally, dirt and uncleanliness also contribute to this. On the other hand, people like us, who are conscious of cleanliness, are not spared such illnesses.

Instead of beautiful, bright Armenian eyes, everywhere we go we see red, pus-filled, bleary eyes infested with black flies, which spread the infection to those who are still healthy. Fortunately, the eye problem of the Armenians is not so serious as the one troubling the Circassians. It usually goes away in ten or fifteen days, thanks to a red liquid, the secret of which only Sarkis the barber knows.

For a few days now my eyes have also been infected. I cannot open my eyelids when I wake up in the morning. They're stuck together. Outside, when I gaze at bright spots my eyes hurt. As a result, I have stayed home for the last three days.

18 June, 1917

Because of the bad weather, the wheat harvest is very small this year. Not even one bag of wheat is brought to the market all day long. Should an Arab happen to bring in half a bushel of wheat, the profiteers from Damascus snap it up immediately, then sell it to us in the winter at four times the price.

For the past three days I have been going to the end of the village so I can catch people carrying wheat before they arrive at the market, but the Damascus Arabs have also planted their employees there. If I try to avoid these men by going farther, I get quite far from the village and then instead of wheat I find thieves, and lose my money and clothing.

If you consider that I can't get wheat, even with my money, what can all the other families do, many of whom don't have a penny to spend? Their only nourishment is the grass in the fields, but these days even grass has become scarce, because of the extreme heat.

It is the evil fortune of the Armenians that in a land once flowing with milk and honey . . . everything has now dried up, including the springs.

25 June, 1917

Four days ago an Armenian refugee from Marash was driven by hunger to abandon his three-year-old daughter in a deserted field. A Circassian later found the girl and brought her to the village to hand over to the Armenians. After a long search they found her father, but in order to justify what he had done he lied, saying that he had lost her. This monster of a man took his daughter out again, this time to the mountains, and left her there. Today some women from Yazdi brought the clothes of the girl back to the village. They were all torn apart by wolf hounds.

During these past two years our physical, financial, and moral sufferings have been very onerous. We were all pleased, however, that despite all these failures and declines, theft, prostitution, and crime were still unknown among our people. But now another of our traditional values has been smeared with muck: Armenians had never been guilty of infanticide—the case of those who commit suicide with their children is altogether different—and now our images are stained with that sin too.

2 July, 1917

I was sitting beside the mill stream—I had brought half a bag of wheat to have it ground—and I was drawing a bird on a piece of paper to pass the time. I noticed two Bedouins, who were also there to have their wheat ground. They came and looked down over my shoulder to see what I was drawing.

"Do you know what this is?" I asked one of the Bedouins, showing him the picture.

He looked at it for a long while and answered: "Letters. I can't read."

His friend seemed more intelligent. He took my paper and, after examining it closely, said: "A horse."

"A horse?" asked the first Bedouin in surprise.

"Yes. Look (pointing at the bird's tail). This is the horse's head. And this (pointing at the bird's wings) is the horse's tail.

"Yes, you're right," murmured his friend. And after thinking for a moment or two he turned to me and asked, "Why did you draw this? Don't you feel sorry for the animal?"

"What animal?" I asked, confused.

"This horse," replied the Arab. "Look, it has legs, but it can't walk. It has a mouth, but it can't eat . . . that's pitiful. Poor animal!"

"But it's only a picture," I objected.

"Picture or not, it's cruel to put a breathing being on paper, where it can't breathe anymore," mumbled the Bedouin with a concerned expression on his face.

Seeing that it was useless to discuss the matter, I said no more.

But I'm still thinking. How enigmatic is the soul of the desert dweller . . . he pities the horse without breath drawn on a piece of paper, but on the other hand doesn't mind slitting the throats of humans as though they were chicken!

9 July, 1917

Mohammed was right when he treated hygiene as basic. He tried to teach cleanliness to his followers through the Muslim religion.

I toyed with these ideas today when I saw a group of Fellah women eating at the market. One of them had her child on her knees and wiped the child's bottom with earth—this is a classical method of wiping oneself: rubbing with dirt and then brushing it away—and went right on eating.

It is very common for an Arab woman walking in front of you in the street to squat suddenly on the ground. You soon notice that a river is flowing from under her skirt. The woman then gets up very calmly and, without minding that anyone might have seen her, continues on her way, as if what she has just done was the most natural thing in the world.

It is also well known that the Arabs use their wide-lipped copper vessels to wash both diapers and lambs' entrails, and then knead dough or cook food in them.

It's unfortunate, however, that these people, who live in dirt and foul stench, don't like us and mock us when they see that we don't follow their example.

23 July, 1917

We spend our days like prisoners, hoping and waiting. The only difference is that a prisoner knows when he will be released, but we have no idea.

When will we be delivered from this terrible life? A question which torments every Armenian's mind.

The holy man, Ruhji Bedros, and his followers have now focused their attention on dreams. In the morning, at the market, they ask the first man they see: "What did you dream about last night?"

And people tell each other how a glittering cross came out of the clouds and perched on the crescent; or how an eagle flew into the air with a piece of broken chain in its claws; or a how a column of fire rose on the horizon and shone its mysterious rays on Armenian faces.

"Margos has dreamt this, Pistos has dreamt that, Giragos has seen . . ."

They call on Margos, Pistos, and Giragos to recount their dreams publicly. The elucidators of the Bible interpret them, and people are encouraged to neglect their work.

While other people are dreaming of such momentous things, why do I always have nightmares instead? Since the beginning of the deportations not one night has passed in which I haven't dreamed that I have fallen into a river or a flood or am lying in a dark cave or a cemetery. Sparks ignite, executioners persecute, or skeletons surround me all the time. It's obvious that these are all impressions and reflections of everything that happens during the day. But if they convey a common truth it's this: even in his dreams the Armenian has no respite.

30 July, 1917

One day Vahram and I decided to eat some meat. This decision was almost like deciding to go to Jerusalem, as its realization required a lot of sacrifice. After all, a human being is entitled to commit at least one little folly in a lifetime. So that day we put all our business profits together and had the baker prepare us some *leh majun* with chopped meat in his oven. It was considered one of the most expensive dishes.

We sat between our two counters at the market preparing ourselves to taste this noble food, when from further down, like an alley cat sniffing food, came Muhammad Navash, the brother of one of the seven Beni Hasan chieftains (the dark Bedouins of the Hauran belong to the Beni Hasan clan, which is divided into seven sister communities, each with its own chieftain).

Navash was my friend and customer, so in order to be polite, I said, "Please join us." He rolled his sleeves and approached the food, cut himself a big piece, and put it into his mouth. We had scarcely swallowed our own bites when he finished the rest of the dish and got to his feet.

After the Bedouin left my cousin bawled me out for having invited him to share our food, but it was too late. We would have to divide a treat between ourselves on another, more opportune day.

In time we forgot this incident, but Muhammad Navash didn't. Today he came and left a little roe buck, which he had hunted on his way from the village, between our two counters.

How different the situation of the Armenians would have been if all the chieftains had even half of Mohammed Navash's manners and gratefulness.

6 August, 1917

The refugees who were forcefully taken away on Easter day came back today, after much roaming around and being subjected to massacres and miseries.

Four hours away from the village they were attacked by the Beni Sakhar clan (all of them black); seven of them were killed and the rest were robbed down to their last rag. Now they are all lying in the square at the entrance to the village, presenting a pitiful scene to the beholder. Grown men, children, women, all have been so traumatized at seeing their loved ones slaughtered before their eyes that they scream and cry whenever they see anyone armed walk toward them. Their eyes are all swollen from crying and their faces have a deathly pallor. One need not read Dante to get a picture of Hell: one glance at these blood-drained people says it all.

13 August, 1917

Without pity the police once more threw out these miserable sickly refugees, and added about fifty new undesirables.

When the deportees asked: "You are forcing us to leave, but where shall we go? What will become of us?" the corporal roared, "As long as you don't croak, there's no way out for you. So get lost. Get out of our village."

A couple of hours later there was no shame left. A Circassian who noticed that one of the refugees had left without paying his debt of two silver coins sent a policeman after the caravan and had the "Armenian rogue" brought back. But the policeman brought the entire caravan back so the Circassian could show him the guilty one. The Circassian grabbed his victim and dragged him to his field so he could work there without pay until he had worked off the debt. In the meantime, the exhausted caravan got on the way again, condemned to roam the burning deserts until it disappeared because of thirst, dehydration, and sunstroke.

20 August, 1917

Yesterday about seventy Bedouins attacked a nearby Fellah village called Kiufiurkhan to avenge the killing of a member of their clan. They exchanged bullets for about an hour on the edge of the village, and both sides suffered considerable casualties. We have many compatriots from Zeitoun and Marash in that village. We don't know what has happened to them, caught in the cross-fire between two hostile forces.

There is a rumor that the Bedouins will also attack our village.

27 August, 1917

The Bedouins are stirred up these days. After Kiufiurkhan they also raided the village of Ktdi. There was an alarm here this morning, when we heard that a huge group of Bedouins on horseback were galloping in the direction of Jeresh. The Circassians and Damascus Arabs grabbed their rifles at once and ran to the village limits in order to turn the attackers back and, if necessary, fight them. We Armenians didn't know what to do. We were at the market. A little later a policeman came, showed us a letter asking for auxiliary forces, and asked that one of us take the letter to Irbit.

Kapriel the gun-smith asked, "How can we deliver the letter when the roads are blocked?"

"That we don't know," said the policeman. "This letter must get through to Irbit . . . If not, we'll whip all of you out of the village."

Knowing that the police could use us as ransom and sacrifice us to the Bedouins, we immediately collected 74 coins and asked for a volunteer to take the letter to the governor of Irbit. Sarkis from Moush volunteered, and he and his inseparable friend, Karekin, got on the road at once (these two and six others work at the market place in a newly constructed building under the supervision of Moushegh from Sis, who is a skilled mason).

Just then we heard the deafening singing of the Bedouins, coming from the center of the village. The fight had not yet started. It seemed that they had taken up a position behind the hill and were waiting for reinforcements to arrive.

3 September, 1917

We spent every second of every minute this week under the threat of Bedouin attacks. Fortunately, the danger has almost passed, because mounted gendarmes have arrived from Irbit and are keeping the village under surveillance. Now they keep close watch on the Bedouins who come to the market in groups on the pretext of shopping. If they have the slightest doubt about anyone, they immediately arrest the suspicious person and escort him to the village limits.

Sarkis and Karekin are the heroes of the day. As a reward for their service, the Circassians gave them two pairs of used shoes and the Damascus Arabs a couple of used gowns.

When I asked Sarkis what had they done with the 74 coins, he said: "Since we never ate any nourishing food, even our bone marrow was wasting away. For the last two days now we have been eating a lot of greasy food and drinking a great deal of syrup." Syrup is the elixir of the desert. Whenever a hungry Armenian gets his hands on some money, he immediately buys some syrup to drink, believing that it will restore his lost strength.

10 September, 1917

To offset our 25-coin daily expenses, I make only 5 coins a day, in other words, one-fifth of our general expenses. And that's only our current expenses, because with the rising cost of wheat our expenses are also increasing (a bushel of wheat costs 60 coins at the moment). We try to balance our budget as much as we can with the money we receive from Constantinople and Konia, where we discovered that my maternal uncle had escaped the expulsions. And sometimes also with the money we make by selling small items woven out of wool from our beds.

The wool in our mattresses is our capital for lean days. Whenever we need money, my mother and sisters grab the spinning-wheel and knitting needles for socks and attack the mattresses. And when we go to bed at night, we feel that our mattresses have lost some of their former thickness . . . I don't really know, if our beds keep getting flatter and are finally level with the floor, what we will sell then. Perhaps our shirts! But there is nothing unusual about this. Don't we see countless examples of Armenian families who have been through the same stages?

17 September, 1917

I have been burning up with a fever of 40 degrees for a week. During all that time the fever hasn't gone down, even momentarily. My whole body hurts. My back and my waist pulsate with pain, as though I were being crushed under a huge stone.

If my malaria continues like this, it will eventually kill me. Life no longer holds any delight for me. It's strange, though: the desire to live increases from one day to the next. As if there were a mysterious force hidden deep in our soul. It keeps repeating in our unconscious: "You mustn't die . . . Live! There's still a lot to see!"

24 September, 1917

I've recovered since yesterday and have gone back to work.

Today at the market something pitiful happened. On the wall of the store right across from my counter we sometimes used to see a snake sticking its head out through a crack and watching the passers-by or resting its head on the edge of the hole and snoozing in the hot rays of the sun. Sometime after noon we heard some unusual chirping and automatically raised our heads to look in that direction, where we saw a sparrow in front of the hole. It was beating its wings frantically, and at the same time letting out pitiful shrieks. There was no doubt that the snake had hold of its legs and was trying to pull it in. The bird had opened it wings wide and was trying to remain outside the hole. After a while its wings were destroyed and folded onto its back, and the poor creature was gradually dragged through the dark aperture.

This was a small tragedy of life, but it saddened us. What a similarity there is between the helpless, mangled bird in the bloodthirsty reptile's den and the destiny of the defenseless Armenians in the den of the Turkish monster!

1 October, 1917

Every March and every September the question of the conscription of Armenians comes up again. We spend a few weeks in fear, and then we hear that the evil act has been postponed for another six months and rejoice. Last April they postponed conscription to September, in September it was postponed to March of this year, and then in March it was put off again to September.

This time, however, there is no news of a postponement. They aren't enlisting anybody, though. We spend our days worrying. We are afraid that at any moment we may be arrested and sent to Tfliye.

8 October, 1917

I was sitting in front of my counter this morning when I suddenly noticed the Kurdish corporal and two policemen heading for the end of the market. I immediately sensed danger, grabbed my counter, and ran in the opposite direction. Then I noticed that three policemen armed with bayonets had blocked the entrance of the three streets that open onto the public square, confining us like fish in the net placed by their chief.

I decided to leave my counter at the store of our compatriot, Mihran Vartanian—where I used to store it—and wait for events to develop. Before long we saw the satrap who hated the Armenians. He was walking in our direction with all the Armenians he had arrested. He was using his whip on the backs of those who were falling behind. He had started to arrest them at the entrance to the market. The group of arrested Armenians got larger as they approached us. A policeman raised his whip and ordered me to walk (he said nothing to Vartanian, as he is older).

I left the store and began to walk to the jail with the rest of the Armenians. There were more than forty of us. We were all itinerant merchants, shopkeepers, and skilled workers. We had walked more than half way when I felt somebody pulling me by the arm. I turned around. It was Setrag from Marash, winking at me to indicate "Come, follow me." At that moment the policeman who was walking next to us was busy arresting another Armenian. We took advantage of the opportunity immediately, stepping out of the procession and dashing like lightning into Sheikh Salih's store.

Sheikh Salih was an exception among the Damascus Arabs. When we arrived in Jeresh we sublet our accursed house from him. He always respected my father's memory and he always gave me fantastic discounts when I bought items to put on my counter to sell. So instead of betraying us to the police as the other Damascus Arabs had done, he received us kindheartedly. Seeing my emotional state, he said: "Don't be afraid, they are not arresting you for military service."

"Not for military service?" Setrag and I asked. We didn't believe our ears. "Then why are they arresting us?"

Sheikh Salih smiled and replied: "The police found the corpse of a Turk in a garden. He died of cholera. They are arresting you to make you bury him."

"But why do they need forty people to bury one corpse?"

"Don't you know the corporal's whims?"

Indeed, a bit later, a foul stench spread over the market. We went to investigate and saw the Armenians, some of whom had covered their noses with handkerchiefs and some with the edges of their clothes, bearing the stinking corpse of the Turkish soldier on a stretcher toward the Circassian cemetery. Meanwhile the police followed them from afar and made sure that they didn't drop the corpse and run away.

In half an hour the pallbearers came back. They told us that the pain-wracked bones of the Turkish soldier had at last been put to rest, but that his entrance to Paradise was jeopardized: the *hodja*, afraid of catching cholera, had not blessed the grave.

As life returned to normal in the market, we asked a policeman why they had arrested so many Armenians, instead of Circassians or Arabs, to bury a Muslim.

"What's the difference?" he asked, and shrugged. "Aren't you Muslims?"

Muslims? Yes, that's right . . . We had forgotten that.

15 October, 1917

I spent a sleepless night. My mother, who suffers from heart problems, suffered all day and all night and worried us tremendously. This morning I left her in the same condition and went to the market and saw that the police were again arresting Armenians.

This time the question seemed more serious. I immediately turned around and tried to escape, but a policeman came after me. "Where are you running to?" he asked, and pushed me into the group.

About 100 of us were taken to a former coffee house at the end of the market and were penned up inside, one on top of the other, like lambs.

The police locked the door and left in different directions. They returned in an hour with thirty more Armenians, who had been arrested in their homes, at the mills, and in their gardens.

Then the news spread that those who had been arrested would be conscripted and would leave in a few hours. Automatically I put my hand in my pocket. I had four coins and fifteen *para*. It was not possible to live, even for a couple of days, with only that much money. With the intention of getting a message to my family, I made my way to the only window of the building, but what with the crowd of wailing and weeping women who had gathered outside and the police who were whipping them, I couldn't find a single familiar face to entrust my request to. During this moment of hopelessness, I suddenly noticed my Circassian friend passing by on the other side of the square.

"Reshid Bey! Reshid Bey!" I shouted after him.

The women outside echoed my voice. And Reshid Bey crossed over to talk to me.

"What's this crowd? Why are you in jail?" asked my friend in surprise.

"Reshid Bey, they've arrested us to be soldiers. They're taking us to Dera a bit later. My mother is seriously ill at home. Please, can you get permission for me from the corporal to delay a week? I can get the money you need to arrange it."

"Don't worry, I'll take care of it," said Reshid Bey. Then he turned to the guards and asked, "Where's your commanding officer?"

"He's at the town hall," replied the guard, arranging himself in "on-guard" position.

My Circassian friend left, and in a quarter of an hour he showed up again with written permission exempting me from military service for a week. Reshid Bey had obtained the permission for two silver coins. We went home together, and I paid him immediately.

After Reshid Bey left I didn't even have a chance to catch my breath. My mother, who had heard about my arrest from the neighbors, had another attack and fainted. My sisters and brother couldn't have done anything. And Arshag had run away to Mejdel. I lied to my mother, assuring her that conscription had once again been postponed for six months. Then I had my meal and went to bed, completely exhausted.

This evening they took away all the arrested Armenians.

22 October, 1917

The good news tore through the village like lightning. The conscription of Armenians has in fact been postponed for another six months.

Those who had already been taken to Dera came back late last night.

The Armenians of Jeresh are celebrating.

29 October, 1917

Our insignificant village of two years ago is gradually gaining in importance, first because of its size, and then because it is getting closer to the battle front.

Workers from Irbit arrived today to convert one of the buildings near the market into a telegraph office. Along the roads Armenian laborers are working, putting up telegraph poles. They want to connect Jeresh to Salt (Al Balqa) and Irbit by telegraph facilities.

Every day hundreds of soldiers pass through here on their way to the front. The Turkish soldiers always talk about victory and say that the Russian army in the Caucasus has been decisively defeated and that they are now heading for Persapé (Persepolis) to take care of the English. A Turkish woman was among the soldiers who came through today. Perhaps her officer husband was taking her with him to visit the pyramids and the pharaohs' tombs after they have captured Egypt!

5 November, 1917

When we listen carefully in the silence of the night, we hear deafening noises coming from very far—it seems to be the din of cannons being fired. These roars are sometimes faint and at other times very loud. We assume that we are near a battlefield and that the loud noises are made by British artillery, the faint ones by Turkish—simply because the British cannons are directed at us, whereas the Turkish ones are aimed in the opposite direction.

The local people, however, insist that the British are very far from us and that it's impossible to hear the explosions of artillery all the way from the battlefield. According to them, a battalion of laborers are using dynamite to clear the way for the roads they are building, or perhaps the Turkish army is carrying out maneuvers in the region of Salt. The Armenians don't believe the locals' speculations, but they don't want to argue with them either, thinking that such disputes might turn against us. The optimists are happy, hoping that the British will arrive and liberate us. The pessimists are worried, because they assume that before the British arrive the soldiers of the retreating Turkish army will take out their vengeance on us.

At any rate, do you think we're on the eve of decisive events?

12 November, 1917

When we passed through Yozgad during the deportation, we heard that its Armenian population had been completely exterminated. In fact, the executioners would have done the same thing to us if the orders of the Governor of Chorum, Galib Bey, had not reached Yozgad in time.

We gathered some very detailed information about the Yozgad carnage from a woman named Gadariné, who recently arrived here in a very miserable condition with the group of refugees deported from Dera.

Mrs. Gadariné is barely 30 years old, a vigorous and lively woman, and in outward appearance looks like a Fellah. Her sunburnt face has become very dark, and her cheeks and chin are tattooed with bizarre pictures. Her melancholy looks and her furrowed forehead, however, instantly reveal that she is the child of a suffering people.

Mrs. Gadariné's story has certain resemblances to Mrs. Takouhi's. In both, a Turkish family friend revealed his true colors during the early days of the deportation. Why should we be surprised? Didn't my father's Turkish friend from Chorum remove his mask on the day of our departure? It's clear that, whether they're named Riushdu, Ziya, Batdalzadé, or Abdullah, they're all the same snakes, waiting for a chance to squeeze the life out of their friends. What a pity that our elders didn't get to know them better before it was too late.

* * *

The Yozgad carnage was no different from any other massacres of densely Armenian-populated provinces. One could call them classic slaughters. First they deported about 500 prominent members of the city—among them many of our friends and relatives—and martyred them on the road to Sivas.

Three days later they put another caravan (approximately 400 people) on the road, and a week later another one, and sent them on the same route as their compatriots who preceded them.

Then the rest of the population of the city was ordered to get ready to leave immediately.

Mrs. Gadariné heard that military families were exempt from deportation and sought refuge, together with her sister and her sister's six-year-old son, with Ziya Bey, an elderly Turk who was a business colleague of her husband and her brother-in-law, who were both serving in the army.

Ziya Bey promised to protect them. That same day he went to the city hall to intercede with the police chief, who happened to be a close friend.

At home, Mrs. Gadariné, her sister, and her nephew were spending a lovely time with Ziya Bey's wife, when they heard an unusual clamor coming from the market place.

They ran to the windows and saw people looting an Armenian store. They couldn't hide their astonishment when they spotted certain supposedly honorable and decent Turkish *effendis* in the crowd. Uninhibited by their fezzes or starched collars, they carried bags of sugar on their backs like porters. This went on for about 30 minutes, until the police arrived, dispersed the mob, and locked the store.

In the evening Ziya Bey returned home, disturbed. His efforts had not been successful, but still he was not discouraged. He would see the chief again the next day.

The two sisters and the little boy retired to the room assigned to them. They were scared but hopeful at the same time. Despite the fact that the beds had been made up for them, they fell onto the sofa without even getting undressed. After long hours of brooding, they finally fell asleep. But their sleep didn't last long. They woke in alarm. Somebody was at the door, knocking loudly.

They peeked from behind the curtain, and much to their dismay they saw two soldiers at the door. At the same time they heard the scuffle of Ziya Bey's slippers as he came down the stairs. In a minute the street door opened and a conversation between the landlord and the soldiers ensued. After a little while Ziya Bey came up, pointed at the door of the room, entered, and said in a sad voice: "Mrs. Gadariné, I'm sorry to be the bearer of bad news. The military authorities have been informed that you're staying here with us and have now sent two soldiers to take charge of you. I told them their information was not correct, but it didn't help. The soldiers wanted to come in and search my house. I was afraid they would also find your sister and her son, so I confessed. Then I came to ask you to give yourself up and surrender to the authorities; otherwise you may endanger the lives of the others."

"What do the military authorities want with me?" asked Mrs. Gadariné in surprise.

"Now they are collaborating with the police," replied Ziya Bey. Today they have gone from house to house and collected all the remaining men and women, the elderly and the young, and taken them to the station. Tomorrow morning all of them will leave."

"Ziya Bey isn't it possible to bribe the soldiers and send them away?" asks Mrs. Gadariné's sister.

"I tried, dear woman, but it's impossible. Their orders are very strict. Mrs. Gadariné should surrender for your safety," said the Turk.

"If my surrender will save them, I'm ready to sacrifice myself," said Mrs. Gadariné. Then, wasting no time, she said goodbye to them, hardly restraining her tears, and walked out of the room.

The soldiers arrested Mrs. Gadariné and left in silence, without offering her any impudence. After they had crossed a few streets, Mrs. Gadariné noticed that they were not taking her to the garrison.

She slowed down and asked hesitantly where they were taking her.

"To your relatives," the soldiers replied abruptly.

"But aren't our relatives all in jail?"

"How could thousands of people fit into a prison? They are all being held in a field at the edge of town. Walk, and you'll see." The soldiers dragged Mrs. Gadariné by the arm.

"Leave me alone! I can walk by myself," said Mrs. Gadariné, and with a sudden twist she freed herself from their hands.

The soldiers left her alone. They kept walking for a few more streets, but when they arrived at a deserted street, they tried to hold the woman's hands again and started making lewd comments about her looks.

Mrs. Gadariné grasped their intention and suddenly stopped in the middle of the street and, justifiably angry, she shouted: "Aren't you ashamed to address an honest woman with such filthy language?"

"Don't talk so much. Just walk," replied the soldiers in a deafening roar.

"I'm not one of those women. I can't go everywhere," said the woman.

"When you taste the knife you'll walk," one of the soldiers threatened her.

"Shame on you for tyrannizing a helpless woman," she protested in disgust. "My husband is also a soldier, and if you had the slightest respect for the military you'd treat the wife of another soldier with respect."

The soldiers guffawed.

"What's a soldier who belongs to a treacherous people worth, unless his woman has some value?" they asked. "Walk! It isn't much farther. We'll destroy all of you."

Mrs. Gadariné refused to walk. They dragged her along screaming.

A corporal who was on guard duty in the Armenian neighborhoods at the time heard the clamor and rushed to the spot. The corporal listened to Mrs. Gadariné's account of their violent behavior and warned the soldiers that this was a breech of duty. Then he took Mrs. Gadariné's name and spoke to the soldiers: "Take her to the garrison. I'll see to her tomorrow. And if I hear that you've even touched her, you can expect a lot of trouble from me. Go! There's no time to lose. Tonight all the Armenians must be arrested."

When Mrs. Gadariné arrived at the garrison she saw many other Armenians who had been arrested with no consideration for their gender and were being kept under surveillance. She was informed by acquaintances that her sister had also been brought there a while earlier.

Alarmed she started searching for her sister, and she finally found her in deep depression.

"But where's Arda, your son?" asked Mrs. Gadariné apprehensively.

"Ziya Bey wouldn't let me bring him. He snatched him out of my arms by force," the sister sobbed in a pained voice.

Mrs. Gadariné was not a woman who accepted misfortune easily. She immediately went to see the police chief, told him what had happened, and asked permission to return to Ziya Bey's with the soldiers, so they could bring the child back with them.

The police gave her permission in return for a few pieces of jewelry, provided she returned within half an hour, as they would all be leaving early in the morning.

Mrs. Gadariné rushed to Ziya Bey's home with one of the soldiers. She knocked at the door for a long time. He came out grumbling, and, pretending not to notice the Armenian woman, started shouting at the soldier: "Yes, it's a disgrace! You come and you go . . . We have no rest, even at night."

"Ziya Bey, it's not the soldier's fault. I brought him with me to get the child," said Mrs. Gadariné as she walked up to him.

"But we don't have the child," declared the Turk.

"What do you mean you don't have him? You took him from his mother's arms by force," Mrs. Gadariné insisted.

"That's right, my child. I didn't want him to go with you because you're all going to be slaughtered. Later, though, a soldier came and took the child away," replied the Turk, a false sadness covering his face.

"That's a lie. The child is upstairs. You betrayed us in order to get your hands on him," Mrs. Gadariné shot back, her voice distorted with anger.

"Woman, you're out of your mind!" mumbled Ziya Bey and slammed the door in her face.

* * *

The premeditated crime took place in all its horror in a place called Keller, in a deserted valley. Bandits armed with daggers and hatchets surrounded the caravan. "This is how we slaughter the Armenians. They call us the army of butchers," they said, and they killed everybody without mercy.

Scarcely thirty women, among them Mrs. Gadariné, were miraculously spared. They escaped and found refuge in a nearby Circassian village. The chief of the village, who bore no particular animosity to the Armenians, kept ten of them—the ones capable of working—and turned the rest over to the executioners, who were looking for them. They dragged their victims away and shot them all under a bridge.

Mrs. Gadariné, thanks to her healthy and robust constitution, also escaped this second bloodbath and stayed there serving the Circassians for about a month. She, with her other friends, worked in the fields like a man.

After a month, however, she noticed young Circassian men lingering around the sheep fold where she slept. She and one of her friends disguised themselves as Turkish women with veils and ran away from the village. They walked all day and all night and reached the regions surrounding Caesarea, where they met a group of Armenian refugees coming from the direction of Angora.

She joined them and went with them to Ulu Kishla. After waiting at the station there for two weeks, she was taken by train to the Osmaniye refugee camp. After staying there for quite some time, where her friend died as a result of illness, Mrs. Gadariné took to the road again with many other refugees, walking in the direction of Aleppo.

While they were going through the Kurdish regions of Entilli, the police sold the entire caravan containing Mrs. Gadariné to a ruthless Kurdish chieftain for 300 pounds. His profession was to buy all the worthless skeletal human beings who had been subjected to robberies and misery, and exploit them until their drew their last breaths.

With the help of his men, the greedy Kurd took the caravan to his den on a deserted hill. There he carefully examined each member of the convoy. He knocked all the gold teeth out of their mouths with a hammer and cut open the abdomen of anyone whose stools were found to contain gold.

After this detailed inspection, which lasted a week, the Kurd divided the people into two groups. He sent the healthy ones to provinces in the interior, to be sold as pack animals. He had the sickly and the invalid killed, after shaving off their hair, which could be used to make covers and rugs.

Mrs. Gadariné was sold to a Kurdish mountain dweller for 40 coins. She worked for him for a week, and on the eighth day she went out of the village to cut wood and fled for the second time.

After a great deal of hardship, she reached Islahiye. From there she moved on to Aleppo, and then to Damascus.

It was almost as if her destiny were slavery. During her deportation from Damascus to the interior of the desert, her caravan was attacked by half-savage Bedouins, who first injured a few people, then took 42 women to their tents.

Mrs. Gadariné traveled twice through the arid deserts of Ma'an with this nomadic tribe. The majority of her friends died because of the terrible climate and hard labor. There were only eight of them left anyway. And one day about six months ago, when their caravan was going through the Dera region, Mrs. Gadariné, accepting the risk of imminent death, ran away from the tents. Fortunately, her third escape succeeded.

* * *

As we listened with much anguish to Mrs. Gadariné, we admired her courage and endurance. We congratulated her strength of character, by means of which she had escaped so many dangerous situations. Then we took her and settled her in the garden of one of our acquaintances. We hoped that, after serving the Circassians, Kurds, and Bedouins, she might again be sold as a slave . . . but this time to the British—and that all of us might be sold with her!

19 November, 1917

Recently the Hauran region has been almost emptied of its Armenian inhabitants. The Armenian population, which at one time was about 20,000 strong, has now been reduced to barely 1,000 and then only in three or four major centers. The rest have died of famine and disease, except for a few hundred families who have migrated to Damascus, afraid of the nearby dangers of war.

Some people from our village have also left. However, as Armenians from the surrounding regions have moved here, Jeresh retains it congested character. It is possible to say that from the point of view of the Armenian population, Jeresh is more important than Irbit or Dera.

The departure of well-to-do families has put the orphans, widows, and disabled in a difficult situation. Because if anyone gave a slice of bread to their less unfortunate compatriots, it was them. But now the number of those who can help is decreasing and the number of the needy is on the increase.

At the moment all our hope is in the advancing British army.

26 November, 1917

I heard the thin, weak voice of a child. I went to the window to look, and in the dark courtyard I saw a little boy, who was soaked by the heavy rain. He was asking our Circassian landlord to give him some bread. His teeth were chattering with the cold. Nobody paid any attention to his pleas. The boy gradually crept closer to the Circassian's room, to repeat his wish a bit louder.

All at once the landlord's dog, which was resting in front of the door, jumped at him and pulled him down to the ground, ready to tear him into pieces had I not dashed out of my room and brought my cane down on the animal.

Bothered by the terrible screams of the boy and the barking and yelping of the dog, the Circassian at last came out, but instead of helping the little boy who was lying on the ground, he roared savagely: "That's what you deserve, you little bastard! Let that be a lesson to you never to come here again!"

I could hardly restrain myself from bringing my cane down on the man's head. I lifted the boy up and took him to our room. This was probably a more effective rebuke to the Circassian, if he were capable of understanding it, than hitting him with my cane.

In the room, we laid the boy down in front of the stove. He neither spoke nor moved. His face, legs, and shoulders were bleeding from the dog's bites and scratches. He wasn't even crying. He was in shock. We dressed his wounds, gave him something to eat, and finally revived him. Then we asked him who he was.

"My name is Khatchig," he replied breathlessly—this was the same boy who had just returned to life.

"Where are you from?"

"I don't know."

"Are your parents alive?"

"No."

Tears filled my eyes as I looked at the boy. He was wearing worn-out rags. Like all the abandoned orphans of the desert, he had scrawny arms, emaciated legs, a scraggly neck, and, in contrast to his wasted body, an unusually large stomach. No one knew how it had grown so big. Another contrasting phenomenon caught my attention. The skin on his head was scaly, as if he were a hundred years old and ready for the grave. As I looked at my little guest I was suddenly reminded of the orphan I met about six months ago. He and his brother were grooming each other for insects, which had infested their bodies and clothes.

"Khatchig, where is your older brother," I asked, thinking that he was the younger one.

"He died."

And he said no more. He stretched his ice-cold hands to the fire and warmed himself up, and then, in the carefree manner of a child, closed his eyes and fell into a deep slumber. "What an enviable age!" I thought, but then I realized that there wasn't much to envy.

3 December, 1917

Our landlord's inhuman remark caused a dispute between us the next day. Instead of apologizing for his cruel treatment of the boy, the ill-natured Circassian tried to justify himself by shamelessly declaring that he would gladly see all of these infidels with outstretched hands torn to pieces.

"But how would you feel if it were your child who had fallen into such savage claws instead of a simple orphan?" I asked him.

"He asked for it. He'll never forget it," replied the Circassian, a bit annoyed.

"How could a little child like that know he was dealing with such a pitiless person? He is hungry and it's natural that he should ask for food."

"Then let him ask you."

"How can a seven-year old kid tell the difference between you and us? For him everyone is first and foremost a human being, not a Christian or a Muslim."

"I see that you've become the defender of the Armenians."

"No, it's not a question of defending or not defending anyone. I'm only speaking the truth."

"Go and talk about the truth in your own country. It doesn't work in Arabia."

It was impossible to talk sense to such a senseless person. I left home and looked for another place to live. Three days ago I found and rented a room at the end of the village, and finally we have moved there.

It must be our bad luck. We ran away from the rain into the hail—our new landlord is also an extreme fanatic. Had a wise man seen my move, he would probably have said: "My boy, moving from one house to another is not the way to be saved. The important thing is to get out of this hostile people's land."

10 December, 1917

Yesterday we witnessed another barbaric act that is worth recording. An Armenian from Marash was coming home panting and grunting, carrying two tin containers filled with water. At the market square he ran into a Circassian, who walked up to him and slapped him with such force that the poor Armenian lost his balance and fell to the ground with the water containers. Then the violent Circassian kicked him in the ribs, stomach, and back, and finally he stamped on the tin containers and continued on his way—all the time loudly cursing his victim and his victim's relatives.

The Circassian had given the Armenian these containers free, on condition that the latter delivers four containers of water to him every day. The Armenian had kept his promise for a whole week, but then he had taken to bed and was unable to work.

Today for the first time the Armenian had felt a bit of strength in his legs and had gotten out of bed and gone to fetch some water that he could exchange for some bread. But this wicked man just ran up to him and beat him without asking any questions—assuming that the Armenian had broken his promise.

Those of us who saw what happened were very upset. We went into a store and bought new containers, purchased a few loaves of bread from the baker, gave them to the poor Armenian, and told him to go home and stay there until he had completely recovered. A great many Armenians die because they go back to work before they have completely regained their health.

While the Armenian was going home, all stooped over, a storekeeper from Damascus who had watched this violent attack with his friends alluded to our humanitarian gesture in these words: "Look how the dogs take care of each other!"

17 December, 1917

I haven't been able to work for the past six days because of the continuous rain. Today the weather was better, so I set up my counter in its usual place at the market.

I still hadn't taken the goods out of the boxes when a man in city clothes stopped in front of me. "I inspect cigarette papers," he said. "I want to see if you have the required official stamps on the papers you sell."

When I heard the man's function I was alarmed. Because recently a new stamp law was passed that requires me to put a special ten *para* stamp on each booklet of cigarette paper. The Damascus Arabs do not respect this law, so we're forced to follow their example. If we put a ten *para* stamp on a booklet that's worth only 20 *para*s, the client will buy from the others, where he can pay 20 *para*s instead of 30 for the same thing.

Still, on account of the inspectors who occasionally come, I always keep about ten stamped booklets on my counter and the rest I keep in my pocket to sell secretly. So I showed him the booklets on the counter, pointing out that they were stamped according to the law. The man examined each of them, checked my counter inside out, and started to walk away, convinced that I had no contraband goods. At that moment the storekeeper across from my table gave the inspector a wink. The inspector immediately understood the meaning of the storekeeper's signal and came back to me.

"I'd like to check your pockets."

"I have twenty booklets in my pocket but I still haven't put any stamps on them. That's why I haven't put them on the table."

"I've heard that excuse many times," said the civil servant. "You'll have to pay a fine of one *medjidiyé* (silver coin) for each booklet."

"I make two *paras* from each booklet. How do you expect me to be able to pay in silver?"

"That's your problem . . . it's the law," declared the employee seriously.

"If that's how it is, then the law applies to everybody," I said. "Please, let's go and see the guy who winked at you. There are whole boxes of booklets without stamps on them in his store. If you also fine him, I'll gladly pay my share."

"It's not your place to teach me my job. Either pay up or go to prison!"

"Why should I go to prison when I tell you that I'm ready to pay the fine? But you have to begin with that storekeeper."

As usual, the people at the market surrounded us while we were arguing. A Circassian (later I heard that he was the other storekeeper's enemy because the guy had refused to sell to him on credit) came up to us, looked the civil servant over from head to foot, and said excitedly: "The boy's right. If you've come here all the way here from Irbit to collect fines and stock the government's treasury, why waste time on the small amount of money you'll get from him? Come on please, and first let's begin with the shops of the people from Damascus . . . There you'll find boxes and boxes of contraband goods."

But the employee had probably been bribed by the Damascus people. He refused to search them in public. So he let me go, saying: "I'll let you off this time. But make sure you don't get caught again." Then he abandoned his search, got on his horse, and gloomily left the village.

When the people dispersed, the store-keeper who had betrayed me came over and said, in an attempt to justify himself: "*Malesh ya veled* (never mind, boy). I only did it for a laugh."

24 December, 1917

Battalions of Turkish troops leave for the front every day.

We heard the distant firing of cannons for a while and rejoiced in the hope that we would soon be liberated. The sounds stopped some time ago, however. Now there is only silence. It seems the British have retreated.

A profound sense of hopelessness has enveloped everyone's soul.

1 January, 1918

Another black year has passed in tears and mourning. The year is new. There is not a single hope that the gates of famine, fear, illness, and misery have been shut. Whenever the year is renewed, we naively hope that with it our dreams will come true. Far from it. We still find ourselves confronted with bitter realities.

What kind of surprises await us during the course of this new year? Will it be possible for us to see our age-old wishes realized? Or shall we instead, like thousands of our relatives, shut our eyes to the longing for freedom treasured in the depths of our hearts?

It may be necessary to borrow the allegorical interpretation of our "spiritual" brothers—one should not be surprised, as I have just finished reading the holy book that Ruhji (Spiritual) Bedros gave me—that as a nation we are like a crowd assembled in an immense desert, and that every person has been given a burning candle to hold. The flame of the candle signifies our soul, which should never be extinguished. But on the horizon there are always storms, clouds, thunder, and lightning. The clouds reverberate; the wind blows and extinguishes in one breath the light of thousands of souls. And we, who run away from that horrible hurricane in fright, where can we really run to? How long can we keep our candles burning?

This is the question that troubles the mind of every Armenian.

On the threshold of the new year we have one single wish from the depths of our hearts: may this year see the curtain fall on this tragedy.

4 January, 1918

There is no doubt that the new year is beginning auspiciously.

This morning I took my counter from Vartanian's store and was on my way to my usual spot. I suddenly spotted a new officer passing by, walking quickly right in front of me. He ordered the soldiers who were with him: "Hurry up, boys!"

Thinking that something unusual was going on, I stopped for a moment and looked around. All the roads were blocked by soldiers armed with rifles and bayonets. We were again trapped in their net.

What was the reason for this gathering? After all, conscription has been postponed until next March.

I was turning over such reflections when I noticed that the officer was returning with his soldiers, collecting the Armenians in the market square. When they got to me, one of the soldiers told me to join the group.

"Please give me a minute to leave my counter with one of my countrymen," I said. If I left it there, outside, the Arabs would steal everything that was on it.

"Make it quick," he ordered.

"Thank you."

I went to our compatriot's store and I thought of something. If I didn't go back and join them, what would happen? If worse came to worst, the soldier would come in a frenzy and beat me to death. Wasn't an instant death here better than the torturous death awaiting me in the burning desert?

I had decided. Immediately, without the store owner's consent, I went and hid under the long business counter that ran obliquely across the end of the store. Mr Vartanian, the store owner, had been a close friend of my father and the senior secretary of our business in Chorum, and he would go along with my wishes any time.

I had hardly squeezed myself in on top of the pieces of wood piled under the counter when the commanding officer of the soldiers walked in, holding a whip in his hand. For a second I thought he had come to look for me, and my heart stopped. But no, he had come in to buy some tobacco and raisins.

He bought what he needed, lighted a cigarette, and sat in Mr. Vartanian's chair, about a yard away from me.

"Goddam donkeys! They're nothing but trouble," he yawned lazily, and stretched out his legs toward me.

"What donkeys are you talking about?" asked Vartanian, afraid that the officer's foot would touch me and consequently get him in trouble too.

"In Soueida they gave us 250 donkey-drawn wagons to take to the war front. They were supposed to carry sand and stone to build trenches," the Turk explained. "Although these damned animals looked healthy, they got sick on the road and began to die, one after the other. The soldiers took over and started pulling the wagons like animals. The donkeys kept dying, without stop. Imagine! Many wagons had only one soldier pulling them. And finally, after so many problems, we arrived in Jeresh last night . . ."

"And now you are picking up Armenians to pull the wagons," interrupted Vartanian.

"What can we do? We have to replace the dead donkeys."

Just then an insistent cough started tickling my throat. I made superhuman efforts to suppress it. I was trying to hold in the cough and keep my balance on the pieces of wood. Unfortunately, a piece of wood fell from under me and made a noise.

"What's that?" asked the startled officer. "Do you have mice in this store?"

"Yes, sir," Vartanian stuttered feebly.

"They must be big ones," said the Turk, and got to his feet. "Anyway, let me go and see how many people they've rounded up so far."

The moment the officer left I started breathing freely and let out one cough after the other—that nasty cough almost got me arrested!

"Vahram, it's dangerous for you to stay here. Get away from here," said Vartanian. Then, examining the market place, he said, "Come on, there are no soldiers around. Hurry up!"

"OK. Right away."

I came out of my hiding place and ran like the wind. When I arrived home I found out that the soldiers had searched the home of one of our relatives, Krikor Toramanian, which was separated from our house by a narrow street. Fortunately, they had not found my cousins, Levon and Vahram. As for Mr. Toramanian and my grandfather—my grandfather lived with his son-in-law—they were not taken away because of their advanced age.

Thinking that these soldiers might also visit us, I at once jumped over the low wall around our courtyard and took refuge with my relatives whose house had already been searched. I had just arrived there when we heard that the soldiers had gone to our house looking for me.

This evening the neighbors came to tell us that the soldiers had left and taken about sixty Armenians with them. To find out the exact number we went to the market place and peeked from behind the closed shutters of a store just in time to see them leave. They were all soaked in sweat and dust, some pulling the wagons and others pushing the sick donkeys.

When we saw the horrible condition of these animals—their ribs protruding and their legs all tangled up—we wondered how the Turks could keep up a fight against the British under such conditions. Either the enemy was in worse condition or, as happened in the Dardanelles, they had no intention of advancing. No matter which was the reason, there was no ground for us to be hopeful.

5 January, 1918

Early this morning, Vahram and Levon arrived and said that the soldiers had not been able to go far. So they had camped about an hour from the village and had returned to the village with the intention of arresting more people.

I got dressed immediately and the three of us fled to the hill close to our house, where it was safer to hide.

For a moment after we reached the summit of the hill, where the ramparts of the old city dominated Jeresh, we watched what was going on in the village. We had just turned our heads to look when we saw two soldiers in the courtyard of our house, talking to my mother. Of course we couldn't hear what they were saying, but it was clear that they had come to take me away.

If these soldiers, who were probably asking where I was, had thought of looking toward the hill, they would surely have seen us and could just as surely have popped us off like rabbits with one or two shots. My mother foresaw this danger and invited the soldiers in to search the room, while we took advantage of the opportunity to cross over to the other side of the hill as fast as our legs could carry us.

We wandered about for more than two hours looking for a secure hiding place. Finally we spotted a cave and went there. As we approached it, a couple of Armenians from Yazdi dashed out of the entrance to the cave, screaming their heads off. The poor people thought that we were soldiers and were coming to kill them.

We decided that the place was not terribly safe and, with our new friends, went to the adjacent hill and looked for a hideout in its crevices. We were soon disappointed, however, because a road constantly used by the Bedouins ran by the foot of the mountain. The moment they spotted us they would come and steal everything we had.

We remembered that two years ago Reshid Bey had showed us a mysterious hideout carved into solid rock. We directed our steps there.

As we came out of the valley, we noticed that the soldiers and their donkey-drawn wagons had camped on the road leading to the rock.

After wandering a long time, we at last found a spot covered with bushes and brush. The ground was wet, but we lay down completely, deciding that if we sat up, any passerby might have seen our heads.

We blessed this decision when, on hearing the neighing of a horse, we cautiously raised our heads and noticed a policeman examining the area for fugitives. We lay right back down again, afraid to breathe. Five minutes later, when we checked again, we saw that the policeman had turned his horse around and was galloping away from us.

Our fright didn't end there. The policeman had hardly gone for half an hour when we heard noises from the other end of the bushes. We saw two bare arms and at the end of those arms a couple of shiny daggers cut through the air. Suddenly the arms and the daggers descended, and we heard another noise, as several people lay down.

Were they Bedouins perhaps? Were they lying in ambush to capture us? We were petrified. Then we heard a familiar voice: "Is that you, boys?"

It was the voice of Aharonian, the teacher. We got to our feet at once and went to join our friend from Zeitoun. He was still lying down, with seven other people.

"What are you doing here, armed with daggers?" we asked in astonishment.

"We're cutting wood to keep ourselves warm. When we heard you whispering we were scared that you were the police," explained Aram the barber.

"Warming up isn't a bad idea! Hurry up, we're freezing too," we said.

When it was time to light the wood they had cut we realized that no one had any matches.

"Don't worry," said Mr. Aharonian: "Find me a flint stone and I'll make you a fire."

All thirteen of us left to look around for a flint stone. At last Setrag, who was from Marash, was lucky enough to find one. When we heard his exclamations of triumph we gathered around the wood pile and waited impatiently for Aharonian to start the fire.

The teacher from Zeitoun laid four tiny blades of grass on the flint stone and started to strike it with the dull side of his knife. But in vain.

Despite the flying sparks, the grass did not ignite, as it was still wet from last night's rain.

Despite our discouragement, I thought of something. I saw that the coat our friend from Yazdi was wearing had a number of holes. He had stuffed these holes with cotton. I pulled out a piece of cotton out and gave it to Aharonian.

"Try this."

My discovery was not at all bad. The cotton caught fire at once, and in a little while we were all gathered around a pleasant fire.

This pleasure also was short-lived. Afraid that the smoke of our fire could attract the attention of the police, robbers, and Bedouins, we put it out and again we had to lie on the wet ground, waiting for night so we could return home.

6 January, 1918

We heard that the soldiers had not yet left. Therefore early this morning we and our friends from yesterday went back to the same place. This time, however, we had learned from experience, and we took extra clothes and food with us so we wouldn't get cold or hungry like yesterday.

While running up on that familiar hill—the only dangerous stretch that could be seen from the village—I fell. I didn't break anything, but the pain in my arm and knees was all that I could bear, all day long.

Around noon, we saw Mr. Aprahamian's little boy coming in our direction and shouting: "Father, father! The gendarmes have gone . . ."

We congratulated the courageous little boy. He had come all the way alone and found us. Then we all happily returned to the village, and there we wished everybody a merry Christmas.

An hour later our happiness augmented, when, for the first time in our lives, we saw an aeroplane fly over Jeresh. It was flying so high that there were moments we couldn't see it. If we hadn't heard the faint buzz of its engine, like the buzzing of bees, we would never have known it was there or seen it. We immediately concluded that it must have been a British plane. A Turkish or German plane didn't have to fly that high.

We recently heard the noise of cannons. How we all wished that this aeroplane were the harbinger of our liberation.

14 January, 1918

The soldiers disappeared, but they had a very bad effect on me. While roaming in the hills I got a cold. I now cough all day and all night, as if my lungs were tearing apart. My back and my sides hurt, as well as my knees and my left elbow. These are the results of my fall.

We received good news in the evening. The British have captured Jerusalem and are advancing. We think the blasts of the cannons are getting closer.

21 January, 1918

We had a neighbor when we lived in our previous place. Hampar, the felter from Aintab, was not satisfied with making only felt saddle pads. He also created a unique hat, which he sold to all the Armenians at a very reasonable price, so they wouldn't have to wear the fez, which symbolized the Turks. Hampar the craftsman had sold one of his hats to me also. The only difference from a European hat was that the brim was turned up and glued to the sides, and he would definitely have covered the head of every Armenian in the Hauran if he had not died prematurely.

After her husband's death, Hampar's wife sold the store and all the tools, and left for Damascus with her two grown children. Today we had a sad surprise. We saw that she has returned to our village.

Mrs. Baydzar gave us a very gloomy description of the Armenians who live in the beautiful Syrian capital. Here I would like to relate a curious incident from her journey—a fabulous example of bribery and official robbery—just as I was told it.

* * *

They and a few other well-to-do families left our village and went to Dera, where they waited in tents until they found a way to get to Damascus. One day a policeman showed up and said: "If you give me two pounds I'll allow you to buy tickets to Damascus."

Mrs. Baydzar paid the man and bought the tickets. But when they got to the train station another policeman told them that they couldn't travel because the train was at the disposal of the military authorities that day.

"In that case, why did they sell us tickets?" asked Mrs. Baydzar.

"The ticket agent must not have known about the situation when he sold them," replied the policeman.

"So what are we supposed to do now?"

"Your tickets are void. That's the way it is."

The poor refugees start begging the policeman to allow them to leave. They had spent their entire savings to buy these tickets. If they didn't leave then, they would never be able to move.

"I'm moved by your situation," said the policeman calmly. "Give me a pound and I'll smuggle you onto the train."

The Armenians paid the money and entered one of the cars.

Before the train started moving an inspector arrived and asked for their permits to leave for Damascus. And because these travelers didn't have such certificates the inspector threw their baggage out of the car and beat Hampar's two grown sons on top of it all.

"But where do we get permits?" asked Mrs. Baydzar.

"At the station, from the police chief."

"Just to go to the police station and back takes fifteen minutes. The train is going to leave in five. How could we possibly make it?"

"Well then, give me three pounds and I'll take care of it personally."

They were obliged to pay the inspector. They got back on the train and left. At the next station there was another inspector.

"Vesika (permit)."

"We don't have one."

Another beating. More threats. With another pound they shut the inspector's mouth. But there was a second, a third, a fourth, and the same comedy endlessly repeated itself, all the way to Damascus.

At the train station in Damascus a military policeman showed up and seized the refugees' sack of cracked wheat in the name of the army. Another policeman tried to take their belongings to disinfect them. Until they rescued their belongings and left the station they were in a nightmare.

They hired a carriage and left, but a few minutes later another policeman stopped them and asked where they had come from. When they said they had come from Dera, the policeman wanted to send them back to the train station and return them to Dera. After he had been bribed with a couple of silver pieces, he let them go. A block or two later another policeman tried the same thing, and they were obliged to stop his mouth with another costly morsel.

At last, after a host of difficulties, they managed to take refuge in the house of one of their relatives. Hardly two days passed before a policeman came and took the woman's two sons to a place somewhere outside the city limits, where many Armenians were building a road for the government, without pay.

In the evening the boys returned home, tired and hungry. The next day the same policeman showed up again.

In order to free themselves from this torture, they bribed the policeman. He left, but the next day another one showed up. They bribed him too, but on the third day a different one arrived.

Under these conditions, Mrs. Baydzar changed her house. A week later the police found their new address and asked them for their permit to live in the city.

"We have no permit."

"Then you must go back where you came from."

Mrs. Baydzar had no money left to bribe the police. This latest crew took them to the station, and there, with other Armenians suffering the same fate, they were stuffed into a livestock car and shipped to Dera.

According to Mrs. Baydzar, in Damascus, just as in Aleppo, baneful misery has reached its summit. Sick and hungry people sleep in the streets. They die by the dozen every day . . . And the police sometimes put the living, the dead, and people drawing their last breaths on the train and send them into the desert.

28 January, 1918

The Armenians who delivered the donkey-drawn wagons to the Ottoman army returned to the village completely exhausted. Their journey was terribly hard because before they arrived in Salt the other donkeys also died. They were obliged to take the 250 wagons themselves, pulling and pushing them to a far-off place, one day from Salt.

The merciless officer did not let the Armenians go even then, but tried to take them to the battle front. But at the last minute a commanding officer stopped him, telling him that at the moment there was no need for the wagons. The Armenians delivered all the wagons entrusted to them to the military warehouse and, after performing various other tasks there, were sent back. Those who have returned tell us that the noise of the cannons was much louder where they were, and that near the front the Turkish soldiers were passionate about performing their duties.

4 February, 1918

Today was the fifth time we have seen happy faces on the Armenian refugees around us.

The first time was on 10 April, 1916, when the news of the postponement of conscription for Armenians spread through the village. The second was on 4 December, 1916, when Germany proposed a peace treaty. The third was on 19 February, 1917, when the inspector for the refugees, Mumtaz Bey, distributed money to the poor Armenian deportees. The fourth was on 22 October, 1917, when conscription was again postponed. And the fifth time was today, on the occasion of the wedding of one of the prominent citizens of the village, Reshad Bey. There was a huge banquet for all the poor people of the village without distinction.

We were invited as Reshad Bey's personal guests, but I didn't want to sit at the head table. I went to another table, where I could see the my relatives' elation. One could see the fire of life sparkle in their eyes as they swallowed fat morsels of food. For a refugee who has not seen a piece of meat, a drop of oil or fat, or a slice of bread, and has fed on grass and roots for ages, this banquet was unlimited bliss, the like of which has not been seen for centuries and the memory of which has been completely erased.

Huge tree trunks lying on the ground served as tables, and the crowd was gathered around them. The only noise was that made by the motions of their teeth, lips, and tongues. All of them ate like ravenous animals, devouring their bread and cracked wheat, appetizing cakes, and meat, which for years they had only dreamed of.

And I had thought that I would take pleasure in witnessing their happiness, but instead I was even more saddened. I reflected that the happiness of these people was a momentary spark, and that tomorrow they would again be looking for a slice of bread. Would the day ever come when the nightmare of death from hunger and deprivation would be shattered and all Armenians would have their homes filled with bread and eat until they were full?

11 February, 1918

Today a policeman slapped me because I was speaking Armenian to my friend at the market.

"You have no right to hit me. There is no law in this country forbidding me to speak my mother tongue," I protested.

"There is, and you won't speak it," roared the policeman threateningly, "You aren't in Armenia now."

"Then why are you speaking Arabic? You're in Turkey."

The policeman slapped me again and went away, murmuring curses against my people and religion under his breath.

Even the lowliest civil servant is no different than a janissary. They beat and harass the defenseless refugees as much as they please. But they often torture the poor people even more than others. At the moment we see that they have become more violent, or perhaps it is we who have become poorer, losing the little privileges we used to enjoy.

What can we do but hold our tongues and be patient?

3 March, 1918

The new calendar has been officially adopted. Consequently, I'll also date my diary according to the new calender, and record today as 3 March instead of 18 February.

Famine and disease continue to claim new lives. Today we heard that the only barber in the village, Aram from Marash, has died of typhoid fever. Two days ago Khacher Aghpar from Zeitoun died. In another year one will need witnesses to prove that Armenians ever lived in these regions.

The thieving Bedouins keep invading the vegetable gardens. They have once again entered the garden of our compatriot Artin Aghpar and stolen and ruined everything. Around evening we witnessed another of their evil doings. An Armenian gardener from Alabash, covering his nakedness with a branch, came into the village as if he were entering a Turkish bath. He asked for a piece of cloth to cover his privates.

The cruel thieves had stolen even his underpants—which they usually leave, not out of compassion, but because they don't know what their use is. By stealing them now, the Bedouins are probably trying to say that they are civilized enough to wear such things.

10 March, 1918

The rumors of conscription began to spread from mouth to mouth again.

14 young bachelors—among them our Arshag and Levon—left last night for Salt; from there they are hoping to cross over to the British

side. It's a dangerous venture, but I would gladly go with them if I had somewhere safe where I could entrust my mother, sisters, and brother.

Those who are sick or have reasons not to flee have remained in the village. We all feel as if we are sitting on thorns.

Because of the pending conscription, we live in fear, at every minute keeping careful watch on what is going on around us. We are all ready to flee at the very first sign of danger, leaving everything we have behind.

Personally, I very rarely go out these days.

16 March, 1918

We were awoken by coarse voices and heart-rending screams early this morning. The noise was coming from a couple of houses down, where Dzeron's wife, who comes from Adana like her husband, had a baby a couple of days ago.

Was the baby dead? But surely it was impossible for people to cry that much for an infant, when they were used to the deaths of hundreds of brave and robust young men.

To find out the reason, my sister Manoushag went out to the street. A minute later she came back, breathless, and shouted: "Run! The police are looking for soldiers. They've caught Dzeron Aghpar, and they're beating him."

I had already decided where I would take refuge in case of danger. I immediately got dressed and ran through the rain to the stable across from our courtyard. I had hardly buried myself under the hay I had previously prepared there when my mother came to tell me that the police were also searching the stables and that it was in a similar place that they had arrested Artin Aghpar (our compatriot, who was living in Toramanian's courtyard since losing his garden).

There was no time to hesitate. Knowing that the stable of our relatives had already been searched, I went there immediately and rented it from the landlady, who was a poor Circassian widow. I promised her that if I were caught by the police I'd tell them that I was hiding there without her knowledge.

Once the stable door was locked on me, I found myself in total darkness. Then, gradually, my eyes got used to the dark and I saw that besides me there were a couple of oxen there. "After all, I'm not alone in my prison," I said to myself, with a sigh of comfort.

Then I examined my surroundings. I wanted to see what I could do in the event of a surprise visit by the police. What were the possibilities of hiding or fleeing?

I carefully checked the stable walls, the ceiling, and the attached hay shed. I noticed that it had a window, which had been blocked up. Probably in the old days they used to throw hay through it into the shed. I thought that this was a fabulous feature for me. As soon as the police came in, I could escape through that window and run for the hills. No sooner did I form this idea than I climbed onto the pile of hay and, using pieces of wood and stone—perhaps it would be more accurate to say using my nails—in two hours I removed the bricks that had recently been put there.

After I had secured my escape route, my mind relaxed a little. I crouched behind the door and peeked through the keyhole at the street all day long. Occasionally a policeman passed like a bloodthirsty tiger, without suspecting that his prey was only ten feet away from him.

When it was dark my sister visited me and brought me bread and water. She told me that a minute after my escape the policemen who had captured Artin Aghpar and Dzeron from Adana had come to our house and asked where I was. The police did not believe my mother when she replied that I had gone to Salt, searched everywhere for me, and then left, swearing that they would find me sooner or later.

Since the orders to arrest Armenians are much stricter this time, I thought it safest not to return home at night. So I slept on a corner of the hay stack covered with a blanket.

17 March, 1918

I opened my eyes in fright, feeling a warm sponge passing over my face, and found that one of the oxen had broken its rope and come over to lick my face. I hit animal on the head with my fist and pushed it away. Then, seeing its gentle, pleasant eyes turned on me, I regretted my severe reaction. Who knows? Perhaps the poor animal pitied my situation and came over to console me in its own way.

I got up and went to the keyhole to check what was going on outside. The rain, which had poured continuously for the past three days, had stopped. A bright day was following a dark one.

"I wish the clouds that darken our souls might one day disappear," I murmured.

A little later, the landlady's little boy came to take the oxen to pasture. When the door of my prison opened I deeply inhaled the clean air that poured in—how different the fresh air was from the heavy inside air, which was mixed with the smell of dung and urine.

Then, sitting at my observation post, I watched the street for hours and started questioning the meaning of this meaningless struggle and hectic existence. Was it worth enduring all these deprivations and tortures to prolong a life which even the most pitiful street dog wouldn't envy?

I started brooding, and suffered mental agony for a long while, until I could answer the above question: yes, it was worth it!

Near evening Mrs. Mariam returned in tears from the prison. They have taken all those who were arrested away, including her husband, Artin Aghpar. The news was stupefying.

"Who else was in the group that was taken away?" I asked anxiously.

"Many. Who do you want to know about?" the poor woman sobbed. "Your friends Sarkis from Moush and Karekin from Trebizond were also among them . . ."

24 March, 1918

It seems that the clouds are roaring. From far away the blasts of cannons rattle our windowpanes. Nowadays aeroplanes are frequently seen in the sky. Sometimes eight or ten of them fly over, but extremely high in the sky. We can hear only their rumble.

A strange situation! The more we rejoice as the noise of the cannon blasts gets closer, the more nervous the locals get, persuaded that the enemy is gradually getting nearer.

We hear that in Suveilah (a Circassian village near the front) they have massacred thirty Armenian families, afraid that in case of a British invasion the Armenians might complain to the British about all the tortures they have been subjected to. The Circassians give us this news and warn us not to be happy, because if the British come they will only find our mutilated corpses.

"Why do you want to slaughter us? How have we harmed you?" we ask.

They reply: "The Russians kill all the Muslims in the places they capture, and we'll kill you to avenge them."

It's a pity that the Turkish soldiers—who go through here every day—have poisoned the local people so much that they want to massacre us. They openly say that if the Turks ever retreat the Armenians may join the enemy and give them a harder time.

26 March, 1918

We received surprising news today. The British have invaded Salt.

The news caused us both tremendous joy and fear, especially when we saw the terrified Turkish troops running away from the battle front. Fortunately, they did not do any harm. They were too concerned with saving their own skins! They passed through, all confused and in a rush, taking with them a large number of mules loaded with field cannons, ammunition, provisions, and wounded.

After the disappearance of the last member of the Turkish troops, we came out of our hide-outs. The police were no longer arresting anyone. We congratulated ourselves on surviving another real danger.

At the moment, the liberating flag of a Christian nation blows twelve hours from our village. When shall we have the good fortune of greeting it?

We were discussing this at the market. Sarko the butcher suddenly said: "Boys, I've vowed that if the British come, I'll rush out and kiss the first soldier on the forehead."

"I'll bow down and kiss the foot of the first soldier," said Misag the farrier.

Avak the comb-maker vowed to kiss the eyes of a British soldier, Kapriel the gun smith to kiss the hand of the British commanding officer. Realizing that everybody was vowing to kiss something, I said, "I promise to kiss the British flag."

In the evening we all went to the hill, and for hours we focused our eyes greedily on the firing and landing flashes of the cannon shots—as though they were the first glimmers of the dawning sun after centuries of darkness.

In the annals of Jeresh, the faces of Armenians smiled today for the sixth time.

27 March, 1918

The Bedouins, on hearing that Sherif's soldiers are also advancing with the British troops, immediately formed a battalion and started putting enemy elements to the sword. First of all they attacked Rumman, a Turkoman village between Salt and Jeresh. After a couple of hours of bloody fighting, they succeeded in entering the village and slaughtered the major portion of the male population. Around evening the people who escaped the slaughter started to arrive in Jeresh. Their miserable condition reminded us of our own caravans of victims, with the difference that these people had deserved their misfortune a thousand times over.

They were a little group of Turks settled in Arabia, but their village had become a nest of hatred against Armenians. They were the ones who had poisoned the minds of the Circassians and Arabs with their noxious sermons. And they were the ones who had exploited the forced conversions and married Armenian women. In the meantime, they instigated their Muslim friends to follow their example.

One of the Armenian women who was forced to marry one of them came to us today and entreated us in tears to save her from her despotic husband. "Be patient a bit longer," we said, all the time trying to console her. "It would be dangerous for us to do anything now, before the arrival of the British. If they don't come, Armenians will be in danger, not just you, but all of us. The Armenian woman bowed her head and left. We heard from her that six other women were sobbing under the yoke of the Turkomans.

28 March, 1918

Armed Circassians roam the streets. They want to be ready for a sudden attack by the Bedouins. In the meanwhile they store their valuable furniture in secret places, as protection against plunder.

Following our landlady's example, we also dug a huge hole in the middle of the stable and took advantage of the evening darkness to move our clothes and bedding there, as well as a bag of barley, which is our only source of nourishment. We were afraid that the Muslim neighbors who had seen our activity could come and steal from us, so all night long my mother and I took turns keeping an eye on the stable from the window of our room.

29 March, 1918

I had hardly closed my eyes, just before dawn, when a sudden noise woke me up.

"Help! Help! The Bedouins are coming!"

It was the Armenian women on their way to the mountains to collect wood.

They had seen numerous Arab horsemen, brandishing their swords and singing war songs, rushing toward the village. These women had fled in alarm and come to tell us what was happening.

As soon as the Circassians heard the news, they picked up their arms, ran in the direction of the bandits, and at once took up positions behind walls and rocks.[*] The Damascus Arabs also grabbed their rifles and ran to the critical spot. Remaining in the village were the women, the children, the elderly, and the handicapped, who were screaming pitifully, remembering what had happened to the Turkomans.

A moment later we heard the following song roaring out of the throats of hundreds of Bedouins:

Beye mara, esheri barut (Sell your wife and by a gun)

Beye paras, esheri jemel (Sell your saddle-horse and buy a camel)

They repeated this in a monotonous sing-song whenever they went to war or to a feast—hundreds of times, without ever tiring of it. (At any rate, for a Bedouin war is also an occasion for merry-making).

It is impossible to describe the alarm and dread hanging over the village, especially a while later, when they appeared on the road in the distance, looking just as the Armenian women had described: swords in hand as they rode their horses.

When they had almost reached the village limits they gave a joyful shout: "Don't be afraid. Don't be alarmed. We come as friends . . ."

In fact we soon discovered that they were the sheikhs of the neighboring Fellah villages. They were heading for the Bedouin tents to ask for a peace agreement. On their way there they had decided to come to our village to take some of our leaders with them. This would also make them partners in the financial sacrifice that would be required to win the Bedouins over. After the reason for their visit was explained, the warriors came out from behind their barricades, and half an hour later two Circassians and a Damascus Arab joined the armed band and headed toward the tents of Beni Hasan.

Despite all this, the villagers continued to feel nervous. The local people were not sure their delegates would be amicably received by the people of Sherif.

---

[*] We Armenians lag far behind the Circassians when it comes to self-defense. They are as insignificant as a grain of sand in this huge desert, but they would never surrender without putting up a fight.

31 March 1918

Turkish soldiers fleeing from the front are gradually returning and pitching their tents on the edge of the village, presumably to regroup there.

We notice evil smiles on the faces of Circassians and Turkomans. They tell us that the British have evacuated from Salt and returned to their earlier positions. The representatives sent to the Beni Hasan tribe returned towards evening, with reassurances that the Bedouin would not attack the Fellah and Circassian villages.

The Bedouin would not have given such reassurances if they were not convinced of the advance of Sherif's forces with the British.

The canons that we had heard so close by are now far away. We think that the information from the Circassians is correct. The British have fled.

What awful disappointment after our earlier hopes and celebrations.

4 April, 1918

Numerous Fellah sheiks and their followers dressed in elaborate cloaks and silk gowns have been walking around the market, tapping the silver sheaths of their swords on the pavements. They came to Jeresh with the governor of Irbit and twenty soldiers. From here they are going to Salt, to chase away the British. They gave the impression that they were leaving to fight the Armenians. They poured out their hatred on Armenian artisans by not paying them for their work and by beating anyone who asked to be paid.

They didn't even spare an eight-year-old child who was careless enough to protest when a "noble" sheikh grabbed the grass the child had collected and threw it in front of his horse without giving the little boy a penny. As if it were not enough to beat him, the cruel man cursed all "dirty Armenians," who—in his own words—popped up before him at every step and, with their loathsome existence, desecrated the most sacred ideals of a Muslim.

This afternoon more volunteer companies arrived and joined these most fanatic and heartless creatures. We don't know where they came from. We have seen no one like them in the neighboring Fellah villages.

Before leaving, 150 horsemen had their oath-taking ceremony, which was quite significant, on the market square. They formed a circle, and the governor of Irbit and an older man went around the circle, stopping in front of each horseman and asking what he would do to the enemy if he captured him. One horseman answered the question by drawing his sword and brandishing it in the air, pretending he was slicing off human heads. Another made a gesture indicating that he would gouge out the enemy's eyes with his fingers. And yet another caused his horse to rear, indicating how he would crush the heads of the enemy under its hoofs. After each of them had revealed his hatred and violence in his own way, they prayed and left, shouting: "*Ya Allay, ye Allah*," and shooting in the air.

At the sight of the faces of these terrifying people and the evidence of their hatred, we thought about ourselves: what would become of us if ever they decided to turn their rifles against us, unarmed refugees, for even a minute?

5 April, 1918

Today, an Arab acquaintance of ours came from Salt. He told us that the British had left in great fright and that the Turks, who had recaptured the city, had massacred all the Armenians and Christian Arabs who were unable to flee during the British retreat.

Many young Armenians from Jeresh went to Salt to escape conscription. We don't know what happened to them during the general confusion.

What disturbed us most, however, was the order sent by the military authorities to massacre the Armenians.

"I heard that news from my brother-in-law, who works in the telegraph office in Salt," the Arab explained. He said that the telegram was worded as follows: "Taking advantage of the British advancement, the Armenians have killed 35 Turkish soldiers. Exterminate them all."

"The same thing may happen here in a day or two. Look out for your safety," added the Arab.

We are all in panic. How can we secure our safety? None of us is able to go anywhere. After all, where can we go? The order must have been sent everywhere.

As if we didn't have enough worries; now we have another.

7 April, 1918

After suffering for 48 hours, we finally heard that there was a misunderstanding in the news given us by our friend from Salt. The word emphasized in the telegram was not *Ermen*, it was *Irmen*, a

Christian Arab village close to Salt. It seems that the people of this village had taken advantage of the British advancement to massacre the Turkish soldiers who were retreating. Now the government is recapturing these regions and taking revenge by slaughtering the entire population, with no exceptions.

Nevertheless, the danger of a massacre still exists. Because the storekeepers from Damascus and the Turkoman peasants who have already returned to their ruined houses are so naive that they believe that the British are fighting not to defeat Turkey but to liberate the Armenians. In other words, the Armenians are the reason for all the bloodshed and the ruined cities . . . If it weren't for the Armenians, why would the British be in Arabia, fighting?

The naive Circassians believe this malicious talk and with every passing day their hatred for us increases.

14 April, 1918

Our countryman Artin Aghpar, who was drafted about a month ago, escaped and got back here last night. He told us that approximately 400 people—combined with the soldiers gathered from the other regions of the Hauran—have been sent to a place two days away from the Amman station. Their job there is to repair the roads demolished by the British air raids.

According to Artin Aghpar, the situation of the Armenian soldiers in that scorching region of Arabia is tragic. Because water is scarce, they are obliged to drink dirty, cloudy water from a well. Their daily ration consists of fifty grams of bread, and those who are still hungry pick through horse manure in search of grains of barley to eat. Artin Aghpar says there is no trace of the 800 soldiers who were sent there two years ago. No one knows if they have died, escaped, or moved. Our compatriot thinks that they have all died of thirst and disease—if a few had escaped, they would have sought refuge in our village, like Moushegh from Sis.

Artin Aghpar would have suffered the same fate if he had not escaped from that deadly place by risking his life.

One night he left his tent and pretended he was going far out in the fields to satisfy his needs. A soldier on guard duty saw him and asked where he was going. He answered that he needed to go, and squatted at once. In a second or two, noticing that the soldier had turned his attention elsewhere, he crawled, slowly at first, and then got to his feet and ran away.

Fortunately, the soldier didn't notice Artin Aghpar's escape; otherwise he would have been shot on the spot, like many others who tried to flee earlier. Nevertheless, afraid that they might notice his absence and send a few cavalrymen to look for him, he fled with all his might, until he arrived at a shepherd's tent the following morning.

The shepherd was a kind person. He invited our compatriot to sit in the shade of the tent. Then, realizing that the man was hungry, he gave him milk and bread.

After resting for an hour, Artin Aghpar thanked him and left. He had taken barely fifty steps when he heard the shepherd running after him. "Did I forget something?" he asked himself. He checked his pockets and found nothing missing. Then he's probably bringing me some food, he thought, so I have something to eat on the road. But the man's hands were empty. He then concluded that the man was going to give him information about the road.

Meanwhile, the shepherd caught up with him.

"*Ya khayyo*, compatriot," he said coldly, "take off your clothes before you go."

Artin Aghpar thought that the Arab was joking, and laughed.

"Hey, what are you laughing at?" the shepherd asked angrily.

"But you treated me as a guest just a while ago, and now you're asking for my clothes?" replied Artin Aghpar, all confused.

"I treated you as a guest because then you were on my land," said the Arab. "But now you're no longer on my land. That means that you're now a stranger, and whatever you have belongs to me."

"For God's sake, stop joking."

"Who's joking? . . . get undressed . . . quick, or I'll smash you with this club."

Artin Aghpar realized that the man was serious and was prepared to do anything. So he took off his jacket and pants and gave them to his former host.

"Your shirt too," ordered the Bedouin, "and your shoes."

Artin Aghpar took them off too, and gave them to the man.

The thief checked the pockets of the jacket and pants. He found nothing valuable. Then he checked the clothes inside and out and, having discovered that there were more patches and sewn spots than original material, he returned them. He also returned the worn-out shoes, keeping only the shirt for himself.

After this strange robbery, Artin Aghpar bade the shepherd goodbye and got out of the land of the Bedouins as fast as he could. Consequently, he did not stop at any tent or village. He preferred to eat grass and walk along deserted roads, and finally he arrived in Jeresh in a pitiful state.

21 April, 1918

The suffocating heat is here again, and with it the desert snakes. Today, we found one of them asleep in our room, coiled up under a bundle of underwear. Our landlady assured us that it was not the lethal kind.

But the drying of the grasses as a result of the extreme heat causes a great deal more pain to the Armenians than the snakes. Women and young girls put their lives in danger and go around for hours looking for a bit of grass, and often return empty-handed.

I realize how terrible it is to be deprived of even nature's provisions. Everyday we see a paralyzed woman from Yazdi, who lives in our courtyard. Until her sister fetches wood from the mountains, sells it, and brings a piece of bread home, the intestines of this woman writhe with hunger. Regardless of how much of our own bread we offer her, it's impossible to satisfy her hunger. It breaks my heart whenever I hear her pitiful voice begging my brother to go and fetch her some grass. My brother, who is barely six years old, goes and collects all the wild daisies from the street and brings them back to her.

"You can't eat these," the poor woman says, and, showing him a piece of grass as a sample, adds, "Look, the leaves should be like this. The same color, the same shape . . . Come, my sweet boy, go find this kind of grass for me."

Souren grabs the grass sample and runs to the hill, but there he meets his playmates and forgets his mission. Back at home, the paralyzed woman cries: "Souren, my sweet child, why haven't you come back yet? Come back . . . Quick . . . I'm hungry."

This is one vignette among many in the present tragedy.

28 April, 1918

Nishan Dadrian, the patriarch of our family, died today at the age of 71.

The last years of his life were a series of tragedies. His only son—scarcely 30 years old—was taken away from Samsoun and then slaughtered. His daughter and son-in-law were likewise deported from Samsoun. The latter was killed and the daughter was exiled to the deserts (see my entry for 20 October, 1915, the train station in Hama). The wife and little children of his other son, who died a natural death, were lost during the Amasia deportation.

As though his suffering and pain were not enough, two years ago the government caused him a lot of mental anguish with its conscription policy.

He died and is free.

May his bones rest in peace!

5 May, 1918

Today it is Easter. A red day among all our black ones!

From the depths of our hearts we lament the painful disappointment that we have had to bear for the past month. For a moment we forgot our misery and rejoiced, thinking that soon our tortures would come to an end. But alas! We were wrong.

These days aeroplanes—British and German—fly back and forth over our village. Cannons roar, as if saying, "Wait a little longer. Be patient for another little while," but how can we wait, when each day famine and sickness keep decimating the people?

The question of conscription has become a real enigma. One day the police arrest the Armenians and another day they see them and do nothing. We don't know whether to hide or work to earn our daily bread. The incertitude saps our strength.

At the moment, the British are about twenty hours away from us. There is neither famine, nor massacre, nor persecution over there. People live in peace there, whereas here there is death every single day, mourning, anguish, and tears.

When will this heavy stone be lifted from our graves? Will there ever be a day when the Armenians also come out of darkness and enjoy a miraculous resurrection?

12 May, 1918

We are in financial difficulty. For quite some time now we have not received anything from anywhere. Even my business at the market, which I resumed two weeks ago, brings in no money. Today I bartered a ring with a valuable stone for a bushel of barley, put the sack on my shoulder, and took it to the mill to grind.

I had my first shock when I heard from Hovsep's youngest son that his father is suffering from typhoid fever. I went to my friend's room behind the mill and there I found him, unconscious and hallucinating. His wife was sitting next to him and was continuously changing the wet cloth on his forehead, just as Mrs. Mariam did for me.

I asked how many more days he needed before the crisis would be past.

"Four days," replied Mrs. Parantsem, sobbing.

Although people who have had typhoid fever don't catch it again, I couldn't stay in the room any longer. I cast a last glance at my friend's emaciated face and left, greatly moved.

The second shock I had was when I was eating along the river. A stooped old woman came up to me and asked me to give her the bread I was eating.

For a second I glanced at her wrinkled, suffering face. There was no life left in her eyes, and hunger was permanently stamped around her lips. But how gentle her expression was, reminding me of my grandmother, or of all the grandmothers who once graced Armenian homes.

I gave her the slice I was holding, then I went into the mill, brought out some flour, and gave it to her. I thought this famished woman would grab the bread from my hand and throw it into her mouth at once, but to my great surprise I saw that she went a bit further away, sat down beside the river, and began eating the grass that was growing there.

I was interested. I went up to her and asked why she wasn't eating the bread I had given her. The old woman straightened her curved back as much as possible and replied with a sweet smile: "I'll take the bread to my grandchild, who is sick."

19 May, 1918

Two and a half years ago we had the first Armenian wedding in our village. Our neighbor, Boghos the baker, got married to a girl from Marash, where he was from. My mother and I were invited. As I was in bed suffering another bout of malaria, I couldn't go, but my mother went and at night she brought us a slice of cucumber instead of the usual sugar-coated almond for good luck. They had given one to each of the invited guests.

My mother told me that the wedding was quite festive. Young boys and girls had sung and the bride and groom had danced. The marriage ceremony was performed by my uncle, who was the most suitable person in the village. He had acted as a legal adviser for years.

Late last night we heard that the British had recaptured Salt. How true this news is, we don't know.

26 May, 1918

Whenever the British retreat, the Fellah chieftains turn into lions. They form volunteer companies and go to the front to pursue the enemy. When the British advance, the same Fellahs turn into cats, and return to their villages. It is evident that they have a kind of shallow patriotism, and, at the same time, they like to steal from the dead soldiers. They are leaving for the front again. This means that the British are again retreating.

Today, one of these fickle patriots beat Misag the farrier at the market. Apparently the latter asked to be paid for the work he had done.

"Infidel," said the Fellah, bringing his whip down on him, "Can't you see that we are going to shed our blood in war? And are you not even willing to contribute your services and shoe this animal for free?"

Another Don Quixote tortured Kapriel the gun smith for refusing to repair a broken rifle for free: in his words "trying to sabotage the battle that will be waged against the British!"

We had never before experienced such slander. If people succeed in accusing us of betrayal as well, that will take the cake!

2 June, 1918

Around this area of the Hauran, there is a chieftain named Yusuf (it's a strange coincidence that the name of the chieftain in Chorum was also Yusuf). "Up there is God and down here is Yusuf!" say the Fellahs, trembling whenever they hear his name.

Yusuf's raids are countless. Not a day goes by without his attacking a village, robbing innocent people, or killing somebody. The police are fully aware that he is a bloodthirsty criminal, but they dare not arrest him because Yusuf kills anyone who tries to hurt him in any way.

Whenever Yusuf comes to Jeresh, he buys things from me. Sometimes he doesn't pay for the tobacco or cigarette paper or flints, but he never forgets his debts. When the time comes, he pays everything he owes in one shot.

It's impossible to refuse the friendship of such a dangerous creature. He's like a stroke of bad luck. He imposes himself on you. Of course, his friendship is a lesser evil than his enmity.

One day Yusuf said to me: "Yakub (to Bedouins all Armenians are named Yakub), don't be afraid if our people attack the village. I'll ask one of my men to stand guard in front of your house . . . no one will dare to enter your home." I thanked him, but didn't give him the address of the house he had promised to protect. I knew that the Bedouins were assertive and often visited people without being invited.

So one can imagine how frightened and confused I was tonight when I came home and found Yusuf and three of his friends sitting comfortably in our room.

When my mother, sisters, and brother saw four armed Bedouins whose faces—except for their sparkling wild eyes—were covered with their head cloths, they had fled in alarm. Yusuf and his friends calmed them down, explaining that they were my friends and, after leaning their Mausers against the walls, had sat down on the pillows.

When I walked in, Yusuf got up and said with a smile, "Yakub, the position of this house at the end of the village is excellent. We're going to attack Kiufrendje (a Fellah village). We came here to wait for dark."

"Do you want to use my house as a base for your caper?" I asked, half joking and half complaining. "Yusuf, I beg of you, don't do this again. My mother and the children are petrified."

"Yakub, you know that I am your older brother," declared the thief in protest. "Your mother is my mother and your sisters are my sisters. May the beard of my father be cursed if I ever touch them. Tell them to come in. They don't need to be afraid of us."

Yusuf was happy when the members of my family entered the room, because they had shown that they trusted him. He stayed a little longer, then winked at his friends and left.

After the departure of these uninvited guests we breathed freely, and from the depths of our hearts cursed the Turks, who had made us the brothers of such reprehensible thieves.

5 June, 1918

The sickle of death has reaped another young life. Vartanian's daughter Armenouhi died today. She was an attractive, delicate, graceful, college-educated young girl. She suffered from an insignificant illness that would have been possible to cure if we were living in a city. Unfortunately, her condition gradually became complicated and caused her death.

Two days ago a German physician passed through the village. We asked him to try to cure her. He refused, saying that he had no medicine with him, so his visit would serve no purpose.

And so we took Armenouhi to the ruins and left her in a grave. As the earth gradually covered her delicate cheeks covered with white crepe, I got goose flesh all over my body. It was as if the earth being thrown on her were needles, and they were covering my face. But we threw the earth all the same until her face, hair, arms, legs, and finally her entire body disappeared from our sight. And thus Armenouhi turned into a memory in my mind.

We rolled a huge stone onto the pile of earth. Artin Aghpar engraved a cross on it with the end of his hoe. We all took off our hats and said the Lord's Prayer, then returned home.

9 June, 1918

The terror of the Fellahs, Yusuf the thief, has killed one or two people in Kiufrendje, and goes around the village as usual, without any fear.

This morning he came to buy tobacco and cigarette papers. Scarcely ten steps away from my counter there was the Kurdish corporal, accompanied by ten policemen. He carefully followed Yusuf and suddenly put his gun against the chieftain's back and shouted: "Hands up!"

The entire incident had taken just a few seconds. Yusuf had no time to grab his gun. The policemen suddenly threw themselves on him like dogs attacking a wounded wolf and beat him to the ground with their whips. In a minute this deity of the deserts became an unrecognizable heap of flesh under the kicks and blows of the policemen.

The police took him by the arms, tied his legs, and dragged him off to jail. The corporal stayed on the scene of the operation and made a report. Hundreds of Fellahs gathered around my counter, but were unwilling to become witnesses. They were afraid that Yusuf might take revenge on them later. But eventually, when the corporal emboldened them by assuring them that Yusuf would be sentenced to death and sent to Damascus to be hanged, they started to talk freely. One after the other, they declared that Yusuf had set their village on fire, driven their sheep away, killed a neighbor's son, decapitated the chieftain, etc., etc. The corporal wrote all these allegations down and left, proud of his work.

This evening we heard that the corporal, afraid that Yusuf's friends would attack the prison, had brought the mangled body of the thief out in a wheelbarrow and had sent him to Dera, escorted by four policemen and ten armed Fellahs.

16 June, 1918

One of Yusuf's friends had a clash with a Circassian at the market. He thought the Circassian had betrayed Yusuf. The latter took out his dagger and rushed at the Arab, who grabbed his gun and wounded him very seriously.

When they heard the shooting, all the Bedouins, Circassians, and Damascus Arabs in the market rushed to the spot where the fight was taking place . . . Another fight broke out not far from our counters— it was a violent fight, unlike anything we had seen before. There were more than a hundred people fighting. They all ran at each other, swearing and hitting each other with daggers, using swords and guns . . . At times people grabbed each other like wrestlers and fell to the ground. Daggers glittered in the air, curved knives pierced hearts, and swords split skulls. Blood was flowing from everywhere—faces, hands, and clothing. The wounded and dead were trodden under foot by the frenzied mob.

Gradually more forces arrived from the fields, houses, gardens, and mountains, and reinforced both sides, and the fight took on much larger proportions, almost turning into a real war. Fortunately, the soldiers stationed at the end of the village arrived. At the sight of these soldiers armed with bayonets, the Bedouins retreated, taking their dead and wounded with them. An hour later, the corpses of the local people were also removed. They washed down the market square with lots of water, and peace was restored.

Fortunately, as the Armenians had taken refuge in the stores during the bloody brawl and had not participated in the fight, we had no casualties. We were also lucky that these days all of the soldiers being sent to the front are stationed in our village. If they were not here, despite the existence of an agreement between the factions, the Bedouins would turn Jeresh upside down.

23 June, 1918

The presence of detachments of soldiers in the village is an advantage from the point of view of safety, but it's a decided problem for the Armenians. Among them there are bloodthirsty irregular troops, who instigate the local people against us by telling them how we created real bloodbaths in Anatolia three years ago.[*]

"Ah, the day will come again when we fix the heads of Armenians to the points of our swords and parade through the streets," they tell us in front of the Circassians. "Just wait. After every victory it's customary to make offerings to God and the Prophet . . . If we invade Jerusalem and push the enemy into the sea, on our return we'll take care of you too."

And sometimes they go from words to actions and beat every Armenian they bump into, roaring with laughter at the suffering of their victims.

Then they incite the police to draft the Armenians. "The country is in danger," they say. "We are going to shed our blood. Who are these *giaours*, that they should stay behind and watch us being martyred with the greatest of pleasure? Arrest them and send them to the front. Let them die too."

The situation is very dangerous. The Armenians don't want to show themselves in public and mostly stay at home.

30 June, 1918

We took advantage of the departure of the notorious guerrillas and the restored peace to go out today. We were at our compatriot Vartanian's store, discussing the day's events, when suddenly we heard a heart-rending scream that brought our conversation to an end.

---

[*] The Arabs and Circassians have no notion of the genocidal events of 1915. They think that the Armenians from the interior of Turkey were sent to Arabia for strategic reasons. So when they hear about bloody massacres from these irregular troops, they wonder, and tell us that if the government decided to exterminate us we must have been dangerous elements.

We went out into the street and met the Kurdish corporal, who was beating an Armenian woman with his cane. He hit her so violently that the cane broke over the woman's back and part of it whizzed over our heads.

"You can't fool me by pretending you've fainted," roared the savage, stepping on the woman. Now she was lying on the ground, as if struck by lightning. "Get up, daughter of a whore! I'll kill you if you don't tell me where your husband is!"

Many Muslims had gathered around the corporal, but no one made a move to protest his inhuman behavior. They all looked on indifferently, as if the woman crushed under his monstrous feet were a young viper. At last an elderly Circassian, unable to endure the woman's heart-rending cries, showed some pity and asked what her offense was.

The barbarous Kurd stopped beating her for a second and told the man that two days ago he had received a telegram from the governor of Irbit, ordering him to arrest 34-year old Avak, the son of Aleksan, from Sivrihissar, and send him to Irbit. There was no one in Jeresh by the name of Avak who was 34 years old and whose father's name was Aleksan. There was, however, a 40-year-old Avak from Adana, whose father's name was Baghdasar. That meant that the telegram was wrong . . . . the man from Jeresh wanted by the governor was definitely this Avak.

Acting in accordance with this logical conclusion, the brutal corporal had arrested Avak from Adana and sent him to Irbit with a policeman. The "damned" Armenian, however, had escaped the policeman's custody. If he were indeed not the wanted man, why should he run away?

After being informed of Avak's escape by the policeman, the corporal had gone to Avak's store and asked Avak's wife about her husband. "You arrested him two days ago and took him away," the woman said. "You know where he is better than I do."

"He has escaped from the police . . . where is he now? Tell me at once," the savage thundered.

"But I don't know anything about his escape. How should I know where he's hiding?" the woman replied.

"When I start beating you, you'll sing like a nightingale," shouted the foul man, and brought his cane down on the woman. The woman had run out of the store, crying and screaming. The corporal had chased her to the spot where she now lay unconscious beneath his feet.

The moment the Kurd had finished telling the man his story, the woman suddenly straightened up, got to her feet, and started to flee like a mad woman, all the time flailing her arms senselessly and shouting.

"Didn't I tell you she was putting on an act? She hadn't fainted," yelled the monster, with a diabolic grin on his face. "Look how she's running away . . . Hey woman, wait! I'm calling you, bitch! Wait or I'll . . ."

After ordering her to stop, the sadist took his rifle from his shoulder and started racing after the woman.

"I command you to stop . . . Do you hear?"

But Avak's wife neither heard nor stopped.

He took a huge leap and reached the woman, then hit her savagely on the back with the butt of his rifle. For a brief moment he watched his victim. Then he let out a cry of anger and left.

A little later, when we went over to our friend's wife to help, we saw that she lay there without moving . . . her death was quick.

7 July, 1918

During the deportation we camped at a station on the outskirts of Damascus. Three families stayed there because of illness. Since then we hadn't heard what happened to them. Today we received a letter from my friend Yervant Tintonian. They have moved to a village near Damascus. They have had deaths in the family, but no physical and mental tortures like us. By chance, Yervant met somebody from Jeresh who was originally from Caesarea. Hearing from him that we were still alive, Yervant gave the letter to a traveler who was coming to Jeresh.

He also sent us an Armenian newspaper, something we haven't seen for three years. What surprised us most was one of the news items in the paper, *Jamanak*, dated 3 June: according to it there was a newly formed Armenian Republic in the Caucasus, between Azerbaijan and Georgia. And the Republic had sent three delegates to Constantinople to participate in peace negotiations.

Jamanak doesn't give details about the Armenian government, but why should we need more details? It is a reality that at the foot of Mount Ararat there is an Armenian Republic, and the representatives of that republic have gone to Constantinople to extend their brotherly hands to us.

This thrilling news spread through the village faster that lightning. Men and women rushed to our house and many of them put their fingers on the words *REPUBLIC OF ARMENIA*, just like the Apostle Thomas, and started shedding tears of happiness.

Today for the seventh time the faces of Armenian refugees are smiling. We only hope that this won't turn into an unfounded smile.

14 July, 1918

Sultan Reshad is dead. Sultan Vahdetdin has succeeded him.

I went to the market to see the festivities organized for the occasion of the enthronement of the new Sultan. Ruhji Bedros left the crowd and approached me. "You laughed at our predictions," said my friend from Aintab in an authoritative voice, "but look how our predictions for 1335 have proven accurate."

"What do you mean, accurate? You predicted that the Ottoman Empire would fall in 1916."

"It doesn't matter that our prediction was off by a year or two," said my spiritual friend. "Now, with the realization of 666, our prediction is correct."

"What's 666?" I asked, interested.

"Oh, I see that you don't know. Let me explain. Sultan Vahdetdin is the 36th Sultan of Turkey, right?"

"Yes."

"Good. Then, please write the numerals from 1 to 36 on a piece of paper and add them all up and see what you get."

"Suppose I did that, what would the result be? You tell me."

"Six hundred sixty-six, brother. And our prophet has said that number 666 will be the end. Do you see it now? Sultan Vahdetdin will be the last Sultan of the Empire."

"And if Vahdetdin dies . . ."

"It will be the end of Turkey. Don't laugh! That day is not far off. Take the cannons. The other day I counted 62 of them in five minutes. And the British aeroplanes have become a permanent feature in our skies. Please, mark my words, all the signs indicate that the end is near."

During our conversation the procession of merry-makers was heading for the square before the mosque. We followed the procession.

The man at the head of the procession had climbed up on the shoulders of another man and was brandishing a huge sword in the air and shouting continuously: *"Ilahi illalah."* The crowd repeated these words and fired into the air.

When we reached the mosque a young lad got up on a prayer stone and read verses from the Koran. Every time he stopped to breathe the people shouted Amen in unison. After the reading from the Koran, the head of the village got up on the same stone and gave a speech to mark the occasion—but in fact it was not a speech but a series of nonsensical, irrelevant phrases. Then he stepped down and with solemn, ceremonial steps went and opened the door of the prison, which was across from the mosque.

"You are free," he told the prisoners. "Go, and pray for the prosperity of the new ruler." Seven prisoners, among them a couple of Armenian deserters, came out of the jail and made dramatic appeals.

When Ruhji Bedros noticed the liberation of the Armenian prisoners he leaned toward my ear and said: "See! These are signs that better times are coming."

21 July, 1918

The village superintendent, who was as virulently prejudiced against the Armenians as the corporal, has set the prisoners free in order to prepare a trap for the Armenians.

Today we understood his intention. He wanted to get all the Armenians out of their hiding places and have them register their names instead of letting them go about their daily lives without being disturbed. Using the list prepared in this way, they started to arrest people at noon, and this time they went to the mills, gardens, and fields to do it . . . thinking that whenever they start at the market those who are not there have time to flee.

When the news came to the village, we who were working at the market abandoned our stores and counters and ran like frightened animals in all directions.

I again went to my neighbor's stable, which I feel is a very good hide-out. Two hours later, unable to find anybody at the market, the police went into the streets to search.

As I write these lines our house has already been searched twice.

28 July, 1918

During the week the police made three surprise raids on our room, but they went back empty-handed every time.

I am safe in the stable, but on Thursday a big snake showed up and disturbed my comfort. As usual, I was sitting at the keyhole, spying on the police in the street, when I suddenly heard a noise from the hay stacks. I turned and saw a four-foot long spotted snake, as thick as my arm. After gazing at me for a moment it darted into a hole in the wall and disappeared. It is not a poisonous snake, but considering that it might frighten me at night during my sleep, I have been sleeping in our room for the last couple of days. This is also uncomfortable, since the police might surprise me any time.

We had hoped that the Armenian delegates who are negotiating in Constantinople would perhaps be able to intercede in our favor, but these hopes are gradually disappearing. As for the British, they seem to have forgotten us. We haven't heard any cannons recently.

Late tonight I heard that about 28 of the arrested people have been sent to Irbit.

4 August, 1918

To put an end to my unpleasant life in the stable, we came to an arrangement with the Kurdish corporal. I'll pay him three pounds a month, and he will take into consideration my real age as well as my illness and won't arrest me. So today we sold the carpet in our room and I sent him the money to buy my freedom, through my friend Reshad Bey. Now I roam the streets without fear and I realize how precious liberty is. If it is so very precious under such violence and force, how will it feel to live under a free administration?

A Bedouin who brought smuggled goods from an occupied region to the market told us how happy the Armenians were on the other side of the border. "If you want, I can take you to your kinsmen," he said, in the hope of also smuggling from this side of the border.

"But how can we cross the Turkish line?" we asked suspiciously.

"We know many ways, many roads where there are no Turkish soldiers," said the Bedouin with a sneer.

"We believe you, since you've brought illegal goods from the other side," we said, "but we can't run away. We're not alone."

To tempt us further, the Bedouin said: "And do you have any idea how cheap and abundant sugar and rice are there?"

For an Arab the most valuable thing after life itself is sugar. Without attaching much importance to it, we said, "If we want to go to the British side, it's to attain freedom, which is much sweeter than all the sugar in the world."

The Bedouin replied compassionately: "You Armenians are strange people . . . you say that you love liberty, but you wait for it to come knocking at your door."

Silence ensued.

What other reply could there be to an observation as true as this one?

11 August, 1918

Late yesterday afternoon, while passing through the market place, the ox of a Circassian named Murtaza shied and kicked over the counter of Arshag from Adana. Poor Arshag's raisins and pistachios fell into the dirt. Instead of feeling sorry for him, however, the Circassian hit him with the goad in his hand, claiming that the ox had hurt its leg while kicking the counter over. The outlaw was not satisfied with that, but beat Arshag up, demolished all the counters on the market square, and declared that from then on whoever set up a counter there would have problems with him.

I had no idea of all this: because of a toothache I had not gone to the market. So I set up my counter this morning in its usual place. Murtaza rushed at me like a mad cow, cracked his whip in the air, and shouted: "Take away your counter!"

"Why? What's happened?" I asked, completely surprised.

"I'm warning you, take it away," the Circassian roared like a raging monster.

"But I don't see why I should," I replied. "I pay municipal rent for this spot."

"I know nothing about municipal or whatever . . . It is forbidden, do you hear me?"

"Who has forbidden it?"

"I have."

Realizing that I was dealing with an absolute tyrant, I picked up my table and returned to Vartanian's store.

We were not alive during the feudal period, but I don't think it was any different! In this country law and order exist in name only. However, the real law and order are the local people and their whims.

The municipal authorities prepare a price list. For example, they set a price for vegetables, so they can't be sold for more than such and such price. If the Armenians follow the law, the Circassians, who have now learned gardening, start beating the Armenians up, accusing them of lowering their prices and reducing the Circassians' profits. And if the Armenians obey the Circassians, the government punishes only the disobedient Armenians and never the Circassians.

It is the same with the copper coins. According to government order, they have to be withdrawn from circulation. The Circassians pay Armenians in copper coins, and if the Armenians refuse to accept them, they insist that "the money of the government is always good," and start persecuting them. And if the Armenians pay them in copper coins, they beat them up and shout, "Didn't you hear the government order?"

To say nothing of the paper banknotes, which are now worth fifteen coins.

No matter what we do, or which way we turn, we are met with beatings, disrespect, and hatred from all directions—both from the government and from the local population—whether we sit straight or crooked.

18 August, 1918

When the village chief noticed that the municipal revenues were decreasing, he called Murtaza the Circassian and asked him to allow the Armenians to do business in the market place again. The Circassian kindly agreed to forget his oath. So today we were able to set up our counters again, on condition that we pay 40 *para* in rent instead of 10.

I wish, though, we had not been at the market to see the monstrous crime that took place this afternoon right under our eyes.

The same wicked Murtaza was sitting on his cart, goading the oxen through the crowded market so fast that you'd think he was in a chariot race. Suddenly a nine-year-old girl carrying water in a pitcher got caught in the path of the racing oxen, and the cart hit her so forcefully that she was thrown some distance away. Without even taking the trouble to see whether he had killed the girl, the evil ogre continued victoriously on his way, all the while cursing the Armenians, who prevented people from traveling freely in the market place. In fact, that was precisely why he had been racing like that.

Those who saw the accident immediately ran to the poor girl to help. We stopped, terrified, when we saw blood pouring from her half-open mouth. Fortunately, she wasn't dead. We took her mangled body and delivered her to her mother, who was out of her mind with grief.

25 August, 1918

Everybody knew Zarouhi in the village. She was our parish priest's daughter, and after the death of her father and mother she made her living by carrying water to the Circassian homes. Four months ago she was suffering from typhoid fever and was miraculously snatched from the tentacles of that cruel disease. As she was malnourished, her convalescence took a very long time. When she started working again she had not yet completely recovered.

Zarouhi passed the market place more than ten times as she came back from the spring, carrying a couple of heavy tin containers. After she had climbing the slope leading to the village, it was her habit to stop for a moment at the end of the market and rest. When we saw her frail body we thought that one day, like Christ—who collapsed exhausted under the weight of the cross—she would fall on her face under the weight of her tin containers, and perhaps no one would even bother to go over, take her hand, and help her up.

It's been ten days since Zarouhi disappeared. We who work at the market have been worried, wondering if the girl had fallen sick again. Today we visited the hut where she lived, to find out. There we learned from her Circassian landlord that the girl had been thrown out of the house, as she was unable to pay her rent regularly. Thinking that she might have gone to the caves, we went there, and in fact we found her, but not alive. Her body had been torn apart by wild dogs.

Now we can imagine how she became sick again in her new residence (the cave), called for help, and fixed her eyes on the entrance to the cave, waiting for a human being to show up (these caves are now deserted, their one-time inhabitants having perished long ago). Who knows, perhaps she was hallucinating and in her imagination thought she saw the faces of her loved ones. Perhaps the hungry beasts surrounded her in anticipation of their bloody banquet. Perhaps she felt their blood-scented breath on her face but, incapable of moving, could not chase them away. Or perhaps she saw the foaming beasts rushing at her . . . and let out a sudden, terrified scream, at which her heart stopped beating. We cannot know exactly what happened and the conditions under which our parish priest's daughter died. We only know that she was dead and was torn apart by ravenous beasts.

Oh, if the walls of these caves could talk, and tell us what horrifying events they have seen in all these years!

1 September, 1918

The price of a bushel of wheat is now 140 coins. It's been so long since we could afford it, we've forgotten what it tastes like. For a year now we have been eating barley bread, and there isn't enough of even that. We fill the emptiness in our stomachs with boiled grass or roasted wild chestnuts, which are bitter when we eat them, but taste sweeter when followed with a drink of water.

Today Manoushag went to the fields to collect mallow with some other Armenian women. After half an hour she came back in tears. A Circassian had kicked them out, insisting that the fields belonged to him and nobody had the right to pick grass there.

Wheat bread now seems like a dream to us. We never knew how sweet it was, we never knew how valuable it was. Will the day perhaps come again when we will again fill our stomachs with wheat bread only?

8 September, 1918

Out of an unwillingness to fill my diary with my illnesses, I often don't write anything when I get sick, putting it aside with the rest of my normal daily routine. But sometimes there are cases which cannot be put aside, especially when one has not recovered from one illness before another succeeds it.

My winter cold has been with me for the last eight months. I cough so much that I'm afraid I have tuberculosis. For three days now I've been in bed with malaria again. And today, as if my cough and fever were not enough, my tooth started aching.

This last pain especially is really unbearable. One of my upper molars has a huge cavity. In an attempt to cauterize the nerve that is giving me pain, I pushed a burning hot darning needle into the hole. Tears ran from my eyes, but the pain was not reduced, not even a tiny bit.

In the evening I asked our Circassian landlord what he did when he had a toothache.

"We put some pincer oil on it," the man replied seriously.

"Do you have any of that medicine? . . . could you please give me some?"

"Gladly."

The Circassian went into the shed and returned with a big pair of rusty tongs, sturdy enough to pull my jaw out.

"Do you want them?"

"No, thank you," I said, and pulled the blanket over my head.

15 September, 1918

Something is happening, but we don't know exactly what.

The sound of the cannons is getting closer. We very often see aeroplanes in our skies. Yesterday two German officers came from Salt and are staying at the house of the village head. They say that they look quite worried.

Today they organized a horse race at the end of the village in their honor. I was not in the mood for entertainment, but I went to the horse race with a few friends for a change.

Our ex-landlord, Husein Bey, did quite a few daring tricks, rolling himself under the racing horse and coming up on the other side, bending down while the horse sped and picking up coins from the ground, etc.

We took advantage of the exuberant atmosphere to approach the German officers and tell them our nationality in French. We asked them if they had any good news and if the war would end in the near future.

"*Nein*," replied the Germans—and they immediately walked away from us as if we were lepers.

22 September, 1918

Is this, perhaps, the eve of great changes?

The British have again captured Salt, and now we hear the cannon blasts from very close indeed, as if from behind the hill.

More than a hundred aeroplanes fly over the village every day. According to the rumors that are circulating, the British have bombed the Dera station and the Arabs have taken advantage of the situation to loot the stores.

The Circassians of the village are extremely nervous. Late in the evening a company of Turkish soldiers arrived from Salt.

24 September, 1918

Frightened soldiers running away from the front are going through Jeresh. Among today's deserters there are also Germans. Bedouins attacked them on their way to Jeresh and put twenty-six of them to the sword. According to the Circassians, the Bedouins didn't touch the Turkish soldiers because of their religion.

Of course the massacre is very unfortunate, but what a beautiful lesson for the Germans! The semi-savage Bedouins save the Turks because they are Muslims and slaughters the Christian Germans. The latter didn't even have that much compassion when an entire Christian nation was being martyred before their eyes.

A lot is going on in the village these days, but alas! Because of my yellow fever I can't go out to follow events more closely.

25 September, 1918

Is it a dream or reality we are living? The sounds of cannons come from behind us.

Turkish soldiers, policemen, and government employees fled Jeresh in their nightgowns last night. Dera and Irbit have been captured by the troops of Sherif. The British are beleaguering the enemy who, for the last three years, have squatted on our senseless bodies like a blood-sucking vampire.

Massacre, deportation, pillage, destruction, persecution, famine, sickness, beating, suffering, conscription, misery, and all other misfortunes have therefore come to an end.

It's as if a new life, a new period, a new perspective were opening before us.

Forgetting my illness, I went to the market and was thrilled when I saw numerous men and women—sick people, hungry people—hugging each other with tears in their eyes, shouting hurrahs in honor of the British army, which will undoubtedly be arriving within a few days and will bring us bread and medicine.

The Armenians of Jeresh leap for joy for the eighth time. This, of course, will be the last time.

26 September, 1918

Today I am again suffering from a high fever, and can't go out.

The Arabs have brought all the rifles and bullets that the Turkish soldiers left behind during their retreat. They are selling them a

German Mauser for ten coins and a hundred bullets for one coin. They have also taken the clothes, shoes, shirts, and overcoats of all the soldiers they've killed. They are in an unusually happy mood because of the tremendous devastation they've caused.

A Bedouin who noticed that the Armenians on the market were even happier, asked my uncle how we could be in such a joyous mood when we didn't have the least share in the pillage. The stupid man hadn't considered that we've received the most valuable portion of this victory, for we've regained our endangered lives and our lost human dignity.

27 September, 1918

It was fortunate that the Turkish defeat was sudden and that in their panic they didn't have time to deliberate and massacre the Armenians. They tried, though, in Dera, but failed because the British came quickly to the rescue. As if the ruthless villains had not shed enough blood, during their retreat they fired at four women who were doing their wash in a courtyard. Fortunately, they missed their targets, and a little later, when the city was invaded, they ran away and disappeared.

Here events have followed each other so rapidly that the locals have not even had time to realize when and how Jeresh was emptied and captured.

We aren't quite clear about this either. Despite the fact that the British army has captured Dera and gone even further, nobody has yet come or gone through our village.

28 September, 1918

It's as if the Holy Spirit has descended on our neighboring Circassians. From one day to the next they have changed and become Samaritans. We wonder if these are the unyielding, disgusting Circassians we know. Only yesterday they were crushing an innocent girl under a cart, while today, like a caring mother, they tend the sick, feed the hungry, and try to make friends with the unjustly treated.

The secrets of human nature are incomprehensible. If it's possible for the most evil man in the world to turn into an angel in a day, how did evil ever come to make its nest in his heart in the first place?

29 September, 1919

Still no British or Sherifian soldiers have entered our village. We don't know who controls the village at the moment. Anarchy is everywhere. The Bedouins have been spoiled by Sherif's victory and continue threatening to attack the village.

Today three Circassians went to Amman to explain the situation to the government there and request that they send troops to prevent bloodshed.

30 September, 1918

From a traveler from Dera we learned that high-ranking Turkish prisoners of war have been sent to Egypt by train. At the station they were greeted with *down with*s and *shame on you*s. An Armenian woman came forward from the crowd and shouted: "Where are you going, honorable gentlemen? To displace the people of Egypt?" The Turkish pashas kept their mouths shut as they looked down.

We have not yet seen the haughty Turks lower their eyes in guilt, but we are pleased at what we have seen so far.

1 October, 1918

The Circassians who went to Amman came back with a British flag and raised it in the market square. All the Armenians went to the market to see that gratifying sight.

My heart beats with happiness too, but unfortunately I can't go out. Illness has left me quite weak.

2 October, 1918

Three days ago, the British army occupied Damascus.

The criminal, arrogant soldiers of *yildrim ordusu* (the army of lightning), who have bullied us so much, are now miles away from us, and there is no possibility that they will return and recapture the territory they have lost. The swords of the cursed irregular bands can no longer reach us. We are as happy as if we had been reborn!

3 October, 1918

I felt a bit better today. I got out of bed and went to the market to see the British flag. It is a strange flag: a black cross on a white cloth, which doesn't look much like the English flag. But I was elated when I saw that it flew over Abu Hasan's store. This man from Damascus has tortured countless Armenians, simply because they are Christians. You'd think it had magical powers, that piece of cloth—powers to disarm and control people's seditious inclinations.

I saw the pitiful state of these arrogant despots of Jeresh, and I returned home with a heart filled with unbounded joy.

4 October, 1918

Today by chance I met our ex-landlord, Husein Bey. He is one of those who brought the British flag here from Amman. "What kind of British flag is that?" I asked. "I've never seen a black cross on a white flag."

"The British use that flag in the regions they capture," Husein Bey replied with a smile.

"Joking aside, where did you get that flag?" I insisted.

"Don't tell anyone," uttered my ex-landlord, almost whispering. "We invented that flag, just to frighten the Bedouins."

"But haven't the British entered Amman?"

"They have. But they've left this part to Sherif, and are not terribly interested in our village. So under the circumstances we brought back this flag. If we wait for the Sherif troops to come, perhaps by then the Bedouins will have put the entire village to the sword and burned everything down. You know how the law is respected now. The Bedouins look at the flag and think that the English are here in the village, and they behave nicely."

"It's not a bad idea," I said, "but I wish you'd brought back a real flag."

"We couldn't find one," said Husein Bey, shrugging. "Or to be more precise, we found one but it was so complicated that we couldn't reproduce it. So we made this one and brought it back. What's important for us is not whether it's an authentic flag, it's the moral effect it has."

5 October, 1918

The items left behind by the Turkish army are being sold for next to nothing at the market. Besides shotguns, cartridge belts, bayonets and swords, the items sold by the Bedouins include military boots, cameras, whips with silver handles, binoculars, watches, cigarette boxes, and many other things.

We got a batch of papers from an Arab, and when we went through them we discovered that the Turks had reported any insignificant success as a great victory, thus deceiving the people, including the commanders in Constantinople.

What seemed most significant among these papers was a little notebook. The Bedouin had taken it, among other valuable things, from the pocket of a Turkish officer he had killed. Each page of the notebook has a list of dates, and following each date a couple of words are jotted down, mostly the names of villages or cities. It seems that the officer traveled around Anatolia quite a bit and recorded the names of the places he visited, sometimes adding brief explanations.

Among the Turkish officer's daily entries is the following section, which is a little enigmatic and, at the same time, mysterious:

17 August, 1915—Malatia. In the morning, 620; in the evening, 200.

18 August, 1915—104. Yesterday, with my own hands.

19 August, 1915—Woman and child, 746. Well.

20 August, 1915—19 prisoners.

Are these perhaps the numbers of Armenians killed by the officer himself, or the number of those he had killed?

6 October, 1918

Yusuf, the bandit chief, whom we thought had been sent to the gallows, arrived here today, riding a beautiful mare. At the market he began to beat all the Circassians and Fellahs he suspected of betraying him. When he saw me, he approached and greeted me, "*Ya akhi*" (oh, my brother). Then he told me that after the Turks retreated, the people in Damascus had broken down the doors of the prison and freed all the prisoners.

"Now I know what to do," he said between his teeth: "Yakub, you were with me when I was captured. Did you see who accused me?"

"It's true that there were a few Fellahs there," I replied, "but I don't know them."

"I'll track down all of them," he said, his eyes glittering with hatred. "I've already hunted down Mahmoud and killed him."

"Mahmoud, the corporal?" I asked suddenly, not believing my ears.

"Yes, that son of a bitch of a Kurd," he answered with a triumphant smile.

"But where did you find him?"

"Do you think my friends have been sleeping? He was hiding in Dera. As soon as I came out of the station, the first thing I did was go to his home and cut his head off."

"You're lying, Yusuf."

"Yakub, may my father's beard be cursed if I'm lying."

"This news makes me very happy, Yusuf. Do you know how much evil this lawless man has visited on the Armenians? After exiling hundreds of families to the deserts and sending hundreds of people to the front for their military service, only three weeks after your arrest he killed my friend's wife."

"Wait until you see all that I'm going to do. You haven't seen anything yet!" said the chief of the thieves. "We'll talk about it another time . . . Now, give me a bit of tobacco. I'll pay you later."

"I was liquidating my counter anyway," I said. "Take it, my friend. All that tobacco is yours."

"Then let me have a cigarette holder, a needle, and thread too," said Yusuf, taking the things he had asked for.

"Take this too. A gift from me," I added, and gave him an arm's length of lamp wick.

"Yakub, can you do me another kindness, and also give me a comb?" asked Yusuf, looking at me with imploring eyes. "Do you know that it's been four months since I last combed my beard?"

"I give it to you for free, my friend," I said. "You've taken revenge on him on my behalf. Don't be shy, Yusuf. If you need anything else, take it."

"May you live long, my brother! In that case, lend me 5 coins. I'll pay for everything later, all in one shot."

I also gave Yusuf the money, this time with the greatest of pleasure. Because I no longer had to deal with a criminal, but with a revenging Nemesis—he had, at least indirectly, taken revenge for all the blood shed in Jeresh.

13 October, 1918

Today the British "flag" came down and was replaced by the Sherifian.

Absolute anarchy reigns in the village. An Arab chieftain came and gave orders, proclaimed laws, and left. Then another chieftain arrived, abolished the laws of his predecessor, proclaimed his own laws, and left. Then came an officer of Sherif and established laws which completely contradict those, and likewise disappeared.

The Arab chief of the village, who had disappeared for some time, has resumed his duties. The same with all the Arab policemen, but with a difference: on their Turkish uniforms they wear arm bands in the colors of Sherifian flag. Fortunately, the Kurdish corporal has been assassinated. If he had also resumed his official functions, it would have been a farce.

What have we gained so far with all these changes? Almost nothing! The Bedouins continue to steal from Armenian stores and gardens, and they are again beating and injuring the refugees.

Last night they hurt Khurshid the miller quite seriously.

"Don't say a thing. During the confusion of war such small incidents can happen. You should leave the mills and gardens and live close to each other in the village."

"But these people have to work outside the village in order to make their living," we answer.

"Then just hold your peace. Now that the Bedouins have become so spoiled, they may not obey the law. We are not in a position to object."

"We are not in a position to object!" There it is! That's the answer we received from Miudur Bey, the director of public order in the village.

We have sent people to Salt to ask the British to think of a way to rescue us from here.

20 October, 1918

The Armenians who went to Salt returned last night. They had an audience with the British commanding officer and explained our difficult situation. After expressing his sympathy, the British officer told them that he couldn't arrange our evacuation, and advised that the Armenians move to Salt, finding their own means of transportation.

"But how can we?" asked the Armenians. "Our people are hungry, sick, naked, incapable of moving. And the few families who can provide their own means of transportation are afraid to undertake the journey, because the Bedouins have blocked the road and are asking travelers to pay for right of way."

"In that case, you'll have to wait a bit longer," answered the British CO. "We are now attending to administrative structures in the occupied regions. Of course in the future we'll also turn our attention to your people."

But until the British arrange something for us, our situation here deteriorates from one day to the next.

The Muslims, who thought that the British would look after us right away, now realize that the English are not interested, and have returned to their old policies.

A Damascus storekeeper who has a widow from Aintab working for him has locked her up in a room. The reason for this confinement is that he wants her to marry him and doesn't want her to leave the country. When the woman's uncle went to ransom his relative, the Damascus man threw him out, saying that he would starve the woman and that the uncle had no right to protect her.

If such an unjust incident had happened in the days of our slavery, perhaps it wouldn't have saddened us so much, but after our liberation, it's unbearable . . . So we went to the chief administrator and requested that the woman be freed.

"Be patient," he said, after listening to our protest. "Naturally, all these problems will gradually be taken care of."

"How can we wait, when the man from Damascus is using force on the woman?" we asked, justifiably.

"I'll tell him to be a little easier on her," the man replied calmly. "However, if the woman wishes to convert to Islam, naturally we can't interfere."

"But if the woman wished to convert and marry him, why would the man have to imprison her?"

"Who knows? Perhaps it was to protect her from her uncle."

"No sir, what you say isn't the case. You're trying to protect the kidnapper," said Kapriel the gun smith.

"Why should I want to protect the kidnapper?" protested the chief angrily.

"Because if you were a just man you wouldn't keep the three Armenian girls you brought from Wadi Mousa."

"Is it wrong to save three lives from the massacres that were taking place there?"

"You would do much better to stop using these girls of 12, 14, and 15 years of age as wives, and return them to their people. The Turkish government no longer exists, sir. Let's face it."

"You are depending on the British government. That's why you talk so freely," the man barked, with a sudden burst of hatred. "Get lost! Go wherever you want to, and see what you can do."

Having said this, the former employee of Turkey slammed the door in our faces, just as the governor of Dera had done when we went to complain about the lack of bread. But that incident took place three years ago. We thought that since then at least something had changed in world history.

22 October, 1918

Abu Hasan of Damascus, on whose store the British flag was raised, encouraged by the administrator's antagonistic attitude to us and following his compatriot's example, has kidnaped the girl from Deort Yol who worked for him. The girl who used to make her living carrying wood (see the entry for 29 January, 1917).

As soon as the Armenians heard the news, they went to see him to ransom the girl. He refused their demands. The Armenians dragged him out of his store and handed him over to the police.

This morning we heard that Abu Hasan had been bailed out and had disappeared with the Armenian girl. Thinking that he might have taken refuge in the home of one of his relatives, a few young men armed with pistols and truncheons decided go there. They were arrested by the police, charged with disturbing the peace, and taken to the village administrator.

"We're not the ones who are disturbing the peace. The people from Damascus are," the youths protested to the administrator. "Instead arresting us, arrest those men of violence."

"That's my business. You have no right to create a government within a government," the administrator declared quite severely.

"We're not creating a government, we're . . ."

"Then who gave you the right to carry firearms, to raid homes?" the administrator interrupted menacingly. "Come to your senses, Armenians. This is an Arab land. If I want to, I can send you to the gallows this very minute. Nobody can interfere."

"But . . ."

"There's no *but* about it . . . Either you behave yourselves or you leave this country at once."

"We are behaving ourselves," said one of the arrested boys. "Tell the people from Damascus to leave us in peace."

"I don't take orders from you . . . Get lost! . . . Out of my sight! And make sure that you don't have to deal with me again!"

The protesters bowed their heads and left. There is now a very tense relationship between the Armenians and the Arabs from Damascus.

27 October, 1918

About a hundred refugees left for Salt this week.

The Bedouins continue to plunder the Armenian vegetable gardens. They tortured a pregnant woman in a garden three days ago. The woman miscarried and is now on her death-bed.

On the other hand, the provocations of the Damascus storekeepers continue. They have declared a boycott against Armenians and refuse to sell us anything.

Today an old woman clutching her money begged a Damascus butcher to sell her a few bones (here the butchers sell the meat and the bones separately).

"It's to make broth for my sick daughter. Please, I beg of you," the old woman was saying.

"Die, pigs!" the storekeeper barked, shoving the woman roughly. "It's our fault for not skinning you alive when we had the opportunity. But just you wait. The tables will turn again."

We don't believe our eyes and ears when we see and hear such things.

3 November, 1918

The police have not yet rid themselves of the habit of harassing Armenians. Today they went to the shop of Kapriel the gun smith and confiscated the two rifles that were there, on the pretext that the Armenians don't have the right to keep firearms.

"But these rifles aren't mine. The Bedouins brought them to be repaired," Kapriel protested.

"We don't know that," the police replied. "We found them in your shop, and we're confiscating them as your property."

After the police had gone, the Bedouins arrived to pick up their shotguns. When they heard Kapriel's explanation, they attacked him, thinking he was lying to them in order to steal their firearms. With great difficulty, Kapriel persuaded the Bedouins to go with him to the government house, to prove his explanation. Fortunately, the police returned the rifles to them, and that was the end of the incident.

When the Bedouins got their guns back and were leaving, they made the following reproach to those of us who were present: "You may give away your soul, but never give away your rifle. You Armenians are a weak people, and have no right to live."

The words of this Bedouin warrior reminded me of the Bedouin shepherd's justifiable observation: "If the enemy invaded your country, why didn't you fight? Why didn't you kill them? Why did you run away to your country?"

On foot, on camels, on donkeys, and in carriages, group after group of Armenians leaves for Salt every day. We are told that the British there put the Armenians in trucks and send them to Jerusalem.

We are also ready to leave, but because of the continuous rain we are postponing our journey.

The Damascus man who disappeared with the girl from Deort Yol is back in the store today, and sarcastically tells us that our friends, the British, should come and arrest her.

Jeresh and all its evil inhabitants fill us with total disgust, and can't take it any more.

Part Three

RETURN FROM THE DESERT

15 November, 1918

When we woke up on the morning of 2/15 November, 1915, we found ourselves in Jeresh. Exactly three years later we are leaving Jeresh.

Yes, three years have passed since those dark days. Three long years of mourning and worries and horror.

The persecution by the government—conscription into the army, exile, imprisonment, the hatred of the local people, murder, kidnapping, pillage—and natural calamities such as starvation, destitution, and sickness, devastated the population. Thus, out of the 20,000 Armenians in the area only 450 were able to survive—and those survivors were sick, skeletal wrecks. . . . They are the ones who now painfully move toward free horizons, in the hope of finding peace for the remainder of their days.

We were almost the last of the caravans. The few rags we had with us were loaded on seven camels and ten donkeys. We ten families hit the road very early this morning. We were going to Salt, the first station of salvation for the remnants of the Armenians in the Hauran.

Our departure from the village took place under noteworthy circumstances. Circassian families we knew had come to bid farewell, repeating the same slogans as they had used all month: *i.e.*, that we shouldn't leave, that it would be better if we stayed in the village, that they would give us free room and board, etc. Some of them even cried, probably wondering how and to whom they could now rent their worthless stables and chicken coops. Who would plow their land? Who would build their houses and stores? Whom could they ask to mend their clothes and shoes? Who would repair their plows and coulters? To whom could they sell their sheep and grain?

Their behavior did not surprise us. For years and years we had told them, but they had never grasped the importance of the Armenians in their land. The store owners from Damascus often used the Circassians to persecute us. They tortured us relentlessly. Now they were acknowledging their wrongdoing, but it was too late!

"Even if you were to promise us all the riches the world, you could never persuade us to remain in this land. We'll go to Armenia, to rebuild our resurrected homeland," we answered them as we left.

While passing the site of the ruins, we looked for a long time at all the mounds of earth under which lay the bones of our compatriots. For a moment we visualized thousands and thousands of familiar faces—from Marash, Aintab, Zeitoun, Adana, Sis, Caesarea, Chorum, and elsewhere—with whom we were once acquainted. We had shared each other's fates, until one day they were wiped out of our lives as if in a dream.

Did they really live? Were they real faces or only imaginary ones, which we got to know while reading a novel? Yes, there's no doubt they were human beings with nerves and muscles, but they weren't lucky enough to see the defeat of Tyranny and the victory of Justice.

The road gradually declined and the columns of the ancient ruins disappeared from our view like the masts of a sinking ship. We saw only the towering gate of the old city. It was the only thing still tying us to the gloomy memories of our past. After a short while, that too was wiped from our view, and we found ourselves face to face with the present reality.

The elderly, the children, and the sick rode on the animals. The rest of us walked, just as we had done three years ago when we first came to Jeresh. How spiritually different were these two journeys! Then we were like convicts walking to the scaffold. And now we were like convicts saved from hanging!

We no longer minded the muddy and thorny roads. These were the last roads, and soon would all be forgotten.

We came to the Zarga river at noon. We crossed it by putting the women and children on the camels. The rest of us took off our clothes and walked hand in hand through the shallow waters. On the opposite bank we rested for a while, then got up and resumed our journey.

Late at night we reached Rumman, the famous village of the Turkomans, where we slept in a stable.

16 November, 1918

Our trip today was extremely tiring and bothersome. The camels couldn't walk safely on the roads because the pouring rain had opened up huge holes. So we had to carry earth and stones to fill the holes. Despite our attentiveness, one of the camels fell down while climbing an incline. Although it wasn't hurt, the owner got mad and threatened to leave us. He insisted that he would keep his word and leave us at the top of the hill if we failed to win him over with monetary gifts.

Around dusk we finally ended our dangerous trip—dangerous in two respects: the roads were rough, and were frequented by bandits. We finally reached the gravel road that connected Salt and Amman.

Although there was no danger of getting stuck in the middle of this gravel road, it still wasn't something we could cover merely by walking. Sometimes a car with its headlights on would whiz past us like the wind. We'd look back and realize that we had progressed no more than twenty yards.

Finally, tonight we reached Salt, totally exhausted.

The camel owners left us in front of a building and walked away cursing us. We didn't know where we were in the utter darkness. We lay down on the stones and closed our weary eyes.

17 November, 1918

The day we had arrived in Jeresh, when we had opened our eyes in the morning, we were surrounded by Armenian refugees who pointed us out to each other as the "ones in pants."

But we were in Salt, and when we woke up there, we were British soldiers around us saying, "The refugees are here!"

"Hello, what news?" we asked them, using the few English words we knew.

"All right," they replied with a glimmer of satisfaction, nodding their heads.

We remembered that we had sworn among ourselves to do certain things if and when we saw a British soldier.

Sarko the butcher and Misag the farrier were not with us, as they left for Salt before us. We didn't know what had happened to Avak the comb-maker. He hadn't returned to the village after fleeing from the road in Irbit. Only Kapriel the gun smith and his family were with us.

"OK, my friend, carry out your oath," we goaded him. "You vowed to kiss the forehead of the very first British soldier who came your way."

Kapriel looked furtively at the soldier who stood nearby. His arrogant posture intimidated him.

"Let me correct you. I never vowed to kiss the forehead of a British soldier—what I promised was to kiss the hand of the British commander!"

"How are we going to find you a commander?" we asked.

"Why don't you keep your oath?" asked Kapriel, turning to me, "Why don't you kiss the eyes of the soldier beside you?"

"If I were to try, he'd probably put out my eye with a single punch of his fist! And besides, my vow was to kiss the British flag."

While we were joking we noticed two men and a woman who was dressed in civilian clothes and carrying a handbag approaching us. They were employees of the Near East Relief Committee. They gave each of us a coin to help us out. One of them, who knew Arabic, informed us that there is an armistice and that Constantinople has already been occupied by the Allies.

We immediately ran to the market to buy bread and dates with the money we'd been given.

After these purchases, the boys were looking around for a British officer or flag, for we had to carry out our oaths. Just then the youngest Vartanian boy came running up to us, exhausted.

"Hurry, hurry! The British have come with their cars to take us to Jerusalem. They are whipping the women and the old people, to get them on the road as quickly as possible."

"They are actually hitting them? Are you serious?"

We were angry.

"I swear, they're hitting them," insisted Yervant, "Hurry!"

"Yes, we're coming," we answered, "just to pull your ear."

We put off kissing the British soldier and flag for the time being and hurried back to where we were staying. . . . And what did we see? A British officer was threatening the women with his whip, urging them to put their belongings in the trucks. Since the women were unable to lift the heavy bundles, the officer was hitting them. When he saw us— the men from the caravan—he got angrier and started to kick us, at the same time cursing us as only the Kurdish corporal in Jeresh had ever done.

"Where have you been, you good-for-nothings? I've been waiting for you for the last two hours.... Hurry up.... Get into the carriages...Go on, you bloody . . . !"

With heavy blows of his fists, kicking, and whipping, in three minutes he had us all in the three trucks, randomly throwing our belongings at us. Then he slammed the doors of the cars and ordered the drivers to start moving.

We took to the road in great confusion. Had the preceding events actually taken place, or was it all a dream? It wasn't possible that we all had the same dream. The welts from the whip lashes that marked our faces and our backs were undeniable evidence.

Suddenly we were filled with utter despair. Were these really the British?

Such doubt could destroy us, so we decided that the sergeant had been drunk at the time.

"Or he was nervous," added my uncle, who is an eternal optimist. "Before we got there, he probably advised the women to get ready for the journey. But the women couldn't understand what he was saying, so they didn't move. The sergeant must have thought that they were deliberately not obeying him, so he took out his whip, and when we turned up he lashed out at us too, to get revenge."

"Yes, that's it," said other optimists in the group. "We don't think the British would treat us so roughly. It's our own fault, for wandering through the markets this morning when they planned to take us elsewhere."

"But no one told us what they were planning," others objected. "It's only reasonable that if they give us money we'll go to the store to satisfy our hunger."

"The people who gave us the money were Americans. They don't have anything to do with our being transferred."

And so we assumed all the guilt, preferring to deceive ourselves rather than shatter the ideal notions of our British friends, protectors, and saviors that we had nurtured for many years.

Hour succeeded hour as we crossed battlefields filled with blown-out tires, the barrels of cannons, tangled barbed wire, crosses, and graves. Some places were full of very large bomb craters, others were dominated by piles of silent stones. For a whole year, while we were hearing the incessant explosions of bombs, these fields were being soaked with human blood.

Late at night we reached Jericho, and slept on the ground in a deserted courtyard. We were very thirsty, so we drank from a nearby fountain, then we ate our bread and dates, and turned in.

We thought about our experience today. This was our first encounter with the British, and it had been more intense than we had anticipated.

18 November, 1918

Early this morning the trucks returned to Salt. In a way, it was good that we didn't continue the trip, because almost all of us were already ill from the shaking and the noxious fumes of the trucks. Those fumes mostly affected my mother, who is now lying in the courtyard as if she had fainted.

This afternoon we took a walk in the city and bought a few things. With half the money from the American Relief people we bought rice, which we hadn't seen since the day we were deported. Tonight we sat in a circle and devoured the rice with great gusto. With every spoonful we raised to our mouths, we thought of those three years of starvation, and we gave thanks for these days of prosperity.

19 November, 1918

This morning three trucks stood in front of our inn. We climbed into them without being hit or sworn at, and began the journey.

About an hour later, when we were passing through Jordan, we were amazed that Christ was baptized in these turbid waters.

It was noon when, from the top of a hill, we caught sight of Jerusalem, with its historic fortresses, Solomon's Temple, and the gilded dome of the Russian church. The dazzling view of the city filled our hearts with joy. At last we had left behind the desert dust and were standing on the threshold of civilization and peace!

Half an hour later the trucks stopped noisily in front of the church of the Monastery of St. James (Sourp Hagop).

Other refugees surrounded us. "You're most welcome, where are you from? Where have you traveled from? Have you seen anyone from our town? Where is such-and-such a caravan?" etc., etc.

We tried to satisfy everyone's curiosity, but while we were getting ready to step off the trucks, the English sergeant came running, gave the drivers some orders, and signalled with his whip that we should get back on the trucks and stay there. Remembering the crude behavior of the sergeant at Salt, we obeyed at once, and soon we were on the road again.

We drove through the roads and streets of Jerusalem, crossed town, past the residential areas, and stopped in front of a solitary building in the fields.

"Come down," ordered the drivers.

We got off the trucks.

"Take your belongings too!"

We obeyed that order too. The British said good-bye and drove back.

We looked around in confusion, wondering why we'd been brought to this deserted area. We noticed a cross on the building and came to the conclusion that it must be intended for Armenian refugees. It was really strange, though. There was no movement or noise, such as we had seen at the Monastery of St. James, either inside or outside the building. Nevertheless, we knocked on the door to announce that we had arrived and were asking for asylum.

A hunchbacked Greek priest answered the door, looked us over from behind his glasses, and asked in a surprised tone: "*Ti thelete?*" (what do you want?).

"We really don't know. The British have brought us from the desert and left us here."

"*Kyrie eleison* . . . What could Armenian refugees possibly have to do with a Greek monastery?"

"Where should we go, then?"

"To your own monastery, where all the Armenian refugees are settling."

"We just came from there!"

"Apparently there has been some misunderstanding. You should go back there."

"It's a long way to the city . . . how can we get there with our luggage, our sick people, and the children?"

"Why ask me? What can I do?"

He was right. To prevent remaining in the streets when night fell, we each picked up a piece of luggage and headed into Jerusalem.

By asking people in the streets, we finally found the Armenian monastery and presented ourselves to an employee.

"Sorry, the monastery is too crowded. You'll have to stay in a neighboring building," said the man.

"In that case, why did you let the British take us so far and leave us in the fields?"

"Sorry, we were not informed of your arrival."

"So, can you arrange for us to be transferred from the fields to the city?"

"That's impossible. You have to come on your own. We supply you only with shelter."

And he took us to see our shelter, just a few blocks away. We left our luggage in a room, and went back to the fields to carry more luggage, then more, then more. . . .

With the last load of luggage, we were exhausted and sweating. We started murmuring: "What strange people these British are! Let's say that the sergeant at Salt was drunk, but what about the sergeant in Jerusalem? Was he insane?"

"Yes, most likely."

There was no way we were going to be disillusioned.

20 November, 1918

We opened our eyes to the ringing of the bells of the Monastery of St. James. It was as if peace were flowing into the soul of each of us. Our hearts rejoiced that our awakening today was completely unlike any we had known in the desert. We ran to the windows to fill our lungs with the free air of free Palestine.

A while later, a black-robed monk visited us. We were pleasantly surprised when he turned out to be my cousin Arshag. We had heard no news from him since he had left Jeresh with his friends.

"What's going on?" we asked, stupefied. "Where's Levon?"

"Two weeks after we reached Salt, the British unexpectedly attacked and captured the city, explained Arshag. "Levon became an interpreter in the British army (having studied at the American college in Marsovan, Levon knew English well). His arm was injured during the fighting, and he was sent to Egypt for treatment. He's in Cairo now. As for me, I came to Jerusalem with some other Armenians who were saved, and became a *pokravor* in this monastery."

"What's a *pokravor?*" we asked.

"I am the servant of the senior sexton, Father Tavit."

"We don't understand. Why did you choose a religious profession?"

Arshag sighed. "I have no one left in this world. My mother, my sister, and my younger brother were deported from Aleppo to Deir Zor, where they were killed. My older brother, Haig, died in Jeresh. The one older than him, Parsegh, whom we last saw in Yozgad, was murdered by the Turks under horrible circumstances . . . I was shaken. Believe me, I'm fed up with this world, this life, humanity . . ."

"What's that you say? Is Parsegh dead?"

"He is. A soldier who was miraculously saved from the massacre told me about it. Eight hundred fifty people, all of them Armenian workers, were taken out and killed by their Turkish friends. My brother fell to the ground after being shot in the shoulder. A Turkish soldier saw that he wasn't dead yet, grabbed a stone, and smashed his head in."

A horrible silence engulfed the hall. Hundreds of people who were listening to the story looked at each other, unable to comprehend the gruesome murder.

Poor Parsegh.

I visualized his giant frame, his likable face with its wide forehead and glittering eyes that could penetrate the depths of any man.

He was so enthusiastic about the Armenian freedom movement that he was the first in Chorum to order all the revolutionary songs and pictures. We were little boys at the time. Parsegh used to make us sit beside him and tell us of the heroic exploits of the *fedayeen*, while showing us their photos. He had a special talent for captivating his audience. While he was telling us the story, we could easily picture Antranig, swinging his sword from a great height and beheading the enemy. Then there was Mourad. No enemy sword could ever pierce his body. And Serop, who walked out of the fire in the stable without injury. And Cheylo, who could appear in seven villages simultaneously, terrorizing the Turkish police

When Parsegh finished these legendary stories, we would implore him to tell us once more. He never refused. He told his stories over and over again.

And now? His beautiful head has been smashed by a stone, those honey-colored lips no longer fascinate his listeners, and his magical eyes no longer hypnotize his comrades in action.

The Turks destroyed his head. Among the millions of things they destroyed, there is also the head of Parsegh.

21 November, 1917

Although our faith in God has been completely destroyed, we still went to St. James Monastery to hear Mass.

Our eyes were used to seeing thousands of emaciated faces, our ears to hearing only crying and sobbing, our noses to the stench of corpses, so the sudden atmosphere of the church dazzled our senses. It was as if we had been transported to another world.

The crowds of believers in the church were survivors like us. Yet they were dressed neatly and looked healthy. We observed the red cheeks and huge stomachs of archbishops and priests clad in expensive chasubles and crosses encrusted with diamonds. We beheld the glittering crowns and precious chandeliers. We heard the singing of the choirs and the ringing of the cymbals. And above all, when we smelled the aroma of incense and olibanum, we had the momentary illusion that nothing tragic had happened to us, that the past three and a half years had been just a nightmare hallucination.

Our nation has not yet perished.

This was the exultant message that we heard today from the altar, and we thought that it was worth going to the church not just every day, but every single hour, just to hear this message about the immortality of our nation.

* * *

We heard some interesting stories from the local Armenians concerning the Sourp Hagop (St. James') Monastery.

This is a hospice for pilgrims during their visits to the Holy Land.

The exterior of the monastery looks like a medieval fortress, with high stone walls and no windows. But the interior is like a small Armenian town, with its own church, patriarchate, school, and printing house, its spacious courtyards, gardens, and separate quarters for the clergy and for pilgrims. Most of the refugees in Jerusalem, almost five thousand of them, occupy its hundreds of rooms.

Throughout the centuries the barbarians, who tried to loot its valuable treasures, frequently attacked the monastery. They were always defeated, though. Over the entrance gate is carved the decree of Sultan Saladin, which exonerates the monastery from any wrongdoing.

St. James' Church is a beautiful structure. The inner walls are decorated with beautiful tiles. Although they are centuries old, they are still as smooth and shiny as new. They say that the artisan who made these tiles died without teaching his craft to anyone else.

On the left side is a small chapel, where the head of St. James is buried. Our guide, Father Khoren, told us an interesting story about this place:

The Latins had a tradition of celebrating Mass once a year over the tomb of St. James. On the previous day they used to bring a huge chest containing the vestments of the priest designated to say Mass, as well as the liturgical vessels. One year the Latins put a mercenary in the trunk to steal the relics from the church. At night, the thief came out of his hiding place and started digging with his own spade.

By a stroke of bad luck, the edge of the spade struck something hard. The noise was heard by the Armenian guard. Very quietly he entered the church, attacked and instantly strangled the thief, then put his body back in the trunk.

The next day the Latins said that since the cardinal had fallen ill, the Mass would be postponed until the following Sunday, and the chest should be returned. The Armenians pretended that they knew nothing of the plot, and returned the chest to the messenger.

Neither on the following Sunday, nor in all the years that have ensued did the Latins say the Mass. They neither complain, nor explain the reasons for their absence. From that day on, they have never set foot in the Armenian church!

On the two sides of St. James Church are the chapels of Sourp Sarkis and Sourp Etchmiadzin. There are historic relics in those chapels, such as two stones, on one of which Christ stood while being baptized in the Jordan and on the other of which He sat while distributing the fish and loaves on Mount Tabor.

Within the monastery precinct there are two other churches: Sourp Toros, which was built by King Hetum, and Sourp Hreshdagabed (Holy Archangel). The latter was built exactly where the residence of the high priest Annas was located. The root of the olive tree to which Jesus Christ was tied is also there. Nearby is a small building that is supposedly the only convent of the Armenian Apostolic Church.

22 November, 1918

We registered at the American Relief Committee in order to get bread, rice, soap, clothing, and undergarments. Then we went to the Church of Sourp Haroutiun (the Church of the Holy Sepulcher). It is well known that the grave of Jesus is in this church. It is built on Golgotha, which belongs to the Armenians, the Greeks, and the

Latins. Although the Assyrians, the Copts, and the Abyssinians have a few small privileges, the most important locations belong to the first three nations.

The gravestones of murdered monks in the spacious courtyard of the cathedral, now almost completely covered with asphalt, testify to the way the monks of different nations fought against each other to earn privileges for their Churches. In order to put an end to the everlasting fighting of the clergy, Sultan Saladin issued a decree specifying the privileges of each nation. He appointed a Muslim to the hereditary office of doorkeeper, admitting the Christians who come to pray to their God each day.

The Latins and the Greeks were not satisfied with Sultan Saladin's orders. They have spent huge amounts of money to bribe the mayors and viziers to take away the rights of the smaller nations. They were successful in their intentions until the British conquered Jerusalem and enforced the *status quo,* allowing every nation to keep the rights it had up to that time.

As we enter the Church of the Holy Sepulcher, we find ourselves standing before a raised stone, where the body of Christ was wrapped in a winding-sheet soon after it was taken down from the cross. To the left is the place where Mary, Mother of God fainted. To the right is the Chapel of Golgotha, where, according to tradition, the head of the prehistoric man is kept. On the floor above is a chapel where Mary the Mother of God fasted for forty days. Her statue is behind a glass window. The precious jewelry on this statue dazzles the eyes of visitors. Greek clergy guard these treasures night and day.

Christ's sepulcher is in the middle of the church, right under the dome, which rests on eighteen tall pillars. This dome once collapsed, and the Armenians, Greeks, and Latins competed to rebuild it. Legally, it would belong to whoever rebuilt it. They could not agree, and the church remained without a dome for years. At last the Russian tsar rebuilt it, so the Russians gained some privileges where previously they had none.

The small chapel contains a simple marble burial stone, illuminated by thirty eternally burning lamps. The Greeks have assumed the privilege of guarding the sepulcher. A Greek priest stands between the statues of two angels and guards the place night and day, encouraging visitors to put as much as possible into the alms box.

Facing the entrance to the sepulcher is the precinct of the Greek Church, which has the choicest location in the Church of the Holy Sepulcher. Behind the sepulcher is an altar donated to the Copts by the Armenians. And facing this is the altar of the Assyrian Church, near the tomb of Joseph of Arimathea. To the right of Christ's sepulcher is the precinct of the Latin Church, built over Joseph's garden. The site of the pillar to which Jesus was tied before being crucified is also in this area.

To the left of the sepulcher is the precinct of the Armenian Church, which is exceptional in that it's a gallery. Over the years the Greeks and the Latins succeeded in wearing away the privileges of the Armenians, sending them from the ground to a gallery. Fortunately, the *status quo* was issued; otherwise, the Armenians would have been forced to leave their precinct and have only "air privilege" by the Russian dome. Besides this gallery, the Armenians have the Chapel of the Holy Illuminator, close to the Latin chapel, which is twenty steps below ground. From one of the corners of this chapel there are several steps that lead to the Cross upon which Christ was crucified.

In front of the Chapel of the Holy Illuminator is a semicircular corridor that goes around the back of the Greek precinct and ends by the Chapel of Golgotha. The room where Jesus and the two thieves were imprisoned is in this corridor, as is the place where the Crown of Thorns is kept and where the garments of Jesus were divided.

As we were coming out of the church, we noticed the turbaned doorkeeper coughing and spitting on the ground. He wasn't insulting us. It's simply not considered a disgraceful act—unless it's done in the courtyard of a mosque.

We informed our "Mad *Vartabed*" that we hadn't yet seen the Abyssinian precinct. He's called Mad because he has fought against the Greeks and the Latins and has more than twenty scars. He showed us the roof of the church, telling us that the poor Abyssinians barely had the right to pray on the roof.

We noticed four minarets at the four corners of the church.

"What are they doing there?" we inquired.

"The Turkish government put them up to prevent the Church of the Holy Sepulcher from expanding," replied our guide.

23 November, 1918

Today we walked around Sourp Asdvadzadzin (St. Mary's) Church, which is in the Armenian section of the Garden of Gethsemane, in a valley outside the city. We entered the church by going down sixty steps. To one side of these steps is the tomb of Joseph, the guardian of Christ. The church's altar was built by King Hetum of Cilicia. Yet there is no record of this on the supports of the altar. The Greeks, out of the blue, have come to own this too. Our guide, Father Ashod, explained to us in detail the complicated issue of earning and losing privileges. We have heard a lot about this problem lately, as we visit the holy places.

Years ago the Christian nations, being true believers, did not have this nationalistic hatred of each other, and worshipped in each other's venues. Over the centuries the privileges of the guest nations have become sacred, and they have claimed some sort of ownership in the host buildings. Not being satisfied with this, the guests have gradually expanded their boundaries, thus harming the host nations.

In order to extend a boundary, it is enough to push a rug a bit farther or hang another lamp on the wall. If the defending nation can't stop such transgressions, the place where the carpet is put or the wall on which the lamp is hung becomes the legal property of the confiscator. Over the course of a few years they gradually spread their carpet a bit farther or hung a second lamp on the wall and lo, one day the main privilege-holder is pushed closer to the door, if not all the way out . . . . This is why the clergy have had bloody fights. Whenever the case has been taken to court, the winner has been whoever bribed the judge most.

"So the main thing is to keep watch and never let the other party put up the first nail to hang a lamp," we reasoned. "Otherwise the intrusion will gradually expand, finally expelling the host, as happened to the Armenians in the Church of the Holy Sepulcher."

"Let me tell you a story that happened to me years ago, when I was still a sexton. I used to stand guard and sleep in this very church," said Father Ashod, who is a courageous man from Evereg. Instead of becoming a soldier, he became a clergyman by mistake. "One night," he continued, "I woke up at the noise of a match being lit. I came out of my cell and saw the Greek sexton, who was walking toward the altar with a three-legged ladder. I watched his movements. He looked around, and when he was certain that no one was following him he set up the ladder by a pillar, climbed it, and started hammering in a nail. After each blow he stopped to check if I had heard the noise. To give him more confidence, I began to snore. Then I slowly crept up to his ladder and pulled its legs with such force that the thief of our privilege fell down and, stunned, ran out of the church in his pajamas."

Despite the careful vigilance of the Armenian guards, the foreigners have succeeded in taking away some of our privileges. Most notably, the Greeks have some privileges in the church that belong to the Armenians.

It is surprising that there is no church belonging to the Greeks or the Latins in which the Armenians have earned privileges. We have always been on the losing side. If we still have some property today, it is mainly because of the fists and daggers of courageous clergy like Father Ashod and the "Mad Priest."

The place where St. Stephen was stoned is located in the Greek section of the Garden of Gethsemane. The Latin section includes the historic rock where Jesus prayed before His arrest. Jesus expressed one of His most meaningful thoughts under the tree by that rock: "Put your sword back in its sheath. For all who take the sword shall perish by the sword." (See Matthew 26:52)

The Latin section of the Garden of Gethsemane is beautiful. It's very well taken care of. But the areas belonging to the Greeks and Armenians—especially that of the Armenians—has been neglected.

The Valley of the Last Judgment begins at these gardens. Both sides of the valley are covered with the graves of hundreds of thousands of Jews from all corners of the world, who are buried here in the hope of being resurrected at the Last Judgment.

Across this mountain plain there are many historic places, including the cave where the disciples of Jesus hid the day He was arrested and the tombs of Zachariah and Absalom. There is a hole in the latter's grave, where the pilgrims throw stones in the naïve belief that if their stone falls into the hole their wish will come true.

Below the valley is a brook, where women were washing laundry when soldiers threw St. James down from the high citadel walls of Jerusalem. When the women saw his body rolling down the slope, they tore it to pieces. Now only the tomb of St. James stands there.

After walking through the Garden of Gethsemane and the Valley of the Last Judgment, we climbed the hill called the Mount of the Ascension. There is a stone at the top of the hill on which Jesus stood before ascending into Heaven. The stone has been kissed so frequently that is has taken on the shape of a footprint. Long ago the Armenians had a church in this place, but through the years it collapsed, and the Armenians lost ownership because they didn't rebuild it. A few walls have been built around the stone, and several nations have altars there. The doorkeeper is another turbaned Arab, who is also the guard of the nearby mosque. We have to give him money before we can see the stone where Jesus stood.

On top of the Mount of the Ascension is the famous Russian monastery, with its equally famous tower. We climbed more than three hundred steps to see the panorama of Palestine. Near the Russian monastery is a church foundation covered with beautiful mosaics. We noticed Armenian letters in the mosaic. Probably our ancestors owned these places, built churches, and then, through unfortunate circumstances, lost them. Besides this monastery, the Russians have their famous church with the gilded domes on this same hill. The Greeks and the Latins also have monasteries there.

At night, as we were returning, tired from so much walking, we remembered how fed up we were with walking along interminable roads when we were deportees. But now we realize that walking is not so unpleasant, especially when one's heart is light and one's mind free of worries.

24 November, 1918

Today is Sunday. We went to the Church of the Holy Sepulcher to see how so many nations worship together. It was like being in the Tower of Babel. Each nation competed to drown out the ceremonies of the others with noise. The Latins' organ was roaring, shaking the arches of the church. The Greeks did not lag behind. They were singing their hymns loud enough to tear their throats out. The Armenians were making as much noise as they could to announce their presence in the gallery. The Copts and the Assyrians, although minorities, were making much more noise with their songs than the army of Genghis Khan as it sacked a city.

It was impossible to hear the sermons, readings from Scripture, or songs. After a while we had to run out of the Church muttering the well-known refrain: "O what barbarities are committed in the name of religion!"

25 November, 1918

In order to end the tour of the historic places of the Holy Land, today we visited Solomon's Temple. It's on the edge of the city, near St. Stephen's Gate. It's a magnificent mosque, erected in the center of a big courtyard, and is called Omar's Mosque. It's built on foundations around twenty-three centuries old. We took off our shoes and put on special slippers that the doorkeeper supplies in return for a small gift. We entered the famous temple and were astonished by the dome, which is supported by gilded pillars.

Precious tiles taken from destroyed churches decorate the walls. Very large, valuable rugs cover the floor. Located exactly under the dome is the rock upon which Abraham was ready to sacrifice his son Isaac, if a ram hadn't been provided to take his place. It's in this temple that Mary the Mother of God prayed on her knees. After giving us all the necessary explanations, the guiding *hodja* showed us a stone building at the end of the courtyard. It was the palace of Pontius Pilate.

On the other side of the wall surrounding this mosque is the Weeping Wall, against which the Jews beat their heads every Friday, bemoaning not only their lost independence, but also the loss of the temple.

After the Temple of Solomon, we visited the Pool of Bethesda, which is a huge reservoir fifty-six steps below the ground. Some of us rubbed the miraculous water on their lips, convinced that they would be cured of their ailments. This reservoir belongs to the Latins. Beside it is Saint Anne's Church. On the walls of the courtyard are written, in eighty-four languages, the words of the New Testament describing all the miracles of Bethesda (John 5:2-4).

In this same church the Latins have a statue of the Infant Jesus made of pure gold, lying in a cradle that is also made of pure gold (apparently with the progress of civilization, the Latins have turned the humble manger of Christ into a cradle.)

Later we toured the church of the Armenian Catholics. They showed us a historic stone, where Jesus sat on some occasion or other. Then we went to St. Veronica's Church, also a Latin church, where Simon was made to carry the cross of Jesus, and where Veronica wiped the sweat off His forehead. We ended up visiting another Latin church, where Pontius Pilate washed his hands.

All these churches are located on the way from Gethsemane to Golgotha. Father Khoren, our guide, showed us a stone at the corner of a street, where Christ rested His knee while carrying the cross. We were really surprised that there was no church built over this stone. This much-kissed stone, covered in mud and dust, has assumed the shape of a knee.

Finally we went to a house that Kelegian Khan purchased and gave to our nation. Excavations have revealed a floor made of mosaic, with the figures of birds, flowers, vines, and the following inscription in Armenian: "In memoriam: for the salvation of those whose names are known to the Lord." There is a tomb below this mosaic floor that contains the bones of thousands of Armenian soldiers who fell before the gates of Jerusalem during the invasion of the Crusaders. We bowed in reverence to their memory, yet we thought that if these courageous soldiers had defended the land their ancestors had walked upon instead of this land where Jesus walked, who knows? Perhaps we would have been spared the indescribable sufferings that have clung to us for six hundred years!

1 December, 1918

The surviving Armenians of Syria are congregating in Jerusalem, Beirut, and Aleppo. That's why every day there are new incidents of "rediscovery." Countrymen, friends, members of the same family, who were separated under dire circumstances, with a bit of luck meet each another, and cries of joy and laughter fill the air. Today we were lucky enough to find our cousin Eugenie, whom we thought had died a long time ago.

Her story is truly heart-wrenching. I'll just summarize it, to avoid repeating hundreds of similar stories.

She was deported from Samsoun, along with her husband and brother, in a caravan of well-to-do Armenians. They left in a horse-drawn carriage, carrying their valuables and what they needed for a long journey.

Two days into the journey, at a place called Tavak, the soldiers stopped the caravan. They made all the travelers get out, took all the males over thirteen, and killed them on the other side of a hill, then forced the women and children to leave their belongings behind and continue their journey on foot.

During this march the soldiers inspected the women more than twenty times, thinking that they might have some jewelry hidden on them, and during the process of these inspections they committed unspeakable acts of violence upon them. Turkish and Kurdish peasants finished what the soldiers began by kidnapping all the pretty girls and widows.

During these attacks a lot of Armenian women committed suicide, others were murdered, and still others could not withstand the hardships of deportation and died "natural" deaths. Those who survived continued walking, without rest or comfort. Wealthy women, who were not used to walking so far, were forced to wrap their feet in rags, whipped on by the soldiers.

The Turkish soldiers threw the sick, the elderly, and the children who fell behind off bridges or promontories. Those who were unable to keep up with the horses and fell on the ground they burned with dried grass. They reached the height of their barbarism one day when they separated out the boys aged nine to thirteen, still in their school uniforms, who cried and hugged their mothers, begging them not to abandon them to the executioners. In vain the mothers struggled to keep their children. The soldiers pulled them away . . . A small boy with a pale face asked Eugenie: "Auntie, are they taking us away to kill us?" Despite superhuman efforts, Eugenie couldn't save him.

After horrible deprivations and tortures, out of the thousands of deportees, only thirty stayed alive long enough to reach Aleppo.

On the road my cousin took care of Mrs. Messerian, a wealthy woman from Samsoun, who had a young boy in Germany. When they got to Aleppo this woman sent a telegram to her son, describing their situation. He sent his mother financial assistance immediately. The money saved Mrs. Messerian and her friends.

Then Eugenie was exiled to Hama, and from there to Damascus. She was probably in the caravan of people from Zeitoun. They had a horrible accident on the train though her recently saved life was saved again.

She reached Damascus with minor injuries and with great effort. She got a job in a factory and stayed there until the British occupied the city.

It's strange that Eugenie was in Jerusalem even before us. Despite the fact that she saw her cousin every single day in church and he saw her, they never recognized each other. Time and suffering had totally altered their appearance.

8 December, 1981

We found another lost sheep.

As I was going to the market this morning, I noticed a British soldier coming in the opposite direction. I was totally surprised when I recognized my cousin Levon Toramanian.

"Levo-o-o-on!" I called, running up to him and taking his hand.

"I just arrived from Egypt and was on my way to St. James Monastery to find you. Is our family alive?"

"We're all alive. After you left our grandfather passed away. We lost him, but we found Eugenie a week ago."

"My aunts are alive, apparently."

"Yes, let's go to the monastery. Your folks are living there."

We reached the monastery and went to the Cham Quarter, where his parents were living. I left my cousin at the foot of the stairs and burst into their room like a bomb.

"I have very happy news, but I won't tell you what it is unless you promise me a present."

"News from Levon . . ." they exclaimed and surrounded me.

"I won't tell until you promise me a gift," I insisted.

"We'll give you anything you want. Just tell us the news," pleaded Levon's mother, father, brother, sister, grandmother, and two aunts.

This was my chance to satisfy one of my wishes. I took off my felt hat and said: "Buy me a hat!"

"We will. What's the news?"

"Haven't you guessed? Levon . . ."

At that instant Levon entered and kissed the members of his family one by one, with tears in his eyes.

This evening Mr. Toramanian took me to the market and bought me a nice hat.

Ever since I was a young boy, I have always dreamed of wearing a European hat. I am glad that my wish was fulfilled on the occasion of meeting my cousin.

9 December, 1918

The incessant ringing of the bells of St. James announced that something unusual was happening.

We ran to the monastery and learned that today is the anniversary of the capture of Jerusalem. Although other communities sent only delegations, it was decided that the entire Armenian population would go to congratulate and express our gratitude to the representatives of the allies.

By noon there was a huge crowd in the main courtyard. After receiving orders to stay orderly and calm, the procession moved forward.

Leading the procession was a bailiff in official attire, with a big British flag in his hand. Behind him was another bailiff, waving an Armenian tricolor of the same size. The national orchestra followed in their uniforms, then more than twenty bishops and priests, dressed in their cowls and with beautiful crosses hanging on their chests. The people followed, waving small paper flags, while the church bells rang and the orchestra played "*Lousin chgar*" (there was no moon).

It was an unbelievable scene. Were these the remnants of our emaciated refugees? Were these the young men who were vomiting blood on the paved streets? Were these the Armenian women who wandered aimlessly, almost naked and disheveled? Were these the children who cried, "I'm hungry"? Overnight they have turned into energetic young men, grasping the Armenian flag tightly in their fists, their heads held high with visible pride. It was unbelievable for us to watch a crowd of Armenians with no soldiers, no whips, no daggers or hatchets. Instead of sobs and moans, cries of happiness filled the air. Instead of beating our chests or knees, we were joyfully clapping. Instead of marching toward death or the desert, we were marching toward life and a rosy future.

The procession had come out of the monastery street into the big avenue, when we heard a short and effective order:

"*Erga* . . ." (stop)!

A corpulent guard from a nearby police station barred the road.

"What's this? Where are you heading, all of you, young and old, with flags and fanfare? Don't you know that it's forbidden to hold a demonstration in this city? Turn back!"[*]

---

[*]. In fact, the Jews had tried to hold a demonstration about a month earlier, but young Arabs had grabbed the flags from the demonstrators and broken the flag staffs over their backs. In order to prevent similar unpleasant incidents, the British mayor had strictly forbidden any kind of demonstration.

"This isn't a political demonstration," said the official translator of the monastery, "we're going to express our respect and gratitude to our saviors."

"Whatever your intention, all kinds of gathering are forbidden. You have to turn back."

"We'll die here if need be, but we're not turning back," complained the people unanimously.

Realizing that he wasn't dealing with faint-hearted people, the Arab commandant washed his hands like Pontius Pilate, and passed on the responsibility to the guards of our community.

Having resolved this issue, the procession went forward, blowing the trumpets and playing the drums more loudly, with a sense of great satisfaction. People threw flowers and candies at us from the shops and houses on the main avenue. People in the street, noticing that we were not Jews, shouted encouragement and clapped for us. Thus supported by many, the procession came to a stop in the front of the city hall, where it sang the British anthem.

Apparently the sheriff had informed the commandant of the city, General Stores, of our march. The latter came down the stairs smiling, and thanked us for our "collective visit." Then he delivered a speech evoking the memory of the Armenian heroes who had worked miracles in Arara. He repeated the words of Field Marshal Allenby: "Although the Armenians were a small ally, the role they played in securing victory was great." He assured us that the allied nations, particularly England, will never forget our service, and will always protect us. Then he spoke encouragingly to us about our reborn homeland, and expressed his heartfelt wish that our suffering was over for good.

Our people welcomed his words with thunderous clapping, while other British officers photographed us from the windows. After this peaceful demonstration in front of the city hall, we headed for the Italian embassy. We were received with similar hospitality there, by the ambassador and several high-ranking officers.

Then we went to the American embassy. They welcomed us with visible joy. The ambassador himself shouted. *"Getsé Hayasdan"* (long live Armenia)! The officers showered us with flowers.

Lastly, we went to the French embassy. General Georges Picot delivered a speech glorifying Armenia. Then he spoke of our national flag: "I see that your flag has the same colors as ours (our flag consists of horizontal blue, white, and red bars). I hope that like ours it will bear witness to glorious pages in world history."

After the singing of the *Marseillaise*, General Picot asked us to sing the Armenian national anthem. Immediately the orchestra started the "*Pam Porodan*." When we saw the French generals saluting our anthem, our hearts were filled with joy and our eyes with tears.

Tonight we made a bonfire in the courtyard of the monastery. We sang and danced and set off fireworks, as the Turks did when they celebrated the anniversary of their sultan's enthronement. We are extremely happy today, because in the courtyard of the monastery the fire is still burning to express *our* joy, to celebrate *our* independence.

15 December, 1918

For some time now strange blisters have been appearing on our faces and arms. Mine is at the end of my right eyebrow. It's deep and porous, like a sponge. It doesn't hurt, but it's annoying. The locals call them Jericho blisters, and say that they're caused by the water of Jericho. "The water contains the eggs of some kind on insect," they say. "Anyone who drinks it without boiling it first gets these blisters."

We remembered that we were so upset at the rough treatment of the British sergeant in Salt, that we had drunk lots of the water, and no one had the decency to tell us it was harmful.

This morning I went to the American hospital to find a cure. Any medication, doctor, or hospital, whether British, Italian, or American, is free for us.

Dr. Martin, formerly head of the American hospital in Marsovan and a good friend of my father, checked my spot and concluded: "No medication has yet been invented to cure this infection. You have to be patient for six months, after which it will automatically disappear, leaving a mark like a vaccination scar."

"Doctor, would you please check my chest?" I asked. "A year ago I caught a cold and started coughing severely. I still have that cough. It bothers me at night and sometimes I am short of breath."

Dr. Martin made me lie down on a stretcher, listened to my heart, made me cough a couple of times, moved the stethoscope back and forth on my chest, and, with a very serious expression, said: "My son, you have chronic bronchitis."

The roof fell in on me.

"Chronic?" I stuttered. "You mean this sickness doesn't have a cure either?"

"The cure is in your own hands. To reduce further complications, you shouldn't get tired or catch cold. You should take especially good care that you eat well."

I left the doctor in deep despair. In the desert I had always comforted myself by saying that once I settled down I would be able to cure my cough by taking some kind of medication. Now it's chronic, and further complications may arise in the future.

Apparently, my face was not meant to wear a smile.

22 December, 1918

Anyone but me would have been very sick this morning. We're used to it, though. These small things don't affect us.

The windowpane above my bed is broken and all night the rain poured down on my face, while the cold weather froze my senses. There are more than fifty of us in one room. There was no place for me to go to avoid this disaster. I had no choice but to stay in bed and freeze.

The first thing I did this morning was sit in the sun for hours, until my body felt better. Then I went to get my share of rice from the Relief Committee, made myself some soup, and felt much better.

The doctor advises me to take good care of my health, but how can I, when we are deprived of the basic necessities of life?

24 December, 1918

The building where we found refuge was so dirty, crowded, and noisy that it was almost impossible to continue living there. Finally, five families found the means and transferred to the Sourp Prgich (Holy Savior) Monastery, which has been assigned to the refugees.

Holy Savior is not far from St. James. It's a comfortable abbey in a big garden outside the city walls. It's on the site of the house of Caiaphas, the high priest, where Peter denied his Lord three times before the cock crowed. The Armenians have an important relic here: the stone cover of Christ's sepulcher, over which they have raised the altar.

This monastery is like a graveyard. All the Armenian patriarchs are buried in the courtyard, and the Armenian cemetery is close to the garden. When we passed like shadows through these unending tombstones and monuments, we thought we saw many dead people, but we never imagined that we would soon be close neighbors to them. Nevertheless, we don't regret transferring here. This deadly silence is preferable to the tumult of the other, crowded house.

1 January, 1919

During our exile, we used to ask the following question at the beginning of each year: "Will we be saved this year, or will we die one after the other, like our relatives and friends?" Throughout those years, and particularly last year, our energy faded away. It was impossible to hope that we would greet another New Year.

Fortunately, we were saved from a horrible fate; before the inescapable took place, the storm calmed down, the darkness dissipated, and the golden dawn spread over us.

Finally, after six centuries of slavery, difficult though the rebirth of the Armenians has been, at last freedom, which we most eagerly desired and longed for, has come. Today we all hope that it will be everlasting, and that not a single dark cloud will darken its radiant horizon.

5 January, 1919

Our abbot, Father Ashod, came from St. James Monastery this morning and said: "Good people, don't even go out today. British soldiers have surrounded the Monastery of St. James. They are forcing the refugees onto trucks, to take them to Port Said. Those who refuse are being beaten."

"Don't tell us that the Turks have come back!" we said, without surprise. "Why do they want to exile the Armenians to Port Said?"

"They think that Jerusalem is already crowded. There is an empty refugee camp in Port Said," answered the priest. But their treatment of Armenians is unacceptable. They are treating them like the Turks, when they deported them from Aleppo to Deir Zor, with whips and threats . . ."

"What threats?"

"They say they will cut off aid to all who refuse to go to the refugee camp."

We remained in the monastery until evening. We thought about what would happen to us if the British cut off aid. At last we have recovered physically and the number of people dying every week has fallen to two or three, while in the desert we had twenty to thirty deaths a week.

It seems we are returning to the misery of former times. It may very well be. We live in a city where there are no jobs, and life is so expensive that people are selling even the feet and intestines of chickens.

8 January, 1919

I now have no doubt that the Armenian Monastery of St. James is a place where surprising things happen (I should mention in passing that the Armenian relocation to Port Said has been postponed). I never thought that today I would bump into a young man who was thought to be dead.

It was Karekin from Trebizond, and with him was an attractive young woman.

"What a surprise!" I said, running up to my friend. "What a wonderful surprise! Where's Sarkis?"

"We came in from the desert the other day," he answered, hugging me. "He was arrested for carrying arms illegally."

"You mean Sarkis was arrested?"

"Yes. Anyone who carries arms in the city is apparently sentenced to three months in prison. How were we to know that, my dear friend? We barely escaped with our lives from those thieves, the Bedouins."

"Was the lady with you too?"

"Oh, excuse me. In my excitement I forgot to introduce my sister."

"Kohar?"

"Yes, Kohar."

"I'm so happy to meet you, but how has this come about?"

"Come," said Karekin. He took my arm and walked me toward the Bulgur Quarter (the section of St. James Monastery where he lives). It's a very long story."

* * *

As we heard from Artin from Chorum, the Armenian soldiers arrested in the region of Hauran were taken to a deserted section of the Hijaz railroad to rebuild the roads demolished by British fire. Because of the terrible conditions, within a week the majority of them got sick. Insisting that these Armenians were malingering, the Turkish soldiers dragged them to the edge of the road and whipped them to make them work. Four months later, out of 400 people only 150 were still alive. The others had died mainly of sunstroke, hunger, and torture.

One evening the Armenians who were still alive returned from work and lay down in their tents. A corporal rushed up and ordered: "Quick! Clean everything up. The captain (who lived about an hour from the camp) has decided to pay us a visit."

The Armenians came out of the tents at once. Some of them grabbed the water containers and rushed to a nearby well, others grabbed brooms and started sweeping the floors and the ground, and still others tidied up the tent poles and picked up the garbage.

In an hour, everything was ready. The full moon had risen in the sky and shone like the noonday sun, illuminating the dreary area as if it were broad daylight. Everything was clean. Not even the tiniest speck of dirt could be found, except for the Turkish soldiers.

Before long they noticed a couple of cavalry soldiers in the distance, galloping in their direction. All the Armenian soldiers formed a straight line and awaited their arrival.

The riders got quite a bit closer. One of them was their Turkish captain and the other a German officer. The captain pointed his whip at the tents and the railroad, and explained something to the German officer. The latter nodded his head in agreement. They soon arrived at the encampment, got off their horses, and inspected the rank of Armenian soldiers.

"Do any of you speak any European languages?" the captain asked.

A deep silence ensued. Nobody dared step forward. Everyone was afraid that he might fail a language exam, be accused of lying, and be punished.

"Isn't there at least one of you who speaks a foreign language?" asked the captain in surprise.

"I do," answered a young man, none other than Karekin.

"Come closer. What language do you speak?"

"French."

"No, that won't do. The German officer here knows that language but doesn't want to speak it. Don't you know any English or German?"

"I know a bit of English."

"English?"

The German officer questioned Karekin and, pleased with his replies, said in English: "I'm taking you as my interpreter."

Then the captain asked the Armenian soldiers a second question: "Do any of you play a musical instrument?"

"Me, me, me," came replies from everywhere.

"What do you play?" the captain asked the first soldier.

"The flute."

"No, that won't do. And you?"

"The piano."

"That won't do either. Where would we find you a piano in the desert? And you?"

"Tar."

"Is there anyone who can play the violin?"

"I can," replied Sarkis from Moush.

"European or Turkish music?"

"Both."

"Good! Then I'll take you into my service. Tomorrow morning, both of you come to the station and await my orders at the military office there."

The Turkish officer then gave a few orders to the commander of the camp, got on his horse, and left, accompanied by his German colleague.

That night Karekin and Sarkis were so happy they couldn't close their eyes. In the morning, accompanied by a Turkish soldier, they went to the train station and that night they assumed their new duties, Karekin with the German and Sarkis with the Turkish officer.

* * *

Karekin's task was very easy. He accompanied the German officer everywhere and served as his interpreter and translator, because at that station nobody but the Turkish captain knew a foreign language.

On the other hand, Sarkis' duties were quite hard. During the day he worked as a servant and shopped for the officer, going to the market several times a day, and at night he would play the violin until dawn to entertain his master's guests—the Turkish employees of the station, military commanders, etc.—who ate and drank all night long. Nevertheless, he was also pleased with his situation, considering that what he was doing was at least a hundred times easier than working in the scorching desert sun all day.

One day the German officer called Karekin. "I've received a letter from Constantinople. I'm leaving tomorrow. Get everything ready," he said.

Noticing that the officer used the singular, "*I'm* leaving," he asked anxiously: "Won't I be going with you?"

"No, you're a soldier. You have duties here," the officer answered coldly.

"Please take me with you. If I return to the encampment it will be the end of me," murmured Karekin. He told him about the hellish life there and that there were only 150 people left out of 400. "Please don't send me back there."

The German officer was moved by Karekin's story and said: "Very well, I'll go to see the captain. Perhaps I can arrange to take you with me."

As soon as the German left, Sarkis entered. "Where's your man?" he asked. "I've brought him a letter from the captain."

"He left for your place just a moment ago," replied Karekin. "Did you know, Sarkis, that we're leaving for Constantinople tomorrow?"

"Really?" exclaimed Sarkis, surprised and happy at the same time. "Don't tell me you're going to be saved from this hell-hole."

"Yes, if my officer can convince the captain, I'll be saved," replied Karekin. "But I'll also have to leave you behind, and that causes me great pain."

"Don't worry about that. You just try to save yourself," Sarkis consoled his friend. "Every Armenian saved from this hell is a gain for the Armenian people. But I forgot to tell you: I discovered this morning that there's another Armenian here besides you and me. Even better! An Armenian woman!"

"An Armenian woman?"

"Yes, my captain's wife. Only this morning I had the opportunity of talking to her. She is a very beautiful woman . . . the captain kidnapped her from a caravan."

Karekin was suddenly alarmed. He was filled with compassion for this unknown Armenian woman, who had suffered the same tragic fate as his sister. But before he could say anything the German returned. Sarkis delivered his master's letter and left. As if he already knew the content of the letter, the officer put it in his pocket and said to Karekin: "There's a train to Damascus in half an hour. Take the trunks to the station. We're leaving immediately."

"Aren't we leaving tomorrow?"

"No, right away. Hurry up."

Karekin immediately packed, put the luggage on his back, and left for the train station. Not even a minute passed before the train arrived, blowing its whistle. The train whistled sharply once again and left in a deafening uproar.

Karekin watched the captain's house from the train window for a long time, hoping to see either Sarkis or the captain's Armenian wife. But he saw no one, either in the deserted street or at the windows of the house.

"Goodbye," he exclaimed, waving his handkerchief.

When the station disappeared from sight, he sat and let out a deep sigh.

* * *

The train arrived first in Dera and then in Damascus.

At the first station in Damascus, Kadem Station, where there had once been a refugee camp, a military policeman put his hand on Karekin.

"Get off the train."

"I'm this officer's translator," said Karekin, indicating the German.

"Get off the train! Armenians are not allowed to go to Constantinople."

Karekin looked at his boss, as though asking for help.

"We can't break the law," said the German with a shrug. "Since it isn't allowed, you can't go."

Without further resistance, Karekin got off the train.

"Follow me," said the military policeman.

"What is it now?"

"Don't talk so much. March!"

Karekin followed the soldier in silence. They soon arrived at a police station. Karekin was put into a cell for a few hours. Sometime in the afternoon another soldier arrived, opened the cell door, and winked at him.

"Follow me."

Karekin came out and followed the soldier. Seeing that the latter was a simple peasant, he asked in a friendly manner: "Where are we going, my friend?"

"Where your brothers are," answered the soldier, motioning to the end of the road with his chin. "They're building a road over there."

When they passed a shop, the soldier bought some bread, cheese, and tobacco. After walking a short distance he said: "There's no rush. Let's sit here until I finish eating."

They sat in the shade of a tree near a well. The soldier put his rifle down next to him, opened his little parcel, and voraciously devoured everything. Then he reached for the flask hanging from his belt to get a drink of water. Noticing that it was empty, he gave it to Karekin and told him to fill it.

Karekin took the flask, walked over to the well, and started climbing down by putting his feet into the little hollows carved into the wall of the well. While filling the flask he noticed that the well water, which was hardly a meter deep, flowed in from a subterranean channel. But where did the channel lead? Suddenly he had an idea. Without further consideration, Karekin stepped into the water and started running quickly in the direction of the current.

"I'll either drown by falling into a reservoir, or I'll come to an open place and be free," he thought. He waded through the water, which by then came up to his chest, in the meantime taking care not to hit his head on the arches of the dark subterranean channel.

Meanwhile, the soldier realized that his prisoner should have returned by then, stood up impatiently, stuck his head in the opening of the well, and shouted: "What's taking you so long, my friend?" Seeing that his prisoner had disappeared, he said: "I see. But if you escape me, my name isn't Mehmet!" And he grabbed his rifle, climbed down into the well, and released a continuous volley of shots.

He shouted: "You son of a *giaour*, wherever you run I'll leave your corpse behind in the water. Just you wait and see."

Karekin ducked his head and almost crawled through the water, following the channel. He took a deep breath only when the channel turned a corner and the bullets started hitting the wall. He had escaped the danger of being shot. The danger now was of being drowned, as the channel was gradually getting narrower and the water was rising over his head.

"Going on is too dangerous," he thought, "I'll have to wait here. If the soldier comes I can fight him to the death. Either he'll kill me or I'll kill him."

He waited for about fifteen minutes, but nobody came. He considered turning back, but thought that the soldier might be waiting for him at the opening of the well, so he gave up the idea.

"Let's go a bit farther," he said to himself. "Let's see where it takes us," and he continued walking.

As he walked forward, the water continued to rise, and eventually reached his mouth. He clamped his mouth shut, kept his head above water as much as possible, and walked on tiptoe, but without hope, until he noticed that the channel was getting brighter. He was approaching the light!

"That means I must be getting close to an opening," he concluded, "perhaps the mouth of another well. Let's keep going."

In fact, he soon reached the opening of another well.

"No," says Karekin to himself, "if the soldier had known about this underground channel he wouldn't have let me come down to fetch him water."

So he gathered his courage and climbed. He stuck his head out of the hole and carefully examined his surroundings. It was dark out there, and deserted. He leapt out and started running away from the direction of the station.

* * *

That evening there was a cool wind. His wet clothes stuck to his skin, and he was freezing. He kept running, in spite of the fact that he had eaten nothing since morning. The mental image of being rearrested and sentenced to hard labor or even being shot as a deserter was so horrible that he fled with all his might, without even knowing where he was going.

After running like that for hours, he stopped in a rough area where there were neither inhabitants nor any cultivated land.

He looked for a fruit tree to get something to eat. He couldn't, however, find even so much as a piece of green grass. He made his way to a rock, took off his wet clothes and spread them on the stone, squeezed himself into a crevasse, and shut his eyes.

He did not sleep too long, but soon opened his trembling eyes, put his clothes on, and examined the area to decide which way to go. Just then he noticed, far in the distance, a flickering light, as small as the tip of a burning cigarette.

"There are no villages around here, so that must be a shepherd," he said to himself. "I should get closer and have a look. If it's a shepherd, I'll go over to warm up and ask for bread. If it's a soldier, I'll just take off again."

With this in mind, Karekin headed for the flickering fire. When he was close enough to get a good look, he bent down and crawled for a while, until he stopped behind a bush. From there he could not only spy on the people sitting around the fire, but even overhear their conversation.

There were seven Arabs, armed to the teeth. They were all lying down, their heads toward the fire, forming a huge star on the ground (lying on the chest like that is quite common among the inhabitants of the desert, especially when they have something important to discuss). There were also nine pure bred Hejin camels. Two of them were loaded and, a bit further up, the others were grazing. The Arabs, whose appearance indicated that they were wealthy travelers, were having the following discussion:

"Where is he? We should have been on our way before dawn."

"Has something bad happened?"

"At any rate, we can't wait too long or we'll be late."

"Yes, let's get on the way at once," said a white-bearded Arab, who seemed to be the leader of the group. "Sherif is waiting for news."

"May God keep his sword sharp!" they all murmured when they heard Sherif's name.

"Yes, let's get going immediately."

The travelers had no sooner risen than one of them spotted Karekin. He grabbed his sword and rushed at him, shouting, "Friends, we are betrayed!" Suddenly the leader of the group screamed, "Don't!"

The Arab who had raised his sword and closed in on Karekin suddenly stopped, as did his five friends, who had grabbed their guns the moment they sensed danger. The old man approached Karekin, turned his scrutinizing eyes on him, and asked in a terrifying voice: "Who are you, stranger?"

"I'm a hungry Armenian refugee," Karekin said, standing up. "I thought you were shepherds. I was coming to ask for some bread and to dry my wet clothes by your fire."

"Your wet clothes? How can that be? It hasn't rained in these parts for seven months."

Karekin briefly related everything that had happened to him.

"Very well," said the chieftain. "I see that you're sincere. I'll spare your life. Here's some bread and there's the fire. Eat as much as you wish and warm up as long as you want. Goodbye."

When he signalled his followers to leave, Karekin took hold of the chieftain's hand and brought it respectfully to his forehead.

"I beg you, in the name of God. Take me with you."

"But what will you do in our camp?" asked the chieftain innocently.

"Oh chief, I know that you're not going to your camp," said Karekin pleadingly.

"What? That means you're a spy."

"No, good chief. I overheard your conversation by chance. I beg you to take me with you to Sherif. I promise to do all kinds of work for you. I can also speak English, a language that you might have need of on your way there. In the name of Mohammed, I beg you again and again not to leave me behind."

"Don't take Mohammed's name in vain, my friend. We are Druzes," revealed the chief.

"So much the better. You have helped the Armenians a great deal. We have always loved and respected you as friends. I swear on the Cross and on the Bible that I will never harm you in any way if you take me with you."

The old mountaineer grew less stern.

"But how can we carry you?" he asked. "Can you follow us on foot?"

"Oh noble chief, what are you saying?" asked Karekin. "Is it possible to keep up with a Hejin camel? You have two extra camels. Why couldn't I ride one of them?"

"But they are carrying our water vessels and provisions. Besides, we always need extra animals as reserves."

"My master, their loads are so light that we could put both loads on one camel. Please allow me to ride one of them and lead the other by the reins. If you need the camel I'm riding during the journey, I'm prepared to get off and accept my fate."

The Druzes probably didn't want to leave behind anyone who knew their secret. On the other hand, having been convinced that the Armenian was innocent, they didn't want to kill him. So, after a short consultation the chieftain said: "Very well. Come with us. But take care, my boy. If you're joining us to spy on us, the moment we have the slightest doubt I'll kill you. You can be sure of it."

"If I do anything like that, do whatever you wish to me. May my blood be yours in that case," murmured Karekin.

"*Inshallah*, so be it," said the Druzes in unison.

Before long they all got on their camels and sped through the desert like the wind, until the sun gradually rose behind the bushes and rocks.

* * *

For three days they rode south.

One night Karekin noticed that they had crossed the Hijaz railroad and were heading west. According to his calculations, they were about six hours away from the barracks of his soldier friends.

At dawn, they entered a vast expanse of sand. The mild morning wind blew and rippled the surface of this immense tract. Although Karekin had roamed the desert quite a bit, this was the first time that he had seen the sand moving. Just as the surface of a body of water ripples when touched by the wind, the surface of the desert moved in constant ripples and created ever-changing shapes and patterns that it was impossible not to admire, especially since the newly risen sun gilded the summit of every billow, creating an enchanting play of light and shade.

The Druzes, however, didn't pay any attention to this extraordinary phenomenon of nature. Wrapped in their large open-fronted cloaks, they continued their journey quietly, thinking and worrying about only one thing: reaching their destination and goal as soon as possible.

They continued like that all day. In the evening they noticed outcroppings of soil and rocks. Half an hour later they left the sand and entered an arid plateau that contained not a single breathing creature—not even a bird, a snake, or an insect.

"Let's stop here to rest and eat," ordered the chieftain.

They all brought their camels to an immediate halt and got down.

"My master," said Karekin a moment later, going up to the chieftain, "how many more days do we have to travel before we get to Sherif?"

"I hope we'll cross the line of fire tomorrow morning," answered the chief.

"That means that tomorrow our journey will be dangerous," said Karekin. "It's conceivable that we'll run into Turkish soldiers. Is it possible for me to have a rifle to protect myself if a fight breaks out?"

"First of all, there are no Turkish soldiers in this area," said the Druze reassuringly. "Besides, we can't put a rifle into your hands, because we don't know you."

"To tell you the truth, your doubts offend me," retorted Karekin. "I don't understand why you're so reluctant to trust me."

"We don't have to explain ourselves to you," said the Chief. "If we're attacked, we're capable of defending ourselves. You will only be a witness. But I want to remind you again, young man, if I ever notice a suspicious movement on your part, I'll bash your skull in."

"I hope we reach our destination without harm," answered Karekin, "but if something bad happens you'll see how faithfully I serve you."

Within two hours they got going again. They passed through a rough and stony mountain field. The moon had just risen on the horizon when one of the Druzes suddenly reined in his camel.

"Friends, way over there, behind those piles of stones, I see a shadow."

They were all surprised, and looked at the spot he had indicated. Karekin also gazed in that direction, but he saw only bushes and stones.

"Not one, but three," said the Druzes, whose eyes have an extraordinary ability to distinguish things far in the distance.

"Five," corrected the chief gravely, "and they're soldiers."

"Sherifian or British?"

"It's impossible to tell. We'll have to be careful."

Meanwhile, the shadows disappeared behind the rocks.

Karekin's heart beat faster with excitement, fear, and joy. It was a life-and-death situation.

"The soldiers have taken cover," said one of the Druzes. "They must be coming to attack us."

"Or they saw us and ran away," said his companion with bravado. The conspirators stopped for a second, undecided whether to advance, wait, or retreat.

While they were still debating what to do they heard the distant buzzing of an aeroplane. They lifted their heads and noticed a tiny spot coming in their direction. The plane gradually got closer, circled over their heads, and then flew back where it came from.

"We're saved," shouted the Druzes joyfully. "That was a British plane."

"The fact that the plane was British and was flying very high proves that we're at the Turkish border," said Karekin. "We must be careful. I think that the shadows we noticed a while ago were Turkish border guards or reconnaissance forces."

"So?"

"I humbly suggest that we wait here until we know for sure."

"What you're saying is typical of a cowardly Armenian," said the Druzes, laughing. "Even if we wait here for ten years, we won't find out. It's better to face the danger. If they're Turkish soldiers, we'll soon take care of them. If they're Sherif's forces or British soldiers, there's no problem."

"There's another danger in staying here," said the chief. "Maybe those soldiers went to call their friends. It will be easier to cross the border before larger forces arrive than to wait here and try to go through a cavalry blockade. Come, let's go. There's no time to lose."

Having said this, the Druze chieftain whipped his camel. His friends followed him, as one person. Karekin also followed the group, and they galloped like a storm, ever onward. When they had ridden only about half an hour, they heard a dry explosion from behind the rocks on the side of the road, followed by others, which soon turned into a barrage.

The attack was so sudden that the Druzes didn't even have time to get off their camels before two of them fell. The others, though, without losing their heads, jumped off their camels, took cover behind bushes, and started shooting.

Karekin, seeing that it was dangerous for him to stay on the battlefield without a rifle, pulled on the camel's reins and changed direction, still leading the second camel behind him, and started retreating. He kept going until he was out of the battle zone. When he came to a safe place he got off the camel and hid behind a bush, waiting for the battle to end.

Watching carefully, Karekin noticed that there were not five but a dozen Turks—he no longer doubted who they were—divided into two groups of six. They ambushed the road from both sides and showered a constant barrage of bullets on Karekin's traveling companions.

Fortunately though, the latter, after sustaining two casualties, were able to take cover behind dense shrubbery and succeeded not only in protecting themselves but also in killing three of their opponents, who were not cautious enough and stuck their heads up from behind the rocks. Fifteen minutes later, two more Turks were silenced. The soldiers were completely confused by this counter-attack and tried a flanking and encirclement manoeuvre by combining both sides and attacking their enemy from behind.

The Druzes, however, grasped the danger and suddenly sprang out of their entrenched positions, mounted their camels, and rushed forward. The Turks likewise came out of their hideouts and followed the Druzes, under fire.

A while later, everyone disappeared behind the rocks, bushes, and stones. From the sound of the gunfire Karekin concluded that the soldiers were quite far away by then, but that they would probably return to collect the slain.

Not wanting to be captured by the Turks, Karekin decided to flee. If he were taken prisoner by them, his punishment would be death. He went over to his camel, which was grazing a little further down. Before getting on the animal, though, he had an idea. Why escape empty-handed when his dead friends had rifles, clothes, shoes, and many other things that he would need on his journey? If he didn't take them, they would be picked up by the Turks.

And so, without wasting any more time, he ran to his fallen friends, took their rifles and clothes, and disguised as a Bedouin, got on his camel, kept hold of the reins of the second camel, and tore down the road in the direction they had just come from.

* * *

Karekin traveled all night, alone in the solitude of the steppes. At dawn he reached the desert, the sand of which was still moving in waves at the touch of the wind. He had no time to stop and admire the phenomenon. Perched on the edge of the limitless expanse, he didn't know which direction to take.

"If I find the railroad, I can orient myself," he thought. "We traveled west after the railroad, so now I have to head east."

Karekin stopped for about an hour to feed the camels. He also had a light breakfast, then decided to get moving. He had only the sun as a compass.

It had been only a week since he had left Sarkis. But during that short period he had had so many adventures and had been so occupied with saving his life that hadn't had time to think about his friend and what he had said.

The captain's wife was an Armenian . . . Her sister had also been kidnapped by a captain. Karekin knew how horrible it was to be raped. He had to find Sarkis and make a plan for escape.

Karekin checked his pockets—in other words, the pockets of his dead traveling companions—and he found quite a bit of silver and gold in them. In addition, he had two rifles, two guns, two swords, two daggers, and two camels. Sarkis and he could take turns having the Armenian woman on their saddles and escape to a free sea port.

The more Karekin thought about his sister's kidnapping, the deeper his hatred of the Turkish officer became. Who knows how many other people he had harmed while abducting his wife? And the more he thought about the unknown Armenian woman in a harem and her suffering, the harder he whipped his camel so he could get there as fast as he could and save her from the chains of enslavement and dishonor.

All day and all night Karekin planned his revenge and how to go about it. At midnight, to his great joy, he saw the railroad stretching out before him from one end of the desert to the other, like a black snake. Standing on the edge of the railroad, he debated whether he had to go north or south to find his friend's barracks.

"Probably north," he said to himself, and whipped his camel.

A couple of hours later he arrived at a station. He learned from the passersby that the place he was looking for was another five hours to the east.

In the morning, Karekin stopped in an open field, a short way from the captain's house. He got off his camel, took the load from the back of the second camel, tied the animals with a loop of string, and sat in the shade of a fallen wall. In Arabia it is very common to see Bedouins resting their animals in the streets or public squares. They seem to think that these places are inns, and they live there for weeks, making fires, cooking, lying down, and sleeping. Nobody pays any attention to them, and so nobody was interested in our "Bedouin," who now made himself a temporary abode a bit further down from the station, on an unclaimed piece of land.

Only an hour after he had settled down, he saw Sarkis coming out of the captain's house with a basket in his hands. He was heading for the market. The young "Bedouin" carefully followed his friend to the market, went up to him in a deserted corner, and said: "Sarkis, don't say anything. It's Karekin."

Sarkis from Moush rubbed his eyes in amazement.

"But Karekin, what is all this?"

"I'll tell you later. I came to take you and captain's wife away. Is the Armenian still there?"

"Yes, and do you know who she is? Your sister, Kohar."

Karekin's hands and knees began to tremble with emotion.

"Is it true?"

"Yes."

"How do you know?"

"After you left I had another opportunity to see her in secret. I found out that she was from Trebizond and your sister."

"Does she know I'm alive?"

"Yes, I told her everything. She was very happy that you were saved by going to Constantinople with the German officer. She asked me to take her away from the captain. I've been thinking about that day and night recently, but I always run into difficulties."

"What kind?"

"First of all, the captain doesn't leave me alone, not even for a minute. Besides, there are two black maids in the house, who never leave Kohar alone. Two Turkish soldiers also survey the house continuously, for fear of Bedouin attacks. Despite all that, I was prepared to do something crazy. Fortunately, you've come to help out."

"And how! . . . Do you know that I have at my disposal two pure bred camels, arms, money, clothes, and enough provisions for any long journey?"

"Don't tell me! Where are they?"

"Across from your house, in the open area."

"Good, then, Karekin. Now leave me alone. Someone might notice our conversation. Later, when I find an opportune moment, I'll come to talk things over with you."

"But tell me, is Kohar at home now?"

"Yes, the captain too."

"Embrace her for me. If you get the chance, tell her to go to the window and look for me. I'll always be there, lying in the shade and pretending to be asleep."

"Yes, yes, go. Go in peace."

* * *

Karekin went back to his camels and, as he told Sarkis, he pretended to be asleep and secretly watched the captain's windows in the hope of seeing his sister by chance. But no window curtain moved. Half an hour later, Sarkis returned home, his basket filled with meat and fruit.

"Now Kohar will know," said Karekin to himself. Now the curtain will move and I'll see her face soaked in tears. Now, right now, I'll see her."

And his heart beat faster and faster.

An hour went by. Two hours. It was noon. Still the curtain didn't move. Probably Sarkis hadn't had a chance to see Kohar.

Around two, though, the curtain of one of the upper windows opened and a beautiful female face appeared in the middle of the window frame. Karekin shook, as if he had touched an electrical current. With longing and joy and countless other feelings he watched the radiant woman, who was none other than his sister. Kohar tried to blow him a kiss, then she pulled the curtain shut and vanished from his eyes like a nymph.

"Oh, at last, at last," murmured Karekin, getting up nervously, patting the camels on the comely heads they stretched toward him. "At last, at last, I've achieved what I intended."

As evening drew closer, the suffocating heat of the day subsided. The captain came out of the house, followed by Sarkis, who was holding a mare by the bridle. The officer mounted the horse and headed for the station, while Sarkis ran breathlessly after him in order to be at his master's disposal at all times.

When they rounded the street corner, Karekin had an unbearable urge to go to the captain's house, take his sister in his arms, and free her from her imprisonment. But then he rejected the thoughtless impulse that might have endangered both his own and his sister's lives.

"No, we have to be patient and act cool-headedly," he told himself. "Unless I and Sarkis can decide on a strategy together, our purpose may fail."

His heart, however, beat faster and faster as time went by. He thought that his sister must undoubtedly have been suffering likewise, realizing that she could not throw herself into her brother's arms.

That night Sarkis and the officer returned. Half an hour later Sarkis came out again and headed in the direction of the market. Karekin followed him.

"Don't get too close to me," said Sarkis in a low voice, "Tonight, if you see a light on the first floor, the second window to the right of the door, come very carefully and climb in the window. Bring me a gun. Don't say anything. And go away right now."

Karekin went back without saying a word.

Minutes passed with the slowness of hours, and the poor boy was restless until the signal light appeared in the window at midnight.

Karekin got up anxiously and examined the surroundings. Although the stars and the moon lit everything up as if it were noon, at that time of night there was no one in the streets. He glided under the walls like a shadow and leapt through the window.

"Careful, don't make any noise," whispered Sarkis, taking him by the hand. "They're all in bed, sleeping."

"Is the captain with my sister?"asked Karekin through his teeth. "Let me go and kill the dog. What room is it? Show me!"

"Don't be crazy, Karekin. You'll ruin everything we've planned," sighed Sarkis. "Wait a little. Kohar knows everything. When her husband is sleeping soundly, she'll pretend that she's going to the washroom, and will come down and wait for us. Did you bring the gun? Give it to me!"

Karekin gave it to him, leapt out of the window, and returned to his camels. A little later he saw Sarkis and his sister jump out of the window and head toward him.

"Kohar!"

"Karekin!"

Brother and sister threw themselves into each other's arms.

"Shhh! . . . This is no time for crying or kissing," reproached Sarkis. "Come on, get on the camels. Karekin, take your sister on the saddle with you, so that I can be free to move as I want."

Karekin and his sister got on his camel. Sarkis got on the other one, but they had hardly got the camels to their feet when they heard an unusual noise from the captain's house.

Without wasting a moment, Sarkis and Karekin whipped the camels and galloped out of the city.

Before long the moonlight revealed the captain and two soldiers galloping after them, shouting, swearing, and firing. Sarkis and Karekin turned from time to time, returning the shots, and spurred on their camels.

Before long a bullet wounded Sarkis in the left shoulder. In the heat of the excitement the young man from Moush didn't feel the shot, but he gradually noticed that he couldn't hold the camel's reins the right way to make the animal run even faster. The captain took advantage of this situation and rushed to give his victim a last blow. But at that exact moment the officer fell from his saddle, hit by Karekin's bullet.

When Karekin saw that instead of chasing them the soldiers rushed immediately to the assistance of their superior, he grabbed the reins of Sarkis' camel and, paying no further attention to his pursuers, he darted ahead.

"Sarkis, are you badly wounded?" he asked when they were barely out of the danger zone.

"No, I don't think so," Sarkis murmured. "I'm glad the bastard croaked."

"Brother, let's get off our camel and dress Mr. Sarkis' wound," Kohar proposed solicitously.

"Thank you very much for your concern," said Sarkis, coming over to her. "But Kohar, I'd ask you to do me a favor: from now on, please forget the "Mr." when you talk of me. Always keep in mind that I am you brother's older brother."

With the help of his sister, Karekin got his wounded friend down and made him lie on the ground. Kohar bandaged the wound and asked with concern: "Does it hurt?"

"A wound bandaged by your hands doesn't hurt," Sarkis replied, and he enveloped his benefactress in an affectionate gaze.

* * *

They turned the camels south—the only safe direction—and traveled for three days without encountering a village or a person. Fortunately, they had plenty of water and provisions, so were not bothered by hunger or thirst.

On the morning of the fourth day they caught sight of Bedouin tents in the distance. They went to the place, got off their camels, and introduced themselves as chieftains of Beni Hasan, on their way to Akaba on business. The chief of the inhabitants of these tents received them with pomp and honor, not doubting their identities because Sarkis and Karekin were wearing Bedouin dress and had dark suntans, but most of all because they spoke fluent Arabic, with faultless pronunciation. Kohar also spoke Arabic. Although she was fair, this didn't arouse suspicion, as many Bedouin sheiks marry city women, either kidnapping them or seducing them with their wealth.

"I think the Red Sea is still very far away," said the host sheikh in answer to Karekin's question. "If you don't lose your way, you may get there, perhaps in a month."

"Aren't there any villages or towns in these parts?"

"No, we're in the desert."

"What do you do here?"

"We graze our camels and sheep while slowly making our way to Mecca."

"How long does it take you to get there?"

"*Inshallah*, three months."

"Three months?"

"Yes. What's three months after all?"

And indeed, for people with no notion of time, what is three months? Months, years, decades mean nothing to them. Time passes slowly. Days, months, experiences, and events follow each other with the regularity of a clock. One has no need to rush and make efforts to change the progress of events ordained by Providence or become impatient. Submit to destiny. Let time hold you in its arms and carry you as it carries all of humanity and the entire universe.

The mentality of the desert folk was not unknown to Sarkis and Karekin. In fact, they agreed that such a philosophy was appropriate for this region, since they had no other option—under such circumstances the human being has no choice but to subject himself to time if he wants to get out of this endless expanse. Accordingly, they gave the Bedouin a sack of gold to look after them until they came to an inhabited region. The Arab accepted the proposal and so for twenty days they traveled with these shepherds, eating with them, resting with them, working with them, in other words, doing everything nomadic people do with them.

One day they arrived at a village. They met some Arab soldiers and questioned them. They learned not only that the Turkish army had been defeated, but also that Jerusalem, Beirut, Damascus, Aleppo, and Constantinople had been captured by the Allied forces.

Karekin and Sarkis did not see any need to continue traveling with the Bedouins. So they paid the sheikh and his family quite generously and, after expressing their gratitude, rode eastward.

Near Persepolis one of their camels died and they ran out of money. To obtain money to continue their journey they sold the other camel, as well as their surplus clothing and their weapons—except for a gun that Sarkis kept to ensure security on the road. They got a ride on a cargo truck to Gaza, and from there to Jerusalem.

When they arrived in that city the British police searched them and, discovering that Sarkis had an illegal gun, took him to jail without hearing his objections. Karekin and his sister, on the other hand, came to the monastery. Like us, they were unable to interpret the strange behavior of the British.

* * *

"We could expect anything from the Turks," said Karekin, when he finished his story, "but imprisonment by the British never crossed our minds."

"Why?" I asked with a smile. "Doesn't the tanner beat his favorite skin more rigorously?"

"I can do without that kind of favoritism," Karekin shouted angrily.

"No, don't say that," I said. "We shouldn't criticize their harsh behavior. No matter how unreasonable they might be, we would never have seen these days without their help. Now let's be happy that you too have been delivered alive and healthy out of Hell." Then, turning to Kohar, I continued, "I congratulate you, madam, for having such a brave and courageous brother. I also congratulate you for the admirable perseverance which enabled you to bear your misfortune for years. I hope that you soon forget your suffering and from now on live a happy life, protected by your brother."

"I forgot the good news," Karekin said at once, smiling broadly. "My sister and Sarkis are engaged. They'll be married as soon as he gets out of prison, but we'll talk more about that later."

Then he spoke to his sister: "Kohar, can you set the table? We've talked too much. Let's have a bite to eat with our friend."

10 January, 1919

Today they stopped our rations. Fortunately, my mother and Manoushag found jobs with the American Red Cross yesterday, and they brought home a bundle of cotton and some linen to be sewn. My mother spins the cotton all day long, and my sister sews till morning. The money they make is barely enough to buy dry bread.

We are impatiently waiting for the roads to open so we can leave and put an end to this unbearable penury.

12 January, 1919

Today we saw how much our blessed patriarchs sacrificed for the splendor of the church. We saw chalices studded with diamonds, bright silver crosses, crowns adorned with precious stones, gold-bound Bibles, valuable plates, medals, rings, and all kinds of jewelry, gold and silver antiquities that are all exhibited in St. James Monastery. They say that this magnificent collection of holy vessels and church ornaments is only a fraction of the real treasures, which we ordinary mortals are not allowed to see.

We heard fabulous stories about Jerusalem's treasures, even several from priests. Over the centuries, with gifts made by kings, princes, and royal houses, the collection has grown rich and magnificent. In value and opulence, it can compete with that of any royal museum. It has been robbed and looted on several occasions. It has been reduced by fire and neglect. As a result, many valuable carpets and chasubles were destroyed. Despite all these calamities, however, it has always remained unique, invaluable, and incomparable among the treasures of the world.

It is unfortunate that no one has ever made a list of these infinite treasures and that some of the monks have had the audacity to steal some of them, filling their own and their relatives' pockets. To conceal their thefts, these crooks once even set fire to the treasury, and consequently many old manuscripts, chasubles and other valuable vestments, silk embroideries, and carpets were lost to the flames. Under the ashes they found masses of melted gold and silver. A piece of burnt carpet that had been thrown into a trash can was noticed by chance, rescued, and later sold at an exorbitant price.

In the Chapel of St. Toros more than 3,000 manuscripts are displayed—ancient records, scrolls, etc.—which also represent considerable priceless wealth. They showed us a Bible copied by King Levon (the Leo Gospel). When we saw it we had the same impression that we had when we saw the tombs of the fallen Crusaders. Instead of spending his precious time on the people and the country, the sainted king of Cilicia had wasted it on futilities.

In the Armenian Patriarchate of the Holy City, we admired the paintings of Aivazovsky—especially the one which reproduced the color of flame so skillfully that one particular spot on the canvas seems to be burning. The walls of the council hall are hung with various other oil paintings and tiles. The portraits of Sultan Reshad and Kaiser Wilhelm have been taken down from their honored spots and thrown into a dark room. A friend suggested that they hang them with their faces to the wall, like naughty school children.

"There's no need," we said. "They have committed such horrible crimes that their names are forever inscribed on the rolls of the cursed and dishonored.

19 January, 1919

In the desert, Christmas and Easter came and went like any other, ordinary days. There the cries and sobs of the refugees were always responses to some new fright or alarm. Here, on the other hand, bells and cymbals proclaim that a Messiah has been born to redeem mankind. This is the difference between past and present Christmases.

Yesterday thousands of pilgrims, including my mother and Manoushag, went to Bethlehem according to tradition to celebrate the Birth of Christ. I put off my curiosity to see the manger where Christ was born to another day and instead went to St. James Church. Although a major part of the pilgrims and locals had gone to Bethlehem, the church was full.

Mixed in with the huge crowd of refugee survivors were local Armenians, dressed in Arabic costume and speaking to each other in Arabic, which looked and sounded rather odd. It was strange to see how these people could have lost their national identity so much in a city that contains so many Armenian monasteries, churches, bishops, priests, schools, print shops, and much more.

Who is responsible for this decline? The local population? Or the monastery? I turned this question over in my mind during the ceremony, but was unable to come up with an answer.

26 January, 1919

Today at St. James Monastery an elegant, slim young man with blue eyes was pointed out to me. He was apparently a relative of the famous Father Ghevont. Last year our noble priest made this relative the gift of an emerald torn from a chasuble. The latter went to Egypt, sold the precious stone, and returned to Jerusalem. Despite the fact that he has neither employment nor any other income, according to the earlier refugees, this young man has been living a lavish life for a year, squandering his money on high-class women of dubious character. He has not yet spent all the money he made by selling the church emerald.

Isn't it strange that while some families long for a slice of dry bread, this young man leads a lavish life and grows fat at the expense of the nation? But it is not he who is guilty. As the popular proverb says, here in Jerusalem "the fish rots from its head."

2 February, 1919

The people have never before lived so close to the monks of Jerusalem and penetrated their lives as they do now. The pilgrims who used to come to Jerusalem for Easter and stay here for a short while to visit the historical sites never had time to take an interest in the lives of the clergy. They saw only the exterior gloss and were dazzled by what they were shown. We, as a result of our daily contact, see many things, and I am sorry to report that the interior of the "merchandise" does not correspond to its exterior make-up.

In deference to the very few exceptions, let me first say that the Jerusalem monks, besides being monastic, are factious, disobedient, pugnacious, conceited, and immoral. One is a thief, another tucks his cowl under his arm and runs after women like a street scoundrel. Yet another, despite his advanced years, gets the refugee woman who cleans his room pregnant in exchange for a slice of bread. And another has not set his foot inside a church for the past seventeen years, spending all his days and nights in his cell, drinking.

There's no superior with the authority to discipline them, because even their superior has his own "sins." He is afraid of punishing the guilty, lest many unfortunate secrets be revealed in retaliation.

Then, of course, the question of partiality—partisanship, the familiarity of each other's secrets—has created such anarchy that the cleric finds himself free to live his life any way he chooses. Nobody bothers anybody else. There is neither leader nor subordinate.

Many come to Jerusalem to reinforce their faith and beliefs. If we ever had a grain of faith, we have lost even that.

9 February, 1919

It's common knowledge that the Jerusalem monastery is in debt. The debt is huge. In spite of the fact that every year considerable sums of money are paid to decrease it, the debt always remains the same.

The amount paid barely takes care of the accumulated interest (just like the administration of the public debt of Turkey, to reduce which millions have been paid over the centuries, without reducing the amount owed by a farthing). As we visit the city a certain national pride fills us all. We see numerous buildings on the most exquisite boulevards, the facades of which bear the letters S. H. (*Sourp Hagop*, St. James). We begin to wonder if it is really so expensive to feed a group of fifty monks, sextons, and servants that the revenue from the properties of the Armenian monastery are not sufficient to pay off even the interest on the debt.

What have they done with all the donations made by pilgrims, the fees paid for candles, and the money collected at each Mass and at other religious services? The treasury is like the jars of the Danaïds: always empty despite the generous inflow of national wealth.

The Armenian monastery of Jerusalem does not have the pomp of the Greek or Latin monasteries. The majority of priests get new clothes only once a year, and most of them eat rice paste at least four times a week, which is so insipid that our prior, Father Ashod, gives us his share and goes out to eat, paying out of his own pocket.

So where does the money go? How have they created this fabulous debt? It is not possible to comprehend this puzzling secret.

16 February, 1919

Life here is both dull and monotonous.

The question of making a living bothers me a bit more every day. Armenians can't do anything here but work as laborers, and that I can't do that because I'm terribly weak. Despite the free medicines from the American hospital, my chest is not yet properly cured.

My mother has been sick for a week and can't work. We live on Manoushag's daily wages from sewing underwear. Sometimes I show around the British officers who visit Sourp Prgich. Afterwards I take them around the historical sites of the city and am embarrassed when I accept the money they give me.

Patiently we endure all this, and I console myself, in the meantime, that one day this life of deprivation will come to an end.

23 February, 1919

Today, a young man from Sivas came to Holy Savior Monastery.

During the Great War, like all other young Armenian men, he enlisted in the military, and served at the Dardanelles front. While fighting there in defense of the country, he was taken prisoner by the British, and they sent him to Egypt, the territory designated for prisoners of war. In Egypt the Armenians who survived the Mousa Dagh massacre told him about the extermination of Armenians in Turkey.

He was freed when the Armistice was proclaimed, and went to Port Said refugee camp to look for the members of his family among the survivors who had been brought there. Not only did he not find any of his family, he did not find even a single living soul from Sivas. Hoping to find some of them among the refugees in Jerusalem, he came to this city and applied to St. James Monastery. Even there, however, among 5,000 people—refugees from all parts of Turkey—he has not been able to find a single person from his city. On the recommendation of a priest, he has come to our monastery, thinking we are from Sivas.

After listening to the young man's story I said: "Although Sivas borders on the edges of the Chorum vineyards, our town is in the province of Angora, and we are considered *Ankaratsi*."

"Consider yourself blessed that you were beyond the reach of Bloody Muammer's authority," said the young man from Sivas as he sat sadly on the tomb of the *Shghtayagir* Patriarch.

"Yes, the two-hour distance saved our lives," I said.

"My father, mother, two brothers, sister, wife, and three children have all been lost," sighed the young man, covering his head with his hands. "If I count my paternal and maternal aunts, of the seventy-three members of our family there is no one left. I don't know who to mourn or which pains to endure."

"Don't despair, compatriot," I said. "Go to Beirut and Aleppo. There are refugees there too. Perhaps you'll find one of your loved ones among them." And I told him how we had unexpectedly found a few lost members of our family.

After this young man from Sivas left, I was interested in knowing how many victims we, the fortunate ones, had given to the brutish Turkish Moloch over the past four years. Without counting distant relatives, our family has suffered the following losses:

My grandfather, Parsegh Dadrian, had two brothers: Abraham and Nishan. Parsegh's descendants were two children and a total of fourteen grandchildren. Six remain alive. Apraham's descendants were three children and, again, a total of fourteen grandchildren. Only six of them are still alive. Nishan's descendants were five children (one of whom died before the deportations) and fourteen grandchildren. Only seven remain alive.

In other words, out of forty-two people, twenty-three are dead and nineteen are alive. And to think that we are among the most fortunate of the deportees—fortunate because we did not suffer fire and sword!

2 March, 1919

Today is Carnival. Smiles and folly, dancing and music are everywhere. The Armenian refugees go around wearing masks and amusing each other in the courtyard of St. James Monastery. There is merry-making even in our prior's room. Father Ashod invited me to participate in the celebration, but I refused out of politeness.

As I write these lines I hear Armenian songs being played on gramophones. I've never heard Armenian songs on records before. Enthralled, I listen to them and remember how I used to long for such happy days in the desert.

Now these happy days are here! Why am I not rejoicing? I don't know. An extraordinary melancholy has enveloped my soul.

9 March, 1919

On one of the main boulevards of the city there's a bookstore with a reading room. It was founded by the British. We go there almost every day to quench our thirst for knowledge and at the same time to read the daily news. Today, sitting in the garden adjacent to the reading room, a young man from Rodosto who was miraculously saved from the Deir Zor massacres told us his Odyssey.

Torkom's life has been full of adventure. Their deportation from Rodosto . . . their removal by night in their nightgowns, by cargo boats, with no opportunity to take their furniture, money, or even underwear . . . 150 people in one boat, on stormy seas, in the rain, sailing without food or water for weeks . . . at last going ashore at Izmit, and going from there on foot to Aleppo and then to Deir Zor . . . during which more than half of the 10,000 people perished from hunger, misery, sun-stroke, and police brutality, etc. . . . horrible events in which human beings were eradicated, like brambles.

But I will refrain from describing all of them. I will tell only the Deir Zor part of the story, thus adding another eye-witness account to the horrifying carnage that I have described so far.

* * *

The thousands of Armenians of Deir Zor were, as described previously, led to the banks of the Khabur river like herds of sheep on their way to the slaughterhouse. In the solitude of the desert Enezé and Chechen thieves suddenly surrounded the caravan and began to kill them with swords, axes, and bullets. The attack happened so quickly that a ring of blood circled the caravan and the Armenians did not even have time to realize what was going on.

Suddenly heart-rending cries, pitiful screams, and tearful sobs rose from the center of the ring. The savage howling of the executioners, the blazing of rifles, and the ringing of axes echoed from the edge of the ring, which grew gradually tighter and tighter. Everyone was alarmed. They all pushed, stepped on each other, and fell on top of each other. Those who rushed forward in an attempt to save themselves had their skulls split in two with a single stroke. Others, who remained where they were, looked on in dismay as the murderers mowed their countrymen down and steadily drew closer to them.

The savage and unsparing carnage lasted more than two hours. Corpses were heaped on top of each other, blood flowed in torrents. Then approximately twenty young men climbed over the corpses and rushed toward their encircling slayers. Twelve of them fell lifeless at the feet of the killers. The rest succeeded in breaking through the ring, and fled like lightning to open fields. Bullets rang out after them. One, two, three, four . . . five of them fell on their faces. The three who remained resumed their flight. The killers shot after them a few times but then gave up, realizing that they still had thousands of people in front of them to slaughter.

Torkom and his two friends, Asadour from Divrik and Simon from Bandirma (I call them friends although they had met about only an hour earlier), despite their serious wounds—only Asadour's wound was superficial—fled all night, until they reached an Arab village. Fortunately, Simon had sufficient funds in his money-belt. Without going into the village, they bought some bread and cheese from a shepherd boy and rested awhile before continuing on their way. They were trying to put as much distance as possible between themselves and the deadly slaughter-house of the Khabur river.

They traveled over deserted roads for three days and arrived by night at a Circassian village called Sipka. Torkom had passed through that village two weeks earlier and had seen about 400 refugee families living in tents. They went there and found nobody. They asked the peasants and heard that about a week earlier the Armenians had left for Deir Zor of their own will.

Torkom and his friends disguised themselves in outfits bought from the Circassians and continued on their way.

The next day they arrived in Hamam, where 6,000 refugees used to live in tents. There was no trace of them either.

"Aren't there any Armenians here?" they asked the keeper of the inn where they stayed.

"I've started a carpet shop in the next building. There are thirty girls working there," replied the innkeeper, not suspecting his guests' nationality. "If you wish, I can take you there."

"It's too late now. They must be sleeping," the Armenians said.

"It doesn't matter. We'll wake them up," replied the Turk, most obligingly.

Torkom and his friends realized that the man had misunderstood them. Out of curiosity they went to the adjacent building. The innkeeper lit the lamp and showed them the Armenian girls confined there, who, because of the extreme heat, had bare legs and breasts, and were sleeping calmly on the carpets they had woven or on the bales of yarn.

"This one is from Boursa," said the Turk, indicating a thirteen-year old girl with his foot. She is very beautiful, if you want . . ."

Torkom and his friends glanced briefly at the sleeping girl and left the room as if they did not care for the girl, regretting a thousand times that they had found a young compatriot in such circumstances.

The next day they arrived in Abu Harar. There had been 500 tents there. The people had lived in extreme misery. Every day five or six people had committed suicide by throwing themselves into the Euphrates. Now there was no trace of either the living or the dead.

Two days later they reached Meskene, once a city of 800 tents. Torkom tried to visualize the wide river bank and the 30,000 people spread out upon it, giving it the appearance of an ant-hill to anyone who saw it from afar. Arabs from the opposite bank of the river or from distant places used to bring food on rafts or camels to sell to these starving people at incredibly exorbitant prices. These people had already been robbed several times, and sold everything they had to buy a piece of bread. One sold a gold watch for five coins; another sold her engagement ring, which she had kept until the last minute in memory of her lost fiancé. Another girl sold the embroidery prepared for her dowry. A woman sold her wedding gown, which she had brought with her despite very great difficulties. Countless others sold the clothes they were wearing, their underwear, shoes, and so on, and many unfortunate ones even sold their own children.

Now a deadly silence reigned over the river bank. One would think the ground had split open and that all of these buyers and sellers had been swallowed up into the entrails of the earth.

* * *

And so the days went by. Tortured by the memory of all these events, they arrived one night in a town called El Bab. Thinking that there would surely be policemen in the city, they stayed in a safe place on the edge of the city.

As soon as it got dark, Asadour went to the market to buy food. When he had finished his shopping and was returning to his friends, he noticed that an Arab beggar was following him, not uttering a word. Asadour continued walking, ignoring the beggar. The beggar soon caught up with him, and in a whining voice asked for some tobacco. Asadour handed him his tobacco box. The man rolled a thick cigarette and asked for a light. After lighting his cigarette, instead of going away he continued to walk with him, not talking about anything in particular.

Asadour did not enjoy the company of this impudent man. He tried many times to put an end to the conversation and leave, but without success. The man stuck to him like glue.

Before long, when Torkom and Simon noticed this stranger approaching with their friend, they asked Asadour who he was, as if sensing an impending disaster.

"I don't know," he replied. "He saw me buying bread. It seems he's hungry."

"Why did you bring him here?" Torkom asked. "You should have given him a piece of bread and got rid of him."

"He's very tenacious and won't leave me alone," Asadour replied.

Without further discussion, the three friends sat down to eat, and gave the beggar a share, asking him to eat and leave at once.

Before finishing the meal, however, they heard the pounding of galloping horses and a moment later shouts filled the air: "Surrender, all of you!" These words were spoken by the mounted policemen who were riding up to them.

Torkom and his friends thought that the beggar had betrayed them. They rose to their feet to flee when, to their great surprise, they discovered that the beggar was already running away.

The police pursued the fugitive. "You! Surrender! Surrender or we'll shoot!" they shouted repeatedly. Instead of stopping as the Armenians had done, however, the beggar continued running until he fell to the ground, his body completely riddled with the policemen's bullets.

After killing the fugitive beggar, the policemen—six of them—dismounted from their horses and laid into the Armenians with their whips.

"But what do you want from us? Why are you beating us?" the Armenians protested, shielding themselves against the blows that rained upon them.

"Shut up, thieves!" roared the police. "That's what your victims used to say to you, but you went on killing them, ignoring their pleas. You've terrorized the government for a long time. Now you'll see!"

"But please, there's been a misunderstanding . . . we're not thieves . . . we're peace-loving people."

"You look like Armenians . . . Why are you dressed like Circassians? . . . Where have you come from? Why have you joined the thieves of Abu Bekir?" shouted the policemen, much louder this time, savagely bringing their whips down on them.

At last they told the Armenians to pick up the corpse of the beggar (a thief of Abu Bekir) and led them proudly into the city. After starving them in the jail at El Bab, they sent them to Aleppo in chains, where they imprisoned them for four months, until they were convinced that they had no connection with Abu Bekir's thieves.

Once they were free, Torkom left his friends, went to Damascus, and remained there until the British occupied the city.

The last part of Torkom's story reminded me of my "friendship" with the thief Yusuf. I reflected on how lucky I had been not to have suffered because of that.

16 March, 1919

We saw a strange flag at St. James Monastery today—a horizontal tricolor: red, blue, and orange.

We asked Father Madteos, who was standing next to the flag, whose colors they were.

"Ours," answered the prior of the Holy Archangel's Monastery.

"But isn't our flag red, blue, and white?"

"That flag was created by the Armenian legionnaires in the French army. But the government of Armenia has now officially approved these colors."

Just like a man who falls in love with the first girl he meets, we didn't like the orange of this new flag, especially since the other flag, like that of the French, according to what General Picot said, bore witness to fabulous pages in history.

When we made our thoughts known to Father Madteos, he touched his beard and said: "Don't worry, your eyes will soon get used to this one."

23 March, 1919

The Arabs are upset. To manifest their displeasure with the British, they have attacked the refugee camp in Port Said and killed a few Armenians. They have also assassinated Armenians in Aleppo, Damascus, and Amman. No doubt they mistook the rags of the Armenians for British uniforms!

The Arabs in Jerusalem are also smoldering. British planes fly over the city continuously. English soldiers have placed machine-guns on street corners, sometimes on balconies, even on church bell-towers, and they keep the city under surveillance.

We didn't leave the monastery today, simply for reasons of safety. There is fear and excitement everywhere. A state of war has been declared in every city in Palestine.

30 March, 1919

A cold, bitter wind is blowing.

We live in one of the damp rooms of Holy Savior, where there is neither light nor heat. Every day my mother and sister, soaked by the rain, walk about half an hour to bring work from the Red Crescent. They work continuously until evening, to do as much work as possible.

My chest bothers me tremendously. When I start coughing I get breathless, my heart palpitates, and my sides ache. Today I also have a toothache. On the other hand, the infection beside my eye is getting deeper and making me nervous.

My mood is very changeable again.

6 April, 1919

They announced in the monastery that those who would like to go to Cilicia should apply to the National Association and register. Many of the refugees and two families among our compatriots registered to go.

We are waiting for the road to Constantinople to open so we can go there. Our intention is to live in Constantinople for a while—until I can go to Chorum to liquidate our properties and business—and then to go to Armenia and settle there, under the shadow of Ararat, for good.

The registrations for Constantinople haven't begun yet.

13 April, 1919

The holy season has begun. Today is Palm Sunday.

Every year, from the four corners of the world, thousands of pilgrims arrive in Jerusalem to attend the events of Holy Week. We are such "fortunate" people that, without any expense or difficulty, we are already in Jerusalem. We have been living here for five months.

This morning, in the Church of the Holy Sepulcher, the Armenians, Greeks, and Latins took turns around the sepulcher of Christ holding palm branches. The church was packed. For hours we watched the parade of precious vestments, banners with crosses, diadems, and Bibles.

This afternoon we attended the *Trenpatsek* service in St. James Church. The elderly Catholicos of Cilicia, who is a refugee in Jerusalem like us, presided over the ceremony.

This year, for the first time since the war, about twenty pilgrims have come to Jerusalem. In church they looked at us as if we were strange birds.

Blessed are those who have not been baptized by fire!

17 April, 1919

This afternoon we went to St. James Church for the *Vodnlva* service. Many high ranking non-Armenian dignitaries, English officers, and their wives also attended the Armenian rites. After we had waited for two hours, the curtains of the high altar parted at last, and there they all were: the bishops and priests of the monastery stood in a row, and in their midst was the Catholicos of Cilicia, Sahag Khobayan.

The service began immediately. His Holiness washed the feet of the ecclesiastics in a silver basin, one after the other. The ceremony was so interesting that the English ladies used their binoculars in order not to miss any details.

The service was very short.

After the divine service, a bishop from the Anglican Church asked to come to the altar to say a few words to the Armenian people. And, to make his words more impressive, he requested permission to speak wearing Armenian vestments. The sexton, a real blockhead, giving no consideration to the English bishop's slight build, brought out a diadem as big as a cauldron and a chasuble as large as a tent, usually reserved for fat monastery priests. The stupid sexton put the chasuble on the bishop, making the poor man's body disappear from our eyes, and then placed the diadem on his head, making his head, now the only visible part of the man's body, disappear also.

Holding the cauldron-sized diadem in the air with his hands, the English bishop declared that the Armenian Apostolic and the Anglican Churches are sister institutions and that he was glad the Armenian people and their Church had been able to emerge from this horrific tragedy, just as Gregor the Illuminator emerged victoriously from his venomous pit. His words were received with resounding applause . . . an appropriate response, considering the farce that had just taken place in the church!

Tonight the *Latsi Kisher* service was held in the Chapel of the Holy Archangels.

18 April, 1919

What a difference between the worship of the early Christians and the bizarre ritualism of today, anyone who saw the entombment ceremony held today by the Latins would say! Tonight they placed a life-sized Christ made of wax on top of Golgotha. There, murmuring prayers at each blow of the hammer, they nailed Him to a cross with arms outspread. Then they planted the cross on the summit of the mountain. More prayers. Then they took the wax Christ down and took Him to be wrapped in a shroud. They prayed for another hour as they shrouded the Lord. Then they solemnly carried this "puppet" Christ and placed Him in His grave.

Compared to those of the Latins, the Armenian and Greek ceremonies were much simpler. But they still seemed a little strange to us. Back home we were used to seeing the sepulcher carried into the church on the shoulders of those who participated in the Good Friday procession. Here, on the other hand, the procession filed around Christ's sepulcher, exactly as they say of the Prophet: "The mountain wouldn't come to Mohammed, so Mohammed went to the mountain."

19 April, 1919

The most crucial part of the Easter ceremony is the descent of the light. For centuries the clergy of Jerusalem have persuaded the faithful that on this day light comes down from the sky and alights on Christ's tomb. My grandmother, God bless her soul, came to Jerusalem many years ago, and was exposed to this fraudulent delusion. She was so convinced it was true that she wanted us to believe in the miracle too.

"But it's impossible," we used to tell her skeptically.

"Why is it impossible?" she protested with agitation. The patriarch, bishops, priests, *kahana*s (married priests), deacons, altar boys, in short everybody prays to the Lord with one voice. God hears their prayers, and suddenly light, like lightning, descends from the sky.

"Grandmother, did you see the light come down like that?" I used to ask her.

"Yes, and not just me. Thousands of people saw it at the same time."

The woman never lied. We knew there was something mysterious in that "miracle." But what did the clergy do to deceive the naive worshipers? It was like a riddle to us.

"Did the light appear like this?" I used to say, taking my flashlight out of my pocket and shining it in my grandmother's weak eyes, which could hardly gaze steadily at the flame of a match. My grandmother, blinded by the bright rays of the flashlight, would let out a frightening scream and throw anything she could get her hands on at me, shouting: "May God forgive, forgive, forgive . . . this boy is a devil. One day he'll burn in the flames of Hell."

A month later I played the same trick on her, swearing that I didn't have a flashlight in my pocket. I didn't swear falsely. I'd hidden the flashlight under my arm. And when my grandmother came to the part of the story where God heard the prayers of the clergy and the light suddenly descended like lightning, I pressed the button of the flashlight and shone the rays directly into the poor woman's eyes.

How well I remembered my childhood mischief that morning when I went with a friend to the Church of the Holy Sepulcher to attend the Service of the Light. The miracle would take place at three o'clock in the afternoon, but we wanted to go early to get a place close to the sepulcher. But how? Thousands of people came last night with food, and slept there, not only in the church but also in the courtyard. Needless to say, here people go to church not to pray but to see the ritualism.

Besides all this, today's ceremonies had another interesting aspect: every year there's a competition between the Armenians and the Greeks to see which of them will bring the light that descends on the sepulcher to their patriarch—at that moment seated on their thrones in their respective churches—first.

In order that the light might be transported from the sepulcher to the patriarch without meeting any obstacle, on this day all the Armenian and Greek tough guys, armed to the teeth, supervise the roads leading from the sepulcher to the two churches. In former times, apparently, there have been bloody fights, with people blocking the roads deliberately. But now, since the British occupation of Jerusalem, such scandalous practices have stopped. The Race for the Light, however, has not lost its uniqueness.

This year another situation arose. Last year the Greeks won the race. Now, with thousands of pilgrims—now refugees—living in Jerusalem, it had become a matter of pride and dignity for the local Armenian "braves" that we should win the race. Therefore, they added their support to the Arab and British policemen and very assiduously maintained order by constantly pushing the people back, sometimes by shoving politely, sometimes by uttering disguised threats, and sometimes by showing the ends of their daggers.

Under these circumstances it wasn't possible to enter the church courtyard from the street, let alone the church, of course. Nevertheless, we were still hopeful and, abandoning ourselves to the whims of fortune, joined the crowd. By using the ebb and the flow of the crowd to our own advantage and by constantly using our shoulders and elbows, we managed to get into the courtyard. At around two o'clock we were about twenty feet from the exterior gate of the church, but such was our position that we had become part of the monolithic mass that was the crowd, and could move no farther.

At that very moment of despair and immobility, we heard that the governor of the city, General Stores, and his followers were coming to the church to attend the ceremony. The police had a hard time clearing the way so the dignitaries could pass. As soon as their cortege passed, the passage closed again, just as water closes in again behind a passing boat. Seeing our chance, we leapt after the British, hoping to be carried along in their wake. As it turned out, our calculations—at least my calculations—proved accurate. When I regained my balance, although I had become separated from my friend, I found myself near the chapel of the sepulcher—in other words, exactly where the Ceremony of the Light would take place.

There were six huge candelabra where I was standing, a pair of which belonged to each of the Armenians, Greeks, and Latins. Seeing that three or four people had climbed each of them and were sitting on their arms, I did the same, and was threatened from afar by the Latin clergy with gestures of the eyes, fists, and mouths (the candelabrum I had climbed belonged to the Latins).

Perched on my lookout, I watched the exhausted crowd grow ever larger under my feet, when suddenly all the lights went out—even the thirty golden lamps which glimmer day and night over the sepulcher of Christ—and the service began.

An Armenian and a Greek priest entered the tiny chapel of the sepulcher. A turbaned *hodja* advanced solemnly, locked the door of the chapel behind them, and sealed it with wax. Blind man's bluff! Perhaps these turbaned and hooded jugglers wanted the people to understand that there was no light inside (but who is to say that there were no matches either?), that the chapel door was sealed, and that therefore, if light appeared it must certainly have come down from the sky . . .

At the moment all gazes were directed to two round windows, one at each side of the chapel. In the meantime, the divine service and the chants were gaining frantic momentum. Then there it was . . . suddenly, like fire bursting from a cannon, through the two windows of the chapel beamed two columns of light.

A moment later someone screamed: "Long live the Armenians . . . the Armenians have won . . ."

Instead of prostrating themselves in front of Christ's sepulcher, everyone started to applaud endlessly. They let out "bravos" and exclamations of happiness. On the other side, the Greek "braves" had long faces and were blaming each other for the lost victory.

A bit later thousands of believers, each holding between one and ten candles, lit them from one hand to another and we saw an advancing wave of fire. To escape the suffocating heat of the candles, people were now expending as much effort to get out of the church as they had previously expended to get into it.

This evening there was a Coptic procession around Christ's sepulcher. One man led them while another man sat on his shoulders and brandished a huge sword in the air, continually repeating: "*Ya Allah, ya Allah*," just as the Muslims in Jeresh did during the festivities for the enthronement of Sultan Vahdetdin.

And tonight, on the roof of the Church of the Holy Sepulcher, the Abyssinians had a procession with drums, ringing-instruments, and canopies, giving spectators the impression that they were watching a costume parade.

As I came down from the roof of the church I murmured: "Oh my Lord, Who wore sandals and a shirt and like Fellah shepherds went around without breeches, Who was always modest and preached moderation and humility, now that your Light has dawned, come and look around you. See how your worshipers, adorers, and glorifiers mock You!"

20 April, 1919

I was going to church this morning when I heard that the service had already finished, since it began last night.

Finally Easter is here, in a free land!

How sad we were last year in Jeresh, when we didn't know where to hide for fear of being called up. British planes flew overhead. Artillery roared continuously. And we, in despair, asked ourselves if and when we would be able to celebrate the Feast of the Resurrection.

Now we are here, free. We have shaken off our chains, but alas! Under free skies we are again celebrating Easter without red Easter eggs, without the traditional *pagharch* (unleavened bread), and without sufficient food.

27 April, 1919

We read in the Constantinople papers that one of the butchers of Armenians was given the punishment he deserved: death on the gallows. In the end, however, he was buried as a national hero, with a great deal of pomp. Our hearts take a bit of comfort in the idea that justice sooner or later prevails. But what difference does it make if one, ten, or a thousand are punished, when the entire Turkish nation is guilty of the slaughter?

On the other hand, we pity the "poor" national "martyr." We pity him that he did wrong by obeying orders from above. Wouldn't we have done the same thing if we had been given a similar order, if we had the opportunity? He became a martyr simply because he carried out the orders of the bloodthirsty Envers, Talaats, Behaeetdin Shakirs, and Dr. Nazims to "exterminate the Armenian nation, sparing nobody."

He was indeed a martyr, but an idiot of a martyr!

4 May, 1919

Father Tavit, the chief sacristan, held a reception in his apartment last night. On the table he had silver vessels, succulent food, grilled lamb, *baklava,* and excellent wine.

The inhabitants of the Jerusalem monastery can be divided into two categories: the older ones and the newer ones, or even better, the privileged ones and the destitute ones. The refugees belong to the latter category, along with the novices, who spend their days eating rice soup while those in the first category are fed on butter and honey. As the years go by, however, the arms of the newer priests get longer as they also begin to attain seniority and penetrate the secrets of the ancient clergy—before they get a chance to open their mouths in complaint, they find that they also have been promoted to the privileged class.

One would think they were Freemasons. Those who know the secret are insiders and those who don't remain outside. What kind of professional secret do they share? What kind of mob organization is this? Nobody can understand.

Or perhaps we can understand this much: here is an age-old institution, which from the very beginning has received much from the nation, and today, when that nation's children have fallen into misery and are in need of help, they can't even give them a piece of dry bread.

But why? The reason does not interest us. The result is ten thousand times more lamentable.

11 May, 1919

During its prosperous days, the nation also contributed to the Armenian General Benevolent Union. Today only its name continues to exist, not its mission.

When my father founded a branch of this foundation, he used to praise its function and its national aim. "Just as little children put their savings in a money-box and can use it as capital when they grow up, we also should give generously to the AGBU in our days of prosperity, in order to have something to fall back on in days of difficulty," he used to say when he held a membership or fund-raising drive for it.

The nation has never before suffered like this. But instead of opening its coffers to provide medicine and what have you to its people, the AGBU is using only the interest accumulated on their money—we haven't even see that—as if its mission were to pile up money on top of money rather than to use it for the nation during such difficult days.

Now the most important thing is to save the nation. When the nation is alive, it can give money again. If there is no nation, what good is all that money heaped in their safe? The Armenian refugees of Jerusalem today resemble the adopted child whose father has the key to the safe of St. James Church in his pocket and whose uncle has the key to the AGBU funds, but the adopted child is neglected, suffering, unfed.

The people at the top feast on meat and raise their glasses to the nation.

17 May, 1919

Those who registered to go to Cilicia left. Among those from Jeresh who are mentioned in my diary were the following, who left with the surviving members of their families: Aharonian, the teacher from Zeitoun; Khacher Aghpar's daughter-in-law; Sarko, the butcher from Marash, and his brother Setrag; Boghos the baker, Kapriel, the gun smith from Aintab; Ruhji Bedros; Misag the farrier; Mrs. Baydzar; Arshag from Adana; Khurshid from Kilis; the widow of Hovsep the miller; Mrs Gadariné from Yozgad; Karekin from Trebizond and his sister Kohar; Sarkis from Moush (who remained in jail for a week, was released upon the intervention of the national authorities, and married Kohar); Mihran Vartanian from Chorum; Artin the coachman; and my cousin Arshag, who resigned from his order.

Together with other families from Chorum, we registered for the caravan to Constantinople. The first group will leave in a week.

I went to Bethlehem today, to see Christ's birthplace before we leave Jerusalem. According to tradition, the monastery in Bethlehem was founded fifteen centuries ago by King Tiridates. The original building has gradually been restored and altered. Now it has become a solid fortress with its high walls. You enter it through an unusually narrow, low door. The door is small for a reason: to protect the monastery more easily in case of an enemy attack, and to make it impossible for the enemy to bring in animals to desecrate the place in case of defeat.

Once you enter through the narrow entrance, you find yourself in a large courtyard. On its door shine Armenian letters that indicate that it was built by a king of Cilicia.

The visitor soon enters a large hall with forty columns on each side, where he suffers a sudden disappointment on seeing that the greater part of the monastery is occupied by the Greeks and the Latins. Indeed, the large altar at the end of the hall and the stable where Christ was born beneath it belong to the Greeks, and the two modest altars, one on each side, belong to the Armenians and the Latins.

Using the stairwell on the Armenian side, I went down to the cavern where the Son of God was born. On my right was the manger, which belongs to the Latins, and on the left the spot where Christ came into this world, which belongs to the Armenians and the Greeks.

The sight of the place where Jesus was born gave me a strange feeling. Five hundred million people bow in His memory. For 1900 years billions and billions of people have genuflected, crossed themselves, and prayed in front of His cross and image. But among all these people who have come and gone, how many have practiced and still practice His injunction: "Love one another"?

No one loves others in this world. Everything is based on deceit, selfishness, and profit. So why have these countless people worshipped and why do they still worship this Man, whose precepts basically contradict the principles they believe in?

Poor Christ . . . crucified, tortured, crowned for the salvation of mankind; but these people have built well-frequented, lifeless churches over the place where He was born and placed money-boxes in them, simply to profit from His memory.

What decadence! What desecration! And all in the name of Christ and for Christ!

18 May, 1919

The pilgrims who come to Jerusalem have a tradition. They go to the little store across from the Armenian monastery and there they have a sign (normally a tiny cross) tattooed on their right arm to prove that they have become a *mahdesi* (one who has made a pilgrimage to Jerusalem). The pilgrims take advantage of the occasion not only to have St. Harutiun's, St. Klkhart's and St. Gregory the Illuminator's pictures tattooed on their arms, but also to have their chests tattooed with Armenian coats of arms surrounded by flags or even the Armenian fatherland surrounded by ruins.

I didn't feel like following the example of these fanatics and lying on the table for hours on end to have my chest and arms covered in these ridiculous images. In order to honor my mother's request, however, I had them tattoo just a date: 1919. This would remind me of all the horrible events that occurred before that date.

The tattoo artist is a short hunch-backed Armenian. He is the best in all of Jerusalem. He first applies a special ink to the spot to be tattooed and then starts tapping a needle on the inked spot to draw the requested design. After finishing this operation, which sometimes lasts even less than a couple of minutes, he wraps the wound and demands his fee.

This afternoon we visited the Greek Monastery of the Cross. It is located on the spot where the famous tree stood, the wood of which was used to make the cross on which Christ was crucified. Then we went to another Greek church where the grave of the patriarch Simeon is. Simeon was a kindly old man to whom it was revealed by the Holy Spirit that "he should not see death before he had seen the Lord's Christ." [See Luke 2: 26] We also sighed before his grave: "Ah, that we might not see death before we have seen Armenia!"

It's a strange coincidence that this evening when we returned to the monastery we heard that the Allies have officially recognized the Republic of Armenia.

24 May, 1919

Today reminded me of our departure from Aleppo to Damascus, when 500 of us pushed and shoved each other until we got on the train at the station. The difference was that we were not going to the arid desert to die, but to our own free homeland to live.

At ten o'clock the train left, leaving behind a huge crowd who had come to see us off, waving their handkerchiefs and wishing us all the best.

Gradually we passed the town of Remle, where the Armenians have a church, then Lit, Tul Kerim, etc. It was 6:30 in the evening when we suddenly heard a joyful exclamation in the car: "The sea, the sea . . ."

We all rushed to the windows, and for the first time in our lives we saw the sea, which stretched across the horizon like a blue ribbon.

Two hours later we had already arrived in Haifa.

The moment the train stopped at the station, British policemen came running, pointing with the tips of their whips to a station filled with more than a hundred tents. Then they ordered us to go there.

Why did we have to go there? In Jerusalem they had told us that a ship was waiting for us in Haifa and that it would take us directly to Constantinople. Was there, perhaps, a misunderstanding? Those who spoke English explained the situation to the police, but they ignored our complaints, jumped onto the train cars, and started throwing our belongings onto the platform in a jumble, sometimes hitting travelers who were late getting off the train.

Under blows from their whips we soon arrived breathlessly at the refugee camps designated for Armenians. For a moment we seemed carried back to nightmare scenes in which we were followed by Turkish guerrillas.

Each family entered a vacant tent. In fact, all the tents were empty. Hardly a minute had gone by when everybody ran out of his tent in alarm, calling on all the saints for help. Lice had infested the tents. And such lice! All the lice in Tarsus and all the flies in Katma would not make even one per cent of the lice here, in the Armenian refugee camp in Haifa. Their bites drove people crazy. Men and women, grown-ups and children, all were hopping up and down, shaking their clothes and running madly into the fields, in the meantime scratching their arms and legs, faces and backs.

That night everyone suffered more than the unfortunate man who fell into a leper colony, and remained outdoors in the fields until morning.

25 May, 1919

Like prodigal children who sometimes run away from their paternal homes but then return there, we also returned to our tents this morning. We had no choice but to accept them as our temporary abodes.

Five hundred of us, armed with pieces of wood, stones, and bridle straps, dispatched millions of lice all day long. Then, sweating and completely exhausted, we ran to the water barrels, but it was impossible to drink the water in them—it was so flat and smelled of grass.

In order to lessen our torment, the British distributed bread, rice, and potatoes this evening. The appearance of abundant food made us forget our pain for a while. As many of us had no pots to boil the potatoes in, the British kindly put a cauldron in the middle of the station. Each family tossed its potatoes in it, after stringing them together like beads and holding the end of the string while waiting for the potatoes to cook.

After filling our stomachs tonight, we were preparing to leave for the fields again, but the policemen wouldn't let us go, reminding us that during an exodus it's necessary to maintain military discipline.

"What about the lice?" we asked.

"You killed the lice, and the ones that are still alive are no longer hungry . . . They won't bother you anymore," they replied.

Having no choice, we lay down in the tents and spent another sleepless night in the Haifa refugee camp, in torments similar to those of Tantalus.

26 May, 1919

The British corporal at the refugee camp, the foster brother of the corporal in Salt, posted a notice on the entrance door. It contained the following ten injunctions:

1. To sprinkle and sweep the entire station twice a day;

2. After sweeping, to take the rubbish to the seashore and burn it;

3. Likewise, to collect the excrement from the toilets in pails and take it away to be burnt;

4. To fetch all the water needed by the station from the water reservoir, which is half an hour away;

5. To break stones and repair the station wall that faces the sea;

The rest of the regulations are much the same. Anybody who refuses to fulfill these conditions will lose his or her bread ticket.

This evening some well-to-do refugees went into the city, to stay in hotels. We remained at the refugee camp.

27 May, 1919

After the lice and the water, the next problem at the refugee camp was the question of toilets. At one end of the station there were two sections—one for men and one for women—but they had no doors and no roofs. In each section, raised about half a meter from the ground and slightly separated from each other, they have placed sixteen double cages, with a pail in the middle of each double cage: that constitutes the station rest rooms.

When sixteen people satisfy their needs in the same place, naturally there is no lack of ribald laughter and remarks. Some people can take a joke and some can't . . . So just try to imagine the fights and the swearing that take place there!

During the fighting two refugees come in, take one of the pails, and hang it from a pole, which they place on their shoulders and take away, murmuring between their teeth:

"We had to do all sorts of things on the orders of the Turks, but we've never had to do this before . . . My God, what next?"

And indeed, what *will* happen to us next?

28 May, 1918

There's a military camp for Turkish prisoners-of-war next to our station. The refugee camp and the military camp are separated by a two-meter-high wall. The Turkish soldiers sit on the wall and watch us all day long. Seeing our humiliating work, they shout: "Hey, compatriots, see how the British, whom you worshipped, are treating you! They make you work like galley-slaves and make you empty the toilets of excrement. Over here that kind of work is done by Indian mercenaries. We lie on our backs and rest."

"Shut your mouth, murderer!" an Armenian shoots back. "Do you still have the gall to talk to us? Scram! Stay out of our sight!"

The Turkish soldiers smile impudently and yell: "Don't get upset, compatriot. The day will come when you will miss us."

"May your tongue shrivel up, devil-worshiper."

And the Armenian throws a stone at the Turk. In return the Turks shower us with ten stones. The British police run over and break up the gathering of Armenians with their whips. The Turks look on and loudly taunt: "Enjoy it, compatriots. How do British whips taste? Aren't ours tastier?"

Such incidents are repeated at least twenty times a day.

29 May, 1919

Armenians are not allowed to leave the station, but we managed to obtain permission and went to the city to look around a little, and then we went for a swim in the sea.

We had another surprise from the English today. They distributed meat and olive oil quite generously. The insipid water, the abundance of lice, the torturous work of the station, and especially the mockery of the Turks make us extremely nervous.

We are counting the days, waiting for a vessel to arrive and save us from this hateful place.

1 June, 1919

Today the well-to-do refugees who lived in the city left by boat for Beirut, at their own expense. As Haifa has no landing dock, the vessel anchored quite far from the shore, which caused several accidents during the rush. First a little Armenian child was run over on the quay. Then somebody had his arm crushed under a heavy box on the cargo vessel. While getting on board, a woman fell into the sea. Many bales and packages also fell into the sea. The porters and sailors completed the picture, by making furniture disappear and by mercilessly robbing the passengers.

The British soldiers had a lot of fun today, watching the torments of the poor refugees from a distance.

3 June, 1919

The British corporal came to inspect the tents this morning. When he noticed that the top of a tent was unstable, or the rope loose, or the front dirty, he would spout all the swear words, enter the tent, drag the first man he could grab out, and make him complete the unfinished work under the threat of his whip. As if his cruelty were not enough, after harassing quite a few men like this, he declared coolly: "From now on, with no exceptions, all men, whether healthy or sick, will work for their daily rations."

"How can we sick people work?" we asked in surprise.

"You'll be given sedentary jobs," he replied.

"But people are already doing those jobs."

"You'll work in the supply room of a nearby hospital."

"But the hospital has nothing to do with us."

"Then there will be no bread for you or anybody else."

"Don't give bread to those who don't work, but you have no right to deprive women and children."

"I'll show you whether I have the right or not."

And he left, cracking his whip.

The Turkish soldiers who were sitting on the wall watching us threw us a piece of bread, as if throwing it to a dog, and shouted mockingly: "Don't cry, compatriots. We have enough leftovers for all of you!"

4 June, 1919

We handed a petition to the British governor of the city, complaining about the whimsical decisions of the corporal. The governor kindly promised to look into the situation and see whether we had been treated unjustly. In the meanwhile, again today we had no bread.

In the afternoon, one of the Turks shouted with dreadful impudence over the wall: "*Ulan*! *Kiafirler*! If we had known you'd be left with no one to protect you like this, I swear to God we would have put all of you to the sword!"

"Those days are over, butchers!" we responded with disgust. "Take your swords and put them in museums."

The Turks laughed and changed the subject: "Compatriots, are your stomachs empty? Would you like some more bread?"

We reflect that if the Turks are capable of talking to us like this when they are imprisoned in Haifa, what will they do to us in their own country, where we are going to live temporarily? If there too our liberators are going to protect us like this, all is lost!"

8 June, 1919

Some more refugees left today at their own expense. They left on sailboats, accepting all sorts of danger.

For two days we have been getting bread from the government, provided we all work within the confines of the refugee camp. As I am still ill, I don't have to do any compulsory work. The station doctor has given me a certificate stating my physical condition. Today, however, I took the birch broom and swept for about three hours. This evening I rushed to bed, exhausted.

9 June, 1919

I've had a toothache for about a week. When I woke up this morning I saw that my right cheek was swollen. I went to see the British corporal, showed him my face, and told him that I couldn't work. He sent me to the hospital, where a dentist cut my infected gum with a big knife. After resting for an hour, I returned to the station. When the corporal saw that I had had a little surgery, he gave me a piece of cardboard that authorizes the bearer to receive free bread for a week.

10 June, 1919

Two Jewish policemen were killed last night. There are no suspects.

Recently the relationship between the Arabs and the Jews has become quite tense. The Arabs are protesting the British promise of Palestine to the Jews. We're afraid that to get revenge on the British they might attack us refugees, as they did in Port Said.

As if we didn't have enough worries already, now we have to think about another potential massacre!

11 June, 1919

Since this morning, a fight has been going on between the Arabs and the Jews at the market. Six people have been wounded on both sides.

The local people are extremely agitated, and they demonstrate in the streets and stone the windows of official establishments, shouting: "Down with the English!"

A detachment of British soldiers has taken up positions before the refugee camp. Armenians are strictly forbidden to go out.

12 June, 1919

A small French ship arrived. They put us all on it and sent us to Beirut. It seems that they wanted at least one less worry. We're happy to have been able to leave the Haifa station.

In the evening the ship started to roll on heavy waves, which sometimes came in one side of the boat and poured like waterfalls over the other side.

We were all sea-sick. At this time of night we are all lying like drunks on the floors.

13 June, 1919

We arrived in Beirut at six o'clock this morning. We waited for quite some time in the port before the people from the National Association arrived and took us to the Beirut refugee camp, which was more than congested with refugees leaving for both Cilicia and Constantinople.

In the afternoon I had the pleasant surprise of finding my friend Yervant Tintonian. He had heard about the arrival in Beirut of Armenian refugees from Haifa and had come to look for his compatriots.

Yervant, his parents, and two other families from Chorum moved from Damascus directly to Beirut. Now he was living in the city with his parents, waiting for the peace treaty with Turkey to be signed before moving to Samsoun to resume his business. His father was the Chorum director of Ipranosian.

We thanked our friend for the *Jamanak* he sent us a year ago. We told him that we were now going to Armenia and that they should come with us instead of going to Samsoun.

"You go and settle! Then we'll come to Armenia too," my friend said, and then he invited us to spend the night at their house. We accepted his invitation, and for the first time since the deportation we had a lavish meal and enjoyed all the amenities a comfortable home could offer us.

14 June, 1919

This morning Yervant took us around by streetcar and showed us the interesting sights. We went all the way to Jebel Lubnan, a resort place covered with cedars of Lebanon. Then we visited the government building, the medical faculty, the American College, and St. Nishan Armenian Church, which has become a heap of ruins.

At noon we returned to the city and heard that 450 people would leave for Constantinople on board the SS *Carintia*, an Italian vessel. Our name was on the list of passengers.

We were glad that we would not be wasting time in Beirut as we did in Haifa. We immediately packed our personal effects, bid goodbye to our hosts, and went on board.

The Italian sailors took us to the two holds, which are large halls without windows and doors, down in the belly of the ship. Light and air, as well as people and bales, enter through a little hole in the deck. We had just descended into the hold when the women and children let out alarming cries. They had seen rats as big as kittens, which were equally frightened by the presence of people and the commotion, and were running away over the floor and the walls.

"Catch them . . . They ran this way . . . Here they are! . . . Hit . . . Hit them!" people were exclaiming and hitting right, left, and center with pieces of wood, shoes, clothing, and all sorts of things.

Half an hour later, there wasn't a single rat alive in the hold. We picked them up by their tails with a piece of paper and threw them into the sea, and then we settled into their accommodation. Once again we concluded that might is always right in this world, especially when it comes to the right to live.

There are more than 200 of us in the hold. Every family has spread a carpet or a straw-mat by the wall and sits on it, some in the dark and others by the somber light of a candle. We, unfortunately, had to do without the luxury of a candle, as did our neighbors on our left and our right. The former were a family from Adrianople (Edirne)—a father, mother, and grown-up daughter—and on our left were a young man from Adapazar, his wife, and their two-year-old son.

We used our clothes as pillows, pulled a cover over us, and slept there.

From up above, the iron arches of the hold resounded with the deafening clamor of the derrick wheels and the sailors' and boatmen's shouts. The ship was continuously taking on cargo.

15 June, 1919

At eight o'clock this morning we left Beirut.

At noon we stopped in Tripoli, a beautiful city surrounded by vineyards and trees. After loading cargo and passengers for four hours, the ship got underway again, and sailed all day and all night on the placid waters of the Mediterranean.

As the ship's bow cut the infinite expanse of the water, our hearts overflowed with happiness. We felt that each passing minute was bringing us closer to the final destination of our voyage—the disappearance, at last, of our tribulations.

16 June, 1919

This morning we arrived in Alexandretta.

The city does not have a landing dock, so we anchored far from the shore. We went ashore by rowboat to buy bread and fruit.

On the quay we came into contact with Turks for the first time since our deportation. Among the interested onlookers, a veiled Turkish woman shouted at us: "Come *giaours*, come here, so we can slaughter you again!"

Her vituperative words, spoken under the French occupation, stunned us. We thought that after their defeat, the Turks would be crushed and lifeless. But the taunts of the Turkish prisoners of war in Haifa and now the pronouncements of this Turkish woman in Alexandretta overturned our expectations.

Is it possible that we were wrong?

17 June, 1919

The ship's whistle announced that we were approaching another port. Indeed, when we came out of the holds we saw that we had anchored opposite Mersin.

Again we went ashore by rowboat and did our shopping. The Turks here also looked somewhat less than pleased to see us.

"You're coming back here, but these aren't your lands anymore," said the boatman who took us to the city.

"We're going to Constantinople," we answered.

"It could be . . . But many of your relatives are coming here to settle."

"Why shouldn't they settle here?" we asked. "Isn't Cilicia our homeland?"

"Tomorrow, when the French leave, you'll see whose homeland it is," the Turk replied mysteriously.

This evening, Stepan from Adapazar, who heard our conversation with the boatman said: "They still haven't crushed the heads of these vipers. I think we still have a great deal to put up with from these Turks."

"I agree with you," I said. "Otherwise these people wouldn't use such aggressive language."

"They massacred and slaughtered so much, and they're still not satisfied. What kind of hatred is this, that it's never extinguished?" exclaimed Stepan after a brief pause, letting out a heart-rending sigh.

I realized that my young neighbor had much anguish accumulated in his heart.

"Stepan," I said, "where were you during the deportation?"

"Deir Zor."

"Why, don't you tell me you were among those led to the Khabur river slaughter-house?"

"No. We were led to the gates of death before that."

"What do you mean, the gates of death?" I asked in amazement.

"Stop. I don't want to reopen old wounds," replied Stepan.

"The way you talk, you've aroused my curiosity."

"It's better you don't hear about it."

"I must hear it," I said. "First, we'll stay here in Mersin for 24 hours. To break the monotony of the night we must talk. Then, do you see this notebook? I have six more just like it. They're all full of hundreds of deportation and refugee stories. As soon as I arrive in Constantinople, the first thing I'll do is to put them in order, and then I'll publish them. Don't you think that your story deserves to be published as well?"

"In that case, I'll tell you," said Stepan. It's painful to recall old events, but I don't want them buried in oblivion, like the name of our liberator.

* * *

Stepan paid to be exempted from military service when the war started. Consequently, he was not drafted. One day he saw that the police were arresting all the Armenian intellectuals and political party members in Adapazar. He was also a party member and was hated by the Turks. He had to be cautious, so he decided to take refuge in a distant village for awhile and keep an eye on how events developed from there.

After he had left the city, the police came and tortured his parents, and in place of the son they took the father to the Armenian church, which had been converted into a prison. More than 500 arrested Armenians were already imprisoned there.

Stepan heard that the prisoners were subjected to terrible tortures and, since his father had been put in jail in his place, he decided to return to the city and surrender to the police, putting an end to the suffering of his old father. On his way back he met a peasant woman bent under the weight of the load she was carrying on her back. He understood at once from her clothing that she was an Armenian. He asked her about what was going on in the city.

"They've arrested all the men," the peasant woman sobbed, "including my husband."

"Are they also making arrests in the villages?" Stepan asked in bewilderment.

"Everywhere."

"Where are you going like this?"

"To the next village, where my parents live. Our house and everything we had has been destroyed."

"Then they don't intend to arrest only the intellectuals," Stepan murmured, since they were also rounding up illiterate peasants. That meant that a devilish plot was being executed.

He left the peasant woman, sat down beneath a tree a little further down the road, and started thinking. In the city he had a father, a mother, and a fiancee. What would he do if they also had to suffer massacres and deportation, like the Armenian populations of cities elsewhere? And what would happen to him after he gave himself up to the police?

Lost in such thoughts, he stayed there motionless for a long time. Then he was suddenly aroused. Down the road a couple of policemen were taking a man to the city, beating him repeatedly. From his speech and appearance it was not difficult to tell that the victim was an Armenian from the city, and he was begging them to stop beating him. One of the policemen hit him hard in the face with his fist. The Armenian let out a painful cry and put his hand over his mouth. A moment later, blood started dripping through his fingers.

"Die, you son of a bitch!" the executioner roared savagely.

Noticing that the policemen were gradually getting closer to where he was sitting, Stepan immediately stood up and hid behind the dense blackberry bushes that lined the road. Before long the policemen passed in front of him. He could barely stifle a cry when he recognized their victim as none other than Hrant, his fiancee's brother.

Like him, Hrant had also fled to a village to hide. Clearly the police had found him and were now taking him to the city to throw him into jail with 500 other Armenians. The boy poor, dazed by the blows, walked quietly, constantly wiping away the blood that streamed from his mouth. The policemen walked behind him, glaring at him from hateful eyes. They looked both frightening and threatening.

When Stepan saw his fiancee's brother, he suddenly felt like springing upon the policemen and freeing his friend. Then he controlled himself, reflecting that his interference would be useless, as the policemen were armed and he didn't even have a knife. Such a thoughtless move could well prove fatal to both him and Hrant. The policemen would shoot him at the very first sign of movement and then shoot Hrant, in the belief that Hrant was aware of the attack. So, with a very heavy heart he stayed where he was and let the policemen walk past, and then he followed to see if he could find a way to hinder them.

He had walked for scarcely half an hour when he saw Hrant fall to his knees near a brook unable to take another step.

"Get up, infidel!" shouted one of the policemen, raising his whip threateningly.

"I can't. I'm dizzy," pleaded Hrant in a trembling voice.

"I'll show you what it means to lie down. Let's see. How's this?" The policeman brought his whip mercilessly down on the helpless boy's head.

"Don't hit . . . for God's sake."

Hrant's voice was drowned out by a shower of kicks, blows, and oaths. The poor young man neither called out nor made any move to defend himself. You'd think he was dead as he lay in the dust like a corpse.

It seems the policemen didn't have orders to kill him, because before long they started trying to find a way to get their prisoner into the city. "Dragging him by the legs would be too much work," said one of them. "Let's wait. Perhaps a horse or a cart might pass."

"Yes, let's wait," said the other policeman, squatting at the side of the road and wiping away the sweat that ran down his face.

Before long Hrant regained consciousness. "Water! Water!" he shouted, pointing at his mouth. "Please! Give me some water. My heart is burning."

"*Shiukri,*" said the policeman to his seated friend, "He's speaking Armenian. Do you know what he wants? Water. He's very thirsty. Wet his mouth."

Just then a cart appeared in the distance. The policemen abandoned their evil plan and stood in the middle of the road to get the attention of the driver.

"Compatriot," they called out to him when he was quite close, "Stop. You have to take this wounded man to the city."

"I've just come from the city and am going to the village. I'm late," the driver complained.

"Just shut up, or you'll taste the whip," the policemen said threateningly.

"Hey, who are you threatening? I'm not an Armenian. I'm a Turk," exclaimed the peasant angrily.

One of the policemen slapped the driver in the mouth and roared furiously: "If you're a Turk, do your patriotic duty. Don't you know that these are decisive times for the nation? Every Turk has to help the government if we're going to end this fight in victory."

"Enough, faithless ones! My two sons are already fighting on the battlefield," the vexed peasant protested.

"That's a different kind of fight. Now we have an internal fight," responded the policemen. Ignoring the peasant's protests, they put Hrant's half-conscious body on the cart and goaded on the oxen toward the city.

Stepan followed the cart for a good while. Every time the rough road made his friend's head bang against the wood of the cart, he felt a pang in his heart, as if had been stabbed. When he finally concluded that he couldn't help his friend, he left the road, sat down in a deserted spot, and thought out his strategy.

Should he go to the city or not? If he went, what could he do? And if he didn't go . . .

He was absorbed in this struggle when he noticed another traveler on the road. There, covered in dust, was a burly old man: a blacksmith he knew.

"Ohan *Ammi* (Uncle Ohan), Ohan *Ammi*, " Stepan shouted, calling the old man over to him.

Ohan *Ammi* recognized the voice, went over, and asked reproachfully: "Stepan—what are you doing here?"

"I've heard that my father was arrested in my place, and I'm going to the city to give myself up, so I can save him," Stepan replied.

"Go back, go back! There's no reason to act so foolishly," the old man scolded.

"Why?"

"First of all, your father and a few others have been sent to the military tribunal in Constantinople . . ."

"Ah, in that case they'll hang him," murmured Stepan in bewilderment. "How will my mother survive this blow . . . The poor woman already has a heart problem . . ."

"Stepan, it's very unfortunate, but under the present circumstances we can't hide misfortunes from each other," said Ohan. "The day your father was arrested the police beat your mother quite badly. Two days ago the poor woman . . ."

Stepan was frozen to the spot, unable to express his anguish with a cry.

"My son, there's nothing left for you to do in the city," said the old man. "Go back at once. There's a bounty of 100 pounds on your head."

"On my head?"

"Yes, the police have a list of six people, and you're one of them."

Then the old man sat down to rest for a while and said: "Our situation is terrible. They also arrested my sons Rupen and Papken. So far more than 700 people have been arrested. They're all imprisoned in the church and are tortured everyday to get them to tell the police where they've hidden their weapons. The beatings drove the merchant Nerses out of his mind, and he committed suicide by throwing himself off the roof. They broke Der Mikael's legs when they beat him with clubs. They tore the flesh off Noubar the pharmacist. They pulled out Sahag's teeth and nails. And they tortured Zareh with a red-hot iron bar so much that before the poor man fainted and collapsed he exclaimed: 'I wish I had a friend who'd give me poison.' A moment ago I saw Hrant. The police were taking his corpse away in a cart."

"His corpse?"

"Yes, his corpse."

"Damn the Turks!" exclaimed Stepan, and brought his fist down on his knee. "What happened to Hrant's mother and sister?"

For the time being they're leaving the population alone, but I suggest that you stay away from the city," said Ohan. "The police are looking for the six people on that list. They're searching the houses of their relatives and friends. I'm telling you, if they ever catch you they'll send you to the gallows."

"What happened to your sons? Were they tortured too?"

"Yes. For two weeks now they've been sick and lying flat on their backs in jail. We take them a little food, but the police take it from us to deliver, and eat it themselves instead. Yeghiazarian soaked his shoe leather in water and ate that . . . Their situation is dreadful, absolutely dreadful . . ."

"And where are you going?"

"There's a another rumor that they're going to deport everybody. I'm going around the villages to collect a few unpaid debts. We don't know what might happen tomorrow. We have to be prepared for anything."

After a few more observations about the atmosphere in the city, Ohan *Ammi* stood up, and before leaving he said in a fatherly tone: "Stepan, I'm telling you over and over. Don't ever go to the city."

Confused, Stepan shook his head, but the moment he was alone said to himself, "To run away from danger is weakness. Now that I have only one person left in this world, I can't leave her under the Turkish yoke, just to save my own life. I have to go to the city."

And that same night, taking advantage of the darkness, he entered the city and went directly to his fiancee's house.

* * *

Before I continue the story, it's necessary to digress a bit and introduce an ungrateful cur named Ibrahim, who saw Stepan enter businessman Takvorian's (Araksi's) home.

In the eighties a very serious famine devastated the interior provinces. Numerous families left their villages and took refuge in the cities, hoping to find their daily bread there. In certain regions the misery got so bad that parents who couldn't feed their children left them by the wayside, hoping that a passerby would take pity on them.

Ibrahim had been one of these children. He was four years old when he was abandoned by the wayside. When he awoke he found himself in the middle of a deserted field. He walked along the road, crying and looking for his parents. He hoped to find them at the end of the road.

He came to the edge of a forest, fell down, and remained there, overcome by fatigue and weakness. Almost at once heavy clouds covered the sky, it grew dark, the wind began blowing, thunder resounded, and rain poured down in torrents.

No doubt Ibrahim would have died there of hunger, fright, and cold if a kindly horseman, Araksi's father, hadn't found him the next morning. Takvorian woke the boy out of his numbness and asked who he was and what he was doing there. Between sobs Ibrahim told him his story and added that he had a father and a mother and lived in a far-away village.

Takvorian sat him on his saddle pad and took him to the city. He asked a town crier to find Ibrahim's parents. The days passed, but no one claimed the boy. Then Araksi's kindly father gave the boy to one of his Turkish employees and asked him to take care of him. Takvorian, of course, promised to assume all the expenses.

Ibrahim was 15 years old when the Turk who adopted him died. Despite all the expense and care spent on his upbringing, he had become a lazy and irresponsible boy. Takvorian nevertheless took pity on him and hired the boy to replace one of his employees, who had just died.

Approximately ten years later Takvorian himself died and the business shut down. Ibrahim, who had to some extent learned the business by then, opened a little store with the money he'd saved. Then he married a Turkish woman and started living in a street not far from his benefactor's house, always continuing to enjoy the Takvorians' moral and financial support.

There you have it. This same despicable Ibrahim, who was saved from death by an Armenian and was fed by an Armenian for years, rubbed his hands in joy when he caught sight of Stepan entering his former employer's house.

"What difference does it make now?" he thought. "They're all going to be deported and killed anyway. I'll never see them again. I don't have anything to be ashamed of. I'll go and tell the police, and get the reward."

Ibrahim went to the police station without scruple and, without beating around the bush, said: "You've promised 100 pounds to anyone who can show you the hide-outs of the *komitajis*."

"Yes."

"Good. Give me the reward and I'll give you an important address."

"What kind of proposal is that?" asked the police chief, his expression changing. "Give us the address and let us arrest the man, and then we'll give you the reward."

"How do I know you won't arrest the man and then not pay me?"

"Tell me, my friend, are you mad or just stupid?"

"Neither mad nor stupid. Pay me and you'll get the address."

When he saw that no one was going to pay him, Ibrahim got ready to leave. The policeman sprang after him.

"Hey, where are you going? Give us the address, and then leave."

"I won't give . . ."

The policeman gave him a slap, followed by another. Then a kick in the stomach, followed by another. Ibrahim tumbled to the floor, screaming in pain. The police chief signalled the other two policemen in the room, who took a huge club from behind the door and rushed at the informer. They hit him only twice before he cried feebly: "Stop! Don't hit me again. I'll tell you."

* * *

Sitting in a room on the top floor of the house, Stepan, unaware of what had happened, was talking things over with Araksi and her mother, Mrs. Aghavni, trying to find a way to bypass the danger that threatened their existence. Suddenly they heard repeated knocks at the street door. They looked at each other in fright for a moment. Then, as the knocking didn't stop, they turned off the light in the room and peered out from behind the curtains to see who was there.

There were two people at the door. It was dark outside, but Stepan noticed the shiny yellow buttons of the policemen. He leaned his forehead against the window pane and also saw several other shadows hidden in dark corners on both sides of the street, waiting for the signal to rush forward.

"We're surrounded," whispered Stepan, and ran to the back of the house to see if there were policemen there too.

"Yes, they're everywhere."

"What should we do now?" exclaimed Araksi and her mother in muted voices.

"Does Hrant have any weapons at home?" asked Stepan.

"Yes, a dagger."

"Give it to me."

"But careful, Stepan."

Just then the knocks on the door grew louder. Soon the door gave in to pressure from outside and sprang open, admitting several policemen into the courtyard.

Stepan heard the jingling of their swords and the spurs of their boots. He dashed from the room at once, ran through the kitchen, and jumped out the back window onto the roof of the next house. A bullet from the street behind the house shattered the pane of the window he had jumped through.

Keeping his head, Stepan ran across the tiled roof and leapt onto the upper-story balcony of the house. A second bullet whizzed by under his ear. Stepan shoved open the balcony door with his shoulder, entered the house, and rushed down the stairs. The people of the house were startled and let out terrified cries. Stepan ran through the courtyard and opened the door to the street.

Just then an armed policeman appeared before him. With the speed of lightning Stepan drew his dagger and stabbed the policeman, who howled terribly. Stepan flew away and disappeared into the darkness.

He sped along the twisting roads that led out of the city and returned to the village where he had hidden before going to the city.

* * *

Although Stepan had saved himself, the policemen captured Araksi and Mrs. Aghavni and began to torture them to make them reveal where he'd gone.

"But we don't know where he's gone," the Armenians protested truthfully.

"You're lying. You're protecting a dangerous revolutionary. The government has put a reward of 100 pounds on his life," the policemen yelled savagely. "Come with us. You're in more trouble than you realize."

"Where are you taking us?" screamed the mother and daughter. The police dragged them from the room.

"Walk! If you offer the least resistance, we'll break this whip over your backs."

"But . . ."

"Walk!"

"Where can we go, leaving everything behind?"

"To jail. There we'll beat you until we break every bone in your body unless you tell us where that *komitaji* is hiding."

"But we don't know."

"Walk!"

And the whips descended on the shoulders of the two women.

"You have no right to beat a woman," Mrs. Aghavni shouted rebelliously in their faces, "You ought to be ashamed to call yourself a man!"

"You're vipers!" yelled another policeman, cracking his whip. "When you crush the head of a viper you don't ask its gender."

Thus beating, pushing, and reviling them, the police took the mother and daughter to prison by night and locked them up in a deserted room.

The following morning they were led to the police chief. After a short interrogation they were sent back to their cell. Nobody else visited them all day. Not even the prison guard passed to bring them bread and water. But in fact they had been so very badly tortured that they couldn't even think about bread or water. Their delicate bodies ached constantly from the blows they had received from clubs, whips, kicks, and slaps. And their hearts were torn apart by mental anguish.

In the evening the door opened and they saw the stern face of the prison guard for the first time.

"Araksi, daughter of Takvor, come out of there!" ordered the man.

"Alone? Isn't my mother coming with me?" stuttered Araksi, her throat aching with sobs.

"Yes, alone! Come out!"

"Why? Where should I go?"

"Come out, I told you. In jail you don't ask questions. You just obey."

"I won't be separated from my mother. She has to come with me," declared Araksi, as though she'd been forewarned of a tragedy.

"You talk too much. Come out!" roared the prison guard, pulling her savagely by the hand.

"No, I won't let my daughter go," exclaimed the mother, hugging her daughter like a lioness. "Where are you taking her? The court's not open at this hour."

"Shut up, woman!" the Turk rebuked her in an indescribable barbaric roar.

"I won't let her go! I won't let her!" screamed the mother in terror.

"You won't let her?" He hit her hard in the back with his fist.

"Oh, my eyes, my eyes, my eyes," groaned the woman.

Araksi made a slight movement to try to bend over her mother, when she also felt that she was losing her clarity of vision and of mind. A moment later she felt as if a strong arm were holding her and lifting her up in the air.

When Araksi regained consciousness she found herself in a furnished room in an unknown house. She was lying on a bed, and next to her was sitting a monstrous man with a grotesque face—the police chief—who was bent over her open chest, staring at her lasciviously.

Thinking she was dreaming, the poor girl searched the four corners of the room with bleary eyes.

"But I . . . what am I doing here?" she murmured in a barely audible voice.

Then, all at once her situation dawned on her, and she covered herself out of feminine instinct, let out a heart-rending scream, and fainted again.

An hour later she regained consciousness again. This time the hellish-looking fiend was standing in front of the window, smoking a cigarette. The room was filled with the foul stench of smoke and tobacco.

"Let me go! Let me go," she sobbed, trying to sit up in the bed. But it was impossible . . . as if invisible knots bound her firmly, she lay paralyzed on the mattress. Her head was heavy as lead and glued to the pillow. Her arms and legs were numb, spread eagled on the bed.

She had terrible pains all over her body. Sores from bites and pinches were added to the pains that resulted from being kicked, caned, and hit with fists. The perverted thug's teeth had left red marks on her shoulders, breasts, and legs. Her cheeks burned, as though hundreds of canines had bitten her delicate flesh.

"Leave me, I'll go," Araksi sighed faintly, "Leave me, I'll go."

"But where will you go, can't you see it's dark out?" said the chief police, coming closer. "The streets are deserted and dangerous."

"My mother . . . Where is she . . . . Why did you bring me here?" Araksi sobbed. Then, suddenly realizing what had happened to her, she started crying, "Oh monster, monster, monster . . ."

Instead of getting angry at her insults, the police chief grinned like an animal and then shut her quivering lips with a lecherous kiss.

* * *

When Stepan heard in the village of the arrest and imprisonment of his fiancee and future mother-in-law, he was deeply dejected and frantically beat his head. He felt responsible for their misery.

"Alas! what a disaster! Damn . . ."

But it was no time to cry or sigh. He had to do something. It didn't matter if he lost his life. With his father sent to the war tribunal and condemned to die, his mother killed, and his fiancee sent away and subjected to all kinds of insults, life no longer had any value for him anyway.

Yes, he had to do something. But what?

What could he do alone? He was persecuted and a virtual convict, with a bounty on his head, against a government that was no more than a band of executioners, an army against an entire people?

Oh, what could he do? What?

But it was no time to think either. Action was what was required. Regardless of the consequences of his madness, something had to be done to save his fiancee from the predicament she was in.

Stepan fastened the dagger to his belt and once again took the road to the city, turning over in his teeming mind various courses of action, each more daring than the other.

When he was near the city he waited for darkness to fall, then he passed through a couple of streets almost like a shadow, and stopped in front of a friend's house.

"Vartkes, have you heard any news of our people?" was his first question when he found himself face to face with his old friend (Vartkes had escaped arrest by hiding in the house).

"Stepan, you shouldn't have come to the city," his friend said. "My old mother has told me all about what happened out there. The policeman you stabbed is dead . . . They're looking for you everywhere. Araksi is at the police chief's home. Mrs. Aghavni, on the other hand, was cruelly beaten and chained after her daughter's rape, and unfortunately she 'died suddenly' the following day."

"What's Araksi doing at the police chief's?" asked Stepan through his teeth.

"We don't know. She's being kept prisoner there."

"Vartkes, I'm going to free her."

"Don't be stupid. You'll be arrested the moment you set your foot in the street."

"But how can I cross my arms and sit still when my fiancee is suffering like a slave? I have to do something; I'll either free her or die trying."

"There's no contest. Your death is a foregone conclusion."

"I don't care."

Stepan paced nervously back and forth in the room, clenching his fists and gritting his teeth. His face had assumed a terrifying expression.

"I'll kill him," he droned quietly. "There's no way I'll let that damned monster go unpunished. I'll kill him."

Vartkes tried in vain to calm, advise, and console his friend. Stepan remained in the same frame of mind and repeated over and over: "I'll kill him . . . I'll kill him . . ."

A while later, as if he had suddenly had another idea, he stopped short in the middle of the room and asked: "Vartkes, you had a horse. What happened to it?"

"To save it from being confiscated by the military, I'm keeping it at my aunt's place."

"Get the horse for me."

Without waiting for his friend to reply, Stepan rushed out.

It was night.

He quickly climbed over the garden fence and cautiously crept behind the bushes, heading for a particular house—the police chief's house—which was set far back, at the end of a garden. He opened a window from outside and climbed in. Then he went up to the next floor and looked furtively through a pane of glass in a door.

Araksi was there, sitting alone in the obscurity of the room. The Armenian-eating monster wasn't there. At that time of night he was attending an *Ittihad* (the Young Turks political party) meeting, who knows in whose house? They were doubtless cooking up diabolic ways to exterminate Armenians. It was unfortunate that the bloodthirsty executioner would escape Stepan's dagger. But there was no time for regret. Stepan tapped lightly on the windowpane.

Araksi, who was almost paralyzed, lost in some mysterious dream, was startled. She turned and when she saw her fiancé she could hardly stifle the scream of surprise and fright that rose to her throat.

Stepan, his finger on his lips, warned her to keep quiet and signalled with his head that she should come out. Araksi tiptoed to the window and made her fiancé understand that the door was locked from the outside and that there were a couple of guards on the floor below.

Stepan paid no attention to the pending danger, but wrapped his fist in a handkerchief and broke the windowpane. The window, according to Turkish-Muslim custom, was also covered with a wooden lattice. With a Herculean effort Stepan demolished it, took his fiancé out through the opening, and rushed down the stairs.

They were halfway down the steps when the two guards appeared at the bottom of the stairwell, awakened by the noise and still rubbing their eyes. Before they had a chance to use their guns, Stepan planted his fist in the face of one of the guards and kicked the other in the stomach, and while the police screamed painfully and fell to the floor, he dashed out of the building with Araksi.

* * *

With his fiancé on the back of the horse, Stepan galloped out of the city. He avoided being followed and other nightmares, and finally reached Eskishehir.

He saw that there too the Armenians were being deported, without exception. Stepan joined the first caravan and, after a terribly hard journey—which was the fate of all deported Armenians—he arrived in Konia, Adana, Aleppo, and finally Rakka.

Stepan and his wife stayed in Rakka for a few weeks and then were deported to Deir Zor, finally arriving in a huge tent city. We saw others like it in Osmaniye, Katma, Damascus, and Dera, when we were deported.

More than a thousand refugees from Aleppo and Rakka arrived there every day. The intention of the government was to settle them permanently in the neighboring villages. But because everyone who left returned within a week, robbed of everything, the tent city kept growing bigger instead of smaller, and with it grew the famine and misery of the people.

As everywhere in Arabia, there was also a lack of bread, water, medicine, and doctors. Soon winter came, and 30,000 Armenians died like flies, of hunger, cold, and disease.

Early in the spring a stout rider surrounded by about ten other cavalry soldiers arrived at the tents, introduced himself as the Inspector General of Refugees, and said that he had come to help the Armenians. Despite his freckled face, prominent cheek bones, and Kaiser-like twisted mustache, which gave him an unsympathetic air, he was soon liked by the people.

"Here you'll perish," said the inspector, Khalit Bey. "Up to now the government hasn't been able to take care of you properly because they were preoccupied with other, more immediate and essential questions. But now the time has come for us to find a way to alleviate your problems. Those of you who wish to go to Mosul must register immediately. Tomorrow morning we'll send a thousand of you there. Military shops have been established there, in which men and women will work to earn their daily bread. If we're satisfied with the results, we'll gradually send other groups of a thousand until we've dealt with all the refugees who suffer on the inhospitable edges of the desert."

The joy in the tents was unbounded. In order to escape from that terrible existence as soon as possible, a thousand people registered immediately, and on the next day, after heart-breaking farewells, they left for their promised land.

Two weeks later Khalit Bey and his entourage came back.

"They're all comfortably settled," he said. "Form another caravan of a thousand people."

"Where have they settled?" asked Stepan and a few other Armenians who were well known to the police of the tent city as the representatives of the Armenians there.

"Didn't we say they were going to Mosul? So why do you ask?" asked Khalit Bey.

"Because," replied Stepan, "we had relatives among those who left. They promised to write us so that if they were satisfied with their jobs we'd leave to join them . . . "

"And you haven't received any letters yet?" asked Khalit Bey, interrupting the Armenian. "Don't you know that we're still at war? If your letters arrive in a month, you should give thanks to God!"

And the second caravan also left.

Eighteen days after the departure of this caravan, a few letters arrived at the tent city. The letters were in Turkish. But because of censorship correspondence anywhere in the country had to be carried out in Turkish. The letters were from well-known people. They stated that thanks to the efforts of Khalit Bey they had been saved from the cruel tentacles of famine and disease. When the people of the tent city received these letters from their loved ones, they rebuked Stepan and a few other "pessimists" like him, who had doubted Khalit Bey's kindness and were rude to him.

"But isn't it strange that these letters are from the second caravan?" observed Stepan. "In other words, these letters were written after we complained to Khalit Bey, but we still haven't received a letter from anyone in the first caravan."

"Shut up! Just shut up," voices from everywhere reproached him. "What do you expect us to do if there is no letter from the first caravan—perhaps their letters were lost. There's a war going on, and sometimes letters written earlier arrive after letters written later."

In order not to vex his relatives—who were willing to cling to anything, like shipwrecked persons, even though it should turn out to be a poisonous snake—Stepan shut up. Deep down in his heart, though, he had a suspicion that there was something queer about the military shops in Mosul.

Two days after the letters arrived, Khalit Bey showed up again, and a third caravan left. Ten days later there was a fourth one, all of them containing groups of a thousand.

One evening a man from the fourth caravan, Sebouh from Evereg, arrived back in the tent city, exhausted and breathless.

"They slaughtered us. They slaughtered us," he sobbed, and fainted to the ground.

Everyone surrounded him, out of their minds with alarm and anxiety. Some poured water on his forehead, others rubbed his hands and feet, and still others took a piece of cloth and started fanning his face, which was burnt by the sun and covered in a thick layer of dust.

"They massacred all of them . . . All of them . . . All of them . . . All of them," he murmured when he regained consciousness. "Only I managed to escape . . . And I came to warn you . . . don't go. Khalit is a butcher."

And in sobs and disjointed words Sebouh told them his horrifying, incredible, hair-raising story. His every word penetrated like a red-hot rod into the souls of all his listeners.

* * *

Khalit and his companions followed the caravan, riding south before them like animal herders for about six days. They traveled over dry untrodden roads, constantly driven forward by their whips. Those who fell behind were killed with bayonets.

Around noon on the sixth day, Sebouh had a fit, the result of a terrible illness he suffered from, something like epilepsy. The soldiers thought he was dead and continued on their way, leaving him there. A few kindly women even covered his body with dry branches to prevent ravenous beasts from seeing and smelling the corpse.

When he regained consciousness he removed this cover of branches and looked around in bewilderment to see where he was. He remembered that he had been in the caravan heading for Mosul, and now he found himself in a boundless desert. He got to his feet with difficulty and walked in the footsteps of his fellow travelers. That evening he spotted a couple of tiny specks of light. He directed his steps toward them and soon noticed a fairly big building next to a black rock that rose like a tower in the endless expanse of the desert.

He thought the building was an inn of the type found in the desert for camel drivers, three or four days apart from each other. He decided to go there to ask for water and bread. Almost immediately, however, he retreated in alarm when he had heard Khalit's voice coming from one of the lit rooms: "Get up, faithless girl," he roared like a crazed beast, "Here you obey me. I am Khalit, the god of the desert."

Sebouh listened breathlessly. He heard women sobbing. A woman was either sitting on the floor or lying down and weeping. Sebouh saw Khalit's shadow on the window pane, bending down to the floor and trying to raise his victim. Then he forcefully grabbed the woman by the arm and threw her against the opposite wall.

Sebouh's horrified eyes recognized a half-naked 13-year-old girl, the daughter of Vortig, the carpenter from Angora. She was pressed against the wall, covering her breasts with her arms and trembling with fear. Khalit, drunk in the throes of savage lust, was slowly approaching her.

Sebouh grasped the situation at once. Carpenter Vortig was in this caravan. Sebouh immediately started to examine the footprints on the ground, to discover if the girl were the only person from the entire caravan to be taken there. There were thousands of barefoot footprints, which he had not noticed when he spotted the lights of the inn. Yes, they came up to and ended in front of this mysterious gate. Where had the owners of these footprints gone though? It remained an unsolvable secret.

Sebouh walked around the building to see if there were another passage or means of exit. Walls as high as three men surrounded a courtyard, which probably joined to the black rock. There were no openings in the walls except for a window about three meters high on each side of the gate.

Holding on to the rough sides of the black rock, Sebouh climbed up a bit to see if he could hear voices from the courtyard. He heard nothing, not even a whisper. But it was impossible for a thousand people to be confined there without voices being heard from outside, he thought, and he grew alarmed. They couldn't all be dead either, because if they had killed them why would they have stuffed them all into a courtyard? After all, it would have been much more convenient for their purpose to kill them outside, in the desert. So what was he to think? What had happened to those thousand people who had been led away by Khalit, had come here, and had entered through that gate of death? There was only one explanation. There must be a very deep cavern under that frightening rock, where the people of the caravan were imprisoned.

After coming to this conclusion, Sebouh went back to the door and observed Khalit's room carefully. The light was still on, but there was no noise and no movement. The light was also on in the room on the other side of the gate. But there, he thought, some kind of festivity was going on. A dozen or so men were singing in hoarse voices. Plates and glasses clinked against each other. Heavy boots tapped on the wooden floor and dancing soldiers passed to and fro before the window, tapping each other with the spoons they were holding. And most horribly, amidst this din of castanets, the clinking of glass, singing, and dancing could be heard low sobs and protracted groans that came from the chests of dejected Armenian women.

When Sebouh heard the laments and cries of his sisters who had fallen into the claws of these debauched monsters and when he thought about the disappearance of thousands of his compatriots within a few hours, he was convinced that awful crimes and debauchery were taking place behind those walls. So he frantically ran away from that rank charnel house and came to tell his compatriots who were still alive not to leave . . . Khalit wasn't leading the caravans to the shops in Mosul, he was leading them to that "Gate of Death, from whose threshold no traveler returns." [Hamlet, III, i, 79-80.]

* * *

When Sebouh finished his story a fearful silence descended on everyone present. The nightmare of death weighed once more on their souls. A cold sweat poured down their faces. No one dared make a move or pronounce a word.

"Araksi," said Stepan that evening, taking his wife by the hand, "I'm scared. I no longer have the courage I had last year. This is terrible. Absolutely terrible . . . That beast Khalit is not like the police chief in Adapazar. He has established his den in a forgotten corner of the desert. He'll take all of us there and bury us alive under that black rock. He's coming back tomorrow. I sense danger. But I know of no way to escape him."

In fact, four days later, Khalit and his men stopped in front of the tent city.

"Get the next thousand people ready," he ordered emphatically. "We'll be leaving right away."

"Nobody else wants to go," said Stepan. "Those who were unhappy here have already been gathered together and have gone. The rest of us are staying here."

When Khalit realized that his scheme was going to fail, he dropped the mask of the compassionate benefactor, stamped his foot on the ground, and barked: "No one can stay here. This region has been declared a war zone. The British are threatening Baghdad. We can't leave the Armenians here to be shot in the back. You all have to leave this place. A thousand people must get ready immediately."

When no one moved, Khalit and his soldiers entered the tents and began tearing them down, removing the people by force.

Another caravan of approximately a thousand people got underway, under threat of cracking whips and rifles. An Armenian youth in the crowd rushed at Khalit with his dagger, but he had no sooner taken a few steps than he was stabbed by a bayonet and fell under the hoofs of horses.

Khalit, all the more enraged by this assassination attempt, led the convoy away, beating and torturing his victims—like the starving wolf that grabs its victim from the sheep fold and takes the bleating animal to its den, there to tear it apart mercilessly.

Three weeks later Khalit's deputy, Mahir, and fifteen cavalry soldiers came for the rest of the refugees. This time the bloodthirsty

Khalit had not come. No doubt after the failed assassination attempt he decided to be more cautious.

Again people protested, resisted, and revolted. The soldiers entered the tents once more and set fire to them, raining blows of bayonets, whips, and fists, and kicking right, left, and center. After close to a hundred people had been killed, the rest of the crowd, approximately 3,000 people, were shoved onto the road. All of them were aware that they were going to pass through the gate of death and be buried in that hideous cemetery, but they all bowed their heads and went forward, just like the thousands of unfortunate compatriots who had gone before them.

"Araksi," Stepan said restlessly, "I still have my dagger. The first soldier who touches you will taste its death blow, and you and I will follow."

And they were driven on by the cracking whips for days, without food and without water, exhausted and weakened. On the evening of the sixth day they spotted the black rock and the Gate of Death that stood before it. It rose from the surrounding solitude like a hideous scaffold. Its grisly appearance affected everybody and at once the caravan stopped as one person. Everyone was stunned!

"March!"

Again whips cracked. Again bayonets glinted. Again bullets whistled.

In order to evade the relentless whip blows, everyone rush forward helplessly, but suddenly they all stopped, horrified at seeing a black spot on the horizon that was growing bigger and bigger and bigger . . . It was a company of thirty cavalrymen, galloping like lightning toward them.

Thinking that they were slaughterers and that there was no way to save themselves, everyone fell flat on the ground and lay there. A minute later the riders sped up, led by two young officers. One of them had orders to arrest all the executioners in the caravan.

Khalit's bloodthirsty soldiers were surprised by the order and for a moment remained in complete confusion. Then they tried to resist, but it was too late. In only a few minutes they were all arrested and disarmed.

The Armenians looked around in total surprise. It seemed as if they were dreaming. They couldn't understand why these government soldiers were arresting the slaughterers instead of assisting them. But their surprise didn't last long. The second officer drove his horse forward, his eyes gleaming with vengeance and hate, put his hand on Stepan's shoulder, and shouted: "Don't be afraid, I'm an Armenian. My name is Kourken. We've come to tear down the Gate of Death. Don't stay here! Run away as fast as you can and get out of this area. Don't go to Deir Zor. Run toward Aleppo. Take this money and get away as soon as possible. Run with all your might and don't look back."

After handing a purse to Stepan he continued: "We have about ten camels with us, loaded with clothes. Distribute them among the people who need them. Then put the invalids on the camels and leave immediately."

Then he whipped his horse and rode up to his friend, who was busy tying the hands of the arrested soldiers. After consulting him briefly, Kourken left the prisoners with the cavalrymen and he and his fellow officer galloped over to the Gate of Death.

Confused by this incredible miracle, everyone took the camels and their executioners' horses and ran away without knowing anything about the Armenian officer. How did he come to help them, and what did he do to the Gate of Death and its hellish inhabitants? But because some of them were exhausted, hungry, and weak, they could go no farther than Deir Zor, despite the officer's repeated advice. They stayed there, and a few months later they were once again subjected to the tragic destiny from which they had so surprisingly been saved thanks to that Armenian officer.

Stepan and his wife, though, were among the few fortunate ones who could continue their journey, and arrived in Aleppo after numerous hardships. A month later, they were arrested once more and deported to Hama and then Homs, where Stepan was working as an itinerant photographer when the British occupied the city.

* * *

It was quite late at night when Stepan finished his story. The lights in the hold were off, people were asleep, and a dense darkness had descended everywhere. Suddenly, from a corner, an infant started crying. The glittering flame of a candle appeared there at once. A young woman bared her breast and bent over her child. The crying stopped and a deadly silence again reigned in the hold.

"Well, good night," said Stepan, pulling the cover up to his head. "The unfortunate part of all this is that the end of these terrible days has not yet come."

"Let's hope we're wrong in our suspicions," I said, and I also pulled the cover up to my head. "Good night, my friend."

It was as if I could see the black rock unrolling like a film on the dark wall of the hold, rising like a tower in a limitless expanse of sand . . . And the Gate of Death abutting the Black Rock . . . at the sides of the gate, the two lit rooms . . . in one of the rooms a monstrous Turkish officer, roaring like a crazed beast: "I am Khalit, the god of the desert!" . . . An innocent girl pressed against the wall, covering her nakedness with her arms . . . shivering . . . In another room guttural chuckles, songs, castanets, female sobs . . . Outside in the desert, a caravan of thousands of men, women, and children, advancing quietly . . . then a spot on the horizon growing, bigger, bigger, bigger, and turning into a company of cavalrymen . . . And a young Armenian officer, who yells: "Don't be afraid. I'm an Armenian. My name is Kourken. We're going to tear down the Gate of Death."

And then, and then, and then? Did he kill Khalit? Did he tear down the Gate of Death? Or was his handsome head crushed against the Black Rock?

The mystery tortured me all night as I turned it over constantly in my mind. It was impossible to forget. It was impossible to close my eyes, even briefly.

18 June, 1919

The ship took on cargo in Mersin until four o'clock this afternoon and then raised anchor and left.

Tonight there was a severe storm. Despite the fact that the ship has a tonnage of 25,000, it was tossed like a blade of straw on the wild billows, sometimes, like Noah's Ark, riding on their crests and sometimes descending into their unfathomable troughs. The waves were so wild that when they smashed against the bow of the ship they rose high into the air and then crashed down on our heads like waterfalls.

As a precaution, the sailors shut the hatch in the ceiling, depriving us of air and the light of the stars. At the moment we are buried in deep darkness, as though we were in the catacombs of Rome. We are continuously tossed to the right and left, banging against the walls.

Whenever the ship lists a little bit more to one side or is shaken by strong waves, the women cry out mournfully, fearing that the ship will overturn.

Everywhere there is screaming, shouting, and roaring. Some pray, some throw up, others howl. Others, who want to prove that they are not afraid of the sea or the storm, sing, laugh, and jump up and down, thus creating an unusual tumult and chaos in the hold—an atmosphere that lacks only the Turkish *yatghan* to be complete.

19 June, 1919

This morning the storm had subsided by the time we arrived in Larnaka, a port on the island of Cyprus with beautiful buildings and scenery. We wanted to go to the city to buy things to eat—which usually consists of bread and cucumber, and sometimes . . . cucumber and bread—but the British police would not allow us to go ashore, objecting that it was forbidden for Armenians to step on any soil under British command. And the boatmen didn't bring back any bread to sell. So today we borrowed a piece of bread from our neighbor on our right, who is from Edirne.

20 June, 1919

Around noon the ship anchored in the bay of Adalia. For the first time we saw a Turkish flag, flying over a fortress.

We hired a boat and went to town to do some shopping.

Although Adalia is occupied by the Italians, the Turks don't give the impression of a defeated people. Here too they made threatening remarks.

Many Turkish passengers came aboard at this port. Four hours later, we left again.

21 June, 1919

At 10 o'clock this morning we arrived in Rhodes, a big island in the Archipelago that belongs to the Italians. The old city is surrounded by ramparts and the new part by woods. As this was Italian soil, the police wouldn't let us go ashore.

At four o'clock this afternoon we left.

This evening a rumor circulated among the Armenians that an Armenian servant girl is traveling with a Turkish family who came aboard in Adalia.

22 June, 1919

We would have starved to death if we had not reached Smyrna at 1:30 this afternoon.

The numerous British, French, Italian, and Greek battle ships, as well as more than thirty passenger and cargo vessels, all lying at anchor in the port and flying multicolored flags, made a charming scene.

As soon as the ship came to a halt, hundreds of vessels with Greek flags surrounded us, bringing all sorts of food. Although they took advantage of our hunger to sell their goods at twice the normal price, we were so hungry that we willingly paid whatever they asked.

This afternoon the employees of the National Association came and told us that the ship would stay one whole day in Smyrna, and that they would obtain permission from the Greek authorities for us to go ashore tomorrow.

This evening we watched as the famous boardwalk of Smyrna, the Kordon, flooded with electric lights, filled up with passersby, cars, and horse-driven streetcars.

23 June, 1919

This morning we hired a rowboat and rowed to the shore. The police would not allow us ashore. So we returned to the ship empty-handed. At noon they announced that they had lifted the restriction. We took another rowboat and went to the city.

As we were roaming down Kordon Boulevard, a stampede suddenly broke out, as people began to close store-front shutters and run away. Without knowing what was going on, we also started to run away, and by chance we found the Armenian church of St. Stepanos, where we took refuge. A quarter of an hour later we heard that there had been a misunderstanding. After a bloody fight the Greek military police had caught four or five bandits and brought them to town. The people had understood that Turkish bandits were coming, instead of some of the latter being brought to town. It was a ridiculous misunderstanding, thinking that Turkish bandits were coming to burn the city and massacre the people.

After a while everybody calmed down and normal life was restored to the street.

This evening we returned to the ship, having experienced once again the emotional upset of a Turkish alarm.

24 June, 1919

At dawn, when we emerged from our holds to breathe some fresh air, we saw that the ship had anchored opposite Tenedos, a little Greek island off the shores of the Dardanelles, famous for its wine and vineyards. Near the island a British vessel had anchored, and over it circled an aeroplane fastened to the ship by a rope.

We sailed in the strait for about two hours, looking out on both sides at the mountains where cannons had ceaselessly bombarded the enemy during the war, reaping countless human lives. There was no trace of all this today, apart from ruined villages, graves, crosses, and half-sunk battle ships. Rich vegetation covers the soil that for years was fertilized by absorbing the blood spilled from human veins. British soldiers have now set their tents in the middle of this vegetation, and are busy repairing the demolished roads and bridges.

Around noontime the ship anchored opposite Chanak Kale. About forty Armenians got off there and started to look around in amazement. They were trying to find a trace of their demolished and destroyed houses and stores.

This evening we arrived in Gallipoli. Here too the Armenian quarter has been completely destroyed. Twenty-four Armenians went ashore and with tears in their eyes disappeared behind the piles of stone that once had been their houses.

25 June, 1919

We always arrive early in the morning in all big Turkish cities, such as Adana, Aleppo, Damascus, Beirut, etc. In order, it seems, not to make an exception, we also arrived in Constantinople, the beautiful capital of Turkey, early this morning.

The ship anchored opposite Maiden's Tower (Kiz Kulesi), but because of the fog we couldn't see the city well. A little later, though, the fog lifted, and before us appeared stately Constantinople, from San Stefano to Kadikeoy (Chalcedon) and the Princes' Islands.

At last we had come to the end of our voyage. People began to express their joy and happy agitation, and prepared to go ashore as soon as possible. Despite the advancing hour, however, nobody representing any Armenian national organization showed up to welcome us and lead us ashore.

Around noon a steam tug flying a French flag approached our ship. An officer and four soldiers came up the gangway and headed to the captain's cabin to examine our papers.

Meanwhile a sudden commotion broke out at the other end of the ship. A few hot-blooded young Armenians had taken the Armenian servant girl away from the Turkish family who had come aboard in Adalia. The Turk was yelling and shouting and demanding the maid, insisting and swearing that she was a Turk. Finally the Turk applied to the French officer, complaining that an outrage had taken place. The latter had the kidnapped girl brought to him and in the presence of the Italian captain asked: "Tell me, my girl, are you or are you not an Armenian?"

The shy girl remained silent for a moment, then burst into sobs.

"Speak. Don't be afraid. If you're an Armenian, I'll return you to your countrymen, and if you're a Turk I'll give you back to your employer."

The girl continued crying and made no reply.

"I discern from your silence that you're a Turk," said the French officer, handing her over to the Turk.

"No, she's an Armenian," protested the refugees. "If she were a Turk, she wouldn't hesitate to state her nationality. Her crying proves that she's an Armenian. In fact, she's the one who admitted she was an Armenian when she came aboard in Adalia."

"Why doesn't she admit it now?"

"Who knows? The Turk might have beaten, tortured, or threatened her. At any rate, he has kept her confined because ever since her first conversation with us she has not left their cabin.

"We can't take the girl away from the Turk and give her to the Armenians on the basis of suppositions," said the Frenchman. "Go away now."

"No. We won't allow the Turk to take an Armenian girl away," the Armenians protested once more.

"In other words, you're defying a French officer?"

"We're not defying anybody. We're simply demanding the girl."

The Frenchman gave a curt order to his soldiers, who attacked the protesters. After a short fist fight, the soldiers arrested four people and locked them up in one of the deserted cabins.

Everyone was upset about the incident, and surrounded the cabin to free the imprisoned youths. The French soldiers began to kick and hit the crowd, making noses bleed, breaking teeth . . . eventually the situation would have assumed tragic proportions if the Italian captain had not intervened and the fighters had been not separated.

To satisfy the people's demand, the Italian captain freed the prisoners shortly thereafter, but before that the French officer, taking the Turkish family and the girl with him, had embarked on his steam tug and had already disappeared.

We feel as if each of us has lost a member of our family. The kidnapping of an Armenian girl, especially with the connivance of a French officer, has saddened us beyond imagination. We cannot comprehend the injustice forever committed against us by Turk as well as Christian.

26 June, 1919

Several rowboats surrounded the ship this morning, bringing goods to sell.

"*Djagadamard, Djagadamard*" (Battle Front), called the Armenian newspaper boy. Thinking that there might be some news about yesterday's battle in it, we bought the paper and checked all the pages. The following news item caught our attention: "Yesterday, Armenian refugees arrived in Constantinople from Beirut aboard SS *Carintia*. Some of the refugees are staying with relatives and the rest at the Haidar Pasha refugee station.

After reading this we looked at each other. Did the reporter from *Djagadamard* have supernatural powers, perhaps, which enabled him to predict future events, or was the news not about us? But it was impossible for the news not to be about us, as there was only one Italian vessel called the *Carintia* and it was us who had arrived in Constantinople on it. If there was a little mistake in the news, it was that not only we had not yet settled, but we had also sacrificed another victim.

Around two this afternoon, a small French ship approached ours and a sailor shouted: "Get your belongings and come aboard."

A quarter of an hour later we had grabbed our bundles and were aboard. We left immediately, and it brought us to the Sirkeci wharf. We thought we had arrived at Haidar Pasha and looked around a building that looked as though it might be a refugee station.

A French soldier called: "Line up, come on. March!" Men and women, young and old, we lined up two by two and began to march in military fashion. Before long we arrived at a strange building. Our leader ordered: "Separate . . . women to the right and men to the left."

"What?"

We were all petrified.

The poor soldier didn't realize what horrible memories the words "Women to the right and men to the left" could bring back. "Why are you looking at me like that?" he shouted, getting angry. "Get inside. You are all going to wash while your clothes are disinfected. Take these cards, write your names on them, and attach them to your bundles. Come on, step to it, don't dawdle."

We all did what the soldier said and went and stood stark naked under more than twenty showers. When ice-cold water suddenly streamed down on us, we realized that the French officer from yesterday was getting his revenge . . . But we could do nothing but shower him with our curses.

Two minutes later we were taken from the showers into the adjacent room, where we waited, shivering and shaking, until they gave us back our disinfected clothes, which were all wrinkled.

"Get ready, come on, march!"

We lined up once more and returned military style to the ship. A little later the women who had been separated from us also arrived— after having been subjected to the same punishment. The ship left in half an hour and dropped us on the quay at Haidar Pasha.

Fortunately, an employee from the National Association was waiting for us. He received us very kindly and said: "Come, come, my countrymen. There's your refugee station. Take your belongings and go over there. We've prepared a large barrack for you. I hope and trust that you'll rest there and forget all your weariness. Please, walk, my children."

We all picked up our belongings and headed for the place he had indicated.

While we walked in the midst of the crowd—myself carrying our mattress and the blanket on my back, my mother with the bundle of our underwear under her arm, my two sisters holding the handles of a basket, and my brother carrying a water-can—we reflected that nearly four years ago thirteen of us left Chorum in three horse-drawn carriages, and today five of us are returning to Constantinople, almost bare-foot. But we were not sad. We reflected that the deprivation, bereavement, and suffering of those black days are now over, and that a new life is dawning on us. We are shaking off the dust of the desert and advancing as fast as our legs can carry us, the smile of happiness on our lips, and the prospect of a rosy, beautiful future in our eyes.

THE END

Glossary

Cheté (Slavic.): brigand

Medjidiyé (Tur.): (currecy) a silver coin

Vartabed (Arm.): an Armenian clerical rank of learned priests

Agha (Tur.): (title) for landed gentry

Aghpar (Arm.): a diminutive for brother, usually used as a term of respect

Ammi (Arab.): uncle

Ankaratsi (Arm.): a person from Ankara

Baksimad (Tur.): a hard biscuit

Djehennem (Arab.): Gehenna, Hell

Ermen (Arab.): Armenian

Fedayi (Pers.): freedom fighter, volunteer

Fellah (Arab.): a sedentary Arab peasant

Giaour, giavur (Pers.): infidel, unbeliever, a term of abuse against Christians

Ittihad ve Terakki Djemiyeti: (a political party) Committee of Union and Progress

Kahana (Arm.): an Armenian clerical rank of parish priests

Khan (Pers.): inn, caravansaray

Kiafir (Arab.): infidel, heretic [*kiafirler* (Tur. plural)]. Used as a term of abuse, especially against Christians. Also see "giaour."

Komitadji (Tur.): a member of a secret political society

Kurban Bayram: the Muslim feast of sacrifice

Latsi Kisher (Arm.): Night of Tears, a nocturnal service of the Armenian Apostolic Church, held in the evening of Good Friday

Mahdesi (Pers.): one who has made a pilgrimage to Jerusalem

Miudur (Tur.): public official, director, administrator

Moukhtar (Arab.): the neighborhood or village elder

Namaz (Tur.): Muslim prayer

Oghi (Arm.): alcaholic beverage, Ouzo

Pagharch (Arm.): unleavened bread

Para (Tur.): currency, metal coin

Ruhji (Arab.): spiritual
Shghtayagir (Arm.): chain carrying
Tan (Arm.): liquid yogurt
Tar (Pers.): a plucked string instrument with a leather top, used in Azerbaijani folk music
Trenpatsek (Arm.): a religious ceremony celebrated by the Eastern Churches on Palm-Sunday
Ulan! (Tur.) Hey!
Vesika (Tur.): official document, permit
Vodnlva service (Arm.): the service of Tenebrae, the washing of the feet
Yildrim Ordusu (Tur.): the Ottoman "Army of Lightning"

APPENDIX

The following family trees (see insert) and photographs provide more personal information about the Dadrian family. The family originally came from Germir in Turkey. Nothing is known of the family history there.

There were four Dadrian brothers named Parsegh (the oldest), Abraham, Nishan and Kaloust. (Of Kaloust nothing is known and all family members are deceased). All four brothers were merchants. They moved to Chorum in the 1840s and went into the haberdashery business. They each married, prospered, and raised a family there.

At the time of the deportations in 1915 only Nishan of the four brothers was still alive and is a principal character in the Diary. The children and grandchildren of those brothers are the persons in the story. The author is the grandson of Parsegh, who was a miniaturist and supposedly condensed the Bible into a book no bigger than a matchbox. That book was lost during the deportations.

The principal adult characters in the Diary are Armenag, the author's father and son of Parsegh. Armenag was a successful businessman. Hagop the son of Abraham was an attorney. There was also Levon Toramanian, the son-in-law of Nishan Dadrian, who was a successful businessman and member of the Ottoman Parliament.

The pictures included here are primarily of those family members alive at the time of the deportation.

Armenag and Diruhi Dadrian with grandmother Manoushag
holding the author Vahram Dadrian, 1901.

Armenag Dadrian on left and unidentified business associate on right, on a trip to England, probably in 1912.

Dadrian family in Constantinople.
(Back row): Vahram and Manoushag.
(Front row): Arpine, Diruhi and Souren.
Probably 1921.

Author, Vahram Dadrian
(1900-1948)

Souren Armen Dadrian
(1914-1997)

Diruhi Dadrian
(1878-1959)

Manoushag Dadrian Uznikian with son
Arman Simone, taken on June 20, 1948.

Arpine Dadrian
(1910-2002)

Arshag Dadrian (1909–1941), only child of Elizabeth Dadrian Kaishian who survived the deportation, and wife Veronica (1900–1986), probably 1936.

(Left to right): Filor Derderian, daughter Zarouhi Dadrian Toramanian, sons Vahram and Levon, and husband Krikor Toramanian, probably taken in 1903.

Krikor Toramanian, married to Zarouhi Dadrian,
daughter of Nishan Dadrian.

Levon Toramanian, son of Krikor and Zarouhi
Dadrian Toramanian, taken in 1915.

Vahram Toramanian, son of Krikor and Zarouhi
Dadrian Toramanian.

Zarouhi Dadrian Toramanian with daughter and son Levon
Toramanian, probably taken in 1930.

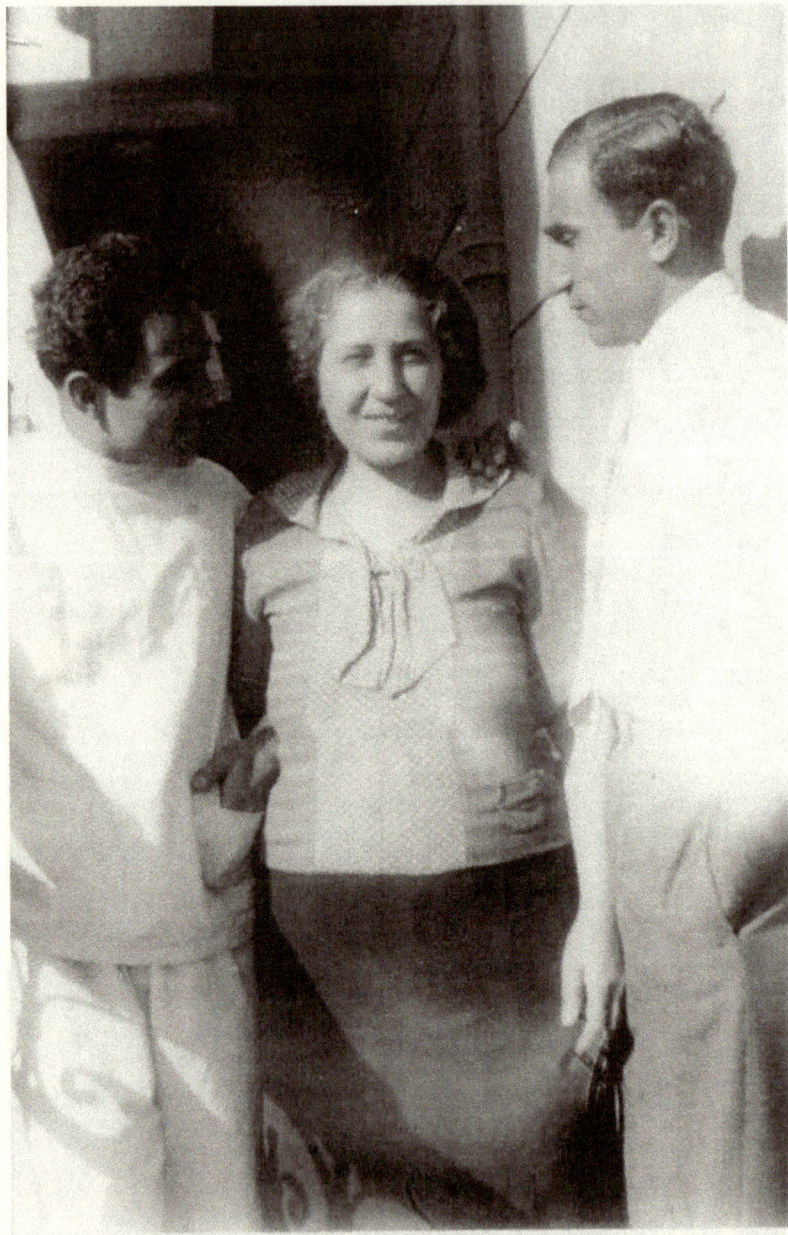

Archam Dadrian (1909-1956) and Hrant Dadrian (1912-1985)
with their mother Lucine Mozian-Dadrian (1888-1978),
taken in Cairo, 1925.

Archam Dadrian (1909-1956) and Hrant Dadrian (1912-1985),
taken in Cairo, 1928.

Hagop Dadrian with first wife Hayganoush and children Adrine and Abraham Dadrian. Also grandmother Santoucht and servant holding Adrine in rear. Picture probably taken in 1909.

Meline, Adrine (1908-2002) and Vahakn Dadrian
(future Armenian Genocide scholar), 1928.

Descendants of Parsegh, Nshan, Abraham and Kaloust Dadrian

Descendants of Parsegh Dadrian

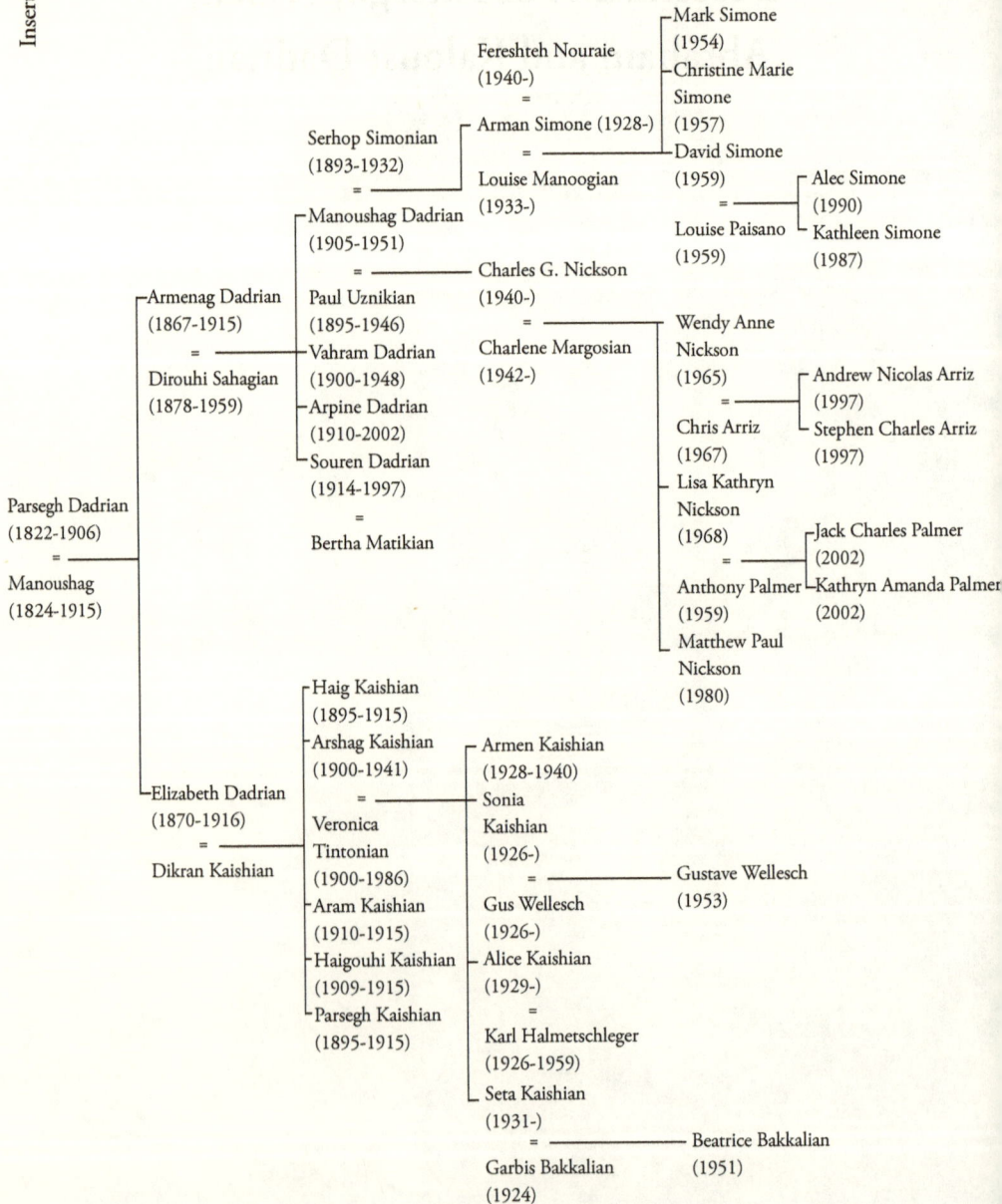

Mark Simone
(1954)

Christine Marie
Simone
(1957)

Fereshteh Nouraie
(1940-)
=
Arman Simone (1928-)
=
Louise Manoogian
(1933-)

David Simone
(1959)
=
Louise Paisano
(1959)

Alec Simone
(1990)

Kathleen Simone
(1987)

Serhop Simonian
(1893-1932)
=
Manoushag Dadrian
(1905-1951)
=
Charles G. Nickson
(1940-)
=
Charlene Margosian
(1942-)

Paul Uznikian
(1895-1946)
=
Vahram Dadrian
(1900-1948)

Wendy Anne
Nickson
(1965)
=
Chris Arriz
(1967)

Andrew Nicolas Arriz
(1997)

Stephen Charles Arriz
(1997)

Lisa Kathryn
Nickson
(1968)
=
Anthony Palmer
(1959)

Jack Charles Palmer
(2002)

Kathryn Amanda Palmer
(2002)

Matthew Paul
Nickson
(1980)

Armenag Dadrian
(1867-1915)
=
Dirouhi Sahagian
(1878-1959)

Arpine Dadrian
(1910-2002)

Souren Dadrian
(1914-1997)

Bertha Matikian

Parsegh Dadrian
(1822-1906)
=
Manoushag
(1824-1915)

Haig Kaishian
(1895-1915)

Arshag Kaishian
(1900-1941)
=
Veronica
Tintonian
(1900-1986)

Armen Kaishian
(1928-1940)

Sonia
Kaishian
(1926-)
=
Gus Wellesch
(1926-)

Gustave Wellesch
(1953)

Elizabeth Dadrian
(1870-1916)
=
Dikran Kaishian

Aram Kaishian
(1910-1915)

Haigouhi Kaishian
(1909-1915)

Parsegh Kaishian
(1895-1915)

Alice Kaishian
(1929-)
=
Karl Halmetschleger
(1926-1959)

Seta Kaishian
(1931-)
=
Garbis Bakkalian
(1924)

Beatrice Bakkalian
(1951)

Descendants of Nshan Dadrian

Nshan Dadrian
(1847-1918)
=
Nor Derderian

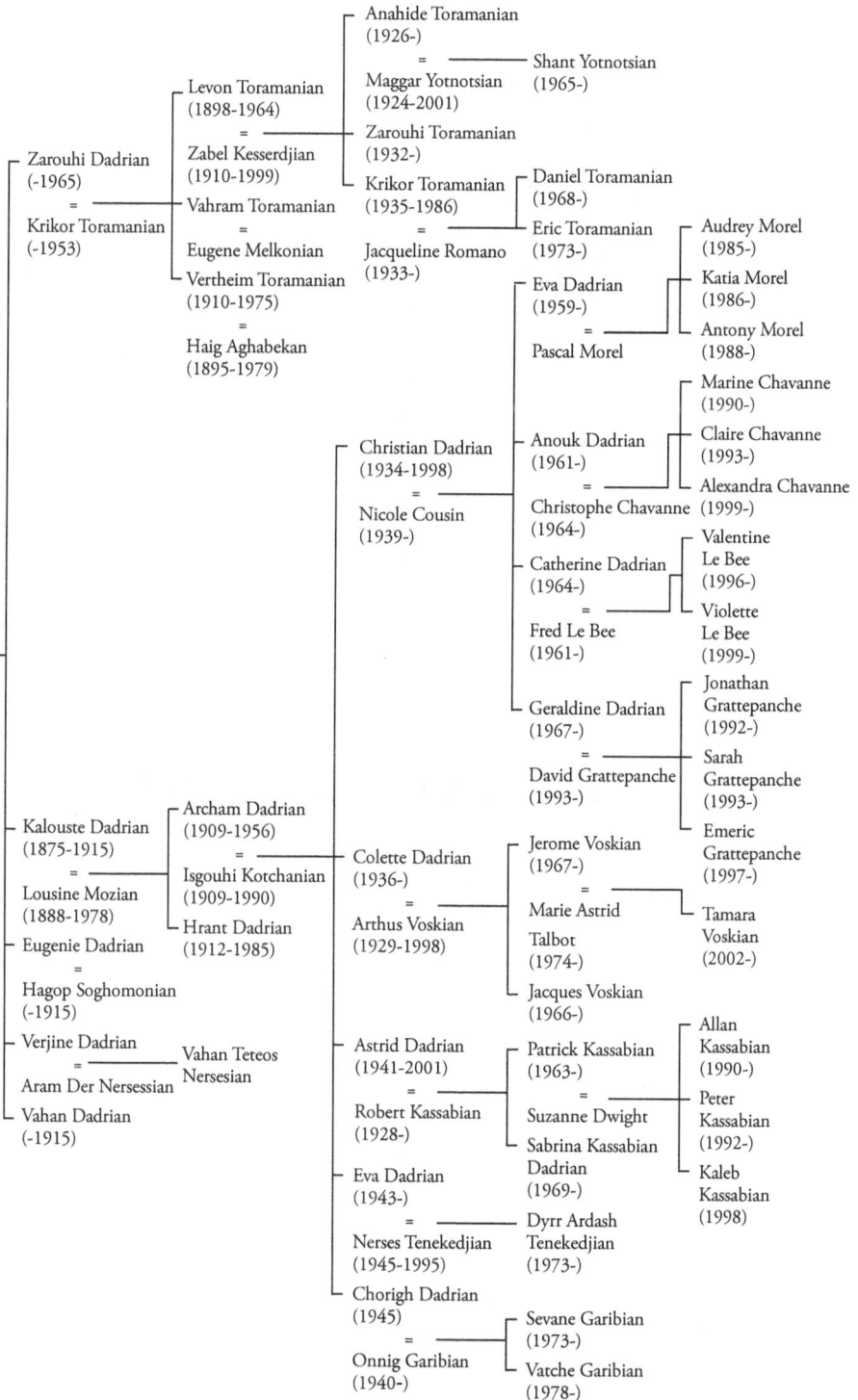

Zarouhi Dadrian (-1965) = Krikor Toramanian (-1953)

Levon Toramanian (1898-1964)
=
Zabel Kesserdjian (1910-1999)

Vahram Toramanian
=
Eugene Melkonian

Vertheim Toramanian (1910-1975)
=
Haig Aghabekan (1895-1979)

Anahide Toramanian (1926-)
=
Maggar Yotnotsian (1924-2001)

Shant Yotnotsian (1965-)

Zarouhi Toramanian (1932-)

Krikor Toramanian (1935-1986)
=
Jacqueline Romano (1933-)

Daniel Toramanian (1968-)

Eric Toramanian (1973-)

Kalouste Dadrian (1875-1915) = Lousine Mozian (1888-1978)

Archam Dadrian (1909-1956)
=
Isgouhi Kotchanian (1909-1990)

Hrant Dadrian (1912-1985)

Eugenie Dadrian = Hagop Soghomonian (-1915)

Verjine Dadrian = Aram Der Nersessian

Vahan Teteos Nersesian

Vahan Dadrian (-1915)

Christian Dadrian (1934-1998)
=
Nicole Cousin (1939-)

Eva Dadrian (1959-)
=
Pascal Morel

Audrey Morel (1985-)
Katia Morel (1986-)
Antony Morel (1988-)

Anouk Dadrian (1961-)
=
Christophe Chavanne (1964-)

Marine Chavanne (1990-)
Claire Chavanne (1993-)
Alexandra Chavanne (1999-)

Catherine Dadrian (1964-)
=
Fred Le Bee (1961-)

Valentine Le Bee (1996-)
Violette Le Bee (1999-)

Geraldine Dadrian (1967-)
=
David Grattepanche (1993-)

Jonathan Grattepanche (1992-)
Sarah Grattepanche (1993-)
Emeric Grattepanche (1997-)

Colette Dadrian (1936-)
=
Arthus Voskian (1929-1998)

Jerome Voskian (1967-)
=
Marie Astrid Talbot (1974-)

Tamara Voskian (2002-)

Jacques Voskian (1966-)

Astrid Dadrian (1941-2001)
=
Robert Kassabian (1928-)

Patrick Kassabian (1963-)
=
Suzanne Dwight

Sabrina Kassabian Dadrian (1969-)

Allan Kassabian (1990-)
Peter Kassabian (1992-)
Kaleb Kassabian (1998)

Eva Dadrian (1943-)
=
Nerses Tenekedjian (1945-1995)

Dyrr Ardash Tenekedjian (1973-)

Chorigh Dadrian (1945)
=
Onnig Garibian (1940-)

Sevane Garibian (1973-)
Vatche Garibian (1978-)

Descendants of Abraham Dadrian

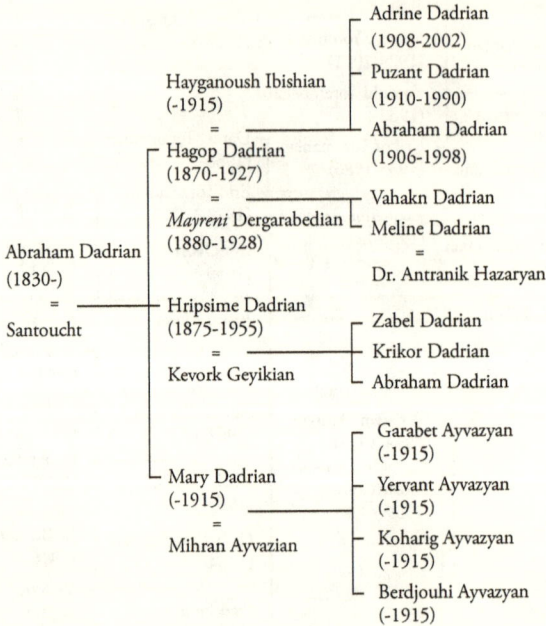

```
                                                    ┌─ Adrine Dadrian
                                                    │  (1908-2002)
                          Hayganoush Ibishian        ├─ Puzant Dadrian
                          (-1915)                    │  (1910-1990)
                          =                          └─ Abraham Dadrian
                        ┌─ Hagop Dadrian                (1906-1998)
                        │  (1870-1927)
                        │  =                          ┌─ Vahakn Dadrian
                        │  Mayreni Dergarabedian      └─ Meline Dadrian
                        │  (1880-1928)                   =
Abraham Dadrian         │                               Dr. Antranik Hazaryan
(1830-)                 │
=                       ├─ Hripsime Dadrian            ┌─ Zabel Dadrian
Santoucht               │  (1875-1955)                 ├─ Krikor Dadrian
                        │  =                            └─ Abraham Dadrian
                        │  Kevork Geyikian
                        │
                        │                              ┌─ Garabet Ayvazyan
                        │                              │  (-1915)
                        └─ Mary Dadrian                ├─ Yervant Ayvazyan
                           (-1915)                     │  (-1915)
                           =                           ├─ Koharig Ayvazyan
                           Mihran Ayvazian             │  (-1915)
                                                       └─ Berdjouhi Ayvazyan
                                                          (-1915)
```

Descendants of Kaloust Dadrian

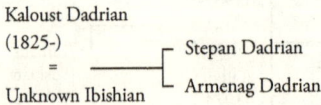

```
Kaloust Dadrian
(1825-)              ┌─ Stepan Dadrian
=                    └─ Armenag Dadrian
Unknown Ibishian
```

www.ingramcontent.com/pod-product-compliance
Lightning Source LLC
Chambersburg PA
CBHW020653270326
41928CB00005B/93